C000114840

LEGAL ADVISER

Your legal questions answered

About the authors

Jeremy Flye graduated from Oxford University in 1984, where he read law at Jesus College. He worked in regional newspapers for a number of years, editing several papers, before becoming a freelance journalist and writer.

Sarah Morgan graduated from Cardiff University in 1994, where she read law, before going on to the College of Law, Guildford. She was admitted as a solicitor in April 1997.

Published by
Law Pack Publishing Limited
10-16 Cole Street
London SE1 4YH

www.lawpack.co.uk

Printed in the Great Britain

ISBN 1 902646 53 3 paperback edition
ISBN 1 902646 54 1 hardback edition

Contents

continued ...

Introduction

The law is an essential part of our society. Literally, it is the fabric that holds society together by laying down rules on the way people, organisations and companies interact together and with the state. The law governs everything we do or say: the way we drive our cars, the way food and drink is served to us, the way we buy and sell houses and even what we read in the newspapers all operates within a framework of legislation. But having evolved over a millennium, the law is not static: it continues to evolve on a daily basis. It is constantly changing and developing as parliament enacts new legislation, or local authorities impose new regulations through by-laws; all of these can impact on you and your family in your home life, your work and your leisure.

Legal Adviser is your guide through the maze of laws. The purpose of this book is to give you an understanding of the law as it affects your everyday life: no heavy legal definitions and academic information here. This is what journalists call 'news you can use': information that is relevant to the way you live your life.

The law acts as both a sword and a shield, protecting you against other people or organisations as well as giving you the power to assert your rights over others. The flip-side of this is that the law also protects other people from, and allows them to assert their rights over, you, too. *Legal Adviser* looks at various facets of your life – your work, your family, your home, your rights, your dealings with the police and your money – and illustrates the law that applies to them by discussing everyday situations that may well arise in an easy-to follow, question-and-answer format, looking at situations ranging from insuring your car to complaining about your local council. In addition to questions about the law, *Legal Adviser* looks at issues that can arise out of the legal process. For example, *You and your family* contains a section on the Child Support Agency, and there is also a section on obtaining credit in *You and your money*. And recognising that some disputes involving legal rights cannot be settled amicably, there is also a section about courts in the UK, including coroner's courts and employment tribunals.

We have deliberately tried to keep the book as jargon-free as possible; the old Latin phrases and law-student approach has been deliberately kept to a minimum, as this is a book for people, not just for lawyers. However, where we have used legal expressions, we explain them in the text, and in addition there is a handy glossary of the most-used terms.

However, while this book is designed to give you guidance about the law, you should never think of it as a way of replacing the family solicitor. There is an old saying: 'A man that represents himself has a fool for a client'. While that may not be true in every case, there are still strong arguments for seeking the advice of a solicitor (or barrister) if your problems warrant it; but by reading this book, you will already have some understanding of your legal position and will be better able to discuss your problems with your lawyer. But some problems you can deal with yourself, for example if you have to complain to a shop about faulty goods. In cases such as these, *Legal Adviser* can point you in the right direction, and suggest ways of resolving your problem without having to take legal action, with all the uncertainty and cost that may involve. In addition, using *Legal Adviser* as a reference may prevent you doing something that may develop into a problem for you some time down the road, for example deciding to extend your house without applying for planning permission. If you have doubts about anything, look it up in *Legal Adviser*.

Acknowledgements

We should like to thank solicitors Robin Williams, Jonathan Bradshaw, Victor Ellis, Emma Keelan and Sonia McGarrigle, barrister Edward Harding (Clerk to the Justices, Gwent Magistrates), and Tracey Kifford and Jamie Ross for their helpful comments on this book.

Jeremy Flye
Sarah Morgan

For convenience (and for no other reason) 'him', 'he' or 'his' has been used in *Legal Adviser* and should be read to include 'her', 'she' or 'hers'.

Chapter 1
You and the law

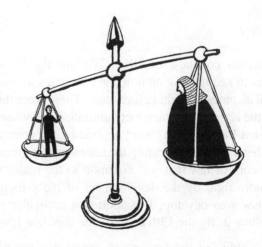

Section 1.1 Sources of law

Despite being a United Kingdom, there is no one source of law for Britain. England and Wales, Scotland and Northern Ireland all have their own systems. England and Wales share the same system, having been tied since the defeat of Owain Glyndwr in the Middle Ages. Northern Ireland is similarly bound, and so these systems are very similar in nature. But Scotland, which only 'joined' the United Kingdom in the 17th century, has a legal system which is in line with English law on broad issues, though with certain differences, for example in the laws of property in relation to buying a house, and in criminal courts where in addition to verdicts of 'innocent' and 'guilty', a third verdict of 'not proven' exists.

Where does English law come from?

England is an old country, with a comparatively stable history. So unlike the US or France, where revolutions (in 1776 and 1792, 1830 and 1848 respectively) led to the drafting of constitutions, in line with which future laws have been framed, we are not tied in the same way and so law has developed piecemeal. Modern English law can be traced to a number of sources – common law, equity, legislation, European law, canon law, mercantile law and local custom.

Common law

After the Norman conquest of 1066, William the Conqueror and his successors sent out representatives to keep an eye on how the different shires and districts were being run; they also adjudicated in disputes brought before them. These were the first royal judges, who derived their powers from the King. These men were untrained and when they visited a shire, they would need to discover what local customs were applied by the courts, and applied it. By rationalising the various local legal systems, rejecting the unreasonable elements and standardising the remainder, a rigid framework of law that was common to the realm was developed. This framework was made even more rigid by the development of the principle of precedent – that when a new principle of law was developed to address a particular problem, all the other judges would henceforth follow it. By the 13th century, the common law of England was developed.

But the very rigidity of the framework meant that the common law could not keep up with changes in society. Cases could only be brought before the common law civil courts (the courts of Exchequer, Common Pleas and King's Bench) if the claim could be made to fit one of the 'writs' that had been devised and kept at the Chancery in London. So, if no writ covered a particular case, the claimant was at a disadvantage. At first, new writs were issued to cover the developing need to dispense justice, but common law judges eventually stopped accepting new writs because a new writ effectively created a new law. This meant that some wrongs went unremedied as a result, although clerks were allowed to amend existing writs to fit new circumstances. This inflexibility led to the development of the Court of Chancery and equity.

Equity

Equity, administered by the Court of Chancery, operated as a sort of fill-in law, plugging the gaps left by common law, to give claimants justice where the existing system could not, for instance if the common law was not sufficiently developed or if common law remedies were not suitable. The Court of Chancery was not bound by the writ system, and considered petitions on their merits rather than on technical issues (such as whether the correct writ was used). Obviously having two systems operating side by side meant that there could be a conflict of laws, with different verdicts coming from either court. But in 1616 it was established that where there was a conflict between common law and equity, equity would prevail.

The flexibility offered by equity meant that chancery courts became popular with litigants, but this very flexibility was also a source of criticism. Because equity was essentially a matter of conscience, two different chancellors might disagree over whether to grant a remedy, making equity less certain than common law. For this reason it was said that: 'Equity varies with the length of the Chancellor's foot.' However, a number of Lord Chancellors sought to add a greater structure to equity's flexibility. Lord Nottingham established that as far as possible equity should follow existing principles rather than operate under an arbitrary discretion, except in the absence of precedent or where the rules conflicted. A later Lord Chancellor, Lord Hardwicke ruled that rules of precedent should apply in equity cases, and Lord Eldon established equity's case law, further strengthening the Court of Chancery. However, having two systems of justice operating side by side was impractical and a series of Judicature Acts passed during 1873–5 reformed the English legal system, by allowing all courts to administer common law and equity side by side, and so ending the vexed question of jurisdiction – which court should you take your case to. The Judicature Acts also confirmed the primacy of equity over common law in cases of conflict, and also established other rights such as allowing evidence to be given orally in civil cases.

As a result all courts could now offer both common law remedies, such as damages, and equitable remedies such as injunctions (an order which prevents someone from doing something) or the contractual remedy of specific performance (which requires a contract to be performed) though the equitable remedies are discretionary.

Acts of Parliament

After the Norman conquest, the feudal system held sway in this country, with the King at the top of the pyramid, with descending levels of lord and earls, barons, knights, freeholders, tenants and peasants all offering allegiance and revenue to their immediate superiors. Lawmaking was the right of the King, who would, in consultation with his council, issue new decrees or amend existing ones to effectively govern the realm. But the King needed money to fight wars, so from time to time a parliament would be called and the most senior lords, bishops and barons would be summoned to meet their monarch. By the 14th century, this parliament brought representatives from cities and towns as well as shires, as Lords Spiritual (bishops) and Temporal (nobles) and Commons met, sometimes together and sometimes separately, to discuss how to respond to the King's demands for money, acting as paymaster.

The paymaster's role gave Parliament leverage, which it exploited by presenting petitions to the King for changes in laws in return for supporting the King's demands. Strong kings and queens were able to bend parliament to their wills, weaker ones could not so a conflict to establish who should rule was bound to happen, first with Charles I and later James II pitting themselves against parliament. The 1689 Bill of Rights regularised the monarchy's function – it could no longer ride roughshod over parliament by ignoring or failing to enact legislation or exercise powers of state without parliamentary approval. Parliamentary power advanced through the 19th and 20th centuries so that the monarch's role is now largely that of constitutional figurehead.

Parliament can legislate in two ways:

1. By statute

Acts of Parliament lay down rules that guide future conduct. Laws are normally introduced in the House of Commons, though the House of Lords can also introduce bills. Once introduced in the Commons, a bill goes through several stages – a first reading, second reading, committee stage, report stage and third reading – where the legislation is reviewed, fine-tuned and polished, with some sections being modified, before being passed to the House of Lords. There it goes through a similar procedure, and if it is amended it then returns to the Commons, which considers the amendments. The Commons can reject the Lords' amendments, though compromise is sought where possible. The Lords cannot hold up legislation indefinitely – the 1911 and 1949 Parliament Acts allow bills to go before the monarch for Royal Assent without agreement from the Lords after a time has elapsed (one year for most bills; one month for money bills). The monarch's permission is really a formality, and once granted, a bill becomes an Act of Parliament.

2. Through delegated legislation

Sometimes parliament cannot devote time to enacting all legislation, so contents itself with laying down the general policies behind some Act, while delegating to another body the responsibility for drafting the exact regulations that will operate within the framework. Such regulations are known as delegated legislation (or sometimes subordinate or secondary legislation) and though they have not been enacted by parliament, they still have the force of law. For example, the Road Traffic Act 1983 empowered the then Ministry of Transport to formulate regulations for road traffic matters. Local government by-laws are delegated legislation, and derive their authority from some Act of Parliament. Delegated legislation offers some benefits – it frees parliamentary time for important matters and allows experts to draft technical regulations – but can be criticised, not least because it allows individual ministers to modify acts of parliament and so undermine the spirit of parliamentary supremacy.

Canon law

After the Norman conquest, the legal system was divided into lay courts which administered the common law, and ecclesiastical courts which dealt with matters such as clergy discipline, offences against morality and church doctrines, marriage and wills. Initially, canon law had a wide jurisdiction and was very important, but once Henry VIII had disestablished the church and state during the Reformation its influence slowly declined, with jurisdiction for matrimonial and legitimacy being transferred to the Divorce Court and testamentary matters to the Court of Probate, both created in 1857.

Mercantile law

Mercantile law was applied by maritime courts and some local courts in market towns, and was effectively the customs of merchants and traders which had been ratified by courts of law and which had become a form of customary law. Maritime courts' jurisdictions included such matters as hiring ships, carrying goods by sea, marine insurance and piracy. Because Britain is an island trading nation, the maritime courts became increasingly important and its jurisdiction increased accordingly.

Local courts dealt with commercial matters, and were often held at towns holding fairs, dealing with such matters as sale of goods, bills of exchange and negotiable instruments. A second group of local courts was the Courts of the Staple, established in towns where staple goods such as wool or leather were traded. Mercantile law offered protection to foreign traders, and the courts were often constituted with one local and one foreign merchant, with the tribunal chaired by the local mayor, dispensing justice swiftly, and making up for the deficiencies in common law in regulating contractual disputes between traders. But the spread of common law courts, following the regularisation of the common law, meant that mercantile courts declined in importance, and by the middle of the 18th century mercantile courts only had jurisdiction over maritime law and prize law (relating to enemy ships captured at time of war).

Local custom

In addition to the common law, some local customs have survived which impose duties and confer rights, even though they differ from the customs of the country as a whole. These rights, many of which have existed before laws were enacted, are enforceable under English law. Examples of local customs are rights of way. For a local custom to have the force of law, it must be reasonable, local and offer certainty in terms of the people or place it refers to, and not be contrary to any statute. The custom must have existed since the commencement of legal memory (though courts will presume that old customs have existed thus unless it can be proved to the contrary) and be continuously observed without interruption. Above all, it must be exercised peaceably, openly and of right. If the custom requires someone's permission to operate, for example the permission of a landowner to walk across his fields, then it is not a right, as it only exists because the landowner allows it to exist.

European Union law

After Britain joined what was then called the European Economic Community in 1971, the European Communities Act 1972 incorporated the laws of the EEC into our legal system. The principles of parliamentary sovereignty mean that EU law is therefore applied as part of our domestic law unless the UK legislation has expressly rejected the EU law. The main principles of EU law that affect our legal system are:

1. **Freedom of movement of goods, services, people and capital.**
2. **Competition law** – which seeks to prevent cartels and price-fixing stopping smaller companies and organisations competing.
3. **Social policies** – which seeks to prevent discrimination, for example over issues of equal pay for work of equal value, or the question of length of the working week.

Section 1.2: The legal system – civil and criminal

A variety of laws regulate different parts of our lives on a day-to-day, month-by-month, year-by-year basis. These can be classified in a number of ways, most of which are of most interest only to lawyers or law students. The ones most likely to affect you, and covered in this book, are:

Criminal law

Criminal law regulates behaviour of individuals towards the state, by making certain wrongs offences against the state. It is important to recognise that crimes are offences because the state says so, not because they necessarily harm another person. Some crimes, for example murder or theft, are obviously offences that harm other people, but some acts are classified as criminal even though the 'victim' doesn't see himself as a victim at all. For example, although boxing is classified as a sport in this country, bare-knuckle boxing is banned. So even though two bare-knuckle fighters consent to having the other fighter try to hit them, when they fight, their act is regarded as an assault and they will be treated accordingly. Another example would be prohibition in 1920s America – though bootlegging (illegally importing and selling alcohol contrary to the Volstead Act) could be said to be a victimless crime in that no-one was harmed, it was still a crime – because the law said it was. Criminal actions are normally brought to court by the police and Crown Prosecution Service, though individuals can also bring private prosecutions.

Criminal law is dispensed through:

- Magistrates' courts.
- Crown Courts.
- Divisional court of the Queen's Bench Division.
- Court of Appeal.
- House of Lords.

The magistrates' and Crown Courts are responsible for dispensing justice in that they hear cases and decide guilt or innocence, and hand down punishment. The Divisional Court, Court of Appeal and House of Lords operate as a review, and if you do not agree with the decision of the lower court, either because the guilty verdict was wrong or the sentence was too harsh, you can seek leave to appeal to the higher court.

Civil law

Civil law governs the relationships of individuals, and their rights and duties, and would include areas such as:

- Torts – civil wrongs such as nuisance, negligence, libel and slander.
- Contract – legally enforceable promises, for example the sale of goods and services.
- Family law – the relationships, rights and duties of family members towards each other.
- Succession – how property is divided when someone dies, with or without a will.

Civil actions are normally brought by individuals, often private citizens or companies, to establish the existence of rights, or to protect them.

Civil law is dispensed through

- County courts.
- The High Court of Justice:
  — Queen's Bench Division.
  — Chancery Division.
  — Family Division.
- Court of Appeal.
- House of Lords.

In addition, the European Court of Justice will rule on matters that affect the treaties that established the European Community, and interpretation of European law including cases where English law appears to be inconsistent with European law.

The county court and High Court of Justice hear cases at first instance, and the Court of Appeal and House of Lords will hear appeals against judgments made by the lower courts.

Administrative law

Administrative law regulates relationships between individuals and the state, local authorities and other public bodies such as local health authorities. Administrative law issues are the health service, education, housing, town and country planning and the environment.

Administrative law is dispensed by:

- The Queen's Bench Division.
- Court of Appeal.
- House of Lords.

More information about courts is contained in Chapter 9.

Section 1.3: Solicitors, barristers and licensed conveyancers

For many years, the legal profession in England and Wales was divided into two distinct branches: solicitors and barristers. At first instance the main difference between them appears to be one of dress – barristers usually wear wigs and gowns in court, while solicitors usually do not! To outward appearances, solicitors' work is essentially administrative while barristers are advocates appearing before courts and tribunals to make arguments; however, solicitors would – and still do – act as advocates at the magistrates' courts and county courts in certain proceedings.

Solicitors

Solicitors are regulated by the Law Society, and any suitably qualified person who has passed Law Society examinations and served a period of up to two years' articles (essentially on-the-job training) can become a solicitor. Once enrolled, solicitors become officers of the Supreme Court and are given a Certificate to Practise, which is renewable annually and allows them to operate as solicitors. In private practice, solicitors can either be sole traders or work within larger firms, either as assistant solicitors or (after some years) as partners. Since 1991, solicitors' firms have been able to set up as limited companies but many firms have chosen not to follow this route because, while the partners would have more protection from exposure should the firm fail, they would have to reveal more information which would be open to public scrutiny. A half-way house has come with the creation of limited liability partnerships, which offer security over financial exposure and limit the amount of information that needs to be revealed. Solicitors also work in industry, commerce, finance, local government and the civil service – indeed, any sphere that might be affected by the law.

What do solicitors do?

You can contact solicitors on a wide variety of matters both legal and non-legal (financial or business). Solicitors will be involved with buying and selling property, the drafting of wills, family matters and managing estates, as well as representing clients in civil and criminal matters. Solicitors in smaller firms tend to be general practitioners, though firms with many partners and many more assistant solicitors will specialise. Solicitors can represent clients (they have 'rights of audience') at magistrates' courts and county courts, and have rights of audience in the Crown Court and Supreme Court. A client-solicitor relationship is protected by privilege. This means that client-solicitor conversations are private, and a solicitor cannot be ordered by a court to reveal anything that has been said or written in the course of a professional relationship.

You can sue your solicitor for negligence over work they have done for you (or not done for you!), for example where your solicitor has failed to issue court proceedings in time.

But bear in mind, that if you don't pay your solicitor's bill, they can sue you for their fees (barristers cannot).

Barristers

Barristers are regulated by the Senate of the Inns of Court, and all barristers must be members of one of the four Inns – Gray's Inn, Lincoln's Inn, Inner Temple or Middle Temple. To become a barrister, a law student must attend their Inn a certain number of times – the process of 'keeping term' or 'eating dinners', and before being called to the bar must pass examinations set by the Council of Legal Education. In addition, they must undergo one year's further on-the-job training, known as 'pupillage', though after six months they have rights of audience in all courts of law in England and Wales.

What do barristers do?

Unlike solicitors, if you want to get hold of a barrister to represent you, you can't just drop in and see him or her, or call to make an appointment. Barristers cannot take instructions direct from 'lay clients,' but only from solicitors – so if you need a barrister, you will need to speak to a solicitor first.

A barrister's primary role is to argue his client's case in court, though it will also involve pre-trial work such as drafting opinions on difficult points of law (which might help you decide that your case is one you cannot win) and giving advice.

London-based barristers tend to specialise whereas barristers in regional chamber are more general practitioners, which means they develop expertise and a reputation in particular areas of the law. Senior barristers can apply to become Queen's Counsel (known as 'silks' because their gowns are silk rather than stuff), which gives them increased status, more important cases and higher fees.

Licensed conveyancers

Under the Administration of Justice Act 1985, the monopoly of solicitors over conveyancing property was removed, and 'licensed conveyancers' were henceforth granted authority to administer all legal formalities connected with land transfers. You can still use solicitors to carry out the legal work involved in buying and selling houses – what the 1985 Act means is that you don't have to if you don't want to, and you can use a conveyancer instead. The Council for Licensed Conveyancers is the regulatory body that oversees this new 'branch', with responsibility for drafting and enforcing rules of conduct and discipline, as well as actually granting licences to conveyancers. Licensed conveyancers cannot enter partnerships with solicitors, but can form a partnership with fellow licensed conveyancers and non-licensed conveyancers.

Section 1.4 Legal Aid

What is Legal Aid?

The cost of bringing legal actions to court – and the cost of defending them – is well-known, but as a matter of public policy it would be wrong that a people cannot defend themselves properly because they can't afford it. The 1949 Legal Aid Act created a mechanism to fund legal action for people whose lack of money might stop them from exercising rights, or mounting an adequate defence in criminal cases. The Act established a Legal Aid fund, funded by the state, which would meet such people's costs. Subsequent Legal Aid Acts have amended this legislation, and now the Legal Aid Board, which administered the Legal Aid fund and, via local committees drew up lists of law firms that could do Legal Aid work, has become the Legal Services Commission, with two arms:

- The Community Legal Service (CLS), which replaces the old civil scheme of Legal Aid, bringing together networks of funders and suppliers into partnerships to provide the widest possible access to information and advice.
- The Criminal Defence Service which will replace the old system of criminal Legal Aid to provide criminal defence services to people suspected or accused of crimes.

For criminal cases, courts grant Legal Aid certificates while in civil cases, the CLS consider applications. Not all solicitors' firms do Legal Aid work, and some of those that do will have a Legal Aid sign. Though there is no longer a Legal Aid Board, for ease and simplicity, this section will continue to refer to state-provided funds for bringing and defending court actions as 'Legal Aid'.

How do I qualify for Legal Aid?

Legal aid applications can be made by people, groups or sole trader businesses. Eligibility is not restricted on grounds of nationality or residence.

To qualify, you have to show that your financial circumstances qualify (the 'means test') and, in civil cases, that the case is worthwhile so costs can be recovered from the other side (the 'merits test'). Your disposable income and capital is checked (this is calculated by looking at your income, expenditure and outgoings) to see whether you fall within the means-tested limits, though different eligibility conditions apply for civil and criminal Legal Aid certificates. Your solicitor will be able to help you fill in the forms; the main form will allow you to outline the basis of your case – this is the section that the Legal Services Commission will examine to decide whether your case is worthwhile. You will have another form to list your financial details – income, savings and any property you own – while self-employed people may have to send in their accounts too. Your employer has a form to fill into certify details of your income and deductions, but they will not be told any of the details of your case, only that you are applying for Legal Aid. You send these forms into the Legal Services Commission; they process your claim and notify your lawyers whether you are entitled to Legal Aid. Normally this takes four weeks or so, but emergency applications can be processed in up to three days. Depending on how much disposable income you have, your Legal Aid certificate may cover all your costs, or you may be have to make some contribution to your costs. If you have too much disposable income, you may not qualify at all. If you apply for Legal Aid, costs can be incurred in submitting the application unless your solicitor is prepared to do the work for nothing, or if you qualify for free advice under the 'Legal Help' scheme. If granted Legal Aid, you can decide whether to accept Legal Aid or not, but if you do, from this point on you are liable for your contributions. Contributions are paid monthly and will be recoverable from the other side at the end of the case if you are successful.

How do I get Legal Aid if I have been accused of a crime?

Everyone is entitled to free advice at a police station after being arrested, and if the case goes to court you may qualify for Legal Aid depending on your income and savings. Once you are brought before a court, you can apply for Legal Aid. Usually, before making any order the magistrates would require a written statement of means – a breakdown of your income and expenditure – to determine whether Legal Aid should be granted.

You will qualify for full Legal Aid if you receive Income Support, Income-based Jobseekers' Allowance, Family Credit or Disability Working Allowance, otherwise you may have to make a contribution, paid weekly. There is a presumption that Legal Aid will be granted where it would not be in the interests of justice for it to be refused, for example in the case of serious crimes where a good defence is most critical. If a case is transferred from magistrates' court to the crown court for the matter can be heard by a jury, Legal Aid can be extended, either by the magistrates' court or by the crown court judge. If a certificate is granted, Legal Aid will cover advice and representation from a solicitor and barrister (but if the case can only be heard summarily (before a magistrate), only a solicitor's costs will be met from Legal Aid funds).

Can I get Legal Aid for civil cases?

Legal Aid is not restricted to criminal cases, and people bringing or defending civil actions may also be eligible for Legal Aid depending on their circumstances and the merits of their case. Legal aid certificates can be issued to cover actions before the House of Lords, Court of Appeal and High Court, as well as the more specialist courts, including county courts and employment appeal tribunals (but not employment tribunals). But Legal Aid will not be granted for:

- Undefended matrimonial proceedings.
- Administrative tribunals.
- Arbitration proceedings.
- Actions for defamation (actions for libel and slander).

The fact that Legal Aid is not available to fund actions for defamation does pose problems for people who feel that their reputation has been damaged by the publication of false information, or by stories that may appear in newspapers, on television or in other media. While a complaint to the Press Complaints Commission may get the false story withdrawn and corrected, damages for loss of reputation can only be awarded by a court – and this requires you to bring the matter to court. And if you can't afford it, the matter might well have to rest there. In 1999, former Conservative MP Neil Hamilton was only able to bring an action for defamation against businessman Mohammed Fayed over the 'cash-for-questions' row because his case was funded by a number of other people. Some of his backers argued the case should be heard because the allegations on which it was based raised a matter of legitimate public interest (but when Mr Hamilton lost his action, the judge directed that his backers should be liable to meet not only Mr Hamilton's costs in the case, but Mr Fayed's costs as well, estimated at some £2 million).

Legal aid certificates will not be granted to fund actions that are too trivial or considered too simple to require a lawyer's help to unravel. The limitation on trivial actions is designed to prevent a flood of vexatious litigants – people bringing actions with little or no merit – and which would put an unfair burden on the Legal Aid system and reduce the funds available to help more deserving cases.

Do I qualify for Legal Aid?

You immediately qualify for Legal Aid if you are on Income Support or Income-based Jobseekers' Allowance, provided any savings or property does not take you above a set threshold. If you receive other benefits, you may qualify depending on how much you receive. If your available income is less than £2,723 a year you will be entitled to Legal Aid without paying any contributions. Once your available income tops £8,067 you will not be eligible for Legal Aid. If your income is between £2,723 and £8,067 a year (after deductions) you may have to pay a monthly contribution towards your Legal Aid of 1/36th of your income between £2,723 and £8,067. Remember, if your partner has income, that will be added to your income when deciding if you are eligible (unless you are suing or being sued by them!). If your capital is under £3,000 (and your income below the threshold already outlined), you won't have to pay any contributions, but if it is more than £3,000 you will have to pay a contribution based on 1/36th of the excess over £3,000. If you have capital of £6,750 or more then you will not qualify, regardless of income.

Different capital rates apply for pensioners:

Income up to £370 per year	allowable capital is £35,000
Income from £371 to £670	allowable capital is £30,000
Income from £671 to £970	allowable capital is £25,000
Income from £971 to £1,270	allowable capital is £20,000
Income from £1,271 to £1,570	allowable capital is £15,000
Income from £1,571 to £1,870	allowable capital is £10,000
Income from £1,871 to £2,723	allowable capital is £5,000

Deductions will be made for tax and National Insurance contributions, as well as for dependent partners and children.

Partner	Deduct £29.75 a week
Child aged 15 and under	Deduct £26.60 a week
Child aged 16 and over	Deduct £31.75

The best way to understand Legal Aid is to think of it like a state benefit. If your disposable income is below a certain level then you may qualify. If your circumstances change, then you should notify the Legal Services Commission at once. A woman who was contesting her former husband's access to their children was granted Legal Aid; she subsequently married a man with a good job and income, but did not notify the Legal Aid Board (as it then was) at once. When she finally did tell them her financial circumstances had changed, the Board reassessed her and revoked her Legal Aid certificate.

Limited Legal Aid certificates

A limited certificate places restrictions on the work your solicitor can do on your behalf. It may require civil cases to be dealt with at magistrates' court rather than county courts (because it could be cheaper to hear), or it may cover all steps up to trial, but not the actual trial itself – in which case your lawyers will have to write to the Legal Services Commission to justify the need for a trial. It may also impose a maximum value of work that can be done on your behalf.

What happens about costs?

In addition to making orders for damages or any equitable remedies such as injunctions, specific performance, etc., courts may also award costs once a case has been concluded. If you are granted Legal Aid for a civil case and you lose the action, you may be liable to meet the opposing side's costs. Normally this is limited to what a court feels is reasonable, taking your financial circumstances into account. But this is unlikely. Should your side win, normally your only financial liability will be any contribution you may have been required to make to the Community Legal Services Fund (which would have been determined when your Legal Aid certificate was granted and which are recoverable). Any costs will be paid to the fund, which also has a first charge on property recovered or retained in the court case (the so-called 'statutory charge'), though in matrimonial cases the first £2,500 you receive cannot be charged in this way. Even if the court awards costs, it will only order your opponent to pay your 'reasonable' costs, so you will have to foot the bill for any work your solicitor may have done that is not considered reasonable (this is known as 'solicitor–client' work).

If you have been paying Legal Aid contributions, you can object to the size of your solicitor's bill because you are partly paying for those costs. Similarly, if you win but have to repay your costs out of damages, you can query the bill. When your solicitor gives you a bill, you can object and get the court to rule how much you pay. You have 14 days (sometimes 21 days) to notify your solicitor that you are objecting, and your solicitor will arrange an 'assessment hearing' where you will explain why you object to the bill. If the judge agrees, the bill will be reduced.

What happens if I am not receiving Legal Aid and the other party is?

If you are not getting Legal Aid and you lose your case, you will be liable for the full costs of both sides. (There is an element of public policy in this – effectively you are 'topping up' the Community Legal Services Fund.) If you should win against a legally aided person, then the court may order that you are awarded costs from the Community Legal Services Fund if:

1. The case has been decided in your favour in court, and not in an out-of-court settlement.
2. The legally aided person brought the legal action in the first place.
3. The court must be satisfied that you will suffer serious hardship unless costs are awarded.

Can I lose my right to Legal Aid?

If the Legal Services Commission decides you are no longer eligible for Legal Aid your certificate may be discharged or revoked. This can happen if your financial circumstances change, or if you fail to provide the board with further information or if your solicitor recommends it be revoked or discharged. Once your certificate is revoked or discharged, your solicitor can do no more work on your behalf under the certificate. 'Discharge' means you do not have to pay for any work your solicitor has done under the certificate up to the date it was discharged; if you want to continue, you will have to reapply for Legal Aid. 'Revocation' means you may have to pay your solicitor for any work done under the certificate. The Legal Services Commission must tell you if it plans to discharge or revoke your certificate; you have 14 days to object in writing.

Is there any other way of getting legal help?

The 1988 Legal Aid Act established the Advice and Assistance scheme, better known as 'the green form scheme' but which will now be known as 'Legal Help'. Under this scheme, you can seek free general legal advice from a solicitor (and in some cases, a barrister) on any problem or question of English law, unless a Legal Aid certificate has been issued in connection with it. If you qualify, your solicitor can carry out two hours' work on your behalf (three hours' if he is acting for you in a divorce). To do more work, the solicitor would have to apply to the Legal Services Commission, which can authorise a further additional hour's work. Once that has been used up, your solicitor will have to apply again. However, this will not be extended indefinitely. Legal Help is applied for using a CLS APP1 form. People aged under 16 can apply for Legal Help advice, but the form will be signed by a solicitor if the applicant's parents or legal guardian won't (or if the problem concerns them). Solicitors can advise anywhere – in their office, a hospital, a prison or a police station – and can draft letters, take statements, draw up documents and negotiate on your behalf and even prepare a written case for you to present at an administrative tribunal. But solicitors cannot represent you in court under this scheme – they can only provide advice, guidance and assistance – unless a court requires the solicitor to do so, for instance acting as a duty solicitor at magistrates' court. However, a solicitor can help prepare an application for Legal Aid in criminal or civil proceedings.

The Legal Help scheme will also not cover conveyancing or making a will, but advice can still be given on general matters arising out of these subjects, such as general property law. Like Legal Aid, Legal Help advice is means-tested, but here the solicitor decides at first instance whether you qualify. If you receive Income Support, Jobseekers' Allowance, Family Credit or Disability Working allowance, you will qualify for advice and assistance provided your capital is not above the £1,000 threshold, and you earn £83 or less per week. In some cases, advice can be given immediately; otherwise the Legal Services Commission must approve the form. If you have a partner (whether married or cohabiting) and you are not actually taking legal action against them, their income will be included when deciding whether you are eligible for green form advice.

Are any changes planned to the Legal Aid structure?

The LSC has come about as a result of changes introduced by the Lord Chancellor, Lord Irvine, in a bid to reduce costs and at the same time make the courts more available to all – not just the very poor or very rich. The other main proposals are:

- To restrict Legal Aid work to those law firms with a contract with the Legal Aid Board, allowing the Board to buy services at a fixed price that has been determined locally.
- To tighten the 'merits test' before Legal Aid is granted. Lawyers will be required to give the Board a precise percentage prospect of the success of the case, and the Lord Chancellor would like to see the merits test stipulate a 75 per cent likelihood of success.
- To set up a special fund for public interest cases, where it is plainly in the public interest for a particular point of law to be examined, or for a precedent to be established.
- To exclude most claims for money or damages from the Legal Aid scheme leaving Legal Aid available for more deserving cases, such as criminal cases; care of children; judicial review; and social welfare cases.
- To extend conditional fee ('no win, no fee') agreements to all civil proceedings, other than family cases. Under conditional fee agreements, lawyers receive no fee if they lose their cases, but receive an 'uplift' – an additional percentage of the fee, agreed with their clients beforehand, limited by statute to 100 per cent of the fees and currently averaging 43 per cent – if they win, but never more than the 25% of the total damages awarded. Check with your solicitor which types of case can be funded by conditional fee agreements.

Section 1.5 Other places to get legal advice

As we have already seen, Legal Aid offers a mechanism to give legal representation to people that might otherwise be unable to protect their rights in a court of law, either in criminal or civil matters.

The 'green form' scheme gives 2–3 hours of free legal advice to qualified people, and Legal Aid will provide state funding for people accused of crimes, or who need to take civil action, which will pay for preparation of a case and in some – though not all – cases the presentation of it in court.

In addition, you can get legal assistance and advice from a number of other places.

Law Centres

Law Centres employ teams of solicitors that will handle your case, including appearing on your behalf in court if necessary – free of charge. At present there are 17 Law Centres in England and Wales; 14 in London and the others in Manchester, Cardiff and Birmingham. The important thing to remember about these centres is that their lawyers will act for you in court – although they will do their best to resolve the matter before it gets that far.

Legal Advice Centres

Here you will be able to get advice about your problems, but staff will not act for you in courts or tribunals, though they will tell you where you can get further advice, and direct you to solicitors that do legal aid work.

Citizens' Advice Bureaux

The CAB has a long and distinguished history of helping people with problems of a legal or quasi-legal nature. Though not legally trained (though some centres employ solicitors) the volunteers will offer a sympathetic ear to your worries and give advice and practical assistance in dealing with your problems, for instance, writing letters to landlords or creditors on your behalf, or drawing up repayment schedules. CABs often work in conjunction with Law Advice Centres, and will offer advice either in person (face-to-face) or over the telephone.

Chapter 2
You and your family

Section 2.1 Births, deaths and marriage

We have just had a child. Are there any formalities that must be followed?

Every child born in Britain must be registered with the registrar for births, marriages and deaths for the sub-district in which the child was born. The register entry can be made by the mother or father if they are married, but if the child is born illegitimately the father's name can not be recorded, unless there is a court order naming him as the father, or the father signs the register as well. The register entry records the child's name and sex, date and place of birth, full names, addresses and place of births of parents, the father's occupation and the mother's maiden name. A copy of the birth certificate entry will be given to you free of charge. If it is more convenient, you can register the birth in another district, for example if you gave birth while on holiday.

If the mother died in childbirth and the father is unknown, who can register the child?

If parents are not able to register the child, the occupier of the property in which the birth took place or anyone present at the birth, for example a doctor or midwife, can register the child.

What happens if a baby is still-born?

Any child born after 28 weeks must be registered, even if it is still-born. But the birth is registered in a separate register and no certificate is given.

How soon after birth do we have to register the child?

All the child's details must be registered by the 42nd day after the child was born. If you fail to register, you can be fined up to £200 at the registrar's discretion.

Can the register be inspected?

The register is a public document and can be inspected locally. Alternatively, all records are kept at the General Register Office and can be searched free of charge during office hours (8.30am–4.30pm, Monday to Friday). Searches at sub-district level are free for specific register entries, though a fee is payable for general searches.

What formalities must be observed if someone dies, or is found dead?

Only a doctor can legally state that someone is dead, so if a sudden death occurs, you should summon a doctor at once. Obviously, if there is any suggestion of foul play you should also call the police. A doctor will check for vital signs and if none can be found, a doctor can in most cases assume the person is dead. The doctor will certify a cause of death and report the death to the registrar. If the cause of death is in any way suspicious, or occurred in police or prison custody, or might have been the result of industrial disease, the death must also be reported to the coroner.

What happens to the body?

The executors or administrators (the next of kin if the dead person died without leaving a will) are usually responsible for arranging a funeral, and though the dead person may have specified his wishes for a burial method or service, they are not binding on executors or administrators. In the same way, regardless of the dead person's wishes, the administrators or executors can decide whether to make organs available for transplant even if the dead person left a donor card. However, a surgeon can overrule the wishes of administrators and executors and can order organs to be harvested, because no damage to the estate is done and no criminal offence is being committed. There was a scandal at a children's hospital after organs were removed from dead children's bodies. But these were not for transplant, but for research.

What formalities are required for disposal of a body?

The registrar must be notified of any death within five days. Three certificates are required in order to bury or cremate a person:

1. A medical certificate of death, signed by the doctor who attended the person during their last illness, and stating the cause of death. If death takes place in hospital, the health authority usually arranges for a death certificate to be issued. This is issued free of charge, and if the doctor does not issue one, relatives who live in the same area or who were with the dead person during their last illness can insist that one is issued. If a doctor other than the attending doctor is called, the death must be reported to the coroner and an inquest may be held.
2. A disposal certificate, issued by the registrar free of charge, which allows the body to be buried or cremated.
3. A death certificate, issued by the registrar on production of the medical certificate. This is needed to claim on life insurance policies, etc.

A death must be registered in person – you can't phone in and mail the certificates. You will need the person's medical card and a medical certificate of death, and in most cases the coroner will record the dead person's name, address, place and date of birth, occupation and whether the dead person was receiving a pension or allowance from public funds and (if married) the age of the surviving spouse. Once this information is provided a disposal certificate will be issued that should go to the undertaker. If the registrar does not feel the death is one that the coroner should be notified of, he may immediately issue a disposal certificate that permits burial but not cremation.

Can a registrar refuse to register a death?

A registrar must refuse to register any death, and must report the death to the coroner if:

- A doctor did not attend the deceased during his or her last illness.
- There is no properly completed medical certificate of cause of death.
- The doctor signing the death certificate did not see the dead person after death or fourteen days before death.
- The cause of death is unknown.
- Death was unnatural, violent, caused by neglect, or was in any way suspicious.
- Death occurred during an operation or before the patient came out of the anaesthetic.
- Death was due to industrial disease or industrial poisoning.

If a death is reported to the coroner, but he feels no formal inquest is required, he will notify the registrar or the next of kin so that disposal and death certificates can be issued.

What happens if a UK subject dies abroad?

Death should be registered in accordance with that country's formalities, but the British Embassy or consulate of that country should also be notified. If the body is to be brought home, the coroner is notified in the district where the body is to be buried before burial or cremation takes place. If he wishes to investigate, he can order an inquest (this can happen even if a local inquest was held and he is not satisfied with its findings).

What happens if a non-UK subject dies in this country?

The death must be registered in the same way as it would for a UK subject, and if the relatives of the deceased wish to take the body abroad for burial they must inform the coroner first. The coroner has four days to decide whether to allow the body to be removed from UK jurisdiction, and if he is not satisfied as to the cause of death he can detain the body while a post-mortem and inquest is held.

What happens to a person's debts and contracts when he or she dies?

Outstanding debts will be met by the estate before it is shared out under a will or rules of intestacy. If the dead man is insolvent, a trustee in bankruptcy may be appointed to wind up affairs. Contracts are personal and end with death, though a maintenance agreement can, in exceptional cases, continue to be paid if a court orders it.

What is marriage?

Marriage is a legal and sometimes religious ceremony that joins a man and woman together, creating a relationship that confers specific rights and privileges on both parties. Under English law, a marriage is only valid if certain legal formalities have been complied with and the religious ceremonies of the place of celebration. Many of these rights relating to property and children can now be acquired by 'common-law marriage' (which is a misleading term in itself), but marriage is a specific commitment. In marriage a man and woman become

husband and wife and in many respects become one legal entity. Each has the right to be supported by the other, and until the extension of the rape laws, a husband had the right to have sexual intercourse with his wife (now, of course, he can be charged with rape if he forces his wife to have sex against her will).

Who can marry?

To get married, you must satisfy a number of conditions:

*   You must be aged sixteen and over – and if you are under the age of eighteen, you will need your parents' permission. If your parents' are married, both parents must consent; if they are divorced or legally separated you will need the consent of the parent you live with. If your parents are both dead, your legal guardian's consent is needed (this can be the local authority if you are in care). If your parents or guardian refuse consent, you could apply to a magistrate for permission, but if he refuses to grant consent then you have no further right of appeal.
*   You must be of the opposite sex. Two men or two women cannot marry – though the UK recently sanctioned a form of 'lesbian' marriage, where, because one partner had undergone a sex change to become a woman but was still legally recognised as a man, in the eyes of the law a man and woman were entering a marriage contract.
*   You must not be already married. If you marry another person while legally married to someone else then you can be charged with bigamy (having more than one spouse) and face

a maximum penalty of seven years' imprisonment. It may be a defence if you thought that you had actually been divorced, or if you thought your husband were dead, but both these beliefs must be reasonable ones.

- You are not so closely related that your marriage is prohibited by law. If you are a man, you cannot marry your mother, mother-in-law, aunt, grandmother, grandmother-in-law, step-mother, adoptive mother, sister, half-sister, daughter, niece, daughter-in-law, step-daughter, granddaughter, step-granddaughter, granddaughter-in-law or adopted daughter. If you are a woman, you cannot marry your father, father-in-law, uncle, grandfather, grandfather-in-law, step-father, adoptive father, brother, half-brother, son, nephew, son-in-law, step-son, grandson, step-grandson, grandson-in-law or adopted son.

Who can perform a marriage ceremony?

The law distinguishes between marriage ceremonies and permission given for a marriage to take place. Various clergy and ministers of different religions can perform the religious ceremony of marriage, but permission can only be granted by an Anglican (Church of England or Church of Wales) clergyman, or by a superintendent registrar for births, marriages and deaths.

If you are planning to get married you (or your intended – only one need attend) will have to make an appointment to see an Anglican clergyman or registrar to fill in the necessary forms, provide proof of identity, marital status, etc.

What formalities would we have to observe for an Anglican wedding?

Church procedures for marrying are very traditional, and require the 'publishing of the banns' – this is where your names are read out in the parish church of the district where you live and where your intended lives, so if anyone knows of a legal reason why you should not be married, they can report it to their vicar – for example if you were already married.

Publishing the banns must take place on three consecutive Sundays, and then you can be married any time within the next three months; if the wedding does not take place within that time, the banns will have to be published again. In the Church of England, the fee for publishing the banns is £15, and £8 for a banns certificate if required. The marriage service itself costs £132, but churches can add additional costs for choirs and bell-ringers, etc.

I don't want the banns to be published. Can I speed things up a bit?

You can apply for a 'common licence' which can be easily obtained from the bishop of a diocese if either of you have lived in the diocese for the past fifteen days. The fee for a common licence is £57 and it allows you to be married in a particular church at any time with the next three months. If you need to marry even faster than that and cannot meet the fifteen-day residency qualification, for example if one of you is very ill and might die, you can apply for a special licence from the Church of England faculty office in London. This licence can only be issued by the Archbishop of Canterbury and you will have to swear statements, provide character references and letters of approval from parents before a special licence can be granted. The licence costs £120 but there will be additional legal fees you will have to pay.

I am not religious; what formalities do I need to observe?

For any marriage ceremony not performed by an Anglican clergyman, either religious or civil, you will need a certificate of notice from the superintendent registrar of the district in which you plan to get married. A certificate is issued after a notice of your intention to marry has been posted in the office for three weeks – the civil equivalent of publishing the banns. Once this has taken place, you can be married any time within the next six months. The cost of publishing the notice is £25, and the fee for the civil ceremony and marriage licence is £37.50. If you undergo a religious ceremony other than an Anglican one, your church – Hindu, Sikh, Jewish, etc. – can advise you of the cost.

If you want to be married more quickly than that, you can get a registrar's combined certificate and licence at a cost of £84 (plus the £25 fee for issuing the notice). To do this, one of you must have lived in the district for the past fifteen days, and the other must be resident in England or Wales in that time.

Can we get married anywhere?

There has been a significant relaxation in the requirements regarding where couples can get married. In days gone by, you could only get married in a register office or a 'registered building' such as a church or other place of worship between the hours of 8am and 6pm. There were exceptions, however – Quaker and Jewish wedding ceremonies could be performed in private houses at any time. Now a greater number of places have been registered, for example castles and great stately homes, so marriages can take place there as well. However, you might want to get married in on a beautiful hillside, or in your favourite football team's stadium. You can have a wedding ceremony there if you want, but for the marriage to have any legal validity you will also have to undergo a ceremony which complies with the normal formalities.

If you get married under special licence (or a Registrar general's licence, which is the civil equivalent) you can marry wherever the licence allows, which is usually hospital or some medical unit.

How many people do I need to be at the service?

Apart from the happy couple and the person that will perform the ceremony – an authorised minister of religion or two registrars for a register office wedding – the only other requirement is to have two witnesses to sign the marriage register. You do not have to know them, so the romantic 'dragging two witnesses off the street' notion is perfectly feasible if you decide to get married in haste, but they do have to be reasonably credible – a young child will not do.

If your minister is not an authorised minister, then a registrar will also have to be present to perform the marriage.

How can I prove I am married?

A marriage certificate is proof that a valid marriage ceremony has taken place. This is a copy of the entry in the marriage register at the church or register office, and shows the names, former marital status, addresses and occupations of husband and wife, and of their parents; it will also record the date and place of the wedding, and the names of the witnesses. If you get married in a religious ceremony, the certificate will also record what religion under which it was performed. You are normally given a marriage certificate at the time of your wedding, or one is sent to you soon after the ceremony; there is a charge. Duplicates can be obtained from the register office where you were married (or in the case of a religious ceremony, where your marriage was registered).

I want to get married abroad. Will that marriage be recognised as legal in the UK?

If you want to get married on a Bajan beach for example, for your marriage to be valid in the UK, it must be recognised as valid in Barbados. So if all the formalities that would be required to contract a legal marriage in Barbados are followed, then you have a valid marriage as far as English law is concerned. Be careful where two ceremonies may be required – for example if you want to have a church wedding in France, remember that the marriage ceremony is civil; so to contract a valid marriage in France that would be recognised in the UK you would need a civil ceremony as well as a church service.

One possible benefit is that if you contract a polygamous marriage (where you have more than one spouse) in a country where polygamy is lawful, then you would not become a bigamist on your return to the UK. But you would not be allowed to contract a further marriage in the UK just because your first two wives were lawful, it would not prevent a third wife married in the UK from being bigamous.

Section 2.2 Separation and divorce

Divorce is a legal step to terminate a marriage so that it is dissolved in the eyes of the law. Many people choose to divorce to invoke the legal process and claim financial relief. Some simply separate without dissolving the marriage in order that certain liabilities and duties continue, for example inheritance, pensions, or for religious reasons.

When can a couple file for divorce?

You cannot divorce until you have been married for at least 12 months, and to have your marriage legally set aside, you must be able to show that it has irretrievably broken down, and cannot be saved.

What is 'an irretrievable breakdown'?

In order to file for divorce as the law currently stands, you would need to be able to establish one of five facts that show your relationship has irretrievably broken down:

- Adultery: Your husband/wife has had sexual intercourse with someone else and you find it impossible to continue living together.
- Unreasonable behaviour: Your husband/wife has behaved in such a way that you feel you can't continue living together as man and wife.
- Two years' separation with consent: You and your husband/wife have been separated for at least two years before you start divorce proceedings, and both agree to a divorce, though you do not have to have lived apart continuously in that time – some couples separate but live in the same house – and can even have attempted a reconciliation of up to six months' duration though a period of reconciliation would not be included in the calculation of the two-year period.
- Five years' separation, regardless of whether the other party consents to divorce.
- Desertion: Your husband/wife withdraws from some or all of the marriage arrangements, without your agreement for two years, for example moving into the spare bedroom.

On your divorce petition you must outline the nature of the 'irretrievable breakdown' in the marriage, for example outlining the 'unreasonable behaviour' or giving the dates you separated, or the approximate date adultery took place (though you do not have name the third party unless you want to).

I am a devout catholic, I don't believe in divorce and at present neither of us wants to remarry. Can't we separate?

If you don't want to divorce but want something more formal than just moving out, you can apply for a judicial separation, which would involve establishing the same 'irretrievable breakdown' as for divorce, but there is no 12-month qualifying period. By involving the courts rather than just splitting up, disagreements about children and property can be addressed, with neither side then being able to breach a court agreement with impunity. The court can make the same financial and children orders in relation for a petition of judicial separation as for a petition for divorce. This would be a formal court order, and any breach would be a contempt of court.

If you can both agree on the issues, your solicitor can draw up a deed of separation incorporating the terms you have agreed, without the court's help. A deed of separation is essentially a contract which is binding in a contractual sense, but does not prevent the court from considering the financial matters in subsequent court proceedings. If you want to 'do your own' separation, you can use an amended divorce petition, striking out any references to the marriage having broken down or getting a decree to end the marriage.

How do I start divorce proceedings if I do not have a solicitor?

If you want to organise your own divorce or judicial separation you will need a petition form from the county court (there is one for each of the different types of irretrievable breakdown, and a general form), or from your solicitor. If you have children you will also need a Statement of Arrangements form. You have to pay a court fee presently £150 for the petition and £20 for the decree absolute (unless you claim Income Support or are being advised by the legal help scheme, as the 'green form scheme' is now called). You will need to send in your original marriage certificate, or a copy of it from the registrar – a photocopy will not do! The Statement of Arrangements form covers your children and the arrangements you propose for them, including school.

What happens then?

Once the divorce petition has been 'filed' at court, a copy is sent to your estranged husband/wife (or their solicitor) together with a copy of your Statement of Arrangements and a form for your husband/wife to complete, acknowledging service and setting out their intentions in respect of defending the petition and costs. The petition is also sent to any co-respondent if you are divorcing for adultery and have named as third party in your petition. The acknowledgement of service should be signed and returned within 14 days (by both parties if applicable); if not, a bailiff can serve the papers personally (or occasionally, notice is served through a newspaper advert).

If the divorce is not contested, the petition can be processed quickly; you will need to fill in and swear – either at your solicitors for a fee or at court for free – a statement of truth which will confirm the contents of your petition. The case is then 'listed' at and examined by a county court district judge; if satisfied the marriage has irretrievably broken down, and the arrangements for the children, if any are satisfactory , a certificate is issued and a date is fixed and the decree nisi announced in open court; provided there are no objections to the decree, a copy of the decree will be sent to both of you. (or a decree of judicial separation if you have applied to separate). Then, six weeks and one day after the date on the decree nisi you can apply for a decree absolute to make the divorce permanent. If you don't your spouse can apply for a decree absolute three months after the date that you could first have applied.

You can apply in your petition for your costs to be paid by your husband/wife and/or any co-respondent. If no agreement is reached over costs, the judge makes a costs order at the nisi hearing.

What if my spouse plans to contest the divorce?

Your husband/wife may object to the divorce for two reasons:

- He/she does not accept that it has irretrievably broken down, and he/she may file an answer to your petition.
- He/she feels that you are to blame for the marriage ending, and wants to petition to divorce you (a cross petition).

In the case of cross petitions, the county court may try to save time (and your money) by granting each of you a divorce based on the other's petition if you both agree, otherwise a date is set for the case to be heard in court.

My wife is divorcing me. What should I do?

The court will send you copies of divorce papers, including a form to acknowledge service (a legal term for the delivery) of the papers, which you must complete and send back. If you are opposing the divorce you should say so on the form, giving reasons why. You may want to seek legal advice at this stage.

My wife and I never made love. Is that a valid ground for divorce?

Apart from arguably being unreasonable behaviour, the fact that you never made love might allow you to have your marriage annulled.

What is an annulment?

An annulment is a recognition that your marriage is not valid, and you can apply to have it set aside by presenting a nullity petition. A marriage might be annulled if it has not been consummated (this is an absolute requirement – so only one love-making session means it has been consummated and you will not be able to have the marriage annulled; making love once in 10 years would be grounds for annulment); if one party were already married to someone else at the time of the marriage; or if the wife is pregnant by another man but is passing her husband off as the unborn child's father, without his knowing the truth.

Annulment can be sought any time after the marriage ceremony but the length of time can be relevant, for example applying for annulment after three days on the ground of non-consummation is unlikely to succeed, whereas it would if you have discovered that you are not the father of the child your wife is carrying.

My wife owns our house. Will I have to leave?

If your wife owns the marital home, your solicitor can protect your interest by registering a notice or caution with the Land Registry, which alerts potential purchasers to the fact that you have an interest in the property, and which stops the property being remortgaged without you knowing, and protects your interest until a judge can decide who should stay in the house, or whether it should be sold (and if you are entitled to any share of the proceeds) or whether to transfer the property to you even if it is not in your name, for example if it is to provide a family home for the children who are living with you.

I walked out of the house. Have I surrendered my rights too?

If you and your spouse own the property jointly, your walking out does not affect that. You are both jointly and severally liable for the mortgage (though splitting payments might be a good idea) and the joint ownership does not end until the house is sold, or one of you agrees to buy the other out, or a court order is made.

Can I stop my wife coming into the house?

If the house is jointly owned, your wife is entitled to return to it, so if you change the locks to bar her coming in, you will have to change them back or give her a key, or she can get a court order forcing you to give her access. If there is a history of domestic violence, you may be able to obtain an injunction order to prevent the wife returning for a period of time, as long as it is not you that has been violent.

I need help to pay the bills now my husband and I are separated and divorcing. What can I do?

You can apply to a judge for 'interim maintenance', paid weekly or monthly (even if you are still living together); sometimes husbands are ordered to pay the mortgage or rent even though no longer living at home. For more on division or property and financial affairs, see Divorce and separation: financial arrangements.

I'd heard that my wife and I would have to go to mediators before getting divorced...

Although the Family Law Act 1996 is on the statute books, the sections dealing with changes to the divorce law have not yet come into force, and the government has announced there are no immediate plans to bring those sections into force. Under this legislation, all you would have to do to get a divorce would be to show that your marriage has broken down, rather than any of the five grounds as such. The changes included the introduction of 'information meetings' where trained mediators would try to reconcile you; then three months later (if one of you still wants to end the marriage) a nine-month 'cooling-off period' (plus a further six months if children are involved, or if one party argues that not all the issues have been considered) would begin before divorce proceedings can be started. Mediation would not be compulsory, but Legal Aid is not available for couples that do not mediate in respect of financial matters, as a result of changes to the Legal Aid system.

Section 2.3 Cohabiting – just like marriage?

It is often said that unmarried couples' rights are just as strong as those of married couples, but in practice this is not strictly true.

My girlfriend has just had a baby. I don't think it is mine, so can she register me as the father without my consent?

If a couple are married, there is an automatic presumption that the husband is the father of his wife's child. For unmarried couples this presumption does not exist, and a registrar can only record the name of the father if the mother has a parental order (formally known as an affiliation order, made by a court following a hearing that has established the man as the 'putative father'), or if the father and mother both attend to sign the register or if the father signs a statutory declaration stating that he is the child's father. So, unless a parental order has been made against you, you cannot be registered as the child's father without your consent. But if you later confirm that the child is yours, you can make a statutory declaration and have your name added to the certificate.

Under the Family Law Act 1986, a child can apply for a declaration that a particular person is his or her parent (if the child is aged under eighteen years, a 'next friend' makes the application on the child's behalf). If the matter goes to court, a judge can order that you and the mother should undergo blood tests, as well as the child. They cannot compel you to undergo testing, however, but if you fail to comply there would be a strong presumption that you are the father of the child.

I never married my partner but we have children together. Do I have any rights?

If you want a say in your children's education or welfare, you will need to apply for parental responsibility which would allow you to make decisions about the children, and be kept informed about matters affecting them, like schooling etc. If your partner agrees, you can draw up your own parental responsibility agreement (or your solicitors can) without going to court, which you both sign and which is binding. If your partner does not agree then you may apply for a Parental Responsibility order from the court.

My partner and I have just split up. We are not married so I won't have to pay for the children...will I?

Oh yes you will. Fathers have an obligation to pay maintenance and the Child Support Agency can and will make an assessment of your liability for maintenance if you do not reach agreement with your ex-partner, or if your partner is claiming state benefits. Even if maintenance has been agreed, either party can ask the CSA to make an assessment at any time.

We're not married and we want to buy a house. Do we both own the property in equal shares, half and half?

It is possible to have an interest in property in two ways: either through the title deeds or though contributions that you make towards a property (which is known as a beneficial interest). The title deed may say that a property is owned jointly, but one partner's beneficial interest may be greater, because they have contributed more to the property. Just because title deeds say the property is jointly owned, it does not follow a court will split the proceeds of sale 50:50; the beneficial interests may (but not always) be reflected in the way the proceeds are shared out. It is generally helpful to have an agreement as to how the property is to be shared to prevent any difficulties if the relationship breaks down.

My partner and I have never married, but we bought a house together. What happens if one of us dies?

When two or more people live in a house together, they hold the property as 'joint tenants' (joint tenancy is a legal term which applies whether you rent or own your home). If your partner dies their share of the property automatically passes to you, regardless of whether they left it to someone else in their will. If you don't want this to happen, you can create a 'tenancy in common' by serving a written notice on your partner that the joint tenancy is split. With a tenancy in common, you both own shares in the property, but you can leave your share to a third party in a will. Unmarried couples should create tenancies in common, as it allows them to determine by will who should get their share of the house or flat.

We are worried about what will happen if we split up. Who gets what?

When relationships end, how does the property get divided? Who gets the house, or the painting? Some people like to deal with such painful eventualities at the start of a relationship, and it is possible to draw up a contract (sometimes called a separation deed) that lays down how money and jointly owned property would to be shared out if the relationship ends. If there is no deed, and you cannot decide how to split your property a court will decide for you, for example, in the case of a house, you can apply for an order to sell the property, and the court then decides what is the value of your interest in the property, and whether you have a beneficial interest greater than your joint ownership reflected in the deeds, for example because only you paid the mortgage or paid a greater share of the deposit.

The house is in my partner's name. What rights if any do I have?

You may still be able to establish some rights to the property in other ways even if your name is not on the deeds. To use a birds' nest analogy, your partner may have built the nest, but you may have been feathering it, for example by paying for improvements to the property, or paying part of the deposit or contributing to the mortgage. All of these could create an interest in the property. You should keep anything that can show you have made contributions to the property, such as bank statements or receipts; these will help establish your claim. If you can establish an interest, the court can order a sale and decide how much you should get from the proceeds. On the other hand, it might order your partner to leave; in such cases the court may order that whoever stays the house takes over all household bills and responsibilities connected with it, but remember that even if you are granted the house, a court may also order you to pay compensation to your partner for having to leave home.

We were engaged. Does that make any difference?

The Law Reform (Miscellaneous Provisions) Act 1970 gives engaged couples that separate the same protection over property rights as a husband and wife. The engagement does not have to be formal – there need not have been an engagement party, an announcement in The Times or even a ring – all that needs to be shown is that there was an agreement to marry which has now been broken. The Act does not empower courts to transfer property ownership between engaged people (though it can order the transfer of tenancies) but does allow them to decide the division of house contents, or order the return of any goods removed from the home.

Do the children have any interest in the house even though I don't?

Under the Children Act 1989, you may be able to apply for a share of the property on your children's behalf, for example if your ex owns the house but the children are with you and you are looking for a new place to live. In these cases a court can order your partner to transfer the property to you as the parent looking after the children; you would then hold the property on trust for the children.

Section 2.4 Separation and divorce : financial arrangements

There are three potential conflicts in terms of financial settlements arising out of a divorce or separation: property, maintenance for ex-partners (married or unmarried) and children, and pensions. Obviously, as a relationship ends there is a redistribution of wealth and finances (and in some cases debt) and a court is often the place where these details are thrashed out – either in front of a judge, or between solicitors before the judge can rule.

How do courts decide how much money should be paid by one spouse to another?

Courts want to be fair to both parties, and to make a fair division, a judge needs to know the full financial picture: details of both parties' income, expenditure and property, plus assets such as savings accounts, shares, pensions and policies of insurance. Receipts such as wage slips, bills, bank statements can give a picture of the state of your finances, showing how much you need to live on and can afford to pay out. The welfare of the children is also crucial, and whoever is looking after them may need more money because of the cost of bringing them up.

Other factors, such as the length of marriage, the ages and occupations of both parties, are also considered. Generally speaking, the shorter the marriage the smaller the settlement, and if a wife is working her settlement is likely to be smaller than that of an older woman that does not work. If you earn more than your ex-partner, you are unlikely to be able to claim from them (though beware as they might always try to claim from you, as in the case of a former Conservative MP, John Browne, who sued his wife for a divorce settlement and had her jailed when she failed to pay). Maintaining your 'usual' standard of living after divorce is also an issue. Courts will look at all these factors before deciding how assets will be divided, whether property will be sold or transferred to one party, and whether any settlement will be a lump sum or by maintenance payments.

Can I claim maintenance for myself?

You can apply for maintenance for yourself as well as for children; it is for the court to decide whether you should get it, and if so whether in periodic payments or in a one-off lump-sum payment.

What if my ex-husband won't pay maintenance for the kids?

Normally if your children's father is refusing to pay maintenance, you apply to the Child Support Agency. But in some cases, you would go to court instead; for example if the children are step-children, or if they are disabled, or if they are aged 19 or over but still in full-time education. You would also apply to court if you want more than the CSA assessment, as it does not give you the standard of living you previously enjoyed; if you want your ex-husband to pay school fees; or if your children are suing the estate of your deceased ex-husband for not having made reasonable provision during his lifetime. (For further information on the CSA, see **The Child Support Agency**.)

How can I ensure the court's maintenance order is carried out?

If the county court or High Court makes a maintenance order, you can register it at the magistrates' court, and this should ensure more reliability in terms of payments. If the order is registered, your ex-partner makes payments direct to court rather than to you; the court then forwards the money (or an order can be made that your ex pays the money into your bank account direct by standing order). If your ex-partner stops paying or falls behind, a warrant can be issued to bring him/her to court to explain why. You would apply to magistrates if you want to increase the amount you receive (and he can apply to them if he wants to have his payments reduced).

The order has been breached. What can I do?

If a court order has been made requiring your ex-husband to pay maintenance (or if the CSA has made an assessment for your children) and he refuses (or stops paying), there are several options open:

- The court (or CSA) can order your ex-husband's employer to deduct maintenance payments from his salary; this is known as 'attaching his earnings'.
- Anyone that is holding money for your ex-husband, or who owes him money, can be ordered to pay some or all of that money to you; this is known as a garnishee order.
- If you suspect your ex-husband is hiding his assets, a court order can freeze bank accounts or stop him moving money around until a judge can assess his affairs and rule on how his assets should be divided.
- If your ex-husband owns another property, you may be able to 'charge' the property, so if it is sold, proceeds of the sale will go to pay off arrears of maintenance. A charge is a registration of your interest in the proceeds of sale in the property, and tells prospective buyers that your ex-husband does not own all the interest in the property. (Once a charge is placed on the property, if you wanted to enforce the order, you could ask the court to order the property be sold and be paid from the proceeds.)

- You could apply to have your ex-husband jailed if he continues to refuse to pay maintenance, as in the case of the wife of ex-Tory MP John Browne.

(All these remedies are also available against wealthier ex-wives that are trying to avoid their responsibilities to their ex-husbands.)

We have reached an agreement over our finances. Do we need to involve the courts now?

If you can sort out your financial matters without going to court, then all well and good. But it might still be wise to make sure that there is some protection so that both sides keep to their part of the bargain. Your lawyers can draw up a consent order, setting out your agreement over the division of assets (and including child maintenance payments if the CSA is not involved); both parties sign, then submit the consent order to court along with a 'statement of information' outlining their financial position as well as any future plans to remarry or live with someone else. If the court is satisfied that the agreement is fair, the order will be stamped and sent back to your lawyers; if either side breaches the consent order, the court can enforce the agreement. If the judge has any concerns about the agreement, he may ask for more information or bring your lawyers to court to discuss the consent order or statement of information in more detail.

What about my rights to my ex-husband's pension?

If your ex-husband has a pension, in days gone by divorce would have robbed you of any entitlement under this pension, but the Pensions Act 1995 and Magistrates' Courts Act 1973 empowers courts to award applicants an interest in any benefits you might have received under their ex-husband's pension scheme. The 1995 Act allows courts to order pension scheme trustees or managers to pay you any benefit that you would have received if the divorce had not happened, for example a widow's pension, or transfer a share of any payments that your ex-husband is entitled to receive early to you, for example a lump-sum payment. If your spouse's pension includes a death benefit – a sum of money to be paid to a nominated person of his or her choice on his or her death – the court can order you be made the beneficiary. In addition, the court can order that you be paid a sum each week or month from the pension once it matures, up to but no more than the amount of the pension. At present, the court can only 'earmark' pensions, and you will not receive your share of the pension until your husband retires; another provision of the 1995 Act will allow the court to 'split' pensions, allowing you to decide when to take your share, but this provision is not yet in force.

My wife and I are divorced, and the children live with me. Who pays maintenance for the children?

If the children are living with you, your ex-wife should pay to help you look after them. If she refuses you can apply to the Child Support Agency.

My partner and I never married. Do I have any rights?

Even if you are not married but have children together, you can still apply for maintenance for them via the CSA. If you own a property together and want to sell it, the courts can be asked to rule whether it should be put on the market. Even if the property is in your ex-partner's name, you may have a beneficial interest in the house (see Cohabiting – just like marriage?). Contributions in kind, such as looking after the children or helping with a business, etc., can also be considered in deciding whether a beneficial interest has been created.

My wife and I have separated. She is living in the family home with our children. Can she ask for money off me to pay the mortgage?

A court can order you to help with mortgage payments until the youngest child is 18, by way of maintenance, if it is justified given your respective financial positions.

Section 2.5 Separation and divorce: the children

Children are the innocent casualties of war when relationships end. Whether married or co-habiting, it is best for all concerned if a couple can agree to do what is best for the children at an early stage of the break-up. However, just as diplomacy is 'war by other means', all too often children get dragged into divorces as parents find they cannot agree on major and minor issues affecting their children's lives after separation.

The Children Act 1989 was brought in to try and protect children more effectively in the aftermath of divorce and separation, whether married or unmarried. If you cannot decide together what is best for the children, the court will decide for you. The court's only concern is what is best for the children – and that may not be what is best for you.

If we separate, where do the children live?

When you and your spouse (or partner if you never married) split up, hopefully you will be able to agree which parent the children will live with, otherwise, you will have to get a court to decide, by making a residence order that will state with whom they should live. You could both apply for a split residence order, though courts do not like to make orders that require children to divide their time between two homes. A residence order gives the parent with residence the right to take the children out of the UK for up to a month at a time without needing the other parent's (or the court's) consent, but not to go abroad for longer than that or to live abroad permanently (this can only happen with the other parent's consent, or if a court orders it).

What if my ex-wife won't let me see my children?

If the children live with your ex wife (or partner) and she won't let you see them, you can apply for a contact order, which allows you to visit your children or have them stay with you for short periods of time like weekends or during the holidays. The contact order can deal with issues such as when and where contact should take place, who collects and returns them, etc. The court can order that contact be supervised if your ex-wife raises concerns that the court feels are legitimate, or that it takes place at a Contact Centre.

The children say they don't want to see their father. What can I do?

Sometimes children decide they don't want to see one of their parents after a separation; this may be because they saw domestic violence during the marriage and have taken one parent's side, or because they were abused or injured themselves, or because they do not want to be disloyal to the parent they live with. If your children don't want to see their other parent, you can go to court to argue why a contact order should not be made on their behalf. But because courts try to ensure that children have contact with both parents if possible (and providing it is in the children's best interests) the court may arrange for a court welfare officer to speak to the children to find out more about why they don't want to see the other parent, and whether the reason is deep-seated and valid or not. The court welfare officer may then produce a report on the situation; in addition, child psychologists may also become involved before a decision is finally made. But remember: the courts will want to be sure that it is your children's honest wish that they don't want to see your partner, and not your wish. Children can sometimes do their best to please the parent they live with by falling in with his or her wishes, so before stopping a parent's contact, the court must be sure that it is the right thing to do.

My partner is talking about going abroad with the children. What can I do?

If your children have already been taken, you can apply for a prohibited steps order that requires your partner to bring them back, and if anyone knows where your partner has taken them, an order can be made ordering them to the children's (and your former partner's) whereabouts. The prohibited steps order is also useful if your partner has not yet left the area with the children, but is only considering it. You may put out a Ports Alert to prevent your partner leaving the country. Once the children are abroad, how easy it will be to get the children home, even with court help, depends on where they are. The UK has agreements with many countries that will help return children that are subject to court orders, including Australia, Belgium, Denmark, France, Germany, Ireland, Italy, Luxembourg, Holland and Spain.

If you believe that your partner is in the UK, you can get a search and find order, which allows police or court officials to enter and search premises where your child might be hidden, and use all necessary force to get them back.

What rights do absent parents have in their children's lives after separation?

If you were (or still are) married, you automatically have parental responsibility over your natural children or children you have adopted, which means you have the right to be kept informed about your children's education and welfare, etc., and make decisions about them.

If you were not married, you would have to apply for a parental responsibility order which, if granted, gives you the right to be involved in making decisions affecting the children, and kept informed about issues affecting them. If you and your former partner agree that you should have parental responsibility, you can draw up your own parental responsibility agreement, witnessed by a court official or magistrate.

Disagreements over specific matters, for example which school will the children go to, or what surname will they use, can be resolved by a specific issue order on that matter, with the court's decision binding both parties.

How do I apply for orders under the Children Act?

The Children Act form C1, which is available from a magistrates' or county court or High Court, is used to apply for a residence order, contact order, specific issue order, prohibited steps order and a parental responsibility order. When you fill in the form, you will have to provide details about you and your children and the order you are applying for. To get an order to reveal a child's whereabouts, you will need to complete a Children Act form C4, and give details of the person you believe has the information you need. A fee is payable.

Once your application has been received, the court will formally stamp it and send a copy back to you (or your solicitor) with a hearing date. It is then your responsibility to send a copy of the processed application and hearing date to your ex-partner (you have to fill in and return a form to show how you served the papers on your ex-partner, so don't try to pretend that you sent them).

You can get emergency orders – for example a prohibited steps order – without your ex-partner having to appear in court (called *ex parte* orders), but courts do not like to make *ex parte* residence or contact orders without hearing both sides. They are generally made for a very short period of time until a hearing for both parties can be arranged.

Can only parents apply for these orders?

Grandparents, other relatives or other people who have cared for the children may also apply for an order, but only if a court gives leave (permission).

What happens at the hearing?

Once you have applied for an order, the court may arrange a conciliation appointment or a directions hearing; both are informal and held in private with only you, your ex-partner, your lawyers, the judge or magistrates and possibly a court welfare officer present (though the children may be asked to attend if they are old enough). At a conciliation appointment, normally 'chaired' by a court welfare officer, you and your partner will be given an opportunity to try and agree a solution (and the children may be interviewed if they attend). If this fails, the court will set a timetable on how to progress the case, and get a second court welfare officer to prepare a report. You should co-operate with the preparation of the report, but are entitled to disagree with its findings, and can express this disagreement in court at the appropriate time; the court does not have to accept the report's findings and may be persuaded by your arguments.

Occasionally, courts decide the children should also be represented by a guardian *ad litem*; this is a person selected from a special panel with experience of dealing with and advising children. The guardian talks with the children to get to know what they want. In some cases, the guardian can appoint a solicitor to act for the children and argue their case, and the children can also instruct their own advocate where they are of an age and understanding to put forward their own views.

If it is felt that a child is old enough to understand what is happening at court, their views will be taken into account (and children aged 12 or over are usually thought old enough to have valid views).

Sometimes decisions go against you, but courts rarely sever all contact between parent and child, even if the other parent hopes that will happen, for example to solve the 'why have I got two daddies, mummy?' issue. Parental sensibilities are not at issue, and if courts feel it is in the best interests of the children to see their biological father then the children will continue to do so. Welfare officers and psychologists have an important role to play because they can often tell that children are doing things to make one parent happy, rather than because they genuinely want to.

What other powers does a court have?

- A court can order that a local authority keep a child in secure accommodation if it fears that he or she will run away (or if he or she has run away in the past).
- A court can order that a child undergo an assessment (either psychological or educational), taking no more than seven days, to decide if he or she is suffering significant harm that would require a care order being made.
- A local authority can seek a contribution order requiring the parents of a child in local authority care pay towards his/her upkeep. The authority must serve a contribution notice that tells the parents how much they should pay, and if they do not, the authority can apply for the order.
- If a child has been removed from the family home or is in serious danger or at risk, in exceptional circumstances the child can be made a ward of court; when this happens, the high court has responsibility for the child and nothing that might affect the child can be done without seeking the permission of the high court.
- A child can be placed under the supervision of an education authority if a court feels that he or she is not being properly educated (but not if the child is already in care).

Social Services have taken my children into care. What can I do?

Taking on local government machinery is very intricate, time-consuming and sometimes soul-destroying work. The professionals at Social Services have a difficult job to do, and no-one takes the decision to put a child into care lightly. But sometimes mistakes can be made, and if you do want to take them on the best advice is to get a solicitor to represent you, so that your case is argued calmly. If you are being accused of being an unfit or violent parent, the last thing you want is to lose your temper before the court.

To get a care order, Social Services must show that your children are likely to be harmed if they stay with you because you are not taking good care of them, or that you cannot control them. You will know about any application for a care order as it will be served on you, so you would be able to oppose the order and either ask the court to let your children stay with you or live with a relative instead (and local authorities have a duty to place children with family members if at all possible, rather than with foster carers). However, the local authority may apply *ex parte* for an emergency care order that only lasts for a week, but a care order must be sought later, which you could oppose. Sometimes the children will not be removed from your care but a supervision order is made for Social Services to monitor the situation to ensure the children are well cared for. Alternatively an interim care might be obtained with the local authority placing the children with you but sharing parental responsibility.

Another option, if you agree, is for a family assistance order, where a social worker will keep in touch with you over a six-month period.

If your children have been removed from your care or a care order is made, you can apply to discharge the care order, but to succeed, you would have to show that things have changed since the order was made; a solicitor can tell you how realistic your chances of success are.

Care proceedings are long and involved. A guardian *ad litem* will be appointed in care proceedings. A interim care order will be obtained if justified but this only lasts for 28 days; therefore you can go back to court every four weeks to challenge the making of a further interim care order (though the number of challenges you can make are limited in number and so must be timed well). A final order is often not made for at least nine months.

Section 2.6 The Child Support Agency

What is the Child Support Agency (CSA)?

For the separated parents of children of school age or in full-time education, maintenance is likely to be an issue. The Child Support Agency was set up by Margaret Thatcher's Conservative Government in a bid to reduce Social Security spending on one-parent families, by making liable parents pay for their children's upkeep, with a corresponding reduction in benefit payments claimed.

The CSA assesses, collects and distributes maintenance for children, and ensures parents that try to evade their financial responsibilities to their children do not do so. The CSA also helps trace and contact parents, resolves paternity disputes, collects and forwards maintenance payments and deals with applications to vary maintenance payments. But critics claim that the CSA has been bogged down in maladministration and inefficiency, which have caused families immense distress, and in some cases to people to take their own life. It was argued that the CSA was going after easy targets, reviewing existing arrangements and pursuing fathers that were paying regularly under maintenance agreements for more money, rather than tracking down non-payers. A more serious criticism was that the system was too rigid and could not take the needs of people with fluctuating incomes, such as seasonal or part-time workers, into account, or deal with frequently changing circumstances, forcing some absent parents into debt.

Who can apply to the CSA for help with maintenance claims?

Parents of children aged under 19 are most likely to have dealings with the CSA. If a child lives with a parent claiming Income Support, Income-based Jobseeker's Allowance or Disability Working Allowance (or whose parent's new partner claims), the parent may have to apply to the CSA for maintenance.*

Many parents have divorced and have paid their maintenance on time and in full; so when they get a letter from the CSA, they may think it is a mistake – but it probably isn't. Applications must be made to the CSA even if a couple agreed a 'clean break' settlement agreement or a court order set out maintenance payments. Parents that are not claiming benefit can also apply to the CSA to assess and collect their maintenance unless they are subject to a written maintenance agreement or court order drawn up before April 5, 1993.

* If your ex-partner is claiming the new Working Family Tax Credit (which replaced Family Credit) and you have a good relationship, you can ask your ex to withdraw the claim for maintenance from the CSA; they have no option but to accept it, and you can then conclude your own private agreement.

My ex-wife says she has applied to the CSA for maintenance. What happens?

You will be sent a form asking for details about your current family, financial circumstances and commitments; this is then used to work out how much maintenance you pay. If the form is filled in correctly and sent back within four weeks of being issued, the start date for your maintenance payments can be deferred for up to eight weeks.

My ex-partner has children by a number of men including me. I am being pursued for child support for all of them, though I adopted none of them.

The CSA form also asks if you are a child's natural or adoptive parent, so if you are not, you should say so clearly on the form. The CSA will need to get more information from your child's mother and if it cannot resolve the matter, you may have to take a DNA test; if this proves you did not father all the children, the CSA will refund the cost of the test. Some fathers dispute paternity, as a delaying tactic, but once paternity is established any arrears run up while the matter was being resolved will have to be paid.

What factors are taken into account when assessing maintenance? I have a new wife and home, and a child on the way...

To calculate how much you have to pay, the CSA deducts essential living expenses for you and any of your children who live with you, plus your rent or mortgage costs. Any new family you may have is also taken into account. Deductions can also be made for the cost of travelling to work if the distance is more than 150 miles per week, or if you transferred property or capital to your ex-partner before April 1993 (but no deductions are allowed for other bills). These deductions will be taken off your net income (your gross pay less income tax, national insurance and 50 per cent of any pension contributions). What is left is known as your assessable income. Maintenance is normally deducted out of half of your assessable income, so if you have £200 a week after deductions, the amount available to pay maintenance would be £100 a week.

Is there any ceiling on how much the CSA can take? Will I have enough to live on?

Normally, the CSA does not take more than 30 per cent of net income (as assessed under their child support rules), or up to 40 per cent if you are in arrears.

Because of concerns over the old system, a reform has been proposed with a simple flat rate: all absent parents, male or female, will pay 15 per cent of their net income as maintenance for an only child, 20 per cent for two and 25 per cent for three or more children. But the proposed system does not consider your ex-partner's financial position; however much she earns, all that matters in calculating how much you should pay is your income. However, this is unlikely to be implemented before 2002.

What if I don't send back the form?

If the CSA does not receive a completed form (or if you do not send in any supporting evidence), your personal circumstances cannot be taken into account to work out how much you should pay, and the CSA will make an interim maintenance assessment instead, which is usually higher than you would normally pay and which stays in force until a proper assessment is carried out and all the information submitted.

What if I don't pay up?

If you don't pay, the CSA has a number of options:

- If you are working, the CSA can get your employer to deduct the money by attaching your earnings (and your employer can charge you £1 for doing this).
- If you are self-employed, once it has obtained a liability order against you, the CSA can instruct bailiffs to seize possessions up to the value of the debt, or place a charge against property (so that when it is sold, cash up to the value of your debt will be paid to the DSS) or against deposit accounts (so banks will have to release funds up to the value of your debt). It can also register the debt, which will affect your credit rating. In extreme cases, you could be jailed for up to 42 days if a magistrates' court is convinced that you have deliberately refused to pay the debt.
- If you are signing on, contributions for child maintenance may be deducted at source from any Income Support or income based Jobseeker's Allowance.

My new partner does not want to give her financial details to the CSA. Does she have to?

Only you and the other parent are required by law to give information to the CSA; your new partner cannot be made to do so.

What do I do if my financial circumstances change?

If your income changes, you should tell the CSA at once, but your assessment may not change, as the CSA will only review your maintenance liability if the assessment changes by £10 a week; this is known as the tolerance rule. The tolerance rule is meant to give both parents financial stability and negate the need for frequent reassessments in the case of minor changes in circumstances. Once several small changes come together to tip you over the £10 threshold, your case will be reviewed.

If my full assessment shows I have been paying too much maintenance, will the CSA repay me in a lump sum?

No. Nor will you be allowed to stop paying maintenance for a while until the overpayment is wiped out. Your regular payments will be readjusted to take into account the error over a period of time, so that your children do not suffer. It's not fair on you, but this way it doesn't hit the children so hard.

Can I appeal if I don't agree with the assessment?

Either parent can disagree with a CSA assessment and appeal in writing, giving reasons why the first assessment may be inaccurate, and it will be reviewed. If you are still unhappy with the result of the appeal, you can appeal again to the Independent Child Support Appeal Tribunal.

My ex-husband has the children living with him. He is working but the assessment says he has no assessable income. How can this be?

If your husband claims Income Support, Income based Jobseeker's Allowance, Family Credit or Disability Working Allowance, then he is regarded as having no income, and unable to contribute to the child's upkeep.

What information does a self-employed person need to submit, and how are earnings calculated?

Calculating self-employed income can be fairly complex, and the CSA needs to establish what the average weekly income is; in doing this, seasonal fluctuations may be taken into account, for example, the construction industry can get quiet over the winter. To calculate an average weekly income, the CSA would need to see a profit and loss account for the year ending in the period of two years prior to the date of the assessment, or details of gross receipts and business expenses for a period of 52 weeks (which can be supplied in the form of cashbooks or day books), and the CSA would also accept a copy of the Inland Revenue's tax computation (or an Inland Revenue print-out) for the period that ends in the period of 104 weeks prior to the relevant week the claim was first made. If you cannot produce these figures, you will need to find out what information the CSA would accept.

I have been self-employed for less than a year. What can I do?

For the recently self-employed, the CSA would want to see evidence of gross receipts and expenses; how much information depends on how long you have been trading, to produce the most accurate figure for your average weekly income.

I can't get my hands on the information immediately. Will I be penalised?

If there is a valid reason why the information cannot be supplied, the CSA may substitute an interim assessment, which allows you to make payments and keep the arrears down while a final assessment is being calculated. Once the final assessment is in place, any arrears will be adjusted accordingly.

Section 2.7 Children

Children occupy a special place in our lives and many laws are set up to protect them, and govern their development. There are special youth courts to hear cases children are involved in, and local authorities can intervene to ensure that children are properly cared for. In addition, since the Children Act 1989, when courts have to rule on family disputes, divorce and separation, they must give great weight to the best interests of the children, even if that may clash with what parents feel are their best interests.

What are the legal requirements for children regarding school?

The law requires that children must be educated at school or otherwise. If you plan to follow the traditional mechanism of educating your children, they must start school at the beginning of the term following their fifth birthday, though some local authorities allow children to start earlier than that. Compulsory education ends at 16, though you can stay on to do further courses, exams and A-levels with a view to gaining vocational qualifications or securing a place at university or college.

Parents who educate their children at school have a duty to send their children to school every day, and if they do not attend, or do not remain in school for full days' teaching, then parents can be taken to court over their child's non-attendance. Obviously there are legitimate reasons why children can be away from school, for example sickness, religious festivals, medical appointments and even a family holiday (despite schools' complaints, children can in fact have up to two weeks away from school term time each year for family holidays). In addition child actors can get an entertainment licence to be away from school to take part in plays or film programmes, provided their educational needs are being met in that time. But unless your child's absence is acceptable, the local education authority will come after you. The local authority may also consider applying for a care order if the absence is significant. Of course, it is possible to remove your child from school and tutor them yourself at home, or get a tutor for them. Nor should this method of education be sneered at, as anyone who remembers how home-tutored Ruth Lawrence found herself at an Oxford college at the age of 13 will recall. But parents can't just pull their kids out of school and keep them at home. You would need to contact your local education authority to tell them that you were planning to educate your children outside the school framework, and then agree a framework of learning for your child. The LEA would then monitor the teaching to ensure that your child's development was not being hampered by the decision to remove him or her from school.

The Children Act has created some anomalies, one of which affects schooling: suppose you and your child argue, and she decides to stay with her best friend and the local authority agrees that this is in the best interests of the child; if she does not go to school, the local authority will then look to take you to court, even though you do not have any day-to-day care and control over your child.

Are there any restrictions on what films, TV, or computer games children can watch or play?

Films, videos and DVDs (digital versatile discs) must be classified by law as to their content, so that parents can ensure that children do not watch unsuitable material. The classifications imposed by the British Board of Film Classification are:

U: Unclassified, no restrictions in law.

Uc: Particularly suitable for younger children (video only).

PG: Parental guidance. General viewing, but some scenes may be unsuitable for young children. Unaccompanied children of any age may watch a 'PG' film or video, but parents are advised to monitor the contents. Some parents take the trouble to watch the film or video first, or seek advice from friends. Others may prefer to watch with their children.

12:   Suitable for persons aged 12 and over. Adult themes may be dealt with but discreetly. Mild swear-words are allowed, as is occasional nudity and brief violence.

15:   Suitable for persons aged 15 and over. Some sexual swear-words, nudity, violence and sexual activity in context.

18:   No under-18s. Films contain violence, swearing, sexual activity, drugs, horror and nudity.

R18: Films supplied from licensed sex-shops only.

At a cinema, a manager can refuse entry to a film if they believe a child is not old enough to see it, and at a video shop it is an offence to sell or rent a film to someone who is under the age classification.

Are there any age restrictions on gambling?

Children under the age of 18 are not allowed to gamble, or work in betting shops or clubs. Adults are not allowed to place bets for under age people. You have to be 16 to buy a lottery ticket.

What regulations govern childminding in the UK?

Registered childminders are professional day-carers who work in their own homes to provide care and education for other people's children in a family setting. Unlike nannies and au pairs, they are inspected and registered by the social services department of their local authority.

Childminders are usually registered to care for no more than three children aged under five, and three under the age of eight (including their own children) subject to local guidelines and personal circumstances. Many childminders look after children up to the age of 14. When childminders apply for registration, the local authority will check the premises where children are to be minded to ensure they are child-friendly, have suitable first-aid and have fire safety equipment. Public liability insurance is also required.

Once childminders are registered, the local authority carries out an annual inspection to monitor standards and premises to ensure that the childminder continues to meet the 'fit person' and 'fit premises' criteria specified in the Children Act 1989. As part of the registration process, police checks are carried out on the childminder and anyone over the age of 16 living at the same address, as well as on visitors who may have regular contact with the children.

At what age do children have to wear seatbelts in cars?

As the law stands, all passengers must use seatbelts if fitted, and all new cars must have front and rear seatbelts fitted as standard. However there are some specific regulations that affect children:

- Children under the age of three must wear child restraints.
- Children over the age of three but under 11 (and less than 1.50 metres tall) must wear child restraints if available, and adult seatbelts (if fitted) if not.
- Children aged 12 and over must wear adult seatbelts if fitted.

When can a young person vote?

The age of majority remains 18 so you cannot vote until your eighteenth birthday, but to stand for public office (as an MP or councillor) you must be aged 21 and over.

What is the age of criminality?

Children aged 10 and above can be charged with criminal offences, provided they can be shown to have understood that they were doing wrong. Children aged 14 and over can be charged with criminal offences.

When can children sue and be sued?

Children and young persons are legally responsible for their actions when they are old enough to be aware of the consequences. Parents can only be sued for the wrongdoing of their children if they share the blame. Children can sue for negligence from the earliest age, even suing their parents for, say, road accident injuries (in reality they will sue the insurance company).

At what age can a child have sexual intercourse?

The age of consent for heterosexual sex is 16. Homosexual males cannot have sex until they are 18, while there is no lower age limit for homosexual acts between females.

If you are over 16 you are entitled to advice and free contraception with complete confidentiality. If you are aged 13 or over you are entitled to advice from your doctor and free contraceptive supplies, but your doctor can tell your parents if he thinks it wise. If you are over 16 you can consent to an abortion without your parents' knowledge; but if you are under 16 your parents will be told.

At what age can a child buy and/or drink alcohol?

At first sight, rules regulating children drinking appear to be very lax: any child aged five or over can drink beer, wine or spirits in a restaurant (but not a public house), provided the child did not buy the drink. But children under the age of 14 cannot enter any part of a pub where alcohol is sold, except to pass through to the toilets, family room or restaurant. Between the ages of 14 and 18, children are allowed in bars but cannot buy or drink alcohol there. But children aged 16 and over can buy beer, lager or cider with a meal in a pub restaurant. A child has to be aged 16 and over to buy tobacco.

Section 2.8 Wills and probate

More than two hundred years ago, the famous diarist Dr Samuel Johnson said that there were only two certainties in life – death and taxes. It is a sad fact of life that it ends in death, and whilst no-one wants to be morbid, it is important to consider what happens when you are gone. You may have split up from your wife or husband, and found love again with another partner though you never remarried; if you die, will your partner be able to claim your estate, or will someone who has not been in your life for many years return in your death to take property you never intended them to have? For that reason you need to consider making a will. It is possible that you may not need a will at all if your estate is small but if you do have any property it as well to direct where it goes for your own peace of mind, rather than hope that the rules of intestacy which govern the division of property after death will channel your property where you want it to go. Another possible benefit of making a will is what is called estate planning, which will allow you to reduce as far as possible the amount of inheritance tax your heirs will have to pay on property you leave in your will. Bear in mind that marriage and divorce affect wills in very significant ways so it always pays to reconsider your will after such an event. The act of marriage or remarriage automatically revokes all former wills, so if you have a will, you will need to make a new one.

Why make a will?

The object of making a will is to state what you want to happen to all your possessions after your death; who you want to handle your affairs and also make any directions as to whom you would like to be the guardian of your children. The will can also express your wishes about funeral arrangements, etc.

Are there any formalities required in the making of a will?

Wills must be drawn up and witnessed correctly, otherwise the courts will treat the estate as though no will were made at all. Wills have to be signed by the will-maker, and two witnesses who cannot be beneficiaries of the will, or husbands or wives of beneficiaries both of whom must be present at the same time. (Strictly speaking, witnesses can be beneficiaries or their spouses, but their bequests will be nullified if they do act as witnesses.) Once a will has been drafted, any alterations must be signed and witnessed before they take effect. Once a will has been made, it can only be changed by codicil or by making a new will which revokes all previous ones.

Who can make a will?

Anyone aged 18 and over, who is of sound mind can make a will to dispose of their property. The key to what constitutes sound mind is whether the will-maker understands what they are doing. Any member of an active military service unit in time of war who is over 14, and underage seamen at sea during peacetime, may also make a valid will.

Do I need to go to a solicitor to make a will?

Solicitors do not charge a great deal for making wills, because they hope to land the probate work later on (which is far more lucrative), but it is a good idea to find out how much you will be charged before going ahead. An alternative is to use a will form or software which you can buy from stores across the country, such as Law Pack's products.

A third option would be to draft your own will yourself. If your estate and wishes are fairly straightforward, there is no reason why you cannot draft your own final testament on a piece of paper. However, if you have complex business affairs, such as being a member of a partnership, you might want a solicitor to advise you so that you do not inadvertently create confusions that might lead to your aim being thwarted, with property you planned to leave to one party going somewhere else. An example might be that you wish to leave your home to your wife, but when she remarries, the property passes to your children. A solicitor could set up a trust to do this for you, but you need to ensure that you don't mis-draft the will so the property would pass absolutely to your wife, because if she then dies without making a will it would then pass to her new husband and not to your children.

An example of a simple will is shown on the opposite page. A couple of things to bear in mind if you write your own will:

- You don't need to say 'last will and testament' although it appears on solicitor-drafted wills and will forms; 'the last will' will suffice.
- If you have made a will before, you must say that you revoke all previous wills; so it might be as well to include it as a matter of course.
- Give the full names of any beneficiaries – it just avoids any doubt as to whom you plan to leave property to.
- Even if you have itemised each possession and valuable you have to leave, you may have forgotten one. So by leaving someone 'the residue' (this is normally your main beneficiary) this acts as a catch-all so all your property is disposed of.
- Witnesses do not have to know the contents of the will, but remember the rule that bars witnesses or their spouses from being beneficiaries.
- By stating that you want bequests to be made 'tax free', you can ensure that the beneficiary receives exactly what you want to leave them, with the estate bearing any inheritance tax costs.

Example of a simple will

LAST WILL & TESTAMENT

PRINT NAME AND ADDRESS
THIS Last Will & Testament is made by me *GILLIAN ROSS*
of *5 MAPLE TERRACE, LONDON SW10 2P2*

I REVOKE all previous wills and codicils.

EXECUTORS' NAMES AND ADDRESSES
I APPOINT as executors and trustees of my will
DAVID PETER ROSS and *THERESA ANN MUNDY*
of *5 MAPLE TERRACE* of *9 KING'S WALK*
LONDON SW10 2P2 *LEAMINGTON SPA LM9 YBL*

and should one or more of them fail to or be unable to act I APPOINT to fill any vacancy

SUBSTITUTIONAL EXECUTOR'S NAME AND ADDRESS
Anthony John Williams
of *17 St George's Crescent, Reading RG7 9XY*

SPECIFIC GIFTS AND LEGACIES
I GIVE *one thousand pounds to my friend Anthony John Williams*
my pearl stud earrings to my sister, Ruth Elizabeth Jones of 11 The Groves,
Aberdeen AB3 4A2
my gold locket to my sister Theresa Ann Mundy

Any legacy to a minor may be validly handed over to his/her parent or guardian.

RESIDUARY GIFT
I GIVE the residue of my estate to *David Peter Ross, Theresa Ann Mundy and*
Ruth Elizabeth Jones in equal shares
but if he/she or (if I have indicated more than one person) any of them fails to survive me by 28 days or if this gift or any part
of it fails for any other reason, then I GIVE the residue of my estate or the part of it affected to
the other residuary beneficiaries in proportion to their shares
other instructions *in family grave at*

FUNERAL WISHES
I WISH my body to be ☑ buried ☐ cremated
St. Catherine's Cemetery, London

DATE
SIGNED by the above-named testator in our presence on the *10th* day of *June* 20 *00*
and then by us in the testator's presence

TESTATOR'S SIGNATURE
SIGNED *Gillian Ross*

WITNESSES' SIGNATURES NAMES AND ADDRESSES
SIGNED *JP Smith*
JOHN PETER SMITH
of *23 DEVONSHIRE ROAD.*
OXFORD
occupation *PLUMBER*

SIGNED *Susan Smith*
SUSAN JANE SMITH
of *23 DEVONSHIRE ROAD,*
OXFORD
occupation *HOUSEWIFE*

Whom should I appoint as my executor?

Whether you make a will yourself or through your solicitor, you will have to appoint an executor. The role of the executor (or executrix to give the correct Latin for female executors) is to wind up your affairs speedily and accurately. Normally the main beneficiary is appointed as an executor, but the role can be quite a strain, so if you know your husband or wife might be worried by the duty, it might be better to appoint someone else, such as your best friend. Remember that if you plan to set up a trust to handle property in your will, you will need to appoint two trustees as well, though executors can also be trustees.

Some people appoint their solicitors as trustees. You don't need to do this unless there is very good reason for doing so, such as a scenario where you want to make sure that a trust for the benefit of children is scrupulously observed. Professionals who act as executors usually have a charging clause inserted in the will which enables them to charge for things which a lay executor could perfectly easily have done, such as negotiating a house sale or liaising with estate agents. Banks and institutions can also be appointed as executors, but they will make professional charges for everything they do, which will make a hole in the estate. For example, if a bank has to dispose of shares, its stockbroking arm will value them – and charge a fee – and there might be a delay in the process which your executor would not have if he or she looked at the share prices in a newspaper and spoke to a broker for himself.

I've made my will. What do I do now?

You need to keep your will safe, so it does not get lost, but also where it can be found when you die. Solicitors very often do not charge for holding a will for safe-keeping (hoping, in general, that they will get the probate work in due course), but if you don't want to use a solicitor, you can deposit it at a bank.

What happens next?

Your part is over. The next step happens after you die, and is known as probate.

What is probate?

Probate is the formal process where the executor (or executors) of a will obtain the formal document which is needed in order to deal with the estate of the deceased. Very often probate is obtained by a solicitor acting on behalf of the executors, but in simple estates or ones of low value there is no reason why it cannot be done by an executor acting personally. An executor should, amongst other things, be chosen for his business-like qualities and so obtaining probate in a simple estate should be within most people's competence. Probate is sometimes contested and that will lead to a formal hearing by a court; but the vast majority of cases is uncontested and obtaining the grant of probate is more of an administrative matter than anything else. If you do not leave a will and die intestate, your next of kin will apply for 'letters of administration' rather than probate, but the process is basically the same.

How does an executor go about being granted probate?

In most cases the executor has to swear an affidavit (an oath) that sets out the fact of the testator's death and other various matters such as the value of the estate. This needs to be lodged with the Probate Registry together with the original will, the probate fee and, depending on the value of the estate, an Inland Revenue account. If everything is in order, the grant of probate will be made within ten days. In straightforward cases the executor can easily make the application himself and the staff at the Probate Registry are usually more than willing to explain the procedure involved and, indeed, on payment of a small fee, even help draft the necessary document.

Once probate has been granted, what is the next step?

Once you have probate, the estate can be divided according to the will. More often than not an executor will ask a solicitor to act in the administration of the estate simply because the executor does not feel competent to do it or, possibly, is too upset. Sometimes, it is done in order to be seen to be fair. In the case of more complicated estates that might involve the sale of properties or negotiations with the Inland Revenue it would be wise to employ the services of a solicitor. (If a solicitor is used, it is wise to agree the basis on which the estate will be charged from the outset, usually an hourly rate; this ensures executors know how much the estate will be reduced by, and avoids any possible bad feeling later.) Often, the administration of an estate will involve selling a property that, quite likely, will be handled by the solicitor administering the estate on behalf of the executors. You need to be sure that your solicitor will not be charging to convey the property on an hourly rate that would be charged to the estate, rather than the more competitive packages normally charged to housebuyers and sellers in his normal course of business.

I want to change my will. How can I do this?

If you want to add additional bequests, you can add a codicil, which is a written statement sworn and witnessed like the main body of the will. If you want to make a major change, it is better to draft a new will, revoking all previous wills.

My father has made a will and has left me nothing. Can I do anything about it?

One often hears of discontented would-be beneficiaries muttering darkly about 'contesting' a will. Apart from proving that the testator was mentally incompetent at the time of making the will, or was forced to assign his property in the way that he did, or that the will itself is a forgery you would only be able to dispute the will if you are a 'dependant' of your dead father who has not been provided for.

The Inheritance (Provision for Family and Dependants) Act 1975 contains details of the persons who are treated as dependants and who can apply to the court on the basis that the deceased has failed to make **reasonable** financial provision for them. The categories include husband/wife or even a former spouse who has not remarried. Any person who has lived with the deceased for two years and was maintained by him/her, for example a common-law wife, partner or partner's child can claim under the provisions of this Act. The court has to consider the financial needs and resources of the applicant and the nature and extent of the deceased's estate. An application for an order must be made within six months of the date of granting of probate or letter of administration.

Can I keep the contents of my will secret?

The contents of a will are confidential until probate has been granted. Once probate has been granted, however, your will becomes a public document, and anyone can obtain a copy of your will by applying to the Principal Probate Registry, provided they can give sufficient information for staff to find it.

How can wills help reduce inheritance tax?

Although the importance of inheritance tax is not confined to wills, it is often an important consideration when it comes to drafting them. Many people do not realise how big an impact inheritance tax can have and just how costly it can be if no steps are taken to deal with it. Inheritance tax is largely an avoidable tax, but can only be avoided if proper consideration is given to it at the right time and if it is not left too late. The tax itself is not payable up to a certain exempt amount (currently £234,000), but thereafter the rate on death is 40 per cent, which many people would consider to be very high, especially since income tax will also have been deducted from any income that helped build up the capital. When the value of a house is added to savings, with shares, etc., it is not unusual for an estate to exceed the exempt amount.

An example of how estate planning can save money: a husband and wife have a joint estate of £434,000, including their house and all other assets. The exempt amount is £234,000. If the husband's will leaves everything to his wife, on his death all the property passes to her but no inheritance tax is payable on transfers to spouses. But if the wife then dies, her estate is worth

£434,000 and her children will have to pay £80,000 inheritance tax on the £200,000, at the tax rate of 40 per cent. This could have been avoided if the husband had left £234,000 to the children in his will instead of leaving everything to his wife. That £234,000 would have been exempt because it did not exceed the limit and, in turn, when the wife died and left her £200,000 to the children that too would be exempt and no tax would have been payable at all. By doing it this way husband and wife could each have taken advantage of their own £234,000 nil rate band instead of the husband wasting that opportunity.

When estates are enlarged by successive deaths, in the absence of a will your children could be poorer as a result. For example, in accidents where husbands and wives die simultaneously, the law presumes that one spouse dies first and leaves his/her estate to the second, who then dies allowing the aggregate estate to pass to the children, leaving them liable to inheritance tax.

Wills can be drafted to solve this problem by adding a survivorship clause in both husband's and wife's wills, so that each can only inherit from the other if they survive the first death by a set length of time, for example 28 days. In the event of simultaneous deaths, the estate of each spouse would then devolve (usually) to the children, but they would do so separately and so each spouse would be able to take advantage of his or her own nil rate tax exemption.

What are living wills?

Although they are not wills as such, living wills are attempts by people to make provision for a time when they may be physically or mentally incapable of taking medical decisions for themselves. The fear of degeneration and/or indignity scares many people as much as, if not more than, death, and in such circumstances a living will can guide medical staff as to your wishes.

Everyone has the right to die in dignity, free from doctors' well-meant efforts to prolong life with the technology available to them. It can be a very heavy burden for doctors and family to decide whether or not to keep a patient alive when there is no real hope. The family and hospital often do not know what to do, and people are left wondering if they have made the right decision. A living will expresses the wishes of the patient at a time when they were rational enough and not afflicted by pain to have their judgement impaired or clouded.

A living will can, for example, indicate whether medical treatment should be directed to saving life at all costs in every circumstance, or if treatment to relieve suffering should be administered, even if such relief could shorten life. Or it may express a wish that a certain person should be involved in decisions about medical care or be contacted if death is imminent – which is very important in the case of co-habiting couples.

A solicitor can draft a document appropriate to the needs of a particular client or, indeed, quite comprehensive forms covering most eventualities can be obtained from organisations listed in the Appendix. Living wills are covered in more depth in the Law Pack 'Power of Attorney & Living Will Guide'.

What happens if I die without making a will?

If no will has been made, then your property will devolve according to the intestacy rules. Those rules are based upon an analysis of what most people actually do in their wills and so they very often correspond to what the testator would have done by will anyway. The rules are periodically revised as will-making patterns change. Under the rules of intestacy, your unmarried partner would not benefit under the intestacy provisions, whereas a will could have ensured he or she would have inherited. Similarly, you might want to leave different amounts to your children, but without a will all your children would take equally.

The most common situations that arise on intestacy are:

- **You leave a husband/wife and no children, grandchildren, parents, brothers or sisters or their children:** The surviving spouse inherits everything.
- **You leave a husband/wife and no children, but surviving parents, brothers or sisters or their children:** The spouse gets all personal property and the first £200,000 and half the balance. The remainder is shared equally between your parents (or to the surviving parent). If your parents are dead the remainder is shared equally between the brothers and sisters (and if they have died, each nephew and niece takes an equal share of their parent's share of your estate).
- **You leave a husband/wife and children and grandchildren:** The spouse gets all personal property and the first £125,000 and a life interest in the remainder. The children get the rest divided equally (and if they have died each child's child (grandchild) takes an equal share of their deceased parent's share of your estate).
- **You leave children or grandchildren:** The property is shared equally between your children, or their children if any of them have died. (Illegitimate children have the same rights as legitimate ones if there is no will, and their children can also inherit if their parent has died, but step-children cannot benefit.)
- **You leave parents:** The parents take the whole estate (if only one survives he/she takes the estate).
- **You do not have any surviving spouse, descendants or parents, but other living relatives:** The estate is divided equally among the brothers and sisters, or their children if any have died. If there are no brothers, sisters, nieces or nephews, property is divided in the following order of priority: half-brothers and sisters and their descendants; grandparents (but not descendants of dead grandparents); uncles and aunts, and their descendants; half uncles and aunts, and their descendants.
- **No surviving relatives:** The estate passes to the Crown.

The widow or widower has some privileges – the right to all personal belongings including furniture, cars, jewellery, clothing and household goods, and can insist on having the family home as part of his or her share.

In the case of intestacy, whoever is dealing with your estate needs letters of administration to deal with it.

Chapter 3
You and your job

Section 3.1 The contract of employment

What is the difference between being an employee and being self-employed?

Every person who works that is not self-employed (whether working for someone else, for a partnership or a company) has a contract of employment, which sets out the rights and responsibilities or worker and employer, and governs their relationship. By contrast, independent contractors are hired under a contract for services (unlike employees who have a contract of service), and which is far narrower in scope. Employees pay income tax on Schedule E (Pay As You Earn), while self-employed people are taxed on schedule D, which allows them to put off more working expenses against tax, but they may pay higher National Insurance contributions. But employees have more rights under employment legislation in terms of employment protection, unfair dismissal and working hours.

How can I tell if I am an employee?

If you should appear before an employment tribunal (formerly, industrial tribunal) to claim you have been unfairly dismissed, and your former employee can show you were never 'on staff', then that's the end of the matter; you are self-employed and the tribunals do not look at disputes involving self-employed people where contracts have been ended. So if your company claims you were a contractor, the tribunal will look at all the factors surrounding your job, including:

- Wages: How were you paid and who looked after your tax affairs? If your former company deducted your tax payments from your salary, you are probably an employee; if you received holiday pay, you were probably an employee, too.
- Work patterns: Did you work as part of an organisation (in which case you are more likely to have been an employee) or was your work ancillary (in which case you were more likely to be a contractor)?
- Supervision: Were you strictly supervised in terms of what you did and how you did it? If so, you were probably an employee. If you had more freedom to decide how to work, you were more likely a contractor.
- Industry practice: What are the industry norms for people doing your sort of job? If it is common for people to work as an independent contractor, then you are likely to be so classified, too.

A crucial element is 'control' – i.e. who tells you what to do and how to do it?

What is a contract of employment?

All employees have a contract of employment, setting out your duties, rights and responsibilities towards your employer, and your employer's duties, rights and responsibilities towards you. Some contracts of employment are unwritten, but they are no less valid for that.

A basic contract employment would have your employer agreeing to pay you a wage for your labours, to provide a safe working environment and to ensure that other employees are competent. There is no duty to pay sick pay or holiday pay or accrued holiday pay, unless it is stated in the contract. Nor is there a duty to provide you with references, but if a reference is provided the employer owes a duty to you to make sure the reference is completed with reasonable skill and care. The employer also owes a duty to the receiver of the reference not to make any negligent statements about you – for example, saying you were 'honest' if you had left the company after being accused of dishonesty.

Your responsibilities under a basic contract of employment would be to agree to carry out the work, co-operate and liaise with your employer and managers, and to act in accordance with your contract and not do anything that might damage the company. The contract will also specify terms and conditions such as working hours and locations, holiday entitlement and sick pay arrangements.

I do not have a written contract of employment. Is that right?

Employment contracts do not have to be in writing to be legally binding; provided that your boss tells you what your job is, how much you will get paid and how much holiday pay you will get then, if you agree (and make it clear that you have accepted), a valid contract of employment exists. But because nothing is in writing, in the case of any future dispute, a tribunal would have to work out what the implied (that is unwritten) terms of your contract are, by looking at the industry and deciding what terms are generally incorporated into contracts of this kind. For this reason it is in everyone's best interests if a written contract of employment exists, as it removes the uncertainty and means no outside body (a court or tribunal, for instance) would have to decide on what terms the contract was ultimately drawn up with.

Even if the contract of employment remains unwritten, within eight weeks of starting your job, your employer is legally required by the Employment Rights Act 1996 to give you a written summary of the main terms and conditions of your employment; if this has not been done, it will be harder for the company to establish what your terms and conditions were in the case of any action for breach of contract or unfair dismissal.

If a written statement is provided, it must include the name of the company and the employee (you), the date you started work, the rate of pay and how often you are paid, the hours of work including any overtime requirements (such as mandatory overtime), holiday entitlement and holiday pay details, company rules over sick pay and absence for sickness, details of any company pensions scheme, notice periods, what your job title is (though not necessarily what that job entails – though most companies do provide it), details of disciplinary rules and procedures, including any rights of appeal, where you would be expected to work, details of any requirement to work abroad for longer than one month, the length of the contract if you have been employed on a fixed-term contract, and (in the case of large groups) any special provisions that exist to preserve your length of service and seniority if you were to transfer between companies.

What are contract terms?

Contract terms are the rights and obligations that bind you and your employer to the contract, and can be 'express' (those agreed with your employer either orally or in writing) or 'implied' (those which have not been spelled out but which both parties would take to form part of the contract). Implied terms are often those that are too obvious to mention or that one would assume would be in the contract from the start. Obvious implied terms are that workers should follow the lawful orders of managers, act in 'good faith' (which can mean working according to the contract, being honest in the course of one's employment, accounting for any profits incurred during one's employment, such as free 'air miles', following a duty of confidentiality, etc.) and not do anything detrimental to the business. Customs and practices of the industry will also be implied terms: for example, many factories close for the summer and it would be an implied term that two weeks of your total holiday entitlement would be taken then.

Express terms are easier to establish – they may be in the written statement of terms and conditions (to which most employees are entitled under the Employment Rights Act 1996), any letter of appointment and statements made by your employer (either verbally or in writing) and accepted by you. Express terms that are included in collective agreements and company handbooks may also be added to the contract of employment.

Some terms may be implied by statute, such as minimum notice periods, and equality clauses implied by the Equal Pay Act 1970; tribunals and courts will recognise them automatically. Attempts in a contract to contract employees out of statutory provisions normally fail and such terms are void.

I was given a contract of employment but never signed it. Can my employer enforce those terms against me?

The general view seems to be that if you have worked under the terms of the contract, and been notified of the terms and conditions in writing, both you and your employer would be bound by its terms, and if any matter went to tribunal it is likely that the tribunal would view the contract as binding on you. However, if you were looking to leave the company early, and your contract of employment specified a six-month notice period, your employer's only course of action against you if you departed before the full six-month notice period would be to sue you for breach of contract in a court. Then, with no contract actually in place, a clever lawyer could argue that only the statutory notice period of one week would apply.

My employer wants to change the terms of my contract, but I don't want to. Can that happen?

Technically, every time you are awarded a pay rise or receive extra holidays, your contract of employment is varied, but you obviously consent to these variations. Of more concern to you are occasions where your employer tries to change your contract and you don't want to, for example varying your working hours, or pay rates going in the opposite direction, or changes in supervision. An employer does not have an automatic right to vary your terms of employment, and just how easily your employer will be able to amend your contract depends on the contract itself. If it contains flexible clauses or has incorporated some allowance for change (such as having a staff handbook incorporated into the contract) then your employer will be able to alter the terms in line with these clauses. Otherwise, the correct procedure must be followed: an existing contract of employment can be varied only with the agreement of both parties. Changes may be agreed on an individual basis or through collective negotiation with a union, and you (or your union's reps) should be fully consulted to explain the reasons for the change and to discuss them. If a variation is agreed and the changes noted in the written terms and conditions, you must be given a month's notice before the changes come into effect. If your contract contains flexibility clauses in which the employer reserves the right to alter your duties, then reasonable changes in your duties will be allowed within your existing contract of employment, without it being varied.

My employer has re-written my contract without my consent. What can I do?

Sometimes, despite consultation and discussion, your employer and you may still not agree about the variation of your contract, with any compromises offered not accepted. If your employer then imposes changes in your contractual terms without your agreement, there is a breach of contract. In these circumstances, you can accept the breach and continue to work under the amended contract – but after a time, you may be regarded as having agreed to the new changes if you continue to work without objection. If the change is fundamental to the contract, for example a pay cut or change of hours of work, you could consider this as a fundamental breach, bringing the contract to an end and allowing you to leave. If you have worked for the company for long enough, you can sue for constructive dismissal at an employment tribunal. Another option is to continue to work under the varied contract under protest, making it clear that you do not accept the terms and regard the change as a breach of contract and termination of the original contract. Then you can sue for damages for breach of contract, or get a court to order your employer to follow the original contract. You might also be able to sue for unfair dismissal if you have worked at the company long enough; in deciding your claim, the tribunal would rule on whether the breach was fundamental and whether your employer acted reasonably in all circumstances.

I'm an employer. I have to vary my workers' contracts of employment, is there any way I can do so?

If, despite negotiations, your employees will not agree to vary their contract, you can, after following the proper procedures, end the original contracts of employment with a proper notice period, and then offer your workers new contracts with the revised terms. There will be no breach of contract if you do this. The proper notice period will be whatever is specified or implied in the contract of employment, or the statutory minimum, whichever is longer. But qualified workers can then sue you for unfair dismissal at a tribunal, whether they refuse to accept the new contract and leave, or whether they come back to work under the new agreement; it will be up to the tribunal to decide if your actions were fair.

Are there any rules to protect employees' rights at work?

Most regulations protecting employees' rights were initially brought together in the Employment Protection (Consolidation) Act 1978, and despite being curtailed somewhat during the Thatcher years, they were restated in the Employment Relations Act 1999. These cover areas such as unfair and constructive dismissal, contracts of employment, maternity leave, notice, time off work, trade union rights and unfair dismissal. In addition, men and women have equal rights under sex discrimination legislation and different ethnic groups' rights are safeguarded under race relations legislation (see **Sex and race discrimination and harassment**). But employment protection is limited; for example, some rules do not apply to workers on fixed contracts of three months or less, or part-timers working less than eight hours a week, or people that have reached retirement age.

My employer wants to deduct cash from my pay for shortfalls in the till. I don't want him to, so can he just take the money?

Anyone handling cash may find shortfalls at the end of the day; this can occur in many ways, not all of them criminal or negligent. But however short-changed your employer may feel, the Employment Rights Act 1996 states that employers may deduct money if, and only if, the employee agrees to this in writing (some firms do this by including a clause in the contract of employment, but this is not always possible.) If your boss deducts from your pay without an agreement, you can sue to recover the money through the courts.

I have been offered a new job. How do I leave my current job?

If you want to leave, normally you should give the notice period specified in your contract of employment, which may be a week, month, three months, etc. But sometimes, workers want to leave early to start a new job, and employers won't play ball. If your contract does not state a notice period, the statutory period of notice applies, which is one week if you have worked for a month or more. If your employer wants to get rid of you, it has to give a statutory minimum period of notice to terminate your contract of employment, if you have been continuously employed for one month. Exactly how much the statutory minimum is depends on how long you worked for the company. If you have worked for one month, you are entitled to one week's notice; if you have worked for two years, two weeks and it carries on with an additional week's notice for every additional year's service up to a maximum 12 weeks' statutory notice (of course, some people's contracts require three or six months' notice). There are specific regulations dealing with redundancy (see **Redundancy**) and dismissal for misconduct (see **Disciplinary hearings and unfair dismissal**).

What are 'restrictive covenants' in employment contracts?

Restrictive covenants are those terms that prevent former employees making use of information gained while working for you to help a competitor, or which try to prevent former employees working for rivals for a period of time. They do not just protect company secrets, but all information that is genuinely confidential to the company, for example a list of customers or a discount structure. To be effective, however, a restrictive covenant has to be well-written, otherwise it could be worthless. General phrases will not do.

What is not protected?

You cannot stop an employee using his 'skill and knowledge', even if he acquired and developed that skill and knowledge working for you. So if your secretary learned to speak German through lessons paid for by the company, you could not enforce a restrictive covenant preventing him working for companies that required him to speak German (though companies have tried to recover the costs of the lessons from the employee).

What types of restrictions can I impose?

You can impose restrictions on area, time and customers. In certain circumstances, a covenant can restrict an ex-employee operating within a given radius for a given length of time, or from seeing specific or general customers. Usually, the more specific the restriction, the more chance of enforcing it; for example, if a salesperson operates in a 20-mile radius of your HQ, a restriction clause with a 25-mile radius would probably fail, though one with a 15-mile radius would probably be valid. The easiest restrictions to enforce are those that prevent ex-staff poaching your customers. Customers are business assets, and courts are happy to enforce restrictive covenants that prevent ex-employees stealing assets they came to know about while working for you.

What can you do if an ex-employee breaches a restrictive covenant?

If an ex-employee breaches a restrictive covenant, you can seek an injunction preventing him and his new employer from breaching the covenant, and also sue for damages for breach of covenant. For this reason, well-drafted restrictive covenants can act as disincentives, discouraging rivals from poaching your staff to get your customer list, but too wide-ranging clauses are likely to be struck out by a court, leaving you with no restriction at all.

I've heard about a lot about 'the minimum wage'. What does this mean?

The National Minimum Wage Act came into force on in April 1999 to enforce a statutory minimum wage – and it is illegal for employers to pay less than the minimum wage. The Act applies to all UK employers, regardless of business size, with a few exceptions.

What is the minimum wage?

The standard minimum wage is currently £3.60 per hour, for workers aged 22 and over (unless they are receiving accredited training in a new job, where for the first six months the minimum wage is £3.20). For workers aged between 18 and 21, the minimum wage is £3 an hour.

Who qualifies for the minimum wage?

Almost all workers qualify for the minimum wage, including full-time workers, part-time workers, casual workers, home workers, freelance workers, temporary and agency workers, people of retirement age or pensioners (if they are working) and piece workers (those who are paid per item they complete, for example in the rag trade), who must be paid the minimum wage for every hour they work. However, some workers do not qualify, such as members of the armed forces, share fishermen, volunteer workers, prisoners working during their sentence and the self-employed.

My employer wants me to become self-employed, to reduce his wage bill and pay me less than the minimum wage. Can he do this?

Employers will not be able to avoid paying less than the minimum wage by making existing employees self-employed. In the same way, the law prevents employers agreeing with staff, in writing or orally, to pay them less than the minimum wage. (In addition, the Inland Revenue would resist this very strongly.)

I'm an employer. What happens if I don't follow minimum wage rules?

You will be served with an enforcement notice by the Inland Revenue or Contributions Agency requesting that you comply with the law within a set time-frame. If you fail to comply, you will be fined £7.20 a day for every worker paid below the minimum wage (a civil penalty). There is also a maximum criminal fine of £5,000 for refusing to comply with the National Minimum Wage Act, failing to keep proper wage records, keeping false records or obstructing officials from the Inland Revenue or Contributions Agency who might be investigating.

How many hours can my employer make me work?

The Working Time Directive came into force in October 1998, and applies to most full-time, part-time and casual workers who have been employed in a job for more than 13 weeks. It does not apply to certain workers such as road, sea, rail and air transport workers and trainee doctors, servicemen, the police and the self-employed. Under the Working Time directive, you do not have to work more than 48 hours per week, averaged over a 17-week period (unless you choose to), and you are entitled to a minimum of four weeks' paid holiday per year. Workers aged 18 and over are entitled by law to a 20-minute break where the working day is longer than six hours, and a rest period of 11 consecutive hours between working days, and a two-day rest period in each seven days. Night-workers will work a daily average of eight hours, averaged over a 17-week period, and be given free regular health assessments to ensure they are fit for night work. Different rules apply to workers aged 16–18. Those that work between the hours of 10 p.m. and 6 a.m. are entitled to health assessments, 12 hours' rest in each 24-hour period worked, and 30-minute breaks if they have worked more than four-and-a-half hours. Anyone selected for redundancy, or dismissed for refusing to work more than 48 hours or during a break period could claim unfair dismissal.

I am an employer. What are my obligations regarding health and safety at work?

The law imposes a responsibility on employers to ensure their employees' safety at work, and much of the regulations regarding safety in the workplace can be found in the Health and Safety at Work Act. As an employer, you must take reasonable steps to ensure the health, safety and welfare of your employees at work; failing to do so could lead to a criminal prosecution at magistrates' or Crown Court. The Health and Safety Executive (HSE) tends to act very quickly, and if someone is injured you will have to show why you are not to blame.

If you fail to ensure that your staff follow safe working practices, you could be sued by an injured employee for personal injury, or in the worst-case scenario be prosecuted for corporate manslaughter should the worker die. There is also an implied responsibility to take reasonable steps to ensure your employees' health and safety are not put at risk; to decide what is reasonable you must balance the level of risk against the cost of eliminating the risk. This responsibility might include a duty to provide safe plant, machinery and premises, a safe system of work and competent, trained and supervised staff. (Some groups need more care and supervision than others, for example disabled workers.)

You are also responsible for the health and safety of customers or visitors that come to your workplace. It would be wise to draw up a written code of conduct regarding training and supervision, and rules on safety procedures, including information on basic health and safety requirements. If you employ more than five workers, you must have a health and safety policy, and were there is a trade union in the workplace that has appointed a safety representative, you must consult that person when drawing up the safety policy. You must also carry out a risk assessment of the workplace and put appropriate control measures in place if necessary.

If you are about to start up a new business, you need to be aware of six important regulations that are now part of UK law as a result of our membership of the European Union:

- The Management of Health and Safety at Work Regulations 1992 oblige you to carry out a risk assessment of your workplace and act accordingly.
- The Health & Safety (Display Screen Equipment) Regulations 1992 introduced measures to prevent repetitive strain injury, fatigue, eye problems, etc.
- The Work Place (Health, Safety and Welfare) Regulations 1992 deal with maintenance of premises, for example floors and corridors, etc.

- The Provision and Use of the Work Equipment Regulations 1992 lay down regulations on guarding dangerous machines.
- The Personal Protective Equipment Work Regulations 1992 deal with the introduction of protective clothing, etc., where necessary.
- The Manual Handling Operations Regulations 1992 deal with the manual handling of equipment, stocks and materials.

You can get help and advice from the HSE and your local authority's environmental health department, which is also responsible for enforcing the Health and Safety at Work Act and the various regulations and can prosecute employers or serve notices on them to improve working conditions, or even close companies down.

Section 3.2 Maternity rights and family responsibilities

I'm pregnant. Do I have a right to take time off for antenatal appointments?

If a doctor or midwife recommends it, you are entitled to paid time off work at your usual rate of pay, to attend appointments and antenatal classes; if you work full-time you are entitled to attend these sessions during your normal working day, and it would be considered unreasonable for your employer to try to stop you going. Part-time workers should try to arrange the appointments outside work hours. But the company is entitled to ask for, and be given, a medical certificate stating that you are pregnant after your first appointment, and proof of future appointments, such as an appointment card.

What are my maternity rights? My contract of employment says they are 'statutory'

Maternity rights for employees changed on 30 April 2000. Women expecting babies on or after that date benefited from these maternity leave changes. Regardless of how long you have been employed, pregnant employees are legally entitled to 18 weeks' 'ordinary maternity leave'; women who have completed a full year's service with their present employer (previously it was two years) can also take 'additional maternity leave', starting at the end of ordinary maternity leave and finishing 29 weeks after the birth (counting from the Sunday at the beginning of the week in which the baby was born). The 'one year' is calculated from 11 weeks before the week in which you are due to give birth. Throughout ordinary maternity leave, women are entitled to receive the benefits of their normal terms and conditions of employment, except for those conditions relating to pay. Some employers will pay your full salary throughout this period, but most women will be entitled to 'statutory maternity pay' or 'maternity allowance'. Throughout any additional maternity leave the contract of employment is deemed to continue, and certain rights such as contractual redundancy rights and notice remain in force.

When can I start maternity leave?

Providing you give your employer at least 21 days' notice before starting maternity leave (or, in the case of a sudden, premature birth, as much notice as possible) you can take maternity leave at any time from the 11th week before the baby is due. Your employer is entitled to ask for written confirmation of the date you wish to take maternity leave from, and the date you expect to give birth. The 21 days' notice is sufficient whether you qualify for ordinary maternity leave or additional maternity leave, and you no longer have to tell your employer that you want to come back to work after maternity leave.

Do I qualify for statutory maternity pay? If so, how much will I be paid?

For you to qualify for statutory maternity pay (SMP):

- You must have worked continuously for at least 26 weeks or more, and the 26 weeks is counted back from 18 weeks before the week the baby is due, and not 26 weeks up to the time you go on maternity leave. But if you go into labour prematurely and had worked at least eight weeks, you may still qualify for SMP if you went into labour more than 18 weeks before the date the baby was due – this protects the rights of woman that would have qualified for maternity pay but went into premature labour.
- You have stopped working because of the pregnancy.
- Your weekly earnings are not below the current rate at which National Insurance contributions must be paid (currently £61 a week). You must have been earning more than £61 at least eight weeks before the 18-week qualifying date you need to count to when your baby is due to be born.
- It is 11 weeks before your 'due date', or you give birth before the start of the 11-week period.

SMP is paid for 18 weeks from the date you go on maternity leave, but this will not be earlier than 11 weeks before your due date, and not later than one week before your baby is due. SMP is paid at two different rates during your maternity leave:

- You are entitled to 90 per cent of your normal weekly pay for the first six weeks. 'Normal weekly pay' is calculated on the basis of what you received before you went on maternity leave.
- After the first six weeks, you are entitled to a current minimum of £60.20 for the rest of your maternity leave.

If your normal weekly pay is less than £60.20, you are entitled to £60.20 for the whole 18 weeks, and your SMP should be paid at the same time as your salary, though your employer will also deduct tax and national insurance.

If you are not entitled to SMP, but have made National Insurance contributions, you still qualify for 18 weeks' maternity allowance at £60.20 a week as an employee (or at a lower amount if you are self-employed). If you also have a contractual right to maternity pay, your employer does not have to pay both the contractual amount and SMP, only the one that pays the most.

You are also entitled to any perks that you normally receive when at work, so if you get private health care as part of your package, check whether pregnancy is covered. If so you could end up 'going private'.

How do I go about returning to work after maternity leave?

If you want to go back to work before the end of your ordinary or additional maternity leave, you must give your company 21 days' notice; otherwise, if you plan to return to work at the end of ordinary maternity leave, you don't need to do anything else. (If you qualify for additional maternity leave, let your employer know when the baby is born so that the company can plan for your return in 29 weeks' time.) If you are claiming additional maternity leave, your company may write no earlier than 21 days before the end of the ordinary maternity leave period to confirm your child's date of birth, and whether you are still intending to return to work after your additional maternity leave. The letter is required to explain how to calculate when the additional maternity leave period ends, and that you may be penalised if you do not reply to the letter within 21 days of receiving it (your employer could take disciplinary action against you).

What protection do pregnant women have?

Dismissing a woman in connection with her pregnancy is automatically deemed to be unfair, and you can complain to an employment tribunal if you are dismissed for any reason connected with your pregnancy or for taking maternity leave. Women are also protected from unfair treatment at work in connection with pregnancy, childbirth or maternity leave, and can complain to a tribunal.

Can I be forced to take maternity leave?

It is normally up to you to decide when to start your maternity leave, but it is illegal for a pregnant employee to work within a fortnight of having given birth. If you breach this, your employer will be fined.

Are there any other restrictions on my right to return to work after having a baby?

Your employer can suspend you if you are pregnant, have recently given birth or are breastfeeding if:

- There are health and safety considerations, working with chemicals such as lead for example.
- If you normally work on a night shift.

Although your company can suspend you, you cannot be dismissed because it would be connected with your pregnancy and so automatically unfair. However, before your employer suspends you, they must consider alternative work for you; if they do not offer you alternative work (if it is available), you can complain to an employment tribunal within three months of being suspended. If you are suspended, it must be on full pay, with all perks and benefits; but if you turn down a suitable offer of alternative employment, your right to full pay is lost.

I've heard about 'parental leave'. What is it?

Parental leave allows parents of children born or adopted after December 15, 1999, to take time off work to care for that child. Both mothers and fathers can claim this right, as can anyone who has been given parental responsibility for a child under the Children Act. As soon as a parent has completed one year's service with their employer, they can start taking parental leave (and parental leave can be taken any time after a child is born or adopted). A parent can take 13 weeks' parental leave for each child, within five years of the child's birth or date of adoption (though parents of disabled children will be able to take parental leave up until the child's 18th birthday). You continue to be employed by your company while on parental leave, and some contractual rights such as contractual notice and redundancy terms will still apply. At the end of the leave period, you are guaranteed the right to return to the same job as before (or if that is not possible, a similar job with the same or better status, terms and conditions as your previous post). If the leave period is for four weeks or less, you are entitled to go back to the same job.

Company and employees can resolve specific issues between themselves (e.g. how much notice? can leave be postponed if it might be to the company's detriment to grant leave?); otherwise a series of fallback conditions apply, which allow a maximum of four weeks' parental leave each year, in blocks or multiples of a week, with 21 days' notice, subject to the employer's right to postpone leave for up to six months if the business cannot cope (but not if leave is applied for as soon as the child is born or adopted). If your company stops – or tries to stop – you taking parental leave, you can take the company to an employment tribunal.

What are family rights?

All workers – full-time or part-time, permanent or temporary – have a right to take time off work to deal with an emergency involving a dependant (e.g. child, spouse, parent). There is no limit on how much time you can take, but it should be for a reasonable period, allowing you to deal with the emergency. But there is no entitlement to pay in this time; that is up to your company. If your company tries to prevent you exercising your 'family rights' you can take them to an employment tribunal.

Section 3.3 Statutory sick pay

I am off work, sick. Am I entitled to pay?

Most employees are entitled to statutory sick pay (SSP) if they are absent from work through sickness, though there are some exceptions, which include workers on strike, workers who do not earn enough to pay National Insurance contributions, new employees, overseas employees, pensioners, pregnant employees, prisoners and short-term employees (on contracts of three months or less).

How much sick pay will I get?

The amount you receive depends upon the terms stated in your contract of employment. The contract may say that when you are absent through illness you will receive your normal salary; therefore you will not receive any statutory sick pay. It may state that you will receive your normal salary minus the amount of SSP. If your contract states that your contractual sick pay is not payable at all, you will then only be entitled to statutory sick pay.

Statutory sick pay falls into bands and is calculated on your normal weekly earnings. Since April 1999, SSP of £59.55 is payable each week for employees who earn enough to pay National Insurance contributions. SSP is not paid for the first three days that an employee is off work, but is paid from the fourth day up to 28 weeks; after that time, if you were still on sick leave, you would have to claim sickness benefit (if you do not qualify for SSP, you may still qualify for Sickness Benefit).

How is SSP paid?

Your employer pays SSP and claims it back from the Benefits Agency. SSP is paid at a weekly rate divided by the number of 'qualifying' days in that week (which is normally your working week of Monday-Friday). So for example, if you fell ill on Monday the first day you could claim for would be Thursday and if you returned to work the following Monday you would be entitled to two days' sick pay (for Thursday and Friday). But in larger companies, you will often be paid your normal salary for the days you were on sick leave. Your contract will normally state which days are 'qualifying days' for sick pay (if it does not, the normal Monday to Friday working week is usually chosen).

Section 3.4 Redundancy

My firm wants to make me redundant. What does that mean?

Redundancy is a situation where your company wants to dismiss you because there is no longer any suitable work for you. This is different to situations where you are sacked for some misconduct, and if you are made redundant, your employer may be obliged by law to compensate you. If you are entitled to redundancy pay, you should be given your redundancy pay on leaving the company, but if your employer tries to avoid paying (by claiming you were sacked or resigned) you may have to fight for your money at an employment tribunal. If your company is insolvent you can claim a redundancy payment from the Department of Education and Employment, the official receiver or the company's liquidator. If employees are 'selected' for redundancy, the company must ensure that its selection process is carried out fairly, or those that feel they have been unfairly selected might sue for wrongful or unfair dismissal. Examples of situations where people are made redundant are:

*   Departmental reorganisations, with fewer people needed to do the work.
*   The business (or part of it) closes.
*   Workers are laid off or put on short-time working.
*   The business relocates.

But you can't claim redundancy if you are sacked, for example if you work in a bar and you don't fit the new image (in that case you could sue for unfair dismissal); or where a company changes working practices, and cuts overtime; or where you are required to work from another site under your contract of employment.

Do I qualify for redundancy payments?

To be eligible for a redundancy payout, you must have worked for the company continuously for two years (24 months). Further, your eligibility depends on your being dismissed or forced out; if you resign of your own accord because you have heard redundancy is in the air, or agree to leave, you have resigned and will not be eligible for redundancy pay.

How does a redundancy process operate?

The first step is for your company to devise a mechanism to decide who will be kept on and who will be made redundant and why. The next step is to notify the workforce as soon as possible to give you (or your union reps) a chance to advance alternative arguments, or apply for other jobs (either with the company or elsewhere). If the workforce can put forward any counter-proposals, the company should consider them as an alternative to redundancy. The company must determine as soon as possible how many workers are to go, and if more than 20 are to lose their jobs, the company is obliged by law to consult with workers' representatives (including unions) to discuss alternatives to redundancy, and what selection criteria will be used for deciding who will be dismissed. (If more than 20 workers are to lose their jobs, the Department of Education and Employment must also be consulted 30 days before dismissal; but if more than 100 workers are to be made redundant, 90 days' notice must be given.) The company can continue the procedures while consultation takes place (for example, sending out redundancy notices) but if proper consultation does not take place, an employment tribunal can order it to pay a protective award; this obliges the company to continue employing the workers and pay their wages for a certain period of time, whether or not they are working.

How does the company select workers for redundancy?

If your company selects a group of workers to be made redundant, the company must show what work the group does and why demand for their skills has decreased or ceased. If only some of the group members were selected for redundancy, the company must show how the selection was made, explaining what criteria were used (which could be 'last in, first out', a scoring system with points being awarded for certain key skills, or some other method). But whatever criterion is used, it must be impartial and impersonal, and cannot be based on any individual view of another employee (for example, the opinions of the line manager). Once set, criteria must be followed (and if possible, criteria should be agreed with worker representatives or the unions; sensible companies will do this as it can defuse potential claims of unfairness later). But any selection criteria involving sex, race, disability, gender or union membership is unfair, and anyone selected for redundancy on these grounds could claim unfair dismissal or discrimination.

Does my employer have to consult me if I have been selected for redundancy?

Yes. Each employee selected for redundancy must be consulted before dismissal notices are handed out; this gives you time to respond, and for a proper consultation to take place, which may end up changing the composition of the group selected for redundancy. You must be told why your job is under threat, and why you may be chosen by the selection criteria (but at this time, the selection should not be completed nor dismissal notices sent out). You should be allowed a few days to respond, and any opinions you express at the time you are first consulted or subsequently should be taken into account; both you and your company should also consider if there is any alternative work you could do or any way of keeping your current post. After the consultation process, the company should call those selected back in to a second interview to break the news and give out the redundancy notice.

I have been selected for redundancy but my boss has offered me an alternative job in the company. Must I accept?

Your company can offer other work instead of making you redundant; it is up to you whether to accept or not. But if you 'unreasonably refuse' an offer, your employer may not have to pay you redundancy pay, for example if you were offered a job identical to your current post or one with similar skills, with similar pay and conditions. Tribunals look at these alternative job offers subjectively; some workers might accept the offer, while others, for their own reasons, would not: for example, if the new job means more travelling for some workers than others. Any alternative job offer must be made before your current job ends and start no more than four weeks after the old job ended. During the first four weeks of the new job, it is effectively a trial period for you, and during this four-week period (or at the end of it) you can still leave and claim your redundancy pay. (The four-week period is a minimum, and you and the company can agree a longer trial period for the new job if you choose.)

How much redundancy pay will I get?

Redundancy payments are calculated by taking into account your age, the number of years' service and your average weekly pay. The weekly pay is limited to a maximum of £220 per week and the maximum number of years that will be considered is 20. However, the years of service also depend upon age:

- For those years' service when you were aged under 22, you will get half your weekly pay (the average week's wage is multiplied by $1/2$).
- For those years' service when you were aged between 22 and 41, you will get your weekly pay (the average week's wage is multiplied by 1).
- For those years' service when you were aged 41 and over, you will get one-and-a-half times your weekly pay (the average week's wage is multiplied by $1^1/2$).

The absolute maximum award is £6,600, which would be paid for 20 years service at £220 for every year, with a multiplier of $1^1/2$. But if you are aged 65 or over, or over the normal retirement age for your particular organisation, you cannot claim redundancy. From workers aged 64–65, the award is reduced by 1/12th for every month up to the age of 65, when no award can be made.

I have a redundancy package specified in my contract...

Some companies outline redundancy terms in their contracts, or your company may already have an agreed redundancy procedure. These are usually more generous than the statutory minimum, but if a large number of staff has to be made redundant, your company might want to exclude staff from the contract arrangement to save money in redundancy pay.

I have been selected for redundancy. Can I appeal?

Most companies have an appeals procedure, so workers who do not want to be made redundant can appeal against their selection, and if such a procedure exists it must be followed fairly. If the whole redundancy process is not followed fairly or if you feel you were unfairly selected, you might be able to claim unfair dismissal. If a tribunal finds you were unfairly dismissed, an award of compensation can be made (though the amount of any redundancy payment made to you will be deducted from the tribunal's award). It can also order you to be reinstated or rehired (but in practice this rarely happens).

If you are not given the notice period laid down in your contract you might be able to claim wrongful dismissal, and you can also take the company to tribunal if you are not paid the correct amount of redundancy pay, calculated by the statutory formula or by the one laid down in your contract.

My employer has asked for volunteers for redundancy. Should I go before I am pushed?

To qualify for redundancy payments you must be dismissed or forced out of your job. So if you volunteer, make sure the company agrees in writing to pay you your redundancy entitlement; if you do not have this agreement in writing, you might find it difficult to convince a tribunal that you did not resign of your own accord, which would make you ineligible for redundancy.

My redundancy notice says I will be redundant in six weeks, but I have just been offered another job – will it affect my redundancy?

If you are under notice of redundancy, you can leave to start a new job before the notice period expires without losing any right to redundancy payments, providing you give the company one week's notice before starting your new job (and which must be served within your own redundancy notice period). But the company can try to stop you leaving, by serving a counter-notice that requires you to stay until your full period of notice is up (most likely to happen if you are a specialist and the company is trying to avoid paying your redundancy by finding you another job within the firm) and may threaten to withhold any redundancy payment, and contest any claim you make at tribunal. Any counter-notice must be in writing, and must reach you before the end of your one week' notice period. If the case went to tribunal, the members would look at how reasonably both sides had behaved.

I am under notice of dismissal and my employer has caught me stealing computer disks. Will this affect my redundancy?

If you commit any offence so serious that it could justify instant dismissal, you can lose all or part of your redundancy payment; after all, if you were working at the company with no threat of redundancy, you would expect to be sacked, wouldn't you? If you are sacked before redundancy notices are issued, you lose all your rights to redundancy pay; but if you are allowed to serve your notice period, rather than be sacked, you might be able to claim redundancy pay (though your company can stop this happening by writing to you to say that you would have been sacked but are being allowed to work your notice). If the offence was committed after redundancy notices were served, you may be able to claim, but only what a tribunal feels is just and equitable in the circumstances – and that could be nothing.

I am on strike, and have been made redundant. Can I claim redundancy pay?

You might be able to claim, though it would depend on a tribunal's judgment. If you go on strike after being made redundant, you will still qualify for redundancy pay, but your boss can make you work extra days to make up the time lost.

Section 3.5 Sex and race discrimination and harassment

What is discrimination?

If an employer treats someone differently because of their sex*, race, colour, nationality, ethnic or national origins or marital status, then that is discrimination. (Sexual harassment can also be discrimination.) If two employees who do the same job are paid different salaries because one is a woman and the other a man, that is also discrimination. It would also be discriminatory to treat disabled people less favourably than their able-bodied work colleagues. It would be discriminatory to treat members of trade unions less favourably than non-union members, and anyone so treated could take their case to a tribunal (but this can also work in reverse, and non-union members can take action if they receive less favourable treatment).

*Compensation is not available for people who are discriminated against because of their sexual orientation (for example gay men or lesbians), because this is not recognised as sex discrimination. But if a gay man is treated differently to a lesbian in the workplace, then this can be discrimination.

How can workers be discriminated against?

Direct discrimination is discrimination by virtue of race or sex (either for employees or candidates for jobs) and tends to be obvious: for example, a female candidate with the best qualifications and experience not getting a job interview; or if she is passed over for promotion, the job going to a less-qualified male worker. In these cases, it does not matter if companies claim they had not intended to discriminate – all that matters is the end result of the company's actions.

Indirect discrimination is less obvious: for example, if a job description is phrased in such a way that it will eliminate people from a particular group on grounds of race or gender. It would also be indirect discrimination if criteria that eliminate a group are not really job requirements, so that candidates on that ground would be able to do the job as well as anyone else. But in order to claim indirect discrimination, you must have suffered in some way because of it.

Are there any exceptions that allow discrimination?

Sometimes, it is possible in cases of indirect discrimination for an employer to argue that though there is discrimination, it is actually required for the job, for example where actors who are needed to play certain characters for authenticity. The same can be true of restaurants, for example an Indian restaurant will want Indian staff rather than white staff. (But in practice, these circumstances do not arise often.) And under sex discrimination law, there are some exceptions where discriminating between the sexes is allowed, usually where it is sensible: for example, in jobs with single-sex situations, such as being the nurse at a girls' school.

Race discrimination laws aim to protect people of 'ethnic origin', but what does that mean?

For a group to have an ethnic origin, it must have certain characteristics such as a long shared history, cultural tradition, common geographic origin or descent from a small number of common ancestors, a common language, common literature and a common religion different from that of its neighbouring community. Tribunals have classed Sikhs as an ethnic group, along with Jews and gypsies, but not Rastafarians.

What is the law with regard to discriminating against disabled people at work?

The Disability Discrimination Act 1995 says that companies cannot discriminate against employees (employed either now or in the future) who have a disability now, or who had one in the past. The Act requires employers to provide supervision, modify handbooks or reference manuals (for example in large print or Braille), allow time off from work that is related to a worker's disability and modify (or buy) new equipment to meet a disabled worker's needs. Any adjustments must be 'reasonable', taking into account factors such as cost, any disruption it will cause and how effective they would be in removing or preventing the disabled employee being disadvantaged. The Act covers any employees (permanent, temporary and contract workers as well as full-timers) with a 'physical or mental impairment' which can affect ability to carry out day-to-day tasks, and it also covers people who have had a disability in the past. But some groups are currently excluded from the Act's provisions: police officers, prison officers, firefighters, servicemen and women, and ship's and aircraft crews. Nor does the Act apply to employees working wholly or mainly abroad or to companies with fewer than 15 employees.

I am planning to employ a new member of staff. What factors should I be aware of to avoid discriminating against anyone, and avoid being accused of discrimination?

Anyone who feels they have been discriminated against in a recruitment or selection process on the grounds of race, sex or disability or membership (or otherwise) of a trade union may complain to an employment tribunal, so your caution is reasonable. As an employer, you want to avoid any discrimination – it de-motivates your workers and can lead to legal actions. And apart from anything else, it is wrong.

Before advertising the position, draw up a 'person specification'; this is a brief description of the ideal candidate for the job which profiles the personal skills and characteristics you will be looking for when you select candidates for interview. Doing this helps clarify issues you may have missed that might be inadvertently discriminatory: could a part-timer do the job? Could one of your existing staff? Decide whether to get candidates to apply with a CV, or whether you want to design an application form instead. A well-thought-out application form can help you sift out unsuitable candidates, but should only ask only for information that is relevant to the job; anything unrelated, and which might give disgruntled unsuccessful candidates an opportunity to complain that they were discriminated against should be avoided. Some people would do anything rather than admit that a better candidate got a job ahead of them, and that includes going to a tribunal. So don't give them ammunition. Asking whether women candidates plan to have children is a definite no-no; it has no bearing on the job and is absolutely discriminatory. Raising the same question at interview would also be asking for trouble – after all, you won't be asking the men, will you? If the woman who plans to have a family is the best candidate, then select her.

A good equal opportunities policy should help ensure that no applicants or employees are treated less favourably on grounds of sex, race, colour, nationality, ethnic or national origin or on grounds of disability.

I think my prospective employer has discriminated against me; what can I do?

To bring an action, you must complain to an employment tribunal within three months of the sex or race discrimination taking place though the tribunal has a discretion to decide exactly when the three months should start, and the guidelines are complex. Legal Aid is not available for cases that go to the employment tribunal, though if the case is subsequently referred to the employment appeal tribunal, Legal Aid may be available. If you win, your legal costs will only be met in certain circumstances, for example if the company is defending an indefensible position.

When you complain to the employment tribunal, it is normal for an official from the Advisory, Conciliation and Arbitration Service (ACAS) to be appointed to try and negotiate a settlement, but if this cannot be done, the case will be heard. You can ask your employer or prospective employer to provide copies of any relevant documents, for example internal memos or notes made during any interview. You can also send your employer a questionnaire, asking questions about the incident. There is no requirement to fill this in, but any answers that are provided can be submitted as evidence; a refusal to fill in the form can also be brought to the tribunal's notice. Tribunals can decide cases on written evidence alone if both sides agree, and can decide cases without a full hearing, for example if the company does not file a defence.

What can a tribunal do if it finds I have been discriminated against?

If it finds that discrimination has taken place, a tribunal has a number of options. It can order your employer to pay compensation (including interest) and with no limit set down by statute, this figure can be large. Damages can also be included for hurt feelings and the loss of opportunity in not getting the new job (which can go beyond the actual salary that was lost). The tribunal can increase the award of damages if it feels that your employer's behaviour was insulting or malicious, and it can recommend that your employer take action to limit the damage done to you. But it cannot order your employer to give you a job or promote you.

I'm a bit worried about having to fund the case myself...

In cases of alleged discrimination, the Commission for Racial Equality (CRE) and Equal Opportunities Commission (EOC) can become involved if the case is a test case, or if it would be unreasonable for you to act alone, for example you are up against a large company with much greater legal resources. Both bodies have codes of conduct and practice, and tribunals take any breaches of these codes into account as evidence in support of your action. In addition, the CRE can investigate your case, requiring the company to provide evidence and documents to rebut your claim.

I am running a company, and some of my workers are picking on a woman van driver. Where do I stand legally?

Racial and sexual harassment are classed as direct discrimination, and hence unlawful (even though neither the Race Relations Act nor the Sex Discrimination Act define them as distinct offences). Workplace harassment is unacceptable, so companies must take steps to prevent it happening. Racial and sexual harassment are not legally defined, but a wide range of behaviour can be harassment, including any physical, verbal and non-verbal conduct which is not welcomed by the 'victim'.

If your workers harass a fellow employee, you can be liable for their actions under the principle of 'vicarious liability'. But it is not always clear whether acts of harassment are 'in the course of employment'; if the harasser is the victim's superior, then it is more likely to be considered as being 'in the course of employment' than if the victim is the superior.

But you will have a defence if you can show that you have done everything reasonable to prevent it from happening. If the company has equal opportunities and sexual and racial harassment policies, these should define harassment and state that harassment is not acceptable; workers should be made aware of the guidelines, and the consequences of breaching them. If an employee complains to you of harassment, it may be that an informal approach to the harasser would be appropriate, for example if the complaint is not very serious or if it is the first instance of it. (You should ascertain whether the victim would be happy if you followed an informal approach, or would prefer that you took a more formal route.) If you decide to follow the informal approach, you should tell the worker that his/her conduct is upsetting another employee, and that the acts amount to harassment and must not continue. You should show the worker the relevant policy (if it is in your guidelines) and warn him that the matter is under review; if the worker does not improve or the harassment continues, disciplinary action will be taken. You should inform the victim of what steps you have taken, and advise them to contact you if the harassment continues.

If an informal approach is not appropriate, or if the complainant wants formal action, then the company's disciplinary procedure should be followed. Get the victim to make a full statement, then (if appropriate) suspend the alleged harasser pending investigation of the complaint. Take statements from any staff that can provide evidence of the alleged harassment (either supporting the allegation or not), and interview the suspended worker, giving him the opportunity to make a statement.

If you find that there is any substance to the complaint, a disciplinary hearing will give the alleged harasser an opportunity to explain, justify or reject the allegations. In most cases, however, there will be no witnesses and it comes down to a question of 'who do you believe?' Disciplinary hearings will be discussed in more detail in **Disciplinary hearings and unfair dismissal**.

If you find that harassment has taken place, the punishment depends on how serious the harassment was; in the most serious cases the worker will be sacked, though in some circumstances a final written warning would be appropriate.

Section 3.6 Disciplinary hearings and unfair dismissal

Companies must be able to impose internal discipline to ensure workers behave in the right way to managers, each other, and to clients and customers. The less serious infractions can be dealt with informally, while more serious breaches may call for a disciplinary hearing. In the most serious cases, breaches of disciplinary codes that amount to gross misconduct can lead to summary dismissal. But if the disciplinary code is not followed, the company may dismiss workers who then sue for unfair dismissal. Unfair dismissal can arise in other ways too, and then an employment tribunal will investigate the circumstances surrounding the claim, and rule whether a worker was fairly dismissed, and it can award damages if unfairness is discovered. Dismissal is unfair unless it can be shown to have been fair. If, for example, the employer can argue redundancy, then the dismissal will, prima facie, be fair, but if the employee can then show improper selection, the dismissal again becomes unfair.

Do all companies have disciplinary procedures?

Companies are not required by law to have a disciplinary code or disciplinary procedure, but if a company does have a procedure, it helps managers deal with disciplinary matters fairly and consistently and reduces the number of claims of unfair dismissal it may face from employees who are questioning disciplinary action taken against them. But any company with more than 20 employees that has a code must refer to it in the written statement of terms and conditions of employment, and must also identify the member of staff workers can appeal to if they want to question disciplinary action taken against them.

What should be covered by the disciplinary code?

The first step for any company is to devise and record some basic rules of behaviour; these will vary from company to company, but will include general conduct, timekeeping and absences (both authorised and unauthorised), health and safety, and the use of office equipment and property. In addition, the code will outline any disciplinary rules that exist, with examples of misconduct and gross misconduct, and information on how such infractions would be dealt with.

What is misconduct?

'Misconduct' is effectively any wrongdoing within a company that can lead to disciplinary action against the perpetrator.

What is 'gross misconduct'?

Misconduct that is so serious that, in the view of managers, it justifies immediate sacking is gross misconduct. However good a worker's previous disciplinary record, if he is found guilty of gross misconduct, the worker will be summarily sacked without notice or payment in lieu. Gross misconduct is the sort of behaviour that damages the relationship of trust between the company and employees, and can include repeated and unauthorised absences, passing on confidential information, bullying, theft, fraud, physical violence, sexual or racial harassment or behaviour that seriously damages the company's reputation. With the spread of technology, it can now include misuse of corporate e-mail systems.

I've been accused of misconduct...

If you are accused of a disciplinary offence – and assuming it is so serious that it is not one that can be dealt with informally – the company's first action will be to tell you in outline what you have been accused of, and what disciplinary action is likely to follow. They may suspend you – and if they do it must be on full pay – while conducting an investigation into the allegations. If there is no case to answer, you will be formally notified in writing and you can return to work. But if they find it a case that requires you to answer, you will have to attend a disciplinary hearing. You must be given notice of any disciplinary hearing so that you can prepare your defence.

I want to take my solicitor in with me, but the company won't allow it. Can they do that?

Most companies don't like washing dirty linen in public, so there is obviously some resistance to letting 'outsiders' become involved in disciplinary proceedings. As a result, some company disciplinary codes specify that only fellow workers be allowed to accompany colleagues to disciplinary hearings, though some companies would doubtless prefer it if employees turn up alone. But the Employment Relations Act 1999 gives workers the right to be accompanied to all disciplinary hearings, and to some grievance hearings. From now on, all workers (with or without written contracts of employment, but not the self-employed) have a right to be accompanied at a disciplinary hearing that could result in a formal warning or some other action being taken by the employer, and at grievance hearings that concern the employer's performance of a duty to the worker. This would include allegations of bullying or harassment, or anything relating to an alleged breach of your employer's duty towards employees. Under the 1999 Act, workers can be accompanied by a fellow worker or a trade union officer (who can be a full-time union officer, lay trade union official or workplace representative). Lay officers or workplace representatives must be certified by the union in writing as being experienced in, or trained in, accompanying people at hearings. Even if the union is not recognised, it doesn't matter – if you want a union rep, you can have a union rep. But not your lawyer.

How do disciplinary proceedings operate?

Different companies have different disciplinary procedures; you will be notified of the form that your company's proceedings take before the hearing. Usually a panel of managers sit in judgment over you, and one manager – normally the one that investigated the complaint – presents the case against you. Prior to the hearing, you will have been sent copies of statements taken from colleagues that form the case against you; you can call them to appear and give their evidence in person if you wish, allowing you to question them about their evidence. In addition, you are entitled to call your own witnesses who can support your case. The panel of managers will almost certainly question you to hear your side of the allegations, before they make a decision. If you are cleared you will be allowed to return to work; but if the allegations are found to be proven, a penalty will be imposed.

What penalties can a disciplinary hearing impose?

Typical disciplinary codes have the following punishments:

*   A formal oral warning in the case of a minor offence.
*   A written warning for subsequent minor offences or a more serious offence.
*   A final written warning for further misconduct, or for very serious misconduct that falls short of dismissal, and which would state that dismissal might follow if you fail to improve.
*   Summary dismissal in the case of gross misconduct.

Written warnings will be recorded and reviewed within a set period of time, and companies should 'clean the slate' if your behaviour is satisfactory.

Can I appeal against the decision?

If you do not accept the findings of your hearing, you can appeal against the decision. The company code of conduct may outline how to appeal against the finding of a disciplinary hearing; normally you must lodge notice of appeal within a short time – often five days – of being informed of the decision and punishment your managers have imposed.

I've been accused of theft, and now my manager has sacked me. Is that right?

Even if you were caught in the act, you cannot be sacked on the spot, as the disciplinary procedure must still be followed, and if it isn't you can sue for wrongful dismissal. But if your employer has evidence, you are not likely to get much sympathy from a tribunal. Small companies may not have a code of conduct, but should still give you an opportunity to mount a defence. If you were to complain to a tribunal, they would examine the way that your 'disciplinary matter' was investigated, and if it were not fair, you might be able to claim wrongful dismissal. If owners of small companies do not have their own code they can follow the procedures outlined in the ACAS handbook *Discipline at Work* (price £2.99, available from ACAS), and if a tribunal is satisfied that a small company has followed these guidelines, it is unlikely to find that a dismissal is wrongful. And of course, you are reading *Legal Adviser*!

What is unfair dismissal?

Dismissal is assumed unfair unless it can be shown to be fair. To claim unfair dismissal, you must prove that you were dismissed from your job, and did not resign – though there is such a thing as constructive dismissal, where you resign but argue that you were effectively dismissed anyway before your resignation. Most full-time workers with longer than 12 months' service qualify for protection for unfair dismissal, and can claim compensation from an employment tribunal if they are unfairly dismissed. Once you have shown that you were dismissed and did not resign, your employer would have to show that your dismissal was fair in all circumstances. So if your employer claimed that you were dismissed for misconduct, the tribunal would look at the misconduct to decide whether it was sufficient to justify dismissal in the circumstances.

How do I qualify to sue for unfair dismissal?

To qualify for unfair dismissal protection:

*   You must be working full- or part-time; the number of hours worked per week is irrelevant.
*   You must have one year's continuous employment.
*   You must be below aged below 65 or the normal retirement age for your job at the date of dismissal.

- You normally work in the UK.
- Your job ended less than three months ago, which runs from three months of the date you are dismissed or your notice expires if you are given notice (if you are paid in lieu of notice, three months is counted from the day you are dismissed). If you appeal against the decision and that fails, the date of dismissal is the date you were first dismissed, not the date the decision was confirmed. The three-month period can be extended, for example if you have been ill, where you were given incorrect advice from Job Centre or employment tribunal staff, where your notification was delayed in the post or where new evidence comes to light later making a claim possible.

Are there exceptions to the 12-month qualifying period?

You do not have to have worked for 12 months to qualify for unfair dismissal if you were dismissed for trade union-related activities (for union activities or for belonging to or refusing to join the trade union) or linked to pregnancy or maternity rights; if you are a shop worker who refuses to work on Sundays; if you are dismissed or made redundant on health and safety grounds; if you are dismissed or made redundant for taking (or trying to take) legal action against the company to enforce your legal rights. If your dismissal involves race or sex discrimination, you should sue for discrimination, not unfair dismissal, as you will get more compensation if you win.

If I bring an action for unfair dismissal, what do I have to prove?

Any claim for unfair dismissal must go through a two-stage test:

- Was the dismissal for a fair reason?

And if the dismissal was for a fair reason, then:

- Was the dismissal dealt with fairly?

This means that your employer can dismiss you for a perfectly valid reason, but if the way in which it was handled was unfair you would be able to bring an unfair dismissal claim.

What are fair reasons for dismissal?

As unfair dismissal means being dismissed unfairly, it stands to reason that your employer can terminate your employment for some valid reasons:

- If you are not capable or qualified to doing the job.
- If you commit gross misconduct that justifies dismissal.
- If you are made redundant.

- If continuing to employ you would be against the law, for example if you were a foreign worker.
- Other valid, miscellaneous reasons which could arise from many situations, for example where your business is being re-organised and some employees refuse to re-organise along with it, or where they are no longer considered suitable.

My managers caught me committing an act of gross misconduct and have dismissed me. How can I show that the proceedings were unfair, and claim unfair dismissal?

The test of fair proceedings is whether your employer used a fair procedure, and whether it was reasonable for your employer to finally decide to dismiss you once the procedure had been carried out. Any employment tribunal would ask:

- Did the company give you a fair hearing?
- What evidence was used at the hearing and was it all used?
- Did you have a representative or trade union rep at the hearing?
- If more than one employee was involved, were all of you treated in the same way?
- Had you committed this act previously?
- Did your employer consider warning you, and have warnings ever been used in a case like this before?
- Did your employer consider your overall performance and your previous work record?
- Could your employer have disciplined you instead of dismissing you?
- Did you have any right of appeal against the decision?
- Was the whole procedure carried out in the same way as previous procedures? If not, how was it different, and why was it different?

If a tribunal decides I have been unfairly dismissed, what can it do?

Tribunals can make a number of orders:

- **Reinstatement**, where the employment tribunal orders you to go back to your old job, and the company pays compensation for loss of wages.
- **Re-engagement**, where you return to a similar job with your employer.

(In practice, it is rare for either of these orders to be made, as tribunals do not like to force an employer to take an employee back.)

- **Compensation**, which is the most usual order, and is divided into two parts: the basic award and the compensatory award.

But your award may be reduced if you did not pursue all avenues of internal appeal before going to tribunal.

How is compensation calculated?

The basic award is calculated by taking an employee's age, years of service and average weekly pay to arrive at a figure. The weekly pay figure is limited to a maximum of £230 per week, with a maximum number of 20 years to be considered. In addition, years of service also depend on the employee's age:

- For years of service below 22 years of age, the weekly pay is multiplied by $1/2$
- For years of service between 22 and 41, the weekly pay is the amount paid.
- For years of service from 41 on, the weekly pay is multiplied by $1\frac{1}{2}$.

Thus the maximum basic award that can be made is £6,900 (20 years at £230 with a multiplier of $1\frac{1}{2}$). For employees aged 64–65, the award is reduced by 1/12th for every month up to 65, when it becomes nil.

The maximum compensatory award is £50,000, and a tribunal would consider factors such as loss of wages, future loss of wages (including an estimate of how long you will be out of work in the future before finding a new job), loss of perks (medical insurance, company car, etc.), the manner of dismissal (whether a public humiliation might make it harder for you to find work in future – but this is not the same as 'hurt feelings'), loss of pension rights and loss of your employment protection in calculating the compensatory award. The compensatory award can be reduced to take into account social security payments, redundancy payments and in those cases where you share some responsibility for your dismissal. If the tribunal finds the dismissal was fair, but carried out unfairly, the award will be reduced. If your employer is ordered to reinstate you, but refuses, the tribunal can make further awards against your employer of 13–26 weeks' pay up to the maximum of £230 per week (26–52 weeks pay of £230 if the refusal is made on sex or race discrimination grounds) in addition to the basic and compensatory awards.

What is constructive dismissal?

Constructive dismissal covers those circumstances where you leave your job because of your employer's conduct: for example, if your manager makes life difficult for you, and you don't feel able to remain in your job. In these cases, your resignation is treated as if your employer actually dismissed you, so you can claim unfair dismissal. Examples of constructive dismissal include:

- Not supporting managers in difficult work situations.
- Harassing or humiliating staff, particularly in front of junior members of staff.
- Changing your job description or terms without consultation.
- Falsely accusing an employee of misconduct, such as theft, or of being incapable of carrying out his job.

Resignation can come over one incident; or as the result of a series of incidents, the last of being the straw that broke the camel's back. But to rely on the incident to establish constructive dismissal, the resignation must follow soon after the incident, and generally speaking the incident must involve a serious breach of contract.

I am unhappy with my company's actions. Can I complain?

Companies that provide a written statement of terms and conditions of employment must identify a staff member to whom you can take grievances against the company; these include issues such as terms or conditions, management or supervisory issues, discrimination on grounds of race, sex, disability, sexual harassment, bullying or health and safety. Most companies outline their grievance procedure in a company handbook or in a separate document, and the simplest procedure would have two stages:

- Raising the grievance informally with your immediate superior or line manager.
- If the matter is not resolved informally, raising the grievance with your employer (accompanied by a colleague or union rep if you wish).

Section 3.7 Companies

I want to start up a business; how can I go about it?

There are three main ways of setting up and running a business: as a sole trader, as a partnership or as a limited company. All three forms of business have advantages and disadvantages attached to them. Section 3.8 will look at partnerships and sole traders, but here we will look at companies.

What are the main advantages of companies?

Whenever you start a business, or while you are trading, there is always the risk something may go wrong – a rival may start undercutting your prices, or suppliers may go bankrupt and owe you stock, or the bottom may fall out of your particular market. If you are a sole trader or a partner in a partnership and the business starts to lose money, your creditors can pursue you for the business's losses – for you are the business – and you could end up not only going out of business, but also going bankrupt.

However, if you form a limited company, you can limit your business liabilities. In law, a company is a legal entity separate from its owners, which holds all the assets of the business and is responsible for any liabilities. The people that set up and run companies are not personally responsible for its liabilities. In practice, if you set up a company and ask a bank to lend the company money, your bankers are likely to ask you to act as guarantor for any loan if the company does not have any assets in its early days; so if the company goes pear-shaped, the bank can recover its loans.

Setting up a company will limit your liability, but you will have to pay out the cost of forming the company, as well as the cost of having your annual returns filed with Companies House. Annual returns must be filed on the last day of the month in which the anniversary of the company's incorporation falls. All companies must submit accounts, but companies with a gross turnover above £350,000 must submit audited accounts.

One obvious drawback about limited companies is that, even though they are private limited companies, their accounts are open to public inspection and scrutiny. So your rivals can come and check through your accounts, to see how well (or how badly) you are doing.

How do I set up a company?

To set up a company, you will have to register it with the Registrar of Companies at Companies House, submitting a number of documents including:

- The 'memorandum of association', which is effectively the company's constitution, and which gives the company's name, the address of its registered office, its business purpose and the maximum amount of capital which may be paid into the company. This 'authorised capital' is then divided into shares. These shares are then given a value, known as the 'nominal value' of the company, and may be sold by the company for that value or more. If shares are sold, their nominal value is known as the 'issued capital'.
- The 'articles of association', which govern the day-to-day operation of the company, outlining directors and shareholders' rights and responsibilities, appointments, etc.

Setting up a company from scratch can take weeks, and a quick way of getting hold of a company is buying one 'off the shelf' which will already have been registered. However, the business purpose outlined in the shelf company's memorandum may not be appropriate, so it will be amended later. This is the normal method of setting up a limited company, rather than going to the effort of creating one from scratch.

How can a limited company limit my liability?

The most usual form of limited company is the 'company limited by shares'. Where a company is limited by shares, each shareholder is only liable for the amount they have paid (or still owe) on their shares. For example, if you hold 1000 shares in a company with a nominal value of £1 each, and you paid £100 when you applied for them, then if the company gets into financial trouble and is wound up, then you will only have to pay the outstanding £900. This would be true whether you were only a shareholder, investor, or you actually ran the company.

If you are a member of a company that is 'limited by guarantee', if the company becomes insolvent and is wound up then you will have to pay out the amount of your guarantee – it does not matter if the company owes more than you have guaranteed, your liability is limited. (Guarantee companies are rarely, if ever, found commercially, and are usually encountered in dealings with charities, etc.)

What is the difference between public and private companies?

Most limited companies are private companies, though larger ones with the initials 'PLC' are public limited companies. Both sorts of company must have at least two shareholders, a director and a company secretary. However, there is a major difference between the two. Private companies cannot offer their shares to the general public, while public companies can do so, provided they have an authorised capital of at least £50,000 (and before it starts trading, a public company must have at least £50,000 in issued capital). PLCs raise money by issuing shares that are traded on the Stock Exchange.

What are shares?

Shares are the capital of the company, and are divided into different classes:

- 'Preference shares', which pay out a dividend at a fixed rate out of company profits, in priority (i.e. in preference) to other share types.
- 'Ordinary shares', which pay out a fluctuating dividend according to company profits.
- 'Deferred shares', which may receive a higher dividend after preference and ordinary share dividends have been paid.

Obviously, if you are looking to set up a company, you should discuss the matter with your solicitor and accountant first to find out whether a limited company will benefit you, and if so, how. See also the **Law Pack** guide on the subject.

What does it mean when a company is 'wound up'?

When a company is 'wound up', it is closed and ceases trading. A company can be wound up either voluntarily (when the members of the company themselves decide to wind it up) or compulsorily, if a court orders it be wound up. The court would do this if one of the company directors, a creditor, or the Department of Trade and Industry presented a petition. Grounds for winding up a company include failing to pay debts and failing to begin trading within a year of setting up. A company can also cease to exist if the Registrar of Companies strikes the company's name from the Register because he is not satisfied with the way it is being operated.

Section 3.8 Unincorporated associations

What is the difference between a corporation and an unincorporated association?

A corporation is a legal entity with a legal personality that is separate and distinct from its members, for example a limited liability company. This means that members of corporations are not responsible for the liabilities of the association or company (unless they have guaranteed loans, for instance). In contrast, unincorporated associations, examples of which would be the local drama club, or the village bowls club or an amateur rugby club, do not have a separate legal identity from their memberships. An unincorporated association is its membership.

Who is liable for the acts of an unincorporated association?

As the law regards unincorporated associations as nothing more than a collection of people, all members are jointly and severally liable for the associations actions – this means that that all bear individual responsibility for the association's actions. So, if you are the secretary of the tennis club and sign a contract for the supply of tennis racquets and balls, you will be personally liable on the contract you signed (as will the members of the committee that authorised you to sign the contract, if any such authorisation took place).

I'm a member of the local rugby club. I accidentally cut through a neighbour's lawn mower power cable while mowing our field. Is the rugby club liable?

If you decided to cut the grass on your own whim, you would undoubtedly be liable in tort for negligence. However, if the rugby club committee authorised you to cut the grass, then the club members would also be liable.

My rugby club wants to buy its playing field. How can we do that, if the club is really the sum of all the members? Will they all own part of the field?

Obviously, ownership of playing fields would present problems for clubs if the pitch were owned by the members individually. So the law allows associations to nominate four members to act as trustees, who will hold the land on behalf of the club. If you are a trustee, you can take legal action in respect of the field you are holding in trust, for instance to sue a contractor who carried out faulty drainage works. But in the same way, trustees can be sued or prosecuted if the way the land is used causes problems for neighbours, or if people were to be injured in a defective stand while watching the game. Similarly, as trustees you will be responsible for breaches of planning regulations, as happened when a local rugby club erected a portable building without planning permission on the side of a rugby pitch.

How can unincorporated associations control members?

Almost all associations have rules in their constitution for electing a committee, which will then meet regularly to transact the group's business. Each year at the annual general meeting, club officers and some or all of the committee will come up for re-election, and the members will be able to ask questions about the club's running. This ensures that members can scrutinise the management of the club. Often, association rules allow the committee to act as a disciplinary body, controlling members and expelling them, if necessary. However, if your committee acts as a disciplinary body, it must observe the basic rules of natural justice, otherwise disgruntled members can complain to the courts.

Section 3.9 Sole traders and partnerships

What is a sole trader?

If you want to set up your own business, you don't need to follow any legal formalities at all, apart from notifying the tax office. This is necessary because your tax affairs will be different. You retain ownership of all the business's assets and goodwill, and you can employ workers and lease or buy property and equipment for the business as you think best. As a self-employed person, you will pay tax on schedule D. However, while self-employed people can offset more of their income and expenditure against tax, they are also liable to pay more National Insurance contributions. You will have to keep books recording all financial transactions so you can be assessed for income tax, and also for VAT if you earn more than £50,000 in a year. (Your accountant will advise you that you will need to retain your records for several years after the relevant tax year, since the Inland Revenue has the right to inspect them.) The main advantage of working for yourself is the freedom to arrange your own time, and the realisation that all the profits are yours. The down side is that all the losses are yours too – and only yours. And if things should go spectacularly badly and you owe money, your creditors can compel you to sell private assets to meet your debts by forcing you into bankruptcy (see **Bankruptcy**).

What is a partnership?

You and a friend can start a business in the same way as you would if you decided to go it alone. You don't need to go through any particular legal formalities to create a partnership, but it is a good idea to have a partnership deed in place to put your relationship on a formal footing and to spell out rights and responsibilities. The Companies Act 1989 has created a new partnership type, the 'partnership company'. In this type of partnership all, or a substantial portion, of the shares in a company are held by or on behalf of its employees, a well-known one being the John Lewis Partnership.

What are my rights and responsibilities as a part of a partnership?

The Partnership Act 1890 regulates relationships between you and your business partner or partners (you can have as many as 20 partners, though professional groups such as doctors and solicitors are exceptions to this – they can form partnerships with as many members as they wish.) Every partner has a right to an equal share of the profits, and has an equal responsibility towards any losses incurred – even if this means you have to sell your house. Partners are jointly and severally liable for any debts incurred by the partnership – so if you and your partner set up a business and run up debts, and then your partner disappears, you are responsible for all of the debt.

Unless you have agreed differently beforehand, all partners will have an equal say in managing the firm. Any agreement into which you enter as a partner, is binding on the partnership as a whole, because the law presumes that as a partner you have the authority to enter into legal relations with other persons or companies.

My partner has done some work that was defective. Can I be held liable?

If one partner does work that turns out to be negligent, the partnership will be liable – and that holds for other torts (civil wrongs), too.

How can I wind up a partnership?

Partnerships can be set up for an agreed length of time or purpose from the very beginning, and the partnership can end on the expiry of that time limit or the purpose being achieved. In addition, partnerships come to an end on the death or bankruptcy of any partner. If you and your partners want to end the partnership voluntarily, you can simply agree that it should end. On the other hand, if one or more of the partners is insolvent and bankrupt, a court can order the partnership to be dissolved.

Section 3.10 Trade unions

What are trade unions?

Trade unions are organisations that represent people at work. They originally came into existence to protect and improve people's pay and conditions of employment. They also campaign for laws and policies to benefit working people. Trade unions exist because individual workers have very little power to influence decisions affecting their jobs. Many different industries and skills are represented by trade unions; some unions represent people who do a particular job or work in a specific industry while other unions include a mixture of people in different jobs and sectors, for example, the GMB, UNISON and the Transport and General Workers Union. People join trade unions to get union protection if there is a problem at work, or to safeguard pay and working conditions.

What is the structure of trade unions?

Trade unions are democratic organisations, which are accountable to their members for their policies and actions. Unions are usually composed of:

- Members, the people who pay a subscription to belong to the union.
- 'Shop stewards' (sometimes called 'union representatives') who are elected by members of the union to represent them to management at their place of work.
- Branches, which support union members in different organisations locally. There is usually a branch secretary elected by local members.
- District and/or regional offices, which are normally staffed by full-time union officials. These are people who are paid to offer advice and support to union members locally.
- A national office, the union's headquarters, which offers support to union members and negotiates or campaigns for improvements in their working conditions. As a rule, at the top of the organisation there is a General Secretary and a National Executive Committee, elected by the union's members.

What do unions do?

Negotiation. Union representatives discuss with management issues that affect people working in an organisation. The union finds out the members' views and relays those views to management. The union then negotiates a solution to the different viewpoints with management. This process is also known as 'collective bargaining'. In many workplaces, unions are 'recognised' for collective bargaining purposes, and they negotiate pay, working hours, holidays and changes to working practices.

Representation. When individual members have a problem at work: for example, if an employee feels he is being unfairly treated, he can ask the union representative to help sort out the difficulty with the employer. If the problem cannot be resolved amicably, it may go to an employment tribunal. Unions offer legal representation to their members; often this is to help people get financial compensation for work-related injuries, or to assist people who have to take their employer to court.

Information and advice. The union can advise on a range of issues such as holiday entitlement, maternity pay and workplace training.

Member services. These include education and training courses, legal assistance, financial discounts and welfare benefits.

What do trade unions do in industrial disputes?

Most collective bargaining takes place quietly, and agreements are quickly reached by the union and the employer. Occasionally disagreements do occur and the two sides cannot agree. In these cases, the union may decide to take industrial action, which can take many forms such as an overtime ban, work-to-rule or strike, and unions must follow strict laws when taking industrial action. Strikes should be seen as the last resort, as both workers and employers have a lot to lose – the company though disruption in production or sales, and workers through lost salaries, because the moment you go on strike you stop working, and that puts you in breach of contract so the company can stop paying you until you begin working again.

My employer does not recognise the unions at work. What does that mean?

There has been a reduction in union membership over the past three decades, as successive Conservative governments passed a series of laws that had the effect of limiting the effects of industrial action. Another effect of the legislation was that employers were no longer obliged to recognise their employees' trade union. This means the employer does not enter into collective bargaining over pay or conditions with the union. Employers can also persuade employees to give up their right to be represented by a trade union, by offering a higher wage to employees who agree to give up these rights. But under the Employment Relations Act 1999, trade unions with more than 20 members in a company can now apply to a central arbitration committee to be recognised by the employer company.

Workers at my company are going on strike. What happens?

For a strike to be lawful, an individual postal ballot of all members must be held, and unions must give employers seven days' notice of a strike. The range of lawful industrial action has been restricted since the days of union unrest in the 1970s and 1980s, and is now mainly confined to matters affecting wages and working conditions. As the law now stands , if you go on strike, your employers cannot sack you for the first eight weeks of the strike simply because you went on strike. However, they can sack you on other grounds, for example disciplinary matters, or if you smashed up your place of work during the strike.

I don't want to strike. Will the law protect me?

If you want to cross a picket line, the strikers cannot legally stop you and if they try physically to compel you to support the strike, they will be breaking the law. However, once the strike is over, it is unlikely that friendly relationships will be rebuilt quickly, if ever, if experience of the miners' strike of 1984-5 is anything to go by; those who returned to work early, or 'scabs' as they are still known, are still regarded badly for not supporting that strike to the bitter end.

Do I have to support financially a political party through my membership of a union?

Since the Trade Union Act 1913, trade unions have only been able to spend money on political activity through a separate political fund. This fund could then be used to campaign on 'political issues', such as opposing a government policy. But since the Trade Union Act 1984, unions must ballot their members every 10 years on whether the union should have a political fund or not. In addition, some 26 unions are affiliated to the Labour Party, and unions pay an annual subscription to them, but this levy is not compulsory and you can opt out of paying it. Labour Party affiliation gives union members a say in Labour Party policy and a chance to vote in elections for the Labour Party leadership.

Section 3.11 Vicarious liability

What is vicarious liability?

Vicarious liability is that curious part of the law where you can be held responsible for someone else's wrongful actions. This is particularly relevant in the case of employers and employees. The general rule is that an employer is responsible for the wrongful action of an employee, if that action is performed in the course of his work. So, if you are a builder and one of your carpenters knocks a wall down while carelessly reversing the company van onto a building site, you, as his employer will be liable in tort for negligence, and the owners of the wall may be able to recover damages from you. Similarly, if you pay a deposit for the purchase of a house to your solicitors and their clerk embezzles the money and disappears, you can sue the solicitors, as the clerk's employers.

But, you will not be liable if your employee does something wrong that is not in the course of his employment. If you run a bus company, and one of your non-driving conductors reverses a bus into a parked car, then the conductor would not be acting in the course of his employment, and so you would not be liable for that wrong. However, if you were that builder (again), and your pesky carpenter took the van to collect fish-and-chips for the builders at lunch and crashed it, then it is likely a court would consider this to be acting in the course of his employment – though driving 20 miles to a favourite chip shop probably would not be.

Even if you have expressly forbidden one of your workers from doing something and they still do it despite your order, you may still be liable for a wrong that ensues if your instructions amounted to guidance on how they should perform a certain part of their duties. If, however, your instruction specifically restricted the scope of your worker's employment then you would not be liable. A good example of this is if you run a garage, and one worker's job is to move cars around the showroom, only by wheeling them. If that worker then drives a car and has an accident then you will be liable, because despite the prohibition on what he did, it did not limit the scope of your worker's job, which was to move cars. But if the worker's job description meant he was not meant to go near or move cars at all, then you would not be liable for his actions.

What about independent contractors?

Here the general rule is that you will not be liable for the wrongs of independent contractors or their employees. This will apply to householders who employ builders or other contractors to work on their homes, as well as to businesspeople. But there are exceptions:

- Where the contract is to do something that is itself a tort. For example, if you employ a company to dig a hole in a pavement when you have no authority to do so, if someone falls into the hole or trips over the stones then you will be held liable.
  Or if you hire a cab and tell the driver to turn into the drive of a property that does not belong to you, you will be guilty of trespass.

- Where a contractor is doing work next to a highway or pavement. For example, if you get a contractor to repair a lamp on the outside of your house, which subsequently falls off because the contractor was negligent, you will be liable in tort.

- Where a contractor is employed to do 'extra hazardous acts', which might include demolishing an old building with explosives. Really this could cover anything out of the ordinary that could involve an element of risk; in one case, taking a picture of a cinema using flash photography was classed as 'extra hazardous' (though this was in the days of magnesium flashes, so using a fixed flash would probably not be regarded as 'extra hazardous' now).

Chapter 4
You and your home

Section 4.1 Buying and selling your home

Should I buy or sell my house without professional help?

Some people fix their own shelves at home, or paint the house. Others will happily service their car rather than going down the road to the local garage, and will spend hours tightening brake shoes, changing oil filters and checking fluid levels. However, if you break your arm, not too many of you will pop next door and ask Mr Jones to re-set it for you.

Some jobs are genuinely better left to the professionals, and it is arguable that buying (or selling) a house is one of them. In theory, the fact that nearly all land in England and Wales is registered land, and hence subject to first registration of title should make it easier for householders to do their own conveyancing (see **What is registered land?**). But there are enough pitfalls to trap the unwary, and it could be said that it is better to use a professional – either a solicitor or licensed conveyancer. Taking a cynical view, this means you will have someone to blame if things go wrong! But there is some truth in that too – for if you miss out something while you are conducting searches at the local Land Registry and only find out that your neighbours have a right to come and dig peat from your garden after you move in, then you will have no-one else to blame but yourself. If a solicitor or conveyancer misses it, however, they may well have been negligent and you would be able to sue them. Another possible barrier to buying your home on your own will be your mortgage lender. If your bank or building society is preparing to lend you a large sum of money over a long period of time, they will want to be sure all the small print is being checked through thoroughly.

What is registered land?

This is one of the main elements of property law reform brought in during 1925–6. Previously, land was unregistered; this meant that ownership of land and property had to be proved through deeds, i.e. legal documents which contain the whole history of the property, and its different owners, with details of when the property was bought and sold, whom by and what covenants or easements applied to it. But unregistered land conveyancing was problematic – every new purchase required a new deed, and papers could be lost, which could lead to defects in title (i.e. ownership) – which meant bad news for the buyer. This was just part of the confusing system of land ownership that had evolved in Britain as a result of the feudal system, and which by the 20th century was ripe for reform.

The Law of Property Act 1925 and the Land Registration Act 1925 brought in a new system, which makes the whole of England and Wales subject to compulsory first registration. This means that every time a property is sold, title to the property must be registered at the District Land Registry by the buyer or the buyer's solicitor/licensed conveyancer. In time, all land will become registered land because as soon as land is transferred, it must be registered. Property and houses that have remained in the same families for many years will have to be registered when the properties are eventually disposed of. When land is registered, all the details about title are registered at the Land Registry, and the register is the owner's proof of title. If the property is owned outright, the owner will be given a copy of his entry called a **Land Certificate**. If the property is bought with a mortgage, the lender is issued a **Charge Certificate**, while the Land Registry retains the Land Certificate.

Does the Land Register give a complete picture of the property?

The Land Registry entry is fine as far as it goes – it will tell you who is the legal owner of the land. So it would be difficult for a con man to try and sell you a swish house, because the real owner's details should be registered (provided the house hasn't remained in the same family for hundreds of years). But the Registry entry doesn't tell you who is 'using' the house on a daily basis – so if you buy a house relying only on the entry, you could end up arriving to move in, only to find the house has been let out to a religious cult, which has a valid lease and is entitled to stay there! Unless you (or your solicitor) make a detailed personal inspection of the property before you buy it, you may take ownership subject to overriding interests that do not appear on any papers.

What are overriding interests?

Overriding interests are third-party rights or interests that override the interests of the buyer or property owner. In theory, they are the sorts of rights that can easily be discovered by physically inspecting the property, though the very fact that this is not always so can be a source of lucrative business for solicitors across the country.

The full list of 12 overriding interests are:

*   Rights of common, customary rights, drainage rights, public rights, rights of way, water-courses, rights of water, *profits a prendre* (the right to take something from land belonging to another, for instance grazing rights, the right to cut turf or a right to fish in someone else's river), public rights and rights of sheepwalk (the right to walk sheep across land).
*   Liability to repair highways by reason of tenure.
*   Liability to repair the chancel of any church.
*   Liability in respect of embankments or sea and river walls.
*   Payments in lieu of title, and charges and annuities payable for the redemption of rent title charges.
*   Rights acquired under the Limitation Acts (or in the course of being acquired).
*   The rights of every person in actual occupation of the land, or in receipt of rents or profits, except where an inquiry is made to these people, and they do not disclose their rights.

- In the case of a possessory qualified or good leasehold title, all estates, rights, interests and powers excepted from the effects of registration.
- Rights under local land charges, unless and until registered or protected on the register in a prescribed form.
- Rights of fishing and sporting, seigniorial and manorial rights of all kinds.
- Leases granted for a term of less than 21 years.
- Rights to mines, minerals, etc. on land registered before the 1925 Land Registration Act.

Nowadays, most of these are of interest mainly to academic lawyers, law students and social historians, but a number of them are still important. You will have to keep an actual look-out for them, whether you decide to convey your house yourself or get a solicitor to do it for you, because it is unlikely your legal representatives will make a physical inspection of the house and gardens.

An example of how this can work – but not in your favour: you buy an old Victorian house with a separate coach house, which is sold as part of the property. But when you move in you discover that a family is living in the coach house who claim they have been paying rent to the house seller for three years, and had made an agreement that they can stay in the coach house for a total of five years. As this is a lease for less than 21 years, it represents an overriding interest and therefore the family can stay until their agreement expires. (In addition, they were in actual occupation at the time of the sale, so they would also have a further right as tenants.) But no one would buy a property without inspecting it first! And of course, any prospective purchaser can ask of vacant possession is to be given.

What about land that has not been registered?

Looking at the Register will be of no use if land has not previously been registered, so there will be no listing of overriding interests on the register of title. But leases or overriding interests affecting unregistered land will be registered on the Land Charges Register under the Land Charges Act 1925. So, if the interest is not registered on the land certificate it is void.

The main steps in buying a house

An outline of the main stages of buying a house:

1. Select the house you want to buy.
2. Speak to mortgage lenders to get the best deal, and get a provisional go-ahead so that you know lenders are prepared to offer you a mortgage, in principle.
3. Make an offer to the estate agent.
4. Inform your mortgage lenders who will probably recommend a surveyor to conduct the survey on the house.
5. Instruct a solicitor to undertake the purchase on your behalf. The first step for them is to carry out local searches.

6. Confirm the mortgage offer will be forthcoming and check that the survey is satisfactory.

7. Check the draft contract of sale prepared by the vendor's solicitors. This can be amended until both sides are happy with the terms.

8. Your solicitor (or you) will send a form of enquiries to the vendor's solicitors. This is a detailed questionnaire that will identify fully what is being sold, to avoid confusion between buyer and seller. This will clear up the question of fixtures and fittings. Most solicitors use a standard form to identify the main enquiries, but if you have any questions or concerns, for example whether the greenhouse is staying or going to be dismantled, now is the time to ask.

9. Your solicitor (or you) will check that the seller has a 'good title' to the property – meaning whether he owns it and can legally sell it to you. This search would be carried out at the Land Registry.

10. If the local authority and Land Registry searches are both satisfactory, and the survey is OK and the mortgage offer is through, then the vendor's solicitor will draw up a contract of purchase in the form agreed by both buyer and seller. Two copies are prepared – one for each side.

11. Contracts are signed and exchanged. This conveys the legal title to the purchaser, and a date is arranged for completion, usually in four weeks' time though nowadays it can be much quicker. The exchange stage also sees the payment of your deposit (normally 5–10% of the purchase price). This stage ties the buyer to the purchase – you cannot back out now without incurring severe legal penalties.

12. Completion is when the balance of the purchase price is paid by your solicitor (after the mortgage lender has previously transferred the mortgage advance to them). Title then passes to you and you have a house! Delays can occur at this stage – if the buyer causes the delay he may have to pay interest on the money owed to the vendor, and the vendor's lawyers can issue a completion notice compelling the buyer to complete within a specified time. If the vendor causes the delay, the purchaser can cancel the contract and demand a refund of the deposit; but he is more likely to go through with the sale and then sue for damages for breach of contract.

13. After completing the sale, you will have to register the property at the Land Registry, for which a fee is payable; you may also have to pay stamp duty (see **What about stamp duty?**) on the purchase.

What is a mortgage?

Most people buying a property will not be funding the purchase from their own pockets and will be going to a bank or building society to obtain a mortgage. A mortgage is a loan secured on the property you buy, with the title deeds held by the lender as security for the loan – this prevents you selling the property and absconding without paying back the mortgage lender, if you were so unscrupulous as to consider such a thing. Different mortgage lenders have different policies on how much to lend, and although they are available, 100 per cent mortgages are not as common as they used to be. Most mortgage lenders offer 90–95 per cent mortgages, leaving you to find the 5–10 per cent deposit which is handed over during the exchange of contracts stage of the purchase. Mortgage lenders now offer a variety of incentives to encourage borrowers to come to them, so you will be able to sign up for the firms that gives you what you need – free legal and professional fees, fixed interest rates and cashback deals are all common now, with virtually all lenders offering better deals for new customers than their existing borrowers. A whole host of financial institutions offer mortgages – banks, building societies and now insurance companies and centralised lenders such as The Mortgage Business – and you can buy these products direct from the companies or through a mortgage broker (but as most brokers make their money through commission on selling you endowment policies to fund your mortgage, you may question the impartiality of any advice you get from them).

How much can I borrow?

Different lenders have different policies but most societies operate a general rule of thumb that a single person can borrow up to three times their annual salary. If you are applying for a joint mortgage as a couple, then some lenders tend to advance up to 2.5 times the joint salary or three times the first person's salary and one times the second person's. So two people earning £20,000 and £10,000 respectively would be able to raise of mortgage of £75,000 using the '2½ × both salaries' method, but only £70,000 using the 'three times the first person's and one times the second person's salary' method. Another limit on how much you can borrow is the age and condition of the house. Older properties might only command a mortgage of 70-80 per cent because of the risks attached to older homes and to borrow more you might have to pay an additional premium in the form of 'insurance'. New homes are less prone to structural defects, and come with a NHBC (National House Building Council) Buildmark which covers 12 months' warranty on mechanical parts like plumbing and heating, 24 months' cover on defects arising out of workmanship that does not meet minimum standards and up to 10 years' cover on items not covered by your own buildings policy.

What sort of mortgage can I take out?

There is a number of mortgage products available on the market:

Repayment mortgage

This is the traditional mortgage loan. You borrow a sum of money and each monthly repayment is made up of part repayment of the capital sum borrowed and part repayment of the interest on that loan. In the beginning you are mainly paying off the interest, but after about 10 years you are starting to reduce the outstanding capital as well. In addition, the borrower will have to take out life assurance, which will be used to pay off the loan should the borrower die before the end of the term of the mortgage.

Endowment mortgage

A more modern financial instrument sees you borrow a sum of money and make monthly interest-only repayments back to the lender. In addition, you take out an endowment policy with an insurance company and make payments that will mature and hopefully generate enough capital to pay off the sum you originally borrowed. Endowment mortgages have been criticised on two main levels:

1. Because the endowment is the main source of revenue that mortgage brokers have, they have come under scrutiny for recommending more endowment mortgages rather than traditional repayment mortgages – are they always the best vehicle to borrow money for individual borrowers?
2. There is always a risk that the endowment may not perform as well as expected, and you will not have enough cash when the policy matures to pay off your mortgage.

Endowment mortgages are either 'with profits' – linked to an inexpensive life policy and which sees additional bonuses paid in depending on the insurance company's performance – or 'unit-linked' – where the monthly premiums are invested in managed funds, with greater potential rewards but a higher risk factor.

Pension-related mortgage

Very similar to the endowment mortgage, with a proportion of your income paid into a pension fund. On retirement, the pension provides you with a retirement income and a lump sum to pay off the capital element of the mortgage. In addition, you will have to make interest-only repayments to your mortgage lender. Pension contributions qualify for tax relief, but while pension-related mortgages maximise your tax benefits they also reduce the pool of retirement income you have available. As with the other mortgages, you will have to take out life assurance.

Why is the survey so important?

When you tell your mortgage lender you have made an offer on a property, they will probably recommend a surveyor that will survey the property for you. The purpose of the survey is to ensure the property will offer sufficient security for a bank or building society to make you a loan to buy it, and to highlight any structural problems and defects that you might need to remedy. There are three main types of surveyors' report:

Valuation report

This is a basic assessment of the property's worth, and is carried out by a qualified surveyor, and really only benefits the lender by determining whether the property offers sufficient security for the loan. The surveyor checks the main structural elements are in place, under RICS (Royal Institution of Chartered Surveyors) or ISVA (Incorporated Society of Valuers and Auctioneers) guidelines. In reaching their property valuation, the surveyor will look at the age and condition of the property, the area, location and local amenities, any restrictions on the property and the local housing market. It would not be wise to rely solely on a valuation report if you are buying an older house – apart from anything else, it is not being written with you in mind and gives no guarantee of structural soundness. If you move in to a property after a valuation report was compiled, and subsequently major defects appear, you might be able to sue the surveyor, but unless the defect was very obvious, you have little chance of success.

Home buyer's report

Unlike the valuation report, this is commissioned by the purchaser and not the lender, and gives more information, collated on standard RICS or ISVA forms. The home buyer's report investigates the interior and exterior of the property, but is not concerned with every defect. Damp and subsidence should be detected, and main walls examined at ground level, but roof spaces will not be checked if it involves significant effort. The home buyer's report bridges the gap between the superficial valuation report and the full structural survey.

Full structural survey

A full survey covers the whole property, building and gardens, with detailed information on everything. It will identify repairs needed and costs involved, and though costly it can help bring down a purchase price by pointing up the defects (and not just the main ones) if the vendor accepted your offer subject to a satisfactory survey.

In addition, it is something of an insurance policy. If a surveyor misses anything that a reasonably competent surveyor would have detected, and you suffer as a result, you may be able to sue for negligence. Surveyors are insured against such claims and may try to further limit their loss by clauses in their contract that attempt to exclude or limit liability, but these clauses may not be valid if a court determines that they are not reasonable, and hence are unfair contract terms contrary to the Unfair Contract Terms Act 1977.

What are local searches?

While you are having surveys carried out on the property and liaising with your mortgage lender to ensure a suitable mortgage offer will be made, your solicitor will not be idle. The solicitors will write to all the relevant authorities and parties to carry out a local search at the local authority; this will (or should) uncover any things such as sewers or proposed new road layouts that may affect your property adversely. But the local authority is not obliged to make a full disclosure – it only has to answer the questions your solicitor asks. So if your solicitor forgets to ask and you buy, it's too late to complain after the event – at least to the council (you can still complain to the solicitor though!). Local searches can be time-consuming, because the local authority may have staffing problems, but you can speed things up by going to the local authority and doing the search work for yourself, or paying your solicitor to get one of his staff to do it for you.

What are fixtures and what are fittings?

Every solicitor has a horror story about the client that moved into a property only to discover that the previous owner had removed all the door handles – and sometimes worse! It may be an irritation, but what comprises fixtures and fittings is a matter for negotiation rather than legislation. One person's beautiful carpet is another's eyesore that will be ripped up as soon as the new owners get their feet onto the floorboards – but the real irritations come when something you expected to stay is actually removed. Fixtures are those things fitted to the property and its land, and are generally included in the purchase price. Examples of fixtures are bathroom suites, wires, fitted fires and fireplaces, fitted kitchen units, door fittings and light switches. Fittings are not fixed to the property and do not automatically comprise part of the sale. Examples of fittings are cookers and fridges (though not if they are part of a fitted kitchen), curtains and carpets, light shades and bulbs. Vendors often leave carpets because they will not necessarily fit into a new property, but they are not automatically part of the asking price. To simplify this process, vendors fill in a detailed questionnaire before contracts are exchanged, describing what is in each room and what is to remain with the property. Fittings can be sold by private treaty, and dealing with items like that can take the overall sale price under stamp duty thresholds, which can lead to substantial savings.

What about stamp duty?

House buyers must pay stamp duty on the transaction. For property transactions over £60,000 but below £250,000, a duty of 1 per cent of the purchase price is currently payable. So, paying a seller £59,000 for the property and a separate contract of £1,200 for the garden shed, fitted carpets, kitchen and other fittings could save you over £600. Above £500,000, stamp duty of 2.5 per cent is payable. Property sales of less than £60,000 do not incur stamp duty.

Can I get tax relief on my mortgage?

Under the old MIRAS scheme, house buyers who bought a home with a mortgage were entitled to tax relief on the interest, provided the home was the purchaser's main residence. Unfortunately, the scheme was scrapped on April 5, 2000 and now no tax relief is available.

What about capital gains tax?

If you are selling your own house, then capital gains tax would not apply. But if you have inherited a house, say under a will, capital gains tax would be payable on the property price. But you will have a tax exemption to set off against capital gains tax; the exemption for the tax year 2000–2001 is £7,100.

Do I need an estate agent to sell my house?

The short answer is 'probably!' While you could put up a board outside your home, and place adverts in the local papers, the cost of doing so would soon begin to hit home – and even though you end up paying an estate agent for the services they provide, the costs are not 'up-front' costs but will be paid out from the proceeds of the sale. More importantly, estate agents are often parts of groups and can circulate your details far more widely than you might do yourself. Estate agents are regulated, and operate subject to laws of contract and agency. The Estate Agents Act 1979 imposes a legal duty on estate agents to find the best available sale, and says it is 'undesirable practice' not to pass on all offers to you as the vendor. Sometimes this does not happen, most recently in the case of an estate agent who deliberately sold a property to a friend, who then sold the property on to another interested party the same day at a much higher price – the end result was that the original seller missed out on the higher price (even though the agent had known of the second offer, she did not tell the sellers) and the agent and her friend split the profit from the dodgy deal.

What happens if a house is not as described?

The Romans had a phrase to warn consumers from the perils of cowboy tradesmen – *caveat emptor* – which means buyer, beware! Flowery phrases designed to attract potential purchasers are one thing – downright untruths are something else again. The Property Misdescriptions Act 1991 provides protection from deceitful agents. If a reasonable person would be misled by a description then the Act has been breached.

How much do I have to pay my estate agent for selling my house?

When estate agents market your house for you, they will obviously charge you for the service. Fees are normally commission-based, and will only be paid on a completed sale. You can negotiate with your agent but most fees are approximately 2–2.5 per cent of the purchase price. For this you will get 'For sale' boards outside your property (if you want), newspaper advertisements, possibly internet posting, sale particulars with a full description of your property and viewings arranged. There is a number of different agency agreements available to sellers, with different benefits and weaknesses. Under a 'sole agency' deal, only one agent sells your home – the agreement normally lasts for 12 weeks initially, and you would be able to try and sell your home privately. Commission costs tend to be lower, but you are restricted in that only people visiting the one agency will see your details. Multiple agency agreements allow your particulars to be displayed in several agencies, with the successful selling agency getting the commission. This type of deal will bring your particulars to a wider audience. Joint sole agency agreements are similar to multiple agency agreements, but the agencies will share the commission if either makes the sale. But avoid agreements with 'sole selling rights' – that means that even if you reach agreement to sell the house privately, the agency will be legally entitled to commission even if it had nothing to do with the sale.

Gazumping

Gazumping is accepting a second (higher) offer on a house after agreeing to sell it to someone else. Neither party is committed to a sale until exchange of contracts, so a seller can accept a higher offer right up to that moment. In addition, your estate agent is legally obliged to get the best offer he can for you. This flexibility can work in the buyer's favour as well. For example, you offer £100,000 for a house, and then discover that the house is riddled with damp; even though the building society may be prepared to lend £90,000 and you have £10,000 for the deposit, you may have to pay another £10,000 to have the damp patches fixed. You might want to negotiate the asking price down, to take this additional cost to you into account, but if acceptance of your offer tied you to the contract then you'd be stuck. As it is, most offers are made subject to a satisfactory survey. In Scotland the system is different, as the offer is seen as binding on the buyer, as is acceptance on the seller. For this reason, it should only be made once a mortgage has been approved, and a satisfactory survey carried out. Clarity of agreement is the advantage, but the downside is the upfront cost in terms of surveys, etc. If anything untoward is revealed during the survey you can pull out before becoming tied contractually – but a few unsatisfactory surveys will soon hit your pocket.

Buying a house at auction

Over the past few years, newspapers have carried stories of buyers snapping up bargains at house auctions – a terrace of houses in south Wales bought for under £100,000 comes to mind. However, the rules of the auction apply – and it's not like buying an old banger of a car. If your bid is accepted, you have to pay 10 per cent of the balance up front, and the rest within 28 days, so between the auction catalogue being published and the sale you would need to carry out searches, obtain a mortgage and get a satisfactory survey. If you do it the other way round, buying the property but then failing to obtain the finance (or indeed, if you change your mind) you can't pull out of the agreement. An auction is a contract of sale so by pulling out – whether through choice or because you can't afford to buy – you will be in breach of contract. At the very least, you will lose your deposit. So take care.

Section 4.2 Domestic and commercial services

Once you are in your house, you need to be able to enjoy it, and that's where you will come into contact with utility companies and tradesmen that will call on you from time to time.

Who supplies my electricity, gas and water?

After the privatisation of the electricity and water companies in the 1980s, a host of smaller regional suppliers arose around the country. Now, with this deregulation, you can shop around for the best possible price and take your water or electricity from another area's regional supplier. In some areas of the country, you can buy your gas from your electricity company. The industry is regulated by the Office of Gas and Electricity Markets or OFGEM (a combination of the older Office of Electricity Regulation and the Office of Gas Supply). In the electricity industry, OFGEM is responsible for setting price controls to ensure that consumers are not charged too much for their electricity, and that companies only charge what is necessary to provide an adequate, well-run business with an adequate return to shareholders.

I want to change my gas or electricity supplier. How can I do that?

Deregulation means you can shop around for your utility services and sign up for whoever offers you the best price or service. OFGEM can advise you as to which energy companies will supply your area, and on how to contact them. Some suppliers have sent door-to-door sellers trying to sign up new customers for their companies, and there have been complaints about high-pressure selling. Ignore them if you can; shop around before signing, then you will have found the best deal for yourself, regardless of any incentives or offers you may 'lose' in the process because, in the long term only by shopping around will you be sure that you have found the best deal.

If you decide to change suppliers, you will usually have to sign a new contract showing you are accepting the new prices, terms and conditions offered by the new company. If you subsequently cancel the new agreement, you would have to give 28 days' notice and change to another supplier again. The new supplier will notify your existing electricity company that you are changing suppliers and of the change-over date, so the meter can be read and a bill sent to you, which if you do not pay may be added to your new electricity provider's first bill and add a charge for the late payment. But if you owe repayments to your existing supplier you may not be allowed to transfer to another company until your debt is paid off. If you choose to change electricity suppliers, the power will still be supplied via the existing cable system and meter; you will just get your bill from a different place.

How can I complain about my electricity service?

If you have any concerns or complaints about the service provided by your electricity company, you should complain to them first and give them a chance to do something about it. Suppliers are required to publish a code setting out their complaints procedure, explaining how to complain and the procedure each company follows. If you are not satisfied with their solution (if any) you should contact OFGEM, who can investigate electricity bills, meters or supply queries.

What happens if I change suppliers and there is a power cut?

When you change suppliers, you will be given a 24-hour emergency number, which you should call if you have any safety fears about meter, cabling or supply, or if your supply is interrupted. If the problems are related to wiring inside your house, you would need to contact an electrician yourself, as the electricity company would not be responsible.

What minimum standards can I expect from my electricity supplier?

Electricity companies are required to meet minimum standards of performance, or pay penalties if they do not:

- Restoring your supply after a fault: within 24 hours or compensation of £50 for domestic customers and £100 for non-domestic customers is payable.
- Connecting your supply and providing a meter: within two working days (domestic) or four (non-domestic) or pay compensation of up to £100.
- Appointments: all appointments to visit must be kept, and can be fixed to morning or afternoon appointments, or within a two-hour time band if customer requests it, or pay £20 compensation.
- Notice of supply interruption: must give at least five days' notice or pay £20 for domestic customers and £40 for non-domestic customers.
- Responding to prepayment meter faults: within three hours on a working day (four hours on any other day), if you notify within working hours, or pay £20 compensation.
- Queries over payments: reply within five days or pay £20.

Can I shop around for gas too?

The same method of changing companies applies, and you should shop around to find the best possible deals for yourself.

How do I complain about my gas service or bill?

You should complain to your gas company first, and their complaints or customer service number will be on your bill. If they can't help, you can speak to the Gas Consumers Council, which will take up valid complaints with the company. If the Gas Consumers Council is not able to resolve the problem (and that is possible, because it can only recommend action, and cannot force the gas companies to do as it asks) because your complaint involves a possible breach of legislation, it will contact OFGEM, which has the power to compel gas suppliers to comply with the conditions under which they were licensed to supply.

I haven't paid my gas or electricity bill. Will I be disconnected?

Non-payment of gas or electricity bills can lead to disconnection, but this is very much a last resort as OFGEM and its predecessors operated codes of conduct that would monitor customer disconnections, giving late payers every opportunity to pay and even offering mechanisms to pay arrears off slowly. But if none of these methods are heeded, disconnection would follow, though customers must be given notice (normally 28 days' notice for the bill and then a further seven days, as in the case of British Gas) and the electricity companies are committed not to disconnecting anyone that is chronically sick, elderly or disabled during the winter months.

And water?

Privatisation set up a number of water companies that provide water supply and sewage services, and are overseen by Ofwat (the Office of Water Services) in terms of providing consumers fairly-priced water and efficient services. These are administered via 10 regional Customer Services Committees which deal with complaints, mostly related to bills and overcharging.

Can I shop around for water?

Deregulation has not hit the domestic water industry in the same was as gas or electricity, partly because there is no national grid as such. As far as deregulation of electricity or gas goes, for the consumer all that matters is that your bill comes from a different company; the generating companies pump the power (or the gas) into the grid or pipeline and customers take it out, and are then billed. But your water comes from a closed regional system. Another issue is public health: if there were a national grid for water, and some toxic bacterium got into the system it would be far more difficult to track back to find the cause of any outbreaks of disease.

Are there any minimum standards that the water services must meet?

The Guaranteed Standards Scheme, overseen by Ofwat, offers customers compensation if certain minimum standards of service are not met. These include keeping appointments (or cancelling them with a minimum 24 hours' notice), responding to complaints within 10 working days, warning you if your supply will be interrupted for more than four hours and making a payment if your property is flooded by sewage. These payments are currently £20 (and £1,000 for the sewage flooding).

How do I complain about my water company?

If you have a complaint about your water company, the first step is to complain to the company direct and in writing, and they will deal with your concerns in accordance with their code of conduct. If you are not satisfied with their response, you can complain once more to the company, who will have the issue reviewed by a more senior manager. Then, if you are still not satisfied, you can ask Ofwat to review your complaint by contacting one of the regional customer service committees, by telephone, in writing or by email or in person (if you make an appointment). The Customer Services Committee (CSC) can recommend courses of action, but these are not compulsory and the water company may not agree, though in most cases they do follow guidance. If you are unhappy about the way the CSC handled your grievance you can write to the Director General, though he cannot intervene in matters that should be dealt with in a court of law or via arbitration.

Can my water supply be disconnected?

You can be disconnected if your bills have not been paid, provided you are given seven days' notice of disconnection. This is very much a last resort, and you will be given every opportunity to pay off arrears before the disconnection is ordered. In addition, your supply may be temporarily disconnected to carry out maintenance and/or repairs to the pipe system.

I'm worried about cowboy tradesmen. What can I do?

Whenever tradesmen, builders, plumbers, carpenters, gas fitters, etc, come to your house, you are relying on their expertise and skills to do a good job. However, for every craftsman there may also be a cowboy who will come to your house, take your money and do a bad job. Unlike the craftsman, the cowboy is a hit-and-run merchant, less concerned with doing a good job and getting asked back to do more. The Supply of Goods and Services Act 1982 requires work to be done to a reasonable standard, using suitable materials of satisfactory quality. The 'reasonable standard' means a level of skill that one might expect from a reasonably competent tradesman of the same type. One way of reducing the risks of using tradesmen is to go for a personal recommendation: if one of your friends knows of a good plumber and has used him, perhaps they can recommend that firm to you. Also check whether the tradesman is a member of a regulatory body: they may have a code of conduct that he will then have to follow which can help if you have to complain. Once you have got a tradesman, insist on a written quotation: this will fix the price legally, and also allows you to get his business name, address and phone number. No reputable tradesman will refuse to give you a written quotation, so if your tradesman does baulk at the suggestion, think about saying bye-bye.

What happens if my extension is botched? Who can I take action against?

To some extent, this depends on how you commissioned the job. If you hired an architect to draw up plans, then took the plans and gave them to a builder who put up the extension, and there is a problem with the plans, you sue the architect or if there is a problem with the building work, you sue the builder. However, if you hired the architect to draw up plans and oversee the building work (selecting contractors and ordering materials) if anything goes wrong then your action is against the architect, as your contract is with him. (If there is shoddy building work, it is for the architect to sue his sub-contractors, and not a matter for you.)

Section 4.3 Letting your home

The property market has picked up over the past few years, but the property slump led to an increasingly important rented property sector, as people who might have wanted to move to bigger, more expensive homes, could not sell their own properties, especially with the problems of negative equity after the 1980s property crash. But you need to be careful when you rent out a house – not following the law to the letter could leave you with a nasty headache in the form of a tenant from hell that you can't get rid of easily, or you could find yourself falling foul of legislation designed to protect tenants from nasty, hard-hearted landlords that are more concerned with getting their monthly rent cheque than providing good-quality accommodation. Nowadays, most tenancies are short-term – usually the Assured Shorthold Tenancy Agreement, created by the Housing Act 1988, which offers benefits to landlord and tenant alike. Whether you rent through an agent, or handle the rental yourself, the tenancy agreement is likely to be one of this type.

Should I use an agent to let my property?

It is easy to rent out your property yourself – all you have to do is advertise it, in the local newspaper or through cards in a newsagent's window. You could show the property to prospective tenants yourself, ask for and check bank and other references, then deal with any queries and problems the tenant has once he has moved in, collect rent, etc. On the other hand, you may decide to let the property through a letting agency – which is very similar to an estate agency except that they 'manage' your property on your behalf, finding you a tenant (who they will credit-check and obtain references from), deal with management issues, collect the rent, inspect the property periodically and deal with legal issues as they arise. Obviously, using an agent removes many of the headaches of monitoring tenants, but how do you know you have chosen the right letting agency? There is a trade association for letting agents, the Association of Residential Letting Agents (ARLA), which regulates members' activity. Members must have two years' experience in the letting industry, carry indemnity insurance, have separate accounts for clients' money and operate from offices (rather than 'a spare room in the house'). Letting agents will find you a tenant, draw up the letting agreement and collect the rent, but most agents also offer a 'property management service' which involves checking the property and undertaking maintenance on top of this. Fees for these services – letting and property management – will normally range from 10 to 15 per cent of the rent, plus VAT.

Obviously, if you use a letting agency or property management company, they will handle the formalities for you, providing documents and leases for you to sign. On the other hand, if you don't want to part with up to 15 per cent of the rent each month, you will need to understand all about assured shorthold tenancies.

Assured shorthold tenancies

This is the main private residential tenancy agreement, and gives the tenant possession of the house/flat for the duration of the lease. The benefit of an assured shorthold tenancy (AST) to the tenant is that he gets exclusive possession of the property, at a market rate, for the duration of the lease. The landlord benefits because the tenancy never confers security of tenure to the tenant. In order to create an assured tenancy, the following requirements must be met:

1. The property that is being let must be a separate dwelling.
2. The tenant (or joint tenants) must be a person (or persons) as opposed to a company.
3. The property is occupied by the tenant as his/her only home.
4. The tenancy is not one specifically excluded by the provisions of the Housing Act 1988 – these include high value property tenancies at a low rent, business tenancies, agricultural tenancies, holiday rentals and tenancies where the landlord lives in the same building.

Prior to 1997, ASTs could only be created if the let was for a minimum of six months, and the landlord had to serve a Section 20 notice that an AST was being created. Now the law presumes an AST is being created unless the landlord specifically gives written notice that it is not. And though the tenancy need not be for a minimum of six months' duration, a court cannot grant an order of possession during the first six months except in limited circumstances:

*   Rent arrears of at least eight weeks (or two months if rent is paid monthly).
*   The death of the tenant.
*   The landlord requires the property as his main home.
*   A mortgagee exercises a power of sale.
*   Demolition or reconstruction of the property.
*   Out of season holiday accommodation.
*   Out of term student let.

If you are a tenant, you will not have an assured tenancy or assured shorthold tenancy if:

*   You are a licensee.
*   You have a resident landlord.
*   You are renting the property for a holiday.
*   You are a student renting from a college or university.
*   The property is let to a company with which you have some connection.
*   You do not pay rent.

In these cases you will have very limited rights.

What do I do when the AST ends?

With ASTs, once the term of the tenancy has expired the landlord has an automatic right to his house as long as a Section 21 notice has been served on the tenant at least two months before the expiry date of the tenancy. The two-month notice period is a minimum, and some landlords serve the Section 21 notice at the beginning of the rental so as not to forget about it. The Section 21 notice is not valid until two months after it has been served – so if the notice is served on the last day of a 12-month tenancy, the tenant effectively has a 14-month AST. If a tenant refuses to vacate after a Section 21 notice has been properly served, you can go to court to get an immediate order for possession.

What if I want the tenancy to continue?

If you want, you can let the tenant remain in possession, and a second assured shorthold tenancy on the same terms will be created, unless the landlord serves noticed to the contrary, in which case, a periodic tenancy is created (which need not be for a minimum of six months' duration). If this happens, notice to end the tenancy is ultimately served under a Section 21(4) notice, again with at least two months' notice if it is to take effect on the last day of the tenancy.

Can I create a tenancy if I live in the house as well?

You can share your house with someone and still create an AST, provided the tenant has exclusive possession of some part of the house – which is usually a bedroom. If all the facilities are shared, a licence is normally granted – in the case of lodgers on a casual basis, for example – but don't try to create a licence to avoid giving a tenant protection. In any case, where the landlord 'lives in', the Protection from Eviction Act 1977 does not apply. But if you move away, an assured tenancy is created, giving the tenant security from eviction.

In 1992, the then government introduced a 'Rent a Room' scheme to allow home owners to let out parts of their home, and provided your rental income is below £3,250 a year you will not pay tax. If your income is more than this, you can either pay tax on the whole amount less expenses (water rates, council tax, repairs and redecoration, wear and tear), or be taxed on your gross income, less the £3,250 allowance.

What rent can I charge for an AST?

The Americans talk about something called rent-control; in England and Wales the test is one of reasonableness. ASTs can only be let at the market rate, and the tenant can take his case to a rent assessment committee if he thinks the rent is too high. In order to set a fair rent, the committee will look at similar property rentals in the area and the rent tenants there are being charged. Once a fair rent is set, it takes immediate effect.

Do I have to give the tenant a rent book?

Rent books must be given to tenants if they pay rent on a weekly basis, but as most ASTs involve monthly rent payments there is no need for a rent book. If you are unsure whether you have to provide a rent book, the Landlord and Tenant Act 1985 outlines when rent books must be provided.

Should I take a deposit?

Most landlords ask for a deposit to cover non-payment of rent and/or breakages and damage to the property. How much you ask for depends on your assessment of the prospective tenant (does he look like the type to hold wild parties?) though deposits of one month or one-and-a-half month's rent are normal. Some tenants try to avoid paying the last month's rent, so you should make sure the deposit is large enough to cover such an eventuality. For this reason, the 'one and a half month's rent as deposit' option might be best for you, in case of additional breakages or the poor condition of the property. The tenancy agreement should outline what circumstances would lead to you keeping the deposit or part of it, and also state when it would be repaid at the end of the tenancy. Taking an inventory will help in this case. At the beginning of the tenancy, you should make a detailed inventory of the property and its contents, and allow the tenant to comment on this and confirm it. At the end of the tenancy you take a second inventory which will identify breakages, repairs, etc. This will put you in a stronger position if you have to retain some of the deposit. Similarly, a deposit can cover what is unreasonable wear and tear; for example if a sofa is too badly stained and cigarette-burned, it may be reasonable to demand a replacement. Equally, if the house is in a very poor condition hygiene-wise, it would be reasonable to use some of the deposit to pay for contract cleaners.

Can the tenant end the AST early?

The AST is a contract that locks you both in for the term of the contract – so if you have a six-month tenancy and the tenant wants to leave after four months, then legally he is still liable for the remaining two months' rent unless you come to an agreement. However, you might want to put a break clause into the contract – though this is only valid in agreements of at least six months' duration – which allows either side to terminate the agreement early (but with a notice period) without the tenant having to pay the remaining rent.

If I rent my property to a tenant, can the tenant then let it to someone else?

Normally, ASTs do not allow tenants to sub-let any part of the property. If your tenant has sub-let the property, the sub-tenant's rights end when the tenant's do – so once the tenant's term has expired, the sub-tenant cannot remain any longer even if he has been granted a longer lease by the tenant. In addition, if the tenant has sub-let contrary to the agreement, you may be able to repossess your property for breach of the agreement.

What about tenancies created before the Housing Act 1988?

The Housing Act excluded tenancies created before January 15, 1989 as being converted into assured shorthold tenancies. These tenancies are covered under the old Rent Acts which give more protection to tenants than assured shorthold tenancies do (although certain types of tenancies, such as agricultural, educational or holiday lettings are excluded). If you are a tenant with a lease created before January 15, 1989, and the tenancy is brought to an end, you will still continue as a statutory tenant if you remain in occupation and it may be harder for the landlord to remove you. A landlord must start court proceedings to obtain a possession order, but before doing so he must serve a notice to quit to end the original contractual tenancy. The notice to quit must be in writing and give at least four weeks' notice, unless the tenancy agreement itself provides for a different notice period (but this must not be less than four weeks). The notice should also include information about your rights. If you (as a tenant) leave the property after the tenancy has been brought to an end you give up your right to Rent Act protection.

Can I create a longer tenancy agreement?

There is nothing to prevent you letting out your home on an AST for longer than a six-month period if you don't want the hassle of setting up regular tenancy agreements, or if you know the person you are letting to. Leases for longer than three years must be created by deed.

Is stamp duty payable on tenancy agreements?

Stamp duty is payable on some tenancies by the tenant, though duty on tenancies of 12 months or less is nominal. Failing to pay stamp duty on an agreement means neither party can enforce it in court (though either side can retrospectively stamp it if they need to undertake court proceedings).

What can I do if I end up with the tenant from hell?

Taking on a tenant is a big step – the law is rightly keen to protect tenants from Rachmanite landlords, but many of these justifiable protections will protect a bad tenant just as much as a deserving case. For this reason, you obviously need to vet your tenants carefully before granting them a lease – references should be taken (ideally three – one from the tenant's bank to show he is good for the money, one as to the tenant's character and one from his employer). But if despite your best efforts you end up with a bad lot, what can you do? Eviction is the answer, but to evict a tenant you will need a court order, however good your grounds. You might think of getting a few 'big friends' to pop round – forget it! Not only will it land you in trouble, but it won't get the tenant out. If you unlawfully evict a tenant, the tenant can apply for an injunction to be allowed back into the house and you could face criminal charges, punishable by an unlimited fine and/or two years' imprisonment. Repossession orders are tricky things, and it might be best to use a solicitor for this; but if not, there are three stages to follow (these are set out in Section 8 of the Housing Act 1988):

1.   Notice of proceedings.
2.   Issue of proceedings.
3.   Enforcement of a court order.

To begin action, you must serve notice on the tenant, specifying the grounds on which you are seeking possession of the property. This notice must be served two weeks before proceedings are issued. If you do not use the correct Section 8 notice, the process could be unenforceable.

The grounds for repossession can be found in Schedule 2 of the Housing Act 1998, and they are divided into mandatory grounds where the court must order possession, and discretionary grounds where the court may order possession:

Mandatory grounds

Ground 1.   Owner occupier.†

Ground 2.   Mortgagee exercising the power of sale.†

Ground 3.   Out of season holiday lets. †

Ground 4.   Out of term student lets.†

Ground 5.   Religious minister's home.

Ground 6.   Demolition or reconstruction of the property.

Ground 7.   Death.

Ground 8.   Substantial rent arrears – 13 weeks' (payable weekly) or three months' (payable monthly). For this to succeed, rent must be in arrears when the Section 8 notice is served and at the date of the hearing.*

Discretionary grounds

Ground 9.   If you can prove there is alternative accommodation available at the date of possession.

Ground 10.   Rent arrears if some rent was owing on the date possession proceedings are commenced, or if some rent was owing on the day the Section 8 notice was served.*

Ground 11.   Persistent delays in paying rent.*

Ground 12.   Breach of covenants – for instance not to keep pets.

Ground 13.   Neglect of the property.

Ground 14.   Causing nuisance to neighbours.

Ground 15.   Damaging furniture because of neglect.

Ground 16.   A former employee of the landlord.

† Courts have an accelerated procedure to seek possession, otherwise actions for possession will go through the county courts.

* A tenant can lawfully withhold his rent if he is forced to carry out essential repairs, which are your responsibility, and any court will take this into account. So make sure that if you have to go to court, your hands are clean! If you accept 'rent' that is owed you, this may suggest you have 'waived' the breach of agreement, and this could affect your chances of securing possession.

Normally, if a tenant owes money landlords will go for possession as a 'bird in the hand' measure – better to get the property back to re-let it than try and get rent you know the tenant has not got. But if you know your tenant has got the money, an alternative would be to sue for the arrears and keep the tenancy going.

Will letting my property affect my household insurance?

You should notify your insurers (who may be tied to your mortgage lender) if you rent out a property; if they agree, your buildings insurance (and your contents insurance) will be valid. Then it is up to the tenant to ensure he has sufficient contents insurance for his belongings. It also follows you should notify your mortgage lender if you plan to let out a property – it is a condition of most mortgages that lets must be approved by the lender.

If I let a property to someone, do I have to pay the Council Tax?

Council Tax is payable by the occupant of a property, which in the case of a rented property is the tenant. However, this is not the case with houses in multiple occupation (HMOs) where the landlord lives in; here, the landlord would be responsible for paying the Council Tax. This is because HMOs are normally large houses divided into smaller bedsits.

Apart from paying the rent, what other obligations has a tenant got?

If you are a tenant, you are obliged to keep the property in good order – and while that does not mean it has to be redecorated before the end of the lease, it does mean it should be clean and tidy, as a reasonable person would understand the term. A landlord may impose other obligations, for example to mow the lawn or keep the hedges neat. It depends on the agreement.

What other obligations have I got as a landlord?

If you let a property for a term of less than seven years, you are responsible for repairs to its structure and exterior. You are also responsible for ensuring adequate water, sewage, electricity, gas and rubbish collections. In addition, if you let your house furnished, the furniture must comply with the Furniture and Furnishings (Fire) (Safety) (Amendment) Regulations 1993. This covers beds, sofas, divans and cushions (but it does not cover bedding and carpets and floor coverings) and new and used furniture, which must pass an ignitability test. Failing to comply with the regulations can lead to a fine, though it does not apply to furniture made before January 1950. Most modern furniture will have a label stating whether the Regulations have been complied with.

All gas and electric appliances including gas-fired boilers, gas fires etc., must be serviced at least once a year by a CORGI-registered tradesman. Failure to comply with this will lead to prosecution. It is now required that an instruction book in English is to be left with each appliance in order that your tenants can see how to use them safely.

I'm a tenant and my landlord is harassing me; what can I do?

Tenants are entitled to live in 'quiet enjoyment' of their home without harassment by their landlord or a person acting under the landlord's instructions. 'Quiet' here means peaceful rather than free from noise. Harassment in the context of tenancies is a criminal offence under the Protection From Eviction Act 1977 and may result in your landlord being fined or even imprisoned. Harassment can take many forms including:

- Entering your home without permission.
- Entering your home while you are out.
- Changing the locks.
- Cutting off utilities, such as gas, water and electricity.
- Tampering with mail or possessions.
- Verbal or physical abuse or threats.

A person who is convicted by magistrates of an office under the Act may have to pay a maximum fine of £2,000 or be sent to prison for six months, or both. If the case goes to the Crown Court, the punishment can be prison for up to two years, or a fine, or both. You should keep a record of any instances where harassment has occurred, names of witnesses or anyone who may have become involved such as neighbours, doctors or the police. Seek advice from your local Citizens Advice Bureau, your local council's tenancy advice officer or a solicitor. In addition to protection under the criminal law, you can claim damages through the civil court for being harassed or illegally evicted.

What is harassment?

Harassment is a very broad term, used loosely to cover a wide range of activities, and it can take many forms short of physical violence. It may not always be obvious to outsiders that particular sorts of activity are intended to drive you from the property. On the other hand there may be cases where a landlord has good reasons for doing things that could be interpreted as harassment. There are defences in the Protection from Eviction Act and the Housing Act for landlords who have a good reason for acting in a particular way, or for thinking you, the tenant, had left the property. A landlord, or his agent, or someone who may or may not be connected with him, may do things that are distressing to you and undermine your sense of security; these activities may or may not amount to harassment as interpreted by the courts. Or he may not do certain things he is supposed to do under the tenancy agreement, either wilfully, because he wants you to leave, or from simple neglect; this neglect might also prevent you from enjoying your rented home and which a court may interpret as harassment.

Section 4.4 Neighbours

Neighbours are just as integral a part of your home as the walls and roof – in one way they form the boundaries of your property, and just as an unpleasant looking fence can ruin your enjoyment of the garden, a nasty neighbour can have the same effect. However pleasant your home, however luxurious the amenities, however sumptuous the furnishings – if the neighbours are pains in the neck then you might as well be living in a trench, because you will feel as if you are under siege all the time. Nightmare neighbours come in all forms, and to some extent what constitutes a nightmare depends on you – if you love barbecues, the smell of sizzling sausages from next door may cause no offence, but if you like the smell of the country on warm summer's day then al fresco cooking may be too much for you. Similarly, younger people tend to accept loud music played late into the night, whereas older couples find it more of a strain; of course, once the young couple becomes a young family, with children trying to get to sleep, that may change too… Obviously, you need to know what sort of neighbours you are getting when buying a house, so visiting the area will help. When you see the house of your dreams, it may be well tended and cared for, and calm. But if the neighbouring houses are run down, with unkempt gardens, you may have a rude awakening. Popping in at different times of day, chatting to locals or friends who live nearby – or even having a drink in the local pub – will give you valuable intelligence. Ask whether there are any busy-bodies, troublemakers or noisy neighbours. You can never get enough information when it comes to deciding whether to move into an area. Hopefully, if you take care and ask questions, you won't make a mistake. Sadly, sometimes you can get it wrong and move next door to a nuisance. And sometimes the nuisances can buy the house next door and come to you.

Who owns the wall/fence between my garden and my neighbour?

The general rule is 'fences mark boundaries, and whoever puts up the fence or wall between two properties owns it'. If you are planning to put up a fence between your and your neighbours' gardens, the first thing to say is that there is no legal requirement to fence – if a fence is required between two properties, it is probably because of a covenant which obliges you to build one. But if you decide you want to build a fence or wall, or fear that your neighbour may have 'stolen' some of your property, the first thing to do is to look at the plan attached to your property deeds (the Land Registry will supply copies of plans for a fee). The boundary will be marked on the plans with a 'T'. If no boundary is shown on the deeds, the usual presumption is that the wall or fence 'belongs' to whichever side of the wall its support posts are on, so if the support posts are on your side of the wall then it belongs to you.

What if the plans show I have less land than I'm entitled to?

If it looks as if your neighbour has 'stolen' some of your land, you can claim it back provided you have not allowed your neighbour to encroach onto your property, and have not given permission for him to do this over the past 12 years. The 12-year period is important – if the neighbours can show that they have 'enjoyed' the use of this piece of land for the past 12 years without objection, they can become owners of through the doctrine of 'adverse possession'. The 12-year period starts from when they (or the previous owners) first 'laid claim' to the property, and once the term has elapsed, they can have the land deeds amended to reflect the new position. Obviously, if you have a dispute with your neighbour over a boundary, it is best to try and talk it through amicably. Most people involved in boundary disputes have not set out to con you deliberately, and it is possible you can solve the matter by discussing it as friends. Get all your facts together first, then have a calm chat about it, avoiding making any allegations of sharp practice or worse. But be fair – let your neighbour make some enquiries of his own too, for it is always possible that your information may be wrong. If this fails, you will have to go to law, to seek an injunction to get your neighbour to move his fence to the legal boundary. Legal action is costly for all concerned, so it would be best to try and find a solution to the problem that doesn't involve a day in court.

What if the boundary follows a road or a stream?

There are specific rules relating to boundaries that follow natural or man-made topographical features:

- **Roads and highways:** the boundary of any land that adjoins a highway runs down the middle of the highway.
- **Rivers:** the same presumption applies to rivers, namely that whoever's land runs down to the river owns the river bed to the middle of the river, except in the case of tidal rivers. There, the river bed is owned by the Crown, and the boundary is the mean high water mark.
- **Streams:** the same presumption applies as for non-tidal rivers.
- **Seashore:** if you have a beach house, you own the coastal strip up to the mean high-water mark, though land reclaimed from the sea always belongs to the Crown.

I'm bothered by my neighbour's trees...

Trees are the property of the landowner that planted the tree, and his successors in title – even if the trunk, roots and branches extend to neighbouring properties. For this reason, if the roots of your neighbour's trees encroach onto your property they are a nuisance, and you can take legal action against your neighbour for nuisance to compel him to stop, by cutting back the root or branch. It may also create a statutory liability, allowing the local authority to issue an abatement notice to force the tree owner to take action. For your action for nuisance to succeed, you have to prove you have suffered damage as a result of the offending branch or root, for example branches destabilising your garden shed, or roots damaging your foundations or blocking your drains. In some cases, simply showing your neighbour's trees are taking water from your soil may be sufficient, if you live in area where subsidence is common when the ground dries out – a clay area for instance. If branches fall on your property and damage it, you can succeed in an action for damages only if you can prove that your neighbour was negligent: for instance, if he knew the tree was rotten and had done nothing to prevent branches falling.

What if I don't want to take my neighbour to court over his trees?

You can take action yourself if your neighbour's trees are bothering you – you can legally remove roots that may encroach on your land, and branches that overhang into your garden – but the parts of the tree remain the property of your neighbour, so legally you are obliged to check with him about how they should be disposed of (if he gets funny, you should really return the branches to your neighbour's garden). But check with the local council that there are no tree preservation orders in place, especially if you live in a conservation area or if the tree is part of a hedgeline or is a protected species; otherwise, you could get into trouble.

My neighbour has put up a screen of Leylandii ...

Over the past few years, a significant number of people are getting frustrated by their neighbours' refusal to reduce the height of Leylandii and other high garden hedges. The problems people encounter with these hedges include loss of light to gardens and homes, loss of view, difficulties in growing plants near the hedges and even worries that the roots of the hedge might lead to property damage through subsidence. In addition, people have to cope with the general stress of the situation. Many also fear that, should they wish to move home, these hedges might affect their prospects of selling their property. The Leylandii can grow up to 1 metre a year, and can be as tall as 30 metres when full-grown. Many neighbourhood disputes have centred on two other conifer types, the Lawsons cypress (which can grow up to 60 centimetres a year, up to 20 metres tall) and the western red cedar (which can grow up to 75 centimetres a year, and be up to 25 metres tall). If your neighbour's tall hedge is causing you problems, there is a number of options open to you. The first step is to talk to your neighbours to draw attention to the problem and ask them to deal with it by cutting the hedge to a reasonable height. If the problem is not resolved in this way, mediation may be able to help. While there will be cases where one party simply refuses to co-operate with the other, over 10,000 neighbour disputes have been settled with the help of mediation in the last ten years. Mediation, when it can be used, is quick, cheap and informal. Mediation UK is the umbrella group for all initiatives concerned with mediation and other forms of conflict resolution. If mediation does not resolve the problem, you may have to take legal action. Where a property carries specific legal rights (such as easements or covenants) which may apply to, or be affected by, a high hedge, it may be possible to resolve these disputes through the civil courts. Anyone thinking of taking such action should first seek legal advice on whether any such legal rights exist and on the best method of enforcing those rights. Advice should also be sought on whether it would be appropriate to have this type of dispute dealt with by means of the small claims procedure. Another approach would be to seek an Anti-Social Behaviour Order, which was introduced by the Crime and Disorder Act 1998. Local authorities or chief officers of police, in consultation with one another, can seek an order from the courts prohibiting an individual from carrying out serious, persistent, anti-social activity which affects a community. The orders are intended to be used for criminal or sub-criminal activity, rather than neighbour disputes. Nevertheless, potentially they might provide a remedy in the more extreme cases where the planting of high trees and refusal to reduce their height are part of a wider campaign of malicious action against neighbours. The government has set up a working party to look into the problems of nuisance hedges and to determine whether a direct government response is required because of public concerns that mediation does not work, and legal action is costly and time-consuming.

My neighbours are noisy – what can I do?

Living next door to noisy neighbours can be incredibly stressful, causing you to lose sleep, suffer depression, and putting strain on your relationships as a result. Noisy neighbours tend to drive even the mildest-mannered men and women to distraction, forcing otherwise totally law-abiding people to take the law into their own hands, often with disastrous results for the people concerned. Noise nuisance is subjective – it depends on where you are and who you are. For country dwellers, the noise of early morning cocks crowing is perfectly acceptable, but if your neighbour in Battersea keeps chickens, you may find their cackling unacceptable. The test in law is one of reasonableness, and what is reasonable will vary from case to case, and from what causes the noise. For example, the noise level made by a milkman at 4 a.m. may be the same as your neighbours partying in the flat above at the same time… but though one is acceptable, the other probably isn't. The first step would be to ask your neighbour to moderate his behaviour, politely and in person, on a friendly basis. That way, if your neighbour is unaware that his actions are causing offence, he would be able to modify his behaviour accordingly. Be reasonable and try to reach a compromise – it often works. But if it doesn't, there is a number of alternative avenues to pursue:

Suing your neighbour for nuisance at the county court

This involves getting an injunction at the small claims division of the county court to prevent the behaviour you are complaining about from continuing, as well as seeking damages for the suffering caused by the nuisance. You will have to convince the judge that your neighbour's noise is unreasonable; this requires evidence, so keep a diary of nuisances and incidents, and see if you can get any other neighbours to give evidence on your behalf. Civil claims for nuisance are uncommon, and can be quite expensive.

Get the local authority involved

The environmental health department at your local council can take action against noisy neighbours. If you can prove a statutory nuisance, which is defined as 'noise emitted from premises so as to be prejudicial to health or a nuisance', then the council can issue a Noise Abatement Notice against your neighbour. This notice orders the neighbour to stop making the noise complained about, and if the neighbour doesn't stop, then the council can begin criminal proceedings at magistrates' court, with a maximum fine of £5,000 and a term of imprisonment. The court can also seize the source of the noise – for instance a stereo. This sounds impressive, but in practice only 3 to 5 per cent of complaints end up in the courts because councils have limited resources. However, if you are convinced that you can prove your neighbours are making a statutory nuisance, then you can take action yourself by summoning them to appear at magistrates' court, by going to court and applying for a summons. The magistrates will require you to produce the same evidence as they would expect from an environmental health officer, but if you argue your case, the same penalties are available as for a council-run prosecution.

Local by-laws

Sometimes by-laws will give you a cause of action against nuisance behaviour, for example allowing the prosecution of owners of persistently noisy dogs, or dogs that foul footpaths.

My neighbour's satellite dish is blocking my light

There is no automatic right to light – but you can acquire a right to light (this means that the owners of one property – the dominant property – have acquired 'the right to light' over a second property – the servient property – without interruption for 25 years). So if your neighbour puts up a satellite dish or something that blocks light to your living room, then you may have an action for damages. But it is all a question of degree – how dark, and how inconvenient? If your normally light living room becomes very dark, you may be able to claim damages, but if it is the lavatory that is only slightly darkened, then you may find the courts less sympathetic. But while you can acquire a right to light over time, you can never acquire a right to a view; so if your neighbour's satellite dish stops you seeing the sun set over a beautiful hill farm there is nothing you can do about it.

My neighbour's dog keeps coming into our garden...

If your neighbour's dog comes into your garden and digs up your prize cauliflower, then provided you can prove your neighbour has been negligent you may have a case against him – and if the owner has good reason to believe that his otherwise docile dog does this from time to time, you won't need to prove negligence, for liability is strict in this case. However, you can't force them to put up a boundary fence to keep the dog (or cat) in. If the dog is a persistent stray, you might be able to bring an action for nuisance.

What if the animal bites my son?

If you – or your family – are injured by an animal when it strays onto on your property, or if it damages your property, you can succeed in an action for compensation if you can prove that the dog's owner did not take reasonable steps to keep the animal under control, or if the owner actively encouraged the animal to damage the property. In addition, the Dangerous Dogs Act 1991 provides protection against 'dangerous' dogs – the act was brought in to combat the perceived menace of the American pit bull, which was a popular breed at that time, but several of which were involved in particularly gruesome incidents involving attacks on adults and children. If a dog is classified as a dangerous dog, then the owner can be prosecuted criminally if the dog was dangerously out of control in a public place, with conviction carrying a fine or jail term.

My neighbours' children keep causing problems

Unruly children tend to grow into teenagers who would rather have their teeth removed without anaesthetic than stay near their homes, so any problems tend to be of limited duration. But while they are close to the nest, children can be brats – and unfortunately some of what they get up to is only to be expected, and is therefore reasonable. A few footballs kicked over the wall into your garden may be annoying, but they would not constitute a nuisance. If a young child continually comes onto your property and damages it, you can sue but only if the child is independently wealthy, for a child's parents cannot be held financially liable for their offspring's wrongdoings. If you think the child is worth suing, the next issue to take into account is the child's age– a teenager would definitely be liable, while a five-year-old probably would not be. You could take action against the parents if you can show that they failed to exercise proper control over the child, and that the damage was reasonably foreseeable. Or you can take action if you can prove the parents encouraged the child to act in a particular way; in this case, the younger the child the more likely you are to be able to get a court to hold parents responsible for their children.

My neighbours' children come into my garden and play without my permission – what happens if one gets hurt?

Unfortunately, the fact that the children are not supposed to be in your garden won't help you much. If features in your garden attract children and they get injured, you will be liable for negligence if it was reasonably foreseeable that children would want to play in this particular part of your garden – that tall tree, for instance – and you had not done anything about the risk.

My neighbours are smelly...

Unfortunately there is not much you can do legally about smelly or untidy neighbours. If the Slobbs move in next door, you will have to grit your teeth, hold your nose and grin and bear it. However, if they are more than 'normally' smelly, you can take action; an overpowering smell can comprise a nuisance – but it would have to be a persistent nuisance; one occasional waft would not be enough, and to succeed in court you would need detailed evidence to support your claim. This evidence could be in the form of corroboration from other concerned neighbours, or the local authority environmental health officer. Similarly if the 'untidiness' is more than 'reasonable' you might be able to get the council to take action if the mess is an eyesore – they can order the neighbour to move the rubbish, or move it and hold him liable for the costs. Your chances of success depend on the locality and the state of repair and sense of civic pride your other neighbours have – as one judge famously stated many years ago: 'what may be a nuisance in Belgravia is not one in Bermondsey'!

What can I do about my neighbour's burglar alarm which keeps ringing at night?

Car alarms and household burglar alarms are designed to get your attention – unfortunately so often do they ring out for the wrong reasons that people tend to do their best to ignore them. But in the wee small hours of darkness, a shrill siren blast from your neighbour's parked car or wall-mounted burglar alarm can be more than just annoying – especially if it doesn't stop ringing. Burglar alarm makers are aware of the problem, and alarms manufactured after 1992 will cut out after 20 minutes' ringing. If an alarm rings for an hour or more, an environmental health officer can get a warrant from a justice of the peace; this gives the officer power to enter the property and disable the alarm, and then leave the property secured. For noisy car alarms, contact the environmental health officer. The EHO will try to find out whom the car belongs to and contact them, but if the alarm continues to ring for more than one hour and the owner cannot be found, the environmental health officer can disable the car alarm, under police supervision (any costs incurred in doing this – getting locksmiths etc. – will be borne by the car owner). Remember, if you take action yourself – by smashing the alarm or hitting it to stop it ringing, you could be accused of causing criminal damage – so get a policeman or environmental health officer to do it for you!

Are my neighbour and I responsible for our drains and sewers?

There are two sorts of sewers – public sewers which are built by the sewerage undertakers (the water company, though local authorities normally act as their agents) or others, and maintained by them; and private sewers, which are sewers built after October 1, 1937 and which connect houses to the main trunk (public) sewer. Private sewers built before October 1, 1937 and which drain two or more houses are classified as public sewers. Householders are thus responsible for sink waste pipes, toilet drains, cesspits, septic tanks and soakaways. If a private sewer serving four houses breaks, then all four homeowners are responsible for repairing it and will share the costs equally, unless one homeowner had been negligent and contributed to the break more than the others. The house that is most affected by the break will probably be the one that will carry out the repairs at first instance – if that is you, check you have insurance cover for sewers (though you probably won't) and notify your neighbours and make it clear that responsibility is joint and everyone will pay equal shares for the repair. Then the work could go ahead, and if your neighbours refuse to take their share of the bill you may have to sue. For fresh water pipes, the water authority is responsible for the main, the supply pipe to the point where it crosses the boundary of your property and the stopcock. All other pipes are your responsibility.

Section 4.5 Trespass and access

Trespassing on someone's land is not a crime – despite the well-known warning: 'Trespassers will be prosecuted' – but a civil wrong or tort (so 'trespassers will be sued'). Trespassers can be sued for civil damages and trespassers can be forcibly evicted by the owner – but trespassers cannot be prosecuted. A person commits trespass when they enter property or a building without the consent of the owner. There is such a thing as implied consent, which allows the postman or newspaper delivery boy/girl to walk up the garden path without fear of being accused of trespass. But if you post a sign outside your house saying 'no hawkers, no leaflets' then anyone who comes up your garden for that purpose is a trespasser because there is no implied permission to come in. Similarly, if someone comes onto your property and you withdraw consent for them to be there, they become a trespasser if they stay. For example, a police officer who knocks on your door has implied consent to be there, but if you refuse access and the policeman doesn't have a warrant, by remaining on your property he becomes a trespasser.

What can I do to stop trespassers coming onto my land?

You have the right to take reasonable steps to stop people trespassing on your land, but not to injure them in the process. A barbed wire fence is reasonable (so is a glass-topped wall) but spring-loaded guns and man-traps are not, nor is an electrified fence if it carries a voltage sufficient to kill. You can keep a guard dog, but if the dog injures a trespasser you may be liable for damages depending on whether a court feels it was reasonable for you to have a guard dog as protection. If a trespasser comes onto your land and refuses to leave after you have withdrawn permission, you, as owner of the property can use reasonable force to eject a trespasser. The precise amount of force that is reasonable is subjective, and will depend on the circumstances. For example, if a young girl trespassed on your property, it would not be reasonable to drive her off with a garden fork; but if masked raiders broke into your home, it might be considered reasonable to force them to flee using a shotgun.

Do trespassers have any rights?

Yes, they do. If you use more force than is reasonable to evict a trespasser, then they could sue you for damages if you injure them in the course of eviction. However, the court must be satisfied that the injuries were caused deliberately and not accidentally. In addition, you may be charged with assault by the police, no matter how sympathetic they may be to your plight. Also, as a landowner, you have to be aware of the safety of trespassers known to be on your property, and avoid recklessly disregarding their safety. For instance, if you have a toxic dump at the bottom of your garden and fail to fence it off, and a child falls in and gets injured, you could be sued.

What happens if I sue for trespass?

If you take someone to court for trespassing on your land, the court will award whatever damages will be required to repair damage caused by the trespasser. A trespasser cannot claim that they did not know they were trespassing – ignorance of the trespass is no defence. Exemplary (i.e. higher damages) will be awarded if officials – for instance police or council officers – committed the trespass, as a form of lesson. Sometimes, it is worth suing for trespass even if no damage has been caused, or if there is no realistic prospect of recovering damages, as a means of settling ownership of a disputed property, between two neighbours, for example.

How can I resolve a dispute with my neighbour when he is trespassing on my land?

If your neighbour persistently trespasses on your land, you should be polite. Ask first and raise the matter, asking them to desist from doing whatever it is that forms the trespass, for example walking across your front garden on the way home from the pub. If your neighbour does not stop, you could sue for an injunction to prevent the act being repeated, and claim for damages caused by the trespass. You should compile evidence before going to law, and try to get witnesses who will back your claim. You will be unlikely to qualify for Legal Aid for this action without making some contribution, and it is rare for damages to be awarded except in the most extreme cases.

Can my neighbour refuse me access to his property if I need to paint my garage?

In law, you need your neighbour's permission to enter his land to do any maintenance on your own property, such as tree pruning or garage painting – if you go without his consent you are a trespasser. But legal action against you is unlikely if you chose to act without permission, not that this book would seek to offer advice that might amount to breaking the law!

If you are refused permission to enter your neighbour's property to carry out maintenance on your own premises, then you can seek a court order from the county court to give you access to do the work, under the Access to Neighbouring Land Act 1992. To get an order, you will have to outline details of the land and why you need access to your neighbour's property, evidence to support your need to go onto your neighbour's land, an undertaking to repair any damage caused, and an estimate of how long you will need access for.

Section 4.6 Squatters

What is a squatter?

Legally, if someone gets into your house without your consent, and without having broken in or in some way forced entry, then they are a squatter. If they have forced their way in they are burglars. Squatting is a trespass, and if you get squatters you can get a court order for possession, unless they are squatting in your usual home.

Can an owner use force to get his own home back?

There is a criminal offence of adverse occupancy, which is committed if a squatter deprives someone of their usual home, or refuses to go when the premises are wanted by the owner for use as a home. The police can be asked to arrest and prosecute squatters in this case.

If you are the resident owner, you do not usually need a court order to claim possession in such circumstances – it will usually suffice to show proof of residence in the form of a sworn statement of housing authority certificate of allocation.

If the squatter refuses to leave, the best course of action is to call the police. But if you want to take immediate possession, you are entitled to use 'reasonable force' to enter the premises or to evict the squatter.

I went away for a holiday, and when I came back squatters had moved into a house I own (but not my own home)

This assumes that your 'squatters' are indeed squatters and did not force their way into the house. You cannot force your way into the house, but if the squatters do not resist, you are perfectly able to go back into the house if the squatters are not there, or if they do not resist your attempts to get in. To evict the squatters you will need a court order. This 'interim possession order' will make it a criminal offence for anyone to remain in the house who is there without your consent. Then the police can arrest them, and if convicted they will be liable to a fine or imprisonment (or both).

How long will it take to get an interim possession order?

The court will normally rule on your application within a few days of your seeking it, so the procedure is fairly swift. However, once you have served the interim possession order, that is still not the end of the matter – you will also have to make an application for possession when you apply for the interim possession order.

How do I get an interim possession order?

You can apply to a county court for an interim possession order if you find that your premises have been occupied by people without your consent provided that:

- The property is a building, a part of a building, i.e. a self-contained room or flat, or land ancillary to a building.
- You have an immediate right of possession to the premises being occupied.
- Your right has existed for the whole time the premises have been illegally occupied.
- None of the occupants is a tenant who has refused to leave after his tenancy or lease has expired.
- You are making your claim for possession within 28 days of the date you first discovered the premises were being illegally occupied without your consent.
- The occupiers are not people granted a legal right to occupy the premises by a legal tenant or lessee.
- You are only making a claim for possession.

You do not need to know the names of the squatters to get a possession order. But because of the potentially serious effects of an interim possession order, courts will want to safeguard the occupiers' rights too, in case they successfully object to the possession order. You will be asked to give two undertakings to court:

- To allow the occupiers back onto the land and pay them damages if an interim possession order is made and the court later decides you were not entitled to that order.
- Not to let the premises to anyone else or damage them, or dispose of any of the occupiers' possessions until the court makes a final decision on your right to possession.

You will have to pay a court fee for the application, and swear a statement of truth containing all the information the court needs to decide whether to grant you an interim possession order. Make sure you present all the facts in your affidavit because you will not be allowed to give additional evidence at your hearing. You can swear an affidavit before a solicitor or commissioner for oaths (for which you will be charged), or an officer of the county court (which is free).

The legal procedures for this are contained in two forms: N130 *Application for possession including application for interim possession* and N131 *Notice of application for interim possession*. They are available from the courts.

What happens next?

You must serve the documents on the squatters within 24 hours of the court issuing your application for an interim possession order. You don't have to hand the documents to the squatters personally; service counts as fixing the papers to the front door or another prominent part of the premises, or pushing them through the letterbox in a sealed clear plastic envelope, addressed to the occupiers. You will have to swear an affidavit stating how the notice was served, with a copy of the notice attached, and send that to court before the court hears your application (or hand it to the judge if you plan to attend the hearing). There is a form N132 *Affidavit of service of application of an interim possession order*.

What happens at the hearing?

The hearing normally takes place in judge's chambers in private; the occupier can attend too, but only if they have filled in their own forms offering their side of the story, and had them sworn at court. Neither side can give more evidence. The judge considers the affidavits and your undertakings before deciding whether to grant an interim possession order. If the judge makes an interim possession order, you will have 48 hours to serve the order on the squatters, in the same way you served the original application, and the squatters have 24 hours to leave the premises or face arrest. If the police become involved, you must give them a copy of the interim possession order and the sworn affidavit of service of that order. The squatters will also commit a criminal offence if they return to occupy the premises illegally again within a year of the order being served. Form N135 *Affidavit of service of interim possession order* is also available from the courts. The interim possession order will have a 'return date' – the date at which the interim order expires and you have to go to court for a possession order. If no interim possession order is made, you will be given a date when the judge will consider your claim for possession of the premises in full.

What happens on the 'return date'?

Here the judge will decide whether to make a final possession order, or dismiss your claim for possession (or give directions as to how your claim should be handled). If the judge decides you were not entitled to an interim possession order, you can be asked to pay compensation to the occupiers, as you said you would in your undertakings. If a final possession order is made, you may ask the court for a warrant of possession if the squatters do not leave the premises.

Can the squatter object to the interim possession order?

The squatters can object to the interim possession order, and ask for it to be set aside, but only if they have complied with it. Once the squatters have left your property they can apply to go back to court before the return date, submitting an affidavit stating why the possession order should be set aside and including any written evidence to support this claim. If the squatters did not attend the first hearing, they cannot ask for the possession order to be set aside on that ground. The judge will decide what period of notice you will have of the application, and may also decide to bring the return date forward and deal with both matters at once.

I'm a squatter – do I have any rights?

Even though you may be occupying premises illegally, the owner must get a court order to get you out. If the owner seeks an interim possession order, he must serve papers on you, and the court will inform you of the date of a hearing for the grant (or otherwise) of an interim possession order.

The court papers and notice don't mention me by name: can I ignore them?

The notice applies to anyone occupying the premises, whether named in the notice or not. If you are occupying the premises referred to in the application and notice, then the papers apply to you.

I think I have a right to be in this building – what should I do?

If you have a legal right to be in the premises – or think you have – you should fill in a form N133 *Affidavit of occupier to oppose the making of an interim possession order*. This will have been served on you along with your notice, and you will be able to fill it in to provide evidence of your legal right to be in the premises. You should also include any agreements, rent books or leases you have been given. Unless you fill in and submit N133 – and make sure the affidavit is sworn – you do not have a legal right to go to the application hearing. Don't forget, you can have the affidavit sworn for free by a court officer. It is not enough that you have nowhere else to go – you must have a legal right to stay.

How do I apply to set the interim possession order aside?

Once you have left the premises, you can get two forms from the court: N244 *Notice of application* and N285 *General form of affidavit*. Fill in both forms, set out your reasons why the interim order should be set aside, and include evidence like a lease or rent book. But you can't have the interim possession order set aside simply because you did not attend the first hearing. If the judge hears your case and agrees, you will be allowed back into the property. The judge will not decide on compensation for you – that can only be decided by the judge dealing with the return date. But if the owner gave undertakings to compensate you and the court decides that you were lawfully in possession of the property, you can be compensated.

Section 4.7 Occupier liability

The occupier of a house, office, shop or any other building has a duty to take care that the premises and any ground belonging to the property are safe for visitors. Failing to do so would give a cause of action for negligence to any person suffering injury or loss if the premises proved faulty. Before 1957, the question of whether occupier liability existed depended on whether the person coming onto your property was an invitee or licensee, but this has been simplified by the Occupiers' Liability Act 1957. Now, there is only one class of person, visitors defined as people with express or implied permission to be on the property, for instance a postman, a shopper or a party guest.

What responsibility am I under as an owner to ensure my property is 'safe'?

Section 2 of the Occupiers' Liability Act states that owners and occupiers of premises owe a common duty to all visitors to take such care as in all the circumstances of the case is reasonable, to see that the visitor will be reasonably safe in using the premises for the purpose for which they are intended or permitted by the occupier to be there. But the section also allows occupiers to contract with visitors to absolve themselves from liability – for instance if you operate a paintball game on your property you might want to limit liability if game players twist ankles, etc., while playing. However, you must expect children to show less care than adults, so it is not enough to say something is idiot-proof – it must also be reasonably child-proof too! So, as occupier, you can be sued if the postman comes to deliver your letters and gets attacked by your pet spaniel. Even though you did not specifically invite them onto your land, they have implied permission to be there.

Have I any defences if my dinner guests sue me for negligence if the ceiling collapses onto them as soup is served?

If you warned your guests, for instance that you were having work done on your house and bits of loose plaster might fall, then that will limit your liability. Applying this to occupier liability generally, if your visitors willingly accept the risks then they cannot subsequently sue you, provided what happened to them was reasonably foreseeable. If you tell your guests not to park their car in a particular part of the drive because slates are falling from the garage roof, then they would not be able to sue you if some slates did indeed hit your car bonnet. On the other hand, if the garage blew up and set their car alight, they could sue you. If damage is caused to a visitor because of faulty building work, maintenance or repairs, you will have a defence if you employed a independent contractor, and you took all reasonable steps to ensure the contractor was competent and the work had been properly done. So, if your ceiling collapses, your dinner guests might sue you as first defendant and the plasterers you employed as independent contractors to fix the ceiling as second defendants. If the plasterers are found to have done shoddy work, they may be held liable for negligence. The Defective Premises Act 1972 also places builders, specialist subcontractors, and developers under a statutory duty of care in respect of new houses, towards purchasers and their successors in title.

Do trespassers have rights?

The general rule is that you do not owe any duty of care to trespassers, and trespassers enter your property at their own risk. You can take steps to make your property secure, with glass on the tops of walls – but not man-traps or spring-loaded guns! But you can owe a duty of care to trespassers if you are aware that there are trespassers on your property, or that they are likely to be on your property; for example if the garden of your house is used as a shortcut by schoolchildren on their way home. If it should ever happen that a trespasser should try to sue you, the court would take into account the reason why the trespasser was on your land in the first place. So a burglar might get very short shrift from the courts; however, a prospective parliamentary candidate might get a different hearing if he slipped on the badly cracked tarmac of your drive.

What about children that trespass?

In general the same rules apply to children as to adult trespassers, but you should be aware that children may not recognise warnings that an adult might understand, and remember that children are less careful than adults. Another point to consider is that if you know children trespass on your land – through a hole in a fence, say – and you do nothing to repair the damage or prevent the trespass, you might be construed as giving implied permission, which would transform the trespassers into visitors.

Another factor to consider with children is that though they might be on your land legitimately as a visitor, they may be forbidden to do some things that might make them trespassers as far as that forbidden act is concerned, for instance to play near the berry trees or by the pond. However, courts have found that notwithstanding the order banning them from playing near the pond or the berry trees, the forbidden thing acts as an 'allurement', and the owners have been found liable for any damage or harm that befalls them. But if you take all reasonable steps to make the allurement as unattractive as possible or secure it, then you should be able to avoid liability.

Will my household insurance cover me for third-party liability?

The costs of personal injury actions can be surprisingly steep – even being sued for a sprained wrist or broken arm can cost several thousand pounds once legal costs (on both sides), days off work and specialists' treatments are taken into account. Check that your household insurance policy includes third-party liability cover. If so, check how much cover it provides, and if not, consider changing your policy. Discuss your needs with an insurance broker.

Section 4.8 The law of trusts

What is a trust?

A trust is the relationship that arises whenever property is held by one person (or group of persons) for the benefit of another person (or group of persons). The person who holds the property on behalf of the other is called the trustee, and it is key to the relationship that benefits do not accrue to the trustees, but to the objects of the trust. Trusts first evolved in feudal times to mitigate the effects of common law rules preventing land from being devised under wills. The important element of trusts is the duality of ownership. The trustee is the legal owner, while the beneficiary is the equitable owner. Trusts are of two kinds: private trusts and charitable trusts.

What are trusts used for?

Trusts can be set up for a variety of purposes that include:

- To allow property to be used to benefit persons in succession.
- To allow two or more people to own land.
- To further charitable purposes.
- To avoid or minimise tax liability – the Vestey trusts that benefit the heirs to the Dewhurst family are famous.
- To hold property on behalf of persons that cannot own the legal title themselves; for instance minors cannot own land legally, but land can be held in trust for a minor.
- To keep property for those not yet born, for instance grandchildren of children that have not yet married.

Private trusts

There are three kids of private trusts:

1. Express trusts
An express trust is expressly created by the settlor (the person who grants the property) for the benefit of one person, or a group of persons. It is created in writing or by deed, or occasionally orally. For an express trust to be created, there must be:

- Certainty of intention: it must be clear that the settlor intended to create a trust – otherwise the person granted the property will take ownership of it absolutely, rather than hold it on trust for the beneficiary in accordance with the settlor's wishes.
- Certainty of subject-matter: it must be clear exactly what property is going to be held in trust – 'the bulk of my estate' is too vague though 'the remainder of my estate after

151

these bequests' is not – and who it will be held in trust for – to say 'some of the property will be held in trust for A and some of the property for B' is too vague.

- Certainty of objects: the persons the trust has been set up to benefit must be ascertainable; if the trustees cannot determine the class of people who are to benefit from the trust, the estate is held on trust for the settlor.

2. Implied trusts

Implied trusts are based on what is presumed to be the settlor's intention, as the settlor may be dead and cannot be asked his intentions. The most usual type of presumed trust is the **resulting trust**, an example of which would exist if a settlor transferred property to trustees to hold on trust for B for life; what happens to the property on B's death? If the settlor has not specified what happens, the property is held on resulting trust for the settlor, and the equitable interest returns to him on B's death, because in such cases ownership will revert to the settlor.

Another example of a resulting trust would occur if X bought property and conveyed it in Y's name; in the absence of any evidence to suggest that it was intended as a gift, equity will assume that a resulting trust exists with Y holding the property for X. (This can operate the other way – if a person buys property and conveys it in the name of his wife or child, it is presumed that a gift was intended and no resulting trust occurs.)

3. Constructive trusts

Sometimes equity decides it knows best and decides that a trust exists regardless of what the parties' intentions might have been. An example of a constructive trust being created was where a trustee held a property lease on trust for a minor; the trustee tried to renew the lease for the child and was turned down, but was allowed to take on the lease himself. Here the courts decided that the trustee held the new lease on constructive trust for the minor.

Charitable trusts

For a charitable trust to be created, three conditions must be satisfied:

1. The trust must be charitable in the legal sense

This means that it must be for the relief of poverty, for the advancement of education, for the advancement of religion or for any other purposes beneficial to the community. This means that trusts for the benefit of rich Oxford colleges are just as charitable as trusts to benefit the poor of Cardiff, and they get the same tax breaks. Another category allows bequests to animal charities, distress funds and other not obviously charitable bequests.

2. It must benefit the public, or at least a section of the public

If the trust is set up to benefit only certain individuals, then no charitable trust can be created, so trusts to provide for the education of the heirs of named individuals are not charitable, nor are trusts to provide for the education of employees of a company, as neither heirs nor employees form 'a section of the public'. A trust to provide sporting scholarships to children from the village of Oakley in Hampshire would be charitable, however. Trusts for the relief of poverty do not need to meet the public benefit requirement.

3.   It must be wholly and exclusively charitable
If the trust can be applied to charitable and non-charitable purposes, the trust is void.

How can I set up a trust?

Trusts are best set up with signed legal documents (this is compulsory for trusts affecting land). The trust document should set out clearly the trust's name, and list all the capital assets and incomes the trust will administer. It should name or accurately describe the beneficiaries, any conditions as to how the trust is to be administered, whether there is any policy affecting investment of assets (into ethical funds, for instance), or the delay before beneficiaries receive their benefits. Unless you specify a time limit for the trust to operate, the maximum duration of a trust is 80 years (or 21 years after the death of someone living when the trust first took effect). This time limit does not apply to charitable trusts. When the trust has been set up and the trustees selected, the assets must be transferred properly – property under seal and shares by transfer document, with the trustees registered as owners.

How do I select trustees?

Anyone over the age of 18 can be named as a trustee, if they agree to serve. Trustees are unpaid unless the trust deed states otherwise (solicitors who are appointed tend to charge their fees). There is no maximum number of trustees you can appoint, except with land when the limit is four. But don't worry about even numbers of trustees freezing decision-making – unless the trust deed specifies otherwise, trustees must be unanimous about decisions they take affecting the trust. Though anyone can serve as a trustee (except a minor), in practical terms you should select practical, intelligent people, ideally with some financial knowledge. Knowing the family history would also be advisable.

Why should I look at setting up a trust?

Transferring assets or income to a trust can reduce taxation, with savings of as much as 40 to 50 per cent of your tax bill. Payments made to beneficiaries of trusts are usually treated as personal investment income, and often the benefit is paid out after tax has been deducted. Speak to an accountant or financial advisor to find out what benefits trusts could have for you.

Is there any control on the way trustees operate?

Trustees are obliged to take the same care of the trust property as an ordinary business person would of their own investments, though professional trustees – solicitors, bankers and trust companies – must show a higher level of skill, that of a reasonably skilled practitioner in their profession. Trustees that are careless, or fail to adhere to the terms of the trust strictly, may be held personally liable for losses the trust incurs as a result of their failure, though they will not be liable for accidental losses or pure errors of judgement. What the trust fund can be invested in is governed by the Trustee Investment Act 1961, which allows trustees to invest up to 50 per cent of the trust fund in companies' ordinary shares. The remainder must be held in safer (less lucrative) securities such as government bonds and gilts, National Savings certificates, etc. Sometimes a specific term of the trust deed may give trustees unrestricted powers of investment. The aim of most trustees is to provide a balance between income-producing and capital-producing investments, so the trust remains viable for the length of its existence. Trustees are not allowed to profit from the trust, though professionals such as solicitors can be compensated for their professional services. While trustees can hire professionals to perform specific tasks, such as lawyers to draft documents or brokers to sell shares, they cannot delegate the operation of the trust – the trustees must always make the decisions. Once all the beneficiaries of a trust are of full age and legal capacity and are entitled to take the whole benefit of the trust, they can ask the trustees to deal with the trust in any manner they wish. Otherwise trustees cannot vary a trust, except in certain cases (for instance where the beneficiaries are of unsound mind) and they have to follow the trust document. If a court is asked to vary the terms of a trust, the judge must be satisfied that variation is in the best interests of the beneficiaries of the trust.

What can I do if a trustee 'betrays his trust'?

If a trustee breaches his trust, you have a number of options:

- You can bring an action against the trustees to compensate the trust for losses sustained.
- In some cases the police can become involved if the breach is criminal.

Trustees are only liable for their own acts, and not those of fellow trustees or people involved with the trust (companies the trustees invested with, stockbrokers, etc.), unless the trustee was guilty of a wilful default, namely a deliberate intention to commit a breach of trust or reckless disregard as to whether there was a breach of trust. If more than one trustee is responsible for a breach of trust, they are, jointly and severally, liable for the breach. This is good news for beneficiaries: if more than one trustee is responsible for a breach of trust, it doesn't matter that, say, two might be poor and unable to compensate the trust for losses; as long as one of them is sufficiently well off to compensate the trust for the whole of the loss, then he will have to pay up the whole amount – even if it wasn't all his fault. Trustees can only be sued for breach of trust up to six years after the date of the discovery of the breach of trust, except where there was a fraud.

Section 4.9 Planning permission

An Englishman's home is his castle, so the saying goes. But sometimes the baron is not satisfied with the depth of his moat or the height of his walls, or he wants to build a conservatory onto his keep! Some people find the concept of building control and planning permission grossly unfair: 'It's my house! Why can't I build that swimming pool at the end of my garden?' But a framework of building control is necessary in order that all householders know the score, and like cases are treated alike. Unfortunately, though the framework exists, application of the laws is patchy, and in fact varies from local authority to local authority, as well as from decision to decision. Whenever you buy a plot of land, or a house, in the back of your mind is the possibility of building a house on it (in the case of a plot of land) or modernising and renovating it. Do you need planning permission? Do you need professional help? Or can you just go it alone?

Who regulates planning matters?

Planning matters are the preserve of the local authority, specifically the district councils. If you apply for planning permission and the council turns you down, you can appeal to the Secretary of State for the Environment (or the Welsh Office or Scottish Office for those outside England), who will appoint a planning inspector to look at your appeal and rule on the merits of the case.

What is planning permission?

You need planning permission for any development, which can be defined as covering things like building an extension or changing the use of a building, from a chapel to a dwelling house for example. Development does not include internal or external improvements that do not materially affect your building's external appearance. Painting the house is not a development but converting your house into an office would be, even if no building work is required, as it is a change of use.

I want to build a house on a plot of land. Do I need permission?

If you want to build a house you will need planning permission, but before you buy the land perhaps it would be as wise to check that you would be able to build there anyway. Some land has been 'zoned' by local authorities, which means it has been set aside for specific uses. It would be a shame to spend a lot of money on a plot of land only to discover the only people able to enjoy the breathtaking views were sheep because the land had been designated for farming. So you should consider applying for planning permission for the land before you buy it. At the very least you should apply for outline planning permission. As the name suggests, this is not a detailed approval of architects' plans, but rather an indication that the council have no objections in principle to you building on the plot of land. (They may have serious objections later on, when you come to submit plans for an alpine chalet in the middle of Pinner, or that Arabian-style villa in Carlisle, but that's another matter.) All you have to do when applying for outline planning permission is to submit plans showing the size and proposed form the building will take.

Can I apply for planning permission even though I don't own the land?

You don't need to own land to apply for planning permission. But if you don't own it, you would need to submit a Certificate B, confirming that the 'real' owners know you are making the application.

I've got outline planning permission; what now?

The next step is to fill in the fine detail in your application, which will need to be approved before you can build. At this stage it might well be wise to get an architect on board, who can draw up the plans, advise on planning policy and help you through the application. Architects are members of the Royal Institute of British Architects (RIBA) who carry indemnity insurance if something goes wrong, and are bound by arbitration rules in the case of disputes. But a local builder might be just as able to recommend someone that can draw up plans for your dream home. This stage is known as 'the application for approval for reserved matters'. There is a number of matters you will need to clarify:

1. **Does your proposal involve demolishing a listed building?**
   You can't knock down listed buildings without listed building consent, in addition to planning permission. Listed buildings are graded from Grade I (those of exceptional interests), Grade II (particularly important buildings) and Grade III (buildings that should be preserved if at all possible). Grade III buildings make up 92–94 per cent of the total number of listed buildings. Getting permission to demolish Grade I (around 6,000 buildings) or Grade II (20,000) will be difficult, even if they are in a poor state of repair. Examples of listed buildings you might not expect to be listed include factories that have particularly stunning architectural features, such as the old Dunlop Semtex factory in Brynmawr, Wales, bridges or even World War II air raid shelters.

2. **Is your plot of land in a conservation area?**
   If so, there will be special scrutiny of your proposals to ensure that it remains in keeping with the area. Special rules also apply to properties in national parks, though these are concerned less with building but ensuring that renovations remain in keeping with the area. To build or retain property in keeping with a conservation area can be expensive – for instance, window frames may have to be wooden rather than UPVC, and roofs may have to be slate rather than tiled.

3.   What are the access arrangements?

Access is an important issue in terms of whether planning permission is granted or refused, with road safety a prime concern.

Do I need planning permission for every change to my property?

While you do need planning permission to build a new dwelling on your land, some developments do not require specific formal planning permission (unless you live in a conservation area, in which case changes need to be made in accordance with the area's general developments). These are contained in the Town and Country Planning (General Development) Order 1988, and though not needing planning permission they still impose conditions on you. A number of them are relevant to householders looking to improve their properties:

Part 1 Developments within the curtilage of a dwelling-house

What counts as a 'dwelling-house' is not defined fully, but flats or apartment blocks do not come under the definition. The curtilage is the land surrounding the house that is used for 'quiet enjoyment' of it (or any other building) although it has not been enclosed. For extensions within the curtilage of an existing house, planning permission is not needed provided the new building work does not exceed set cubic capacities:

- For most houses, planning permission is not needed, provided the new building work doesn't exceed the cubic content of the original building by 70 cubic metres or 15 per cent and provided:
  — The extension will not be higher than the original house (and if closer than 4 metres to the perimeter of the property, it can be a maximum of 4 metres in height).
  — It will not extend beyond the front of the house where it is next to a path or public road.
  — It does not include any alteration to any part of the roof.
  — The area of ground covered by all buildings in the curtilage is no greater than 50 per cent of the total area (and this includes the area of the original house).
  — It does not include the installation, alteration or replacement of a satellite dish.
- For terraced houses, the new building must not exceed the cubic content of the original building by more than 50 cubic metres, or 10 per cent.

Other developments that can be carried out without planning permission, under part 1 of the General Development Order are:

- Porches can be built on the front of your house provided the floor area does not exceed 2 metres, no part of the porch is more than 3 metres above ground level and no part of it is within 2 metres of a boundary adjoining a road or footpath.
- Loft conversions, provided the house isn't enlarged or the shape of the house altered. Otherwise, development is limited to 50 cubic metres, as long as this does not exceed the limits for house extensions (40 cubic metres for terraces).
- Garages can be built without permission, provided they comply with the rules relating to extensions, and no part of the garage is within 5m of the house itself. This also applies to carports.
- Satellite dishes, provided the dish has a diameter of less than 70 centimetres (45 centimetres if attached to a chimney) and is no higher than the highest part of the roof or chimney it is attached to; only one dish per house.
- Television aerials can be erected without permission, but you will need planning consent for radio masts.
- Driveways can be installed without permission if they lead onto an unclassified road, otherwise full planning permission would be required (and it would be wise to talk to the highways authority as well).
- Garden structures – swimming pools, summer houses, greenhouses and sheds – can be built without permission provided they are there for the enjoyment of the house, provided no part projects beyond the front of the house where it faces a public road and its height does not exceed 3 metres (4 metres if the roof is ridged). In addition, no more than 50 per cent of the land can be covered by the new structure built since the erection of the house or since 1948, whichever is later.
- Oil tanks for central heating can be sited as long as the capacity does not exceed 3,500 litres, is no higher then 3 metres tall and is no nearer the road than the original building.

Part 2 Minor operations

This covers a host of minor works, including:

- Walls and fences can be built, repaired and maintained without permission provided they are less than 2 metres high (1 metres if it faces the road). This also includes gates fitted to the walls.
- Internal alterations can be carried out without permission unless they involve a change of use.
- Painting can be carried out without permission, though external painting that comprises an advertisement must be approved.
- Routine maintenance does not require planning permission, and this covers cladding and pebble-dashing that will change the appearance of your property. Note this may not be the case in conservation areas, where external changes will require permission.

Part 3 Changes of use

If you materially change the use of your property then you will require permission from the local authority to do so. For instance, if you start a radio taxi business from your front room and have cars parked up outside, you will need planning permission even though you have not had any building or conversion work done. Obviously, the flow of traffic will increase and this will have a material effect on the neighbourhood. Whether planning permission for a change of use is required is a matter of scale – for instance, running a typing services company from home probably would not require planning permission, while running a masseuse/physiotherapy business would. However, the General Development Order allows changes of use within classes of property use, for example changing a bank into an insurance office would not require permission because both lay within the same class. The use categories are:

    Class A1:   General non-food shops.
    Class A2:   Professional services and financial.
    Class A3:   Premises where food and drink is sold.
    Class B1:   Businesses and offices.
    Class B2:   General industrial.
    Class C1:   Hotels and hostels.
    Class C3:   Dwelling houses.
    Class D2:   Assembly and leisure.

But if the insurance office (A2) were to be turned into a burger bar (A3), then planning permission would be required.

Part 4 Temporary buildings

Temporary buildings that are not connected to the main building are allowed without specific planning permission. For example, if your rugby club is having work done on its stand or clubhouse, you can build a portable cabin to serve as store or site office, provided it is removed at the end of the job. However, the same building would need planning permission if it were to serve as a tearoom for the committee men at half-time.

It looks as if my development needs planning permission; what do I do?

The first thing to suggest is that you go and have a chat, either face to face or over the telephone, with the local authority planning department. Far from being 'jobsworths', most planners are only too pleased to help you with your enquiry – indeed, they may tell you that your proposed development doesn't need planning permission at all. They will be able to give you informal, off-the-record guidance on how to submit your plan. It goes without saying that just like homework, tidy, well-presented and researched planning applications get better treatment than over-elaborate ones. So do your homework properly, and present your application simply. The key word is KISS – or Keep It Simple, Stupid! Collect the forms from the council office, submit them and pay the relevant fee to your local planning authority. Once these have been submitted along with the plans and an ownership certificate – which states you are the owner or are making the application with the owner's consent – the application will be dealt with.

I've got nosy neighbours. Do other people get to hear about my planning application?

If your neighbour decided to convert his home into a funeral parlour, you would probably want to know about it before the first hearse draws up in the street. Local authorities have a planning register where all planning applications are placed, and which is open for all members of the public to inspect. In addition, a site notice might also publicise your planning application, and controversial applications (for example those with a significant environmental impact) will often be advertised in the local paper, so that everyone affected by a planning application is deemed to have been notified about it before councillors discuss the matter.

Can they object to my planning application?

Anyone can register an objection to a planning application, from the man whose garden will be overlooked by your two-storey extension, to the mad battleaxe in No. 24 who never talks to anyone and keeps all those cats. If neighbours want to object to your planning application, they have 21 days to register an objection if they saw a site display notice or if the application was advertised in a newspaper. These objections will be placed before the planning committee when they meet to discuss the application. The objectors will not be allowed to appear in person to argue their case. Planning officers are experienced professionals, able to give sufficient weight to those objections that have serious merit, and those which are downright malicious or unreasonable and which should not be taken seriously.

How long will it take to decide my application?

Planning applications must be considered within eight weeks of being submitted, and the clock starts once you have brought in the papers and paid the fees.

What decisions can the council planning committee reach?

The planning committee can decide to approve or reject your planning application. If permission is granted, the council can still impose conditions on the development; these can be wide-ranging and either very general or very specific – in conservation areas it might even outline the slate with which you need to cover your roof. Even if the conditions are harsh – or appear to be harsh – you might still be able to reach a compromise with the planning officers which you – and they – can live with. Once planning permission has been granted, it is valid for five years from the date it was granted, so you have until then to complete the project. However, there is some discretion for local authorities to extend this; otherwise you will have to apply for planning permission all over again. If your application has been refused, reasons must be given in writing. These will be helpful in determining how you need to amend your application to get it through the second time around.

My application has been turned down; what can I do?

The first step is to get advice. Were your plans turned down because they were flawed or because of a councillor's whim? It might be wise to seek guidance from the planning officers about ways you can spruce up your application and try again. If you fail a second time, you have no option but to appeal to the Secretary of State for the Environment (or the Welsh Office or Scottish Office for those outside England). You have six months to lodge an appeal against a local authority planning decision, and will have to give reasons why you are appealing along with any evidence you are going to rely on. A planning inspector will be appointed to review your application, and he can ask for additional evidence before hearing the case at a public inquiry. The procedure of inquiries is informal, and inspectors can hear evidence and objections from pretty much anyone they feel can offer some insight into the application. An inspector can uphold the council's decision or overturn it and grant you planning permission. If you were granted planning permission, but appealed against some of the conditions that were imposed, remember that the inspector can impose more stringent conditions if he thinks fit. Planning appeals can be time-consuming and expensive, and if your argument is complicated, you may need professional help to guide you through. But remember that the expert advising you on the strength of your case has a vested interest in your appeal if he will be getting paid to represent you. So perhaps an outsider's advice would be valid. A third party who is not so closely involved may see what you cannot – that the council was right to turn your application down. Ask someone that you respect and trust to give you good advice as to what they think are the merits of your application. They might not give you the answer you want to hear right now, but it could be the answer you need to hear in the long run.

My planning application was turned down; what if I go ahead anyway?

You ignore planning decisions of councils at your peril. It would be bad enough if you built something and when questioned by council officers, said: 'I didn't know I needed planning permission!' If your appeal has been rejected and you go ahead anyway, then you are laying yourself open for attack – and for the full weight of planning law to come down on your head. Local authorities can issue enforcement notices against you if your development is a building, a change of use to a house from some other use, or a failure to comply with a prohibition order. They have four years to issue the notice, so if you built a large garage three years ago and the council found out last week, then you're in trouble. An enforcement notice will contain details of the alleged breach, what steps must be taken to remedy the breach by making the development comply with the planning conditions or by restoring the land to its original condition, and what the timescale for compliance is. In the worst-case scenario, the enforcement notice could require you to demolish your unauthorised house or building.

If you decide to really flout the law and fail to comply with the enforcement notice, you can face criminal charges, with the prospect of an unlimited fine at a Crown Court.

What are building regulations?

Building regulations are a separate issue to planning permission, and exist to ensure your property is structurally sound. Building regulations apply alongside planning permission, but most of the developments that do not require planning permission do have building regulations that have to be complied with. They cover things such as chimneys, ventilation, water provision, drainage, structural stability and waste disposal. They can be very confusing. But a builder or architect will be fully conversant with them and can lead you through the maze.

Normally, what happens is that when your builder gives details of the development to the district surveyor, plans and a list of building materials are specified. The building regulations specify what materials can be used in different jobs such as the type of brickwork. If the surveyor wants you to use different materials, he or she must give written reasons for his objections. Normally a compromise can be reached, but in the worst-case scenario you can appeal. Building inspectors will check the work as it progresses to ensure it meets the standards, and they have the power to halt work, or have sections that they are not happy with knocked down.

If you breach building regulations you could find yourself in the same boat as breaching planning regulations, in contravention of the criminal law. However, building regulations allow for a retrospective approval (i.e. after the work has been done) of work contrary to building regulations, provided you have acted in good faith and in ignorance of building regulations (i.e. you did not deliberately flout them). Additionally, the building must have been built to a high enough standard, and sufficiently good materials must have been used to construct it.

Section 4.10 Long leaseholds

Many homeowners don't actually 'own' their homes. For instance, if you live in a block of flats or in one of the smarter waterside developments springing up across the country, you almost certainly have a leasehold property. This means that if you were the original purchaser of the lease, then you have bought the lease to the flat for a period of years (leases normally run for 99 years) after which the property reverts back to the owner (who is often the developer). People can get a bit worried about leasehold properties, but while it is true that in the strictest legal sense you never own your property, if you buy on a long lease you are really in exactly the same position as if you bought the freehold.

What is the history of leaseholds?

The origin of leaseholds derived from the feudal system, under which all land was owned by the Crown. After the Normal conquest, lords and barons were granted estates as 'feudal tenants' of the king. These grants of land, in return for services performed, then were used to create lesser estates as the lords and barons rewarded those knights and others that performed services for them to create the pyramidical feudal systems. At the top was the king who held the land absolutely as the owner. Beneath him were his tenants in chief – the chief barons and bishops. Then came the mesne lords (or middle ranking nobility) and lesser knights and freeholders. At the bottom of the pile came the villeins and serfs, the peasant tenants. The barons, bishops, mesne lords, knights and freeholders held their lands on terms of **free tenure**, performing services such as providing knights to the king, providing crops and animals, providing personal services to a noble or the king or performing religious service. The services they were required to perform were fixed, and once performed, the tenant had the use of the land to himself to use as he wanted. Over centuries these forms of land 'ownership' became known as 'freeholds'. The peasants and villeins held their land on **unfree tenure**, and were under the control and direction of their lord. The services they had to perform were not so clearly defined or limited. They held land because of an entry on the manorial roll, known as copyholders, which gave them their rights to the land. Copyholding was abolished in the 1920s and the land became freehold. When land law was reformed in a series of Acts of Parliament in 1925, two forms of landownership were created: the estate in fee simple absolute in possession (which, cutting through the legal jargon, means you own the land and its freehold) and the estate for a term of years absolute (which, cutting though the jargon again, is an interest in land for a defined length of time, which is a lease). Other interests in land, such as licences were equitable interests, though with the fusion of common law and equity these are as valid as legal interests. So in leasehold properties today, the owner owns the land, and the tenant owns the interest in it for a fixed term of years.

How are leaseholds important in flat developments?

The complex issue of restrictive covenants (see **Covenants and easements**) between neighbours and the realities of communal living in apartment blocks have contributed to the spread of leasehold properties. It's one thing to live alone in the middle of nowhere and let your home go to rack and ruin, with damp patches and poor plumbing. Apartment blocks and developments are communal, however, so if a top floor occupant's bath leaks regularly, the effects will be felt by everyone living underneath. Accidents can happen, and the first time the water runs down you can accept it (probably) but if it soon becomes apparent that the leak is being caused by faulty maintenance or shoddy repairs, something has to be done. But in English law at present, the only landownership to allow a covenant that enforces mutual repairing obligations is a leasehold. Similarly, the owner of the freehold can enforce rights against the leaseholders.

I'm a long leaseholder – I want to buy. Can I?

The weakness of long leaseholds for many is the 'you never get to own it' argument – that after a period of time, when the lease expires, ownership reverts to the owner of the freehold. Another drawback is that as the lease continues, in the last few years the lease becomes increasingly difficult to sell and the property value will undoubtedly fall. But two Acts of Parliament changed that: the Leasehold Reform Act 1967 and the Leasehold Reform, Housing and Urban Development Act 1993.

I want to buy the freehold on my house

The Leasehold Reform Act 1967 allows homeowners with long leases on houses to buy the freehold or extend the leasehold by up to 50 years. There is a number of qualifications:

1. You must have lived in the same house for the past three years.
2. The lease must be a long lease – a long lease is defined as one originally granted for more than 21 years. (This doesn't mean that you have to be the one granted it for 21 years, so if you buy a leasehold from someone, you can still buy the freehold even if there are only eight years left on the lease.)
3. Your property must be a house – this means that the leasehold you 'own' goes all the way up to the sky and to the ground (no-one lives above you or below you in their own property). If a property is divided into horizontal layers, flats are created; but if a large house is divided vertically into separate properties houses are created.
4. If you qualify to buy or extend your house, you cannot be denied that, unless the freeholder is a public body with an identifiable need to develop the property within the next 10 years. Similarly if the freeholder acquired the property before 1966 and can show a greater need to the property than you, they can avoid selling the freehold to you.

How much will it cost to buy the freehold?

The key issue in valuing the freehold is to determine how much the property would be worth with a tenant in possession. Obviously, if the lease only has a few years to run, the leaseholder will get a bargain. Leaseholders buying the freehold will take the freeholder's costs and expenses, namely legal and professional fees.

I want to buy the freehold on my flat

For flat-owners, the Leasehold Reform, Housing and Urban Development Act 1993 granted long leaseholders the right to buy the freehold of their apartment block. This happens if they buy as a group, and will take effect even if the freeholder does not want to sell up. However, if you can't get all your fellow tenants to buy out their freehold, you can still extend your lease for another 90 years on top of your existing lease. In order to extend your lease, or buy the freeholder out with your fellow leaseholders, the original lease must have been granted for more than 21 years (though not necessarily to you) and at a 'low rent'. What is a low rent is calculated thus:

1. If the lease was granted before April 1 1963, the first year's ground rent must have been no more than two-thirds of the letting value of your flat at the beginning of that year.
2. If the lease was granted on or between April 1 1963 and March 31 1990, the first year's ground rent must have been no more than two-thirds of the rateable value of your flat at the beginning of the year. If the flat did not have a rateable value at the commencement of the lease or before April 1 1990, the first year's ground rent must not have been more than £250 (£1,000 in London).
3. If the lease was granted on or after April 1 1990, the first year's ground rent must not have been more than £250 (£1,000 in London).

Surveyors will be able to tell you what letting values applied, while the local authority can advise on rateable values. In addition, for a group purchase, at least 50 per cent of the tenants must have lived in the flats for the last 12 months as their main homes, or at least a total of three years out of the last ten. To extend your lease, you will have needed to live in the flat for the last three years or a total of three years out of the last ten. However, if more that 10 per cent of the building is used for non-residential use (e.g. retail or office space), or if fewer than two thirds of the tenants qualify to buy their leasehold, or if the property only consists of two flats, then you cannot buy the freehold. Other grounds that disbar a property from enfranchisement (a group purchase by tenants) or lease renewal are:

*   The building is on some areas of National Trust land.
*   The building is within the precincts of a cathedral.
*   The building has been given a conditional exemption from Inheritance Tax.
*   The building has been converted to four or fewer flats, and the freeholder has lived on the property for the past 12 months as his/her main residence (this is not a barrier to renewal of your lease).
*   The building is owned by the Crown.

How much will it cost me?

There is no set formula. A number of factors will have to be taken into account in reaching agreement on price:

- How much will the landlord be compensated?
- What is the open market value? In the case of enfranchisement, this will be the value of the interests held by all the tenants; in the case of renewing your lease, this will be the reduction in value of the landlord's interest in your flat.
- The marriage value – the additional value brought about when leasehold and freehold interests in property are married together – i.e. they both vest in one person or group.

Section 4.11 Covenants and easements

What is a covenant?

A covenant is effectively an agreement between two people over the way that they enjoy their respective properties. However, it is drafted in such a way that it passes to subsequent owners of the properties. Examples of covenants are those which restrict hedge heights, or prevent the erection of satellite dishes. Usually covenants are written into property deeds, so purchasers are aware of any restrictions on their land before they commit to a sale.

Are covenants always restrictive?

Most covenants are restrictive in nature, and say 'you are not allowed to do …', as seen in the above examples. However, covenants can also be used to compel behaviour, for example a covenant that requires you to empty your rubbish.

What if I buy the land but don't want to be bound by the covenant?

Tough! You can question the validity of the covenant in a court, but the general rule is that covenants bind new owners just as much as the original owner. So it is safest to assume you will be bound. However, the issue of enforcement means that though you may be bound by the covenant, if no-one takes action against you to enforce the covenant you will get away with it. For example, suppose you buy a new house on a new development that states that no hedges will be higher than 5 feet tall, and you plant Leylandii. They shoot up to 7 feet, but if none of your neighbours complains or takes legal action, the covenant remains unenforced. For a covenant to be enforceable it must 'touch and concern' the land in question – if it does, it can pass as a legal and an equitable right. If you breach a covenant, your neighbour can seek damages for breach of the legal right, and in equity seek specific performance, asking the court to force you to comply with the covenant.

What is an easement?

An easement is a right enjoyed by one landowner over the land of another. Rights to light, rights of way, rights of water and rights of support are all easements. The landowner enjoying the benefit of the easement has the dominant tenement, while the land over which the right is exercised is called the servient tenement. Easements can be positive, giving a right to the owner of the dominant tenement – a right to cut turf, a right to extract water – or negative, imposing a restriction on the owner of the servient tenement – for example, restrictions on using a right of way. Easements cannot compel the owner of servient land to do anything except keep a wall or fence in good repair – the effect on the servient land must only be prohibitive. For an easement to exist, there must be dominant and servient land, owned by different people, and the easement must relate to the 'reasonable enjoyment' of the land, not the people on it. What constitutes reasonable enjoyment is a matter of debate, but it seems to be the case that easements have a more permanent nature and are not merely transitory.

How are easements created?

Easements arise in four ways:

- By Act of Parliament.
- By implied grant. For example, if you sell a plot of land which you had used to gain access to your farm, the land may be sold with an implied right of way.
- By express grant, when you buy an easement from your neighbour.
- By prescription, where a right is exercised by owners of dominant land over servient land without challenge or interruption for 20 years.

If a dispute over an easement arises with a neighbour, try to solve the matter peacefully and amicably, by looking at the land deeds and talking the matter through. The worst-case scenario is where both you and your neighbour look to have a good case – then the lurch to legal action before the Lands Tribunal is almost inevitable, with all the added costs and uncertainty that that involves. The only people sure to win are the lawyers, so it may well be in both your interests to reach a compromise.

Chapter 5
You and the police

Section 5.1 Powers of the police

Since the beginning of the nineteenth century, there have been police forces in Britain. In 1829, Home Secretary Robert Peel set up the Metropolitan Police, and towns and shires were able to establish their own forces since the Town Police Clauses Act 1847. Police officers are ordinary members of the public, but with specific powers of arrest and search granted them by the law.

I'm walking along the street. Can the police stop and search me?

The police are entitled to stop and question anyone they suspect might have committed a crime, or can help them with information about whether a crime has been committed. However, you are not obliged to answer, or even give them your name and address. But, if the police suspect you have committed or attempted to commit a crime, they can arrest you. Normally a warrant would be required, but the police can arrest you without a warrant if they suspect you of committing an offence punishable by five years' imprisonment for a first offence (for instance, theft), taking a car or van without the owner's permission, going equipped for theft, customs offences or going equipped to steal. But  that's not all. Police can arrest you if they suspect you have committed or attempted to commit (or are committing or attempting to commit) any offence at all, provided the 'general arrest conditions' laid down in the Police and Criminal Evidence Act 1984 apply:

- The police officer does not know your name and cannot readily find it.
- The police officer has reasonable grounds to not to believe the name you have given.
- The police officer does not know your address, or has reasonable grounds not to believe the address you have given.
- Arresting you is necessary to prevent you injuring someone, damaging property or blocking the highway.
- Arresting you is necessary to protect a child or someone vulnerable.

A police officer can search you on the street if there are reasonable grounds to suspect you are carrying something suspicious. And the police have other powers of arrest, for example to prevent a breach of the peace.

How does an arrest warrant work?

If the police need a warrant to arrest you they will have to apply to a magistrate, giving a written statement outlining the details of the alleged offence, and reasons why they need a warrant. If the magistrate decides to issue a warrant, the police can arrest you, as the person named in the warrant, at any time of the day or night. They don't need to have the warrant with them when they arrest you, though this is usual; however, you are entitled to see the warrant if you ask, so the police must show you. If you think the warrant is incorrect, or does not refer to you, you can refuse to be arrested; if you are right that the warrant is incorrect and refuse to be arrested, you will be able to sue the police for false imprisonment. However, if the warrant is correct and you are properly arrested but subsequently released without charge, you cannot sue the police, provided they kept you in custody legally and they did not hold you for an unreasonable length of time after deciding not to charge you.

What happens if I am arrested?

If you are arrested, you must be told you are under arrest as soon as you are detained, or as soon as practicable afterwards. It doesn't matter whether you were arrested climbing through a window with the Mona Lisa rolled up under your arm – you must be told you have been arrested. You must also be told why you have been arrested – and again, it doesn't matter whether you were arrested coming through the window with a swag bag on your shoulder. The explanation need not be complete or technical, but must be informative – for instance it is enough to say you have been arrested for assaulting Joe Bloggs, without specifying whether you will be charged with committing grievous bodily harm.

Can the police use force to arrest me?

The police are entitled to use 'reasonable force' to detain you, and use handcuffs if they think you might try to escape, or hurt someone or yourself. If they use excessive force, you might be able to sue them for assault at a later date. What counts as reasonable force depends on the circumstances; if you are walking down the street, a hand on your shoulder is enough, while if you are swinging your arms and legs about, or using a weapon to resist arrest, it might be reasonable for the police to use CS gas spray or batons to subdue you. Remember too that you could be charged with resisting arrest.

If I am arrested, do the police have to caution me?

You should be cautioned if you are suspected of an offence or arrested for an offence unless it is not practical for the police to do so because of your condition or behaviour at the time (you are drunk or fighting). The wording of the caution is:

'You do not have to say anything, but it may harm your defence if you do not mention, when questioned, something which you later rely on in court. Anything you do say may be given in evidence.'

Minor deviations do not constitute a breach of this requirement provided that the essence of the caution is maintained. It is also important to note that you should be cautioned as soon as you are suspected of an offence.

What if police do not arrest me, but want me to 'come down the station'?

The police might ask you to come down to the station to answer a few questions. This is what the media often refers to as 'helping the police with their enquiries'. You do not have to agree, though it may be that they will arrest you if you don't. But if you have gone to the station of your own free will, you can leave at any time provided you have not been arrested while you are there.

If the police try to stop you leaving the station without arresting you, you can sue them for false imprisonment (and assault and battery, if they use force).

I have been arrested. What happens now?

Once you have arrived at the station, either under arrest or voluntarily, you must be told of your rights. They are:

- That you can tell someone you have been arrested and where you have been detained.
- That you may consult a solicitor.
- That you may see the official codes of practice on detention, searches and identification parades.

However, if you are drunk, ill or are behaving in such a way that it would not be practicable to be informed of your rights, this may not happen. Similarly, if you are a juvenile and considered incapable of understanding your rights, you will not be told of them. These codes of practice cover interview procedures and cover your rights including your 'right to silence', and the limits on that right. In addition, the police must keep a custody record, which details every decision taken about your detention at the station including times of interview, decisions to grant bail or release, etc. Once you have been released, you are entitled to see a copy of your custody record. If you have been arrested, the police have a right to search you – and this can mean a strip search. This can only be carried out by an officer of the same sex as you, and only the outer layers of clothing can be removed, unless the police think it is necessary to remove items you will not be allowed to keep while under arrest – for example knives.

An 'intimate body search', which involves a search of body orifices, can also be carried out; but on this occasion the search is carried out by a doctor or nurse, or by a police officer if on the authority of a senior police officer – but only to search for drugs or weapons. You can't carry out an intimate body search to try and locate stolen diamonds, for instance.

Under the Police and Criminal Evidence Act 1984, police are obliged to review your detention regularly, to decide whether to continue holding you. These reviews take place after six, 15 and 24 hours after the detention started. Generally, you should not be held for more than 24 hours without being charged, but this period can be extended to 36 hours on the authorisation of a senior police officer if the allegation is serious.

If the police want to hold you longer than 36 hours, they will need a magistrate to authorise the continued detention. This will allow you to be held for up to four days (or 96 hours).

The police want to interview me about an allegation. Do I need a solicitor?

If the police want to interview you about a criminal offence, either at a police station or your own home, it is wise to ask for a solicitor (if you have not already done so after being notified of your rights if you have been arrested). Until then, it is best to say nothing. You are entitled to talk to a solicitor privately before answering any questions relating to the enquiry. You do not have to provide your own solicitor. Every police station can put you in touch with a 'duty solicitor', who can be contacted by telephone and asked to come to the police station to represent you, as would your own solicitor. A duty solicitor is paid for by the state and is available to anyone regardless of age, income or capital. Just as when you were arrested, you are under no obligation to answer any questions put to you by the police and they will 'caution you' to this effect:

> 'You do not have to say anything, but it may harm your defence if you do not mention now, something which you later rely on in court. Anything you do say may be given in evidence.'

However, the new caution means that although you still do not have to say anything, it may harm your defence if you do not say something when questioned at the police station, that you later rely on in court for your defence. For example: if you are arrested by the police after being involved in a fight with a night club bouncer, and do not tell the police when questioned that the bouncer hit you first and you only defended yourself, then if your case comes to court the court may conclude that you are making it up because you did not tell the police.

Interviews with the police are taped, and anything you say in interview after been cautioned will be recorded or taken down in writing and may be used by the police against you later. Any comments you make to the police at this time, however trivial they may seem, could be extremely damaging and difficult to disprove later. Any tape-recorded interviews can be played in court, so do not say anything in the interview that you would not say if you were actually in court. So if you deny saying something at interview, the police can simply play the tape of your interview in court.

Can the police make me wait for legal help?

Only in some serious cases can the police hold you and restrict your access to a solicitor, and then only if the superintendent agrees. The longest you can be made to wait before speaking to a solicitor is thirty-six hours after arriving at the police station. (This time is extended to forty-eight hours in cases or terrorism, and can be longer if special anti-terrorism laws are in force).

They have finished interviewing me; what happens next?

After you have been interviewed, the police will do one of the following:

- They take no further action. You will be released and the matter is finished with. You will not have a criminal record.
- You are bailed to return. If you are bailed you will be given a date to return to the police station, approximately six weeks later. The police now have the powers to attach conditions to your bail such as a curfew. If you do not return, a warrant can be issued for your arrest. When you return, your case may be dropped, you may be cautioned or your may be charged. If you are charged, you will be given a date to appear at court.
- Young offenders (or the parents) may be informally warned in minor cases; in more serious cases, if the young person has no previous criminal record and is prepared to admit his guilt, the youth may be given a formal reprimand or final warning. This procedure took the place of the old 'police caution' and is the procedure which dealt with Prime Minister Tony Blair's son, after he was found drunk in a London street.
- If there is sufficient evidence and the crime is serious, you may be charged at once and brought before the first available court. This must be the following day, unless the next day is a Sunday, Christmas Day or Good Friday. Once you have been charged, the police will decide whether you will be bailed with conditions to appear before the magistrates, or held in custody.

Can I be held in custody at a police station?

If the police feel the offence you are accused of committing is so serious that you may be a risk to the public if you are given bail, you may be held overnight or over the weekend and taken to the magistrates' court on the following day or on the next day the court is open. The court will then decide whether to bail you or remand you into custody or local authority accommodation. In the cases of young people who are detained overnight, a social worker will try to find a secure placement for them to stay the night.

Can the police enter my house?

The police are only entitled to enter your house*:

- If they have a search warrant.
- To arrest someone they have an arrest warrant for.
- If they suspect someone at the house has committed an arrestable offence or other serious offences.
- To recapture someone that has escaped from custody.
- To save someone from serious injury or death or prevent damage to your house.
- To prevent a breach of the peace.
- To search your house for evidence if you have been arrested.

If the police have one of these reasons to enter your house, they can use reasonable force to gain access, for instance breaking a window if all the doors were locked and barred. If you try to prevent the police entering, you can be arrested and charged with obstruction. If the police do not have one of the above grounds, then they can only come into your home with your permission. And if you give permission, you can change your mind at any time while they are there and they must stop searching and leave at once (giving them a reasonable time to leave the premises). Before they carry out a search, the police must:

- Tell you why they want to search your house.
- Give you a copy of the warrant if they have one and information about your rights.
- Allow you to get a witness, unless prior warning would hinder the search.

The warrant must state the exact address and premises to be searched – if it does not, you are entitled to refuse entry, and can refuse entry to any premises not specifically mentioned in the warrant, an outbuilding or separate flat in your home, for instance. It must also state which laws the search is authorised under, and what articles (if any) the police are empowered to seize and take with them. After the search the police must leave a copy of the warrant, which you should check to make sure it is signed and dated. It is important that you know that searches should be carried out with the minimum disruption to your house. The police must not leave your house unlocked if you are not there.

*In addition to these reasons, the police can search your house if a senior police officer – a superintendent or above – authorises a search on one of four grounds:

- Your house is occupied by someone convicted within the last five years of handling stolen goods or any other offence of dishonesty that is punishable by a jail term.
- The police believe there are explosives in your house that may cause immediate damage or injury.
- The police believe immediate action is needed to look for evidence of terrorism.
- The police believe an offence has been committed contrary to the Official Secrets Act 1911.

I'm out in my car, and the police stop me. Can they do that?

The police have wide powers to prevent motoring offences, in many ways even wider than those they enjoy on pavements! If police officers suspect someone has committed a serious offence, or if someone has witnessed one who may be in a vehicle in the area, they can impose road checks on any or all vehicles in the area. But this requires the written authority of at least a superintendent. In addition, police forces from time to time carry out 'crackdowns', stopping vehicles to check for bald tyres or the like. The most well-known (and regular) crackdown is the annual Christmas drink-drive campaign. A driver must stop and answer questions if asked to do so, but if you want to question the reason you were stopped later, the police must provide you with a written statement giving the reason you were stopped. Police officers can demand to know the name and address of anyone driving a motor car, van, lorry or motorbike on a public road, whether an offence is suspected of being committed or not. The can demand to see your driving licence, insurance certificate and MOT certificate (if your vehicle requires one) or order you to produce these documents at a police station of your choice within five days if you do not have them with you at the time. If you refuse to answer questions or produce your documents, you can be fined.

If a police officer gives me traffic directions, do I have to obey them?

It is an offence to ignore traffic directions given by a police officer in uniform or a traffic warden.

When can the police arrest me if I'm out in my car?

You can be arrested if the police suspect you of any of the following offences:

- Causing death by reckless driving.
- Being unfit to drive through drink or drugs.
- Taking a vehicle without permission.
- Obstructing the highway.
- Refusing to take a breathalyser test.
- Failing to take a breathalyser test.
- Refusing to provide your name and address if committing an offence.
- Driving while disqualified.

A police officer has asked me for help; do I have to help?

There is no general duty to help the police, so if you see a police officer being attacked you do not have a legal obligation to come to his/her aid, and if you do not help you are not guilty of any criminal offence. But, if a police officer asks for your assistance, it is an offence not to do so, and if you are prosecuted you could be fined or imprisoned. You may have a defence if you can show that you were not fit to help out – because you were ill or disabled, for example. However, to say 'I would have been no help, there were too many of them' is not enough to mount a defence to the charge of 'not assisting a police officer'. If you agree to help a policeman – either on his request or voluntarily – and are injured in the process, you might be able to claim compensation under the Criminal Injuries Compensation Scheme. Similarly, there is no legal obligation to volunteer information to the police to help them solve crimes or catch wrongdoers. If you see a crime and don't report it, you are not committing a crime yourself, unless you help the criminal to escape or to avoid prosecution.

I want to complain about a police officer's conduct

Police take complaints against themselves very seriously, and far from wanting to sweep them under the carpet, are very keen to investigate, either internally (for minor complaints) or supervised by the Police Complaints Authority (PCA) for more serious allegations. If you are unhappy with a police officer's behaviour towards you, you should complain directly to the duty inspector at your local station, or write to the chief constable. Any complaint will be recorded and investigated. If the complaint is about a senior officer of the rank of chief superintendent or above, the complaint will go to the local police authority – the body of councillors and magistrates that 'runs' the administration of the force. Otherwise the chief constable will determine whether to deal with the complaint formally or informally. If no criminal or disciplinary charges are involved, and you agree, it is more likely that an informal approach will follow; if this fails, however, a formal investigation follows. If a formal investigation takes place, a senior officer is appointed to investigate, while in the most serious cases, an officer from another force area may be appointed. This is not because any internal investigation might not be above-board, but because the police are keen to show that their disciplinary investigations are open and transparent, and operate fairly towards all complainants. If the complaint involves a senior officer, the police authority decides whether a formal or informal route should be pursued.

What does the Police Complaints Authority do?

The PCA is an independent body set up to supervise the investigation of complaints against police forces and officers. It oversees the investigation of complaints and action taken as a result of the investigations. Complaints alleging involvements in deaths or incidents involving serious injuries are referred to it as a matter of course before investigation, and in some cases the PCA will require a complaint to be referred to it. The PCA can require an investigation to report direct to it, otherwise investigations are referred to the chief constable of the force involved.

The complaint has been investigated, and a report submitted; what next?

Unless a report on a police officer clearly shows that no criminal offences were committed, it is forwarded to the Director of Public Prosecutions (DPP) for consideration. The chief constable will also notify the DPP if he feels a criminal offence has been committed that should result in charges. The DPP takes the decision whether to prosecute. If no law is broken or a decision taken not to prosecute, the chief constable has to decide whether a disciplinary hearing should follow because force guidelines or regulations have been breached. This decision must be reported to the PCA, whether disciplinary action follows or not; but the PCA can order a disciplinary hearing takes place. Disciplinary hearings are normally conducted by the chief constable, but sometimes by a panel made up of the chief constable and two members of the police authority. If the police officer contests the allegation, you (as complainant) will be called to give evidence. The officer may be legally represented at the hearing; you may not – it is like giving evidence at a criminal court case. If the officer admits a breach of the disciplinary code, or is found guilty, he can face a number of punishments, the most severe being summary dismissal or being required to resign. The officer can appeal to the Home Secretary to have the verdict overturned. New misconduct regulations for the police were issued in 1999.

Section 5.2 Crimes of dishonesty

Crimes of dishonesty are normally thought of as offences against property, and many of the common law rules have been codified in the Theft Act 1968. Offences against property include theft, burglary, fraud and robbery.

What is theft?

Theft is defined as 'dishonestly appropriating property belonging to another with the intention of permanently depriving the other of it' (Section 1, Theft Act 1968). So, if you pick up someone's briefcase in the train and take it home, thinking it is yours, you are not guilty of theft because you did not act dishonestly. In the same way, if you borrow someone's lawnmower without their permission you are not guilty of theft, because you only intended to borrow it. Effectively, a theft takes place if you dishonestly assume the rights of the property's owner even if only on a temporary basis and even if you innocently gain possession of the item – and then act as if you are the owner in disposing, or attempting to dispose, of it. You will not be guilty of theft if you take goods in the honest belief that you have a legal right to them, or that the owner would let you have the goods if he/she knew you were taking them, or that you have taken reasonable steps but have not been able to find out the identity of the owner. If you are convicted of theft, a magistrate can impose a maximum penalty of £5,000 and six months' imprisonment (seven years and unlimited fines at a Crown Court).

What counts as property, in terms of whether it can be stolen?

The Theft Act 1968 defines property as 'money and all other property, real or personal, including things in action and other intangible property'. Things in action are items such as cheques. Apart from obvious things, some less usual things that can be stolen include:

- Body products – such as blood and urine.
- Wild plants – if the whole plant is taken, or parts of it are taken for commercial purposes.
- Wild animals that have been tamed or ordinarily kept in captivity – so animal activists freeing zoo animals would be guilty of theft.
- Patents.
- Copyrights.
- Shares.
- Debts.
- An overdraft facility – the amount of credit you have with a bank can be stolen by someone else.

Courts have found that the following items do not contain property that can be stolen:

- Electricity – but for anyone thinking of rigging their meters, there is an offence of abstracting electricity that can punish you just as effectively.
- Confidential information such as business secrets and exam papers – if someone 'steals' these items from you, however, they can in some cases be treated as property for the purposes of civil law and an injunction can be sought to protect your rights.

What acts can count as theft?

Acts that can be counted as thefts include:

- Swapping the price labels on tins of food in the supermarket, so as to pay a lower price.
- Someone looking after an item who offers to sell it.
- A shop assistant who takes money for an item but does not ring it through the cash register.
- A shop assistant who sells goods at less than the correct price.
- Someone taking items from a store shelf and putting them in a bag or pocket.
- Taking the topsoil from land belonging to someone else.
- Removing rubbish from someone's dustbin.

In all cases, someone has assumed the owner's rights over the property and disposed of them in some way.

What if I take someone's theatre ticket, intending to give it back after the performance?

Things like tickets, cheques and vouchers occupy a special case in law because they have value on two levels. The obvious one is the value of the ticket itself in terms of the paper it cost to manufacture, but the other is the value contained in the ticket itself – the money you paid for it. If you get it back after the performance it is effectively worthless. By retaining the ticket until after the performance you have 'borrowed' the ticket for a period of time, which means that you might as well have kept the ticket – it has no value now. And that's theft!

What if I find abandoned property. Does taking that amount to theft?

For a theft to take place, you must take property belonging to someone else, so if it has been genuinely abandoned then you are not guilty of theft. Similarly if you honestly believe that something has been abandoned, you cannot be guilty of theft. However, there is an offence of stealing by finding, if you know that someone is trying to recover their lost property that you have acquired. Council dustmen who remove items that householders or businesses have discarded in their bins are guilty of theft because the property belongs to the local authority once the bin has gone out and is collected; they are assuming the rights of ownership over property that is not theirs.

So taking a car for joyriding is not theft?

While stealing a car to sell on, for example in car ringing, or for keeping for your own use is theft, taking someone else's parked car for a 'burn' around the countryside is not theft according to the definition of the crime. For this reason, an offence of 'taking without the owner's consent' has been created. Taking a motor vehicle without the owner's consent is also known as taking and driving away or TWOC-ing. (See **Motoring offences**).

My bank has accidentally paid money into my account that does not belong to me. Can I spend it?

You can certainly spend it, but you will equally certainly have to pay the money back when the bank finds out its error. If you acted dishonestly to get the money paid into your account you will be guilty of theft. Courts have found that if companies accidentally pay their staff too much, they will be able to recover the money, and if employees act dishonestly to prevent the money being recovered – by withdrawing the money and closing the account, for example, they can be charged with theft. However, if you obtain something in good faith and later it is discovered that it was stolen, you have a defence against theft, for instance if you buy some motor vehicle parts from a 'write-off vehicle' as spares and later discover that they were in fact stolen. But if you then sold on the spares once you knew them to be stolen, even though you would not have been guilty of theft by keeping them, selling them on knowing them to be stolen but not informing the buyer would mean that you could be prosecuted for obtaining the purchase price by deception.

What if I take property with the owner's consent? Can that amount to theft?

Under normal circumstances, taking something with the owner's consent means you are not guilty of theft, but there are occasions when you can be guilty. For example, a taxi driver picks up a foreign visitor to this country and takes them to a destination, for which the fare is only a few pounds. But the visitor does not understand English currency and holds open his wallet, and the taxi driver removes – with the owner's apparent consent – a £20 note. The House of Lords has held that this constitutes a case of theft (which is really open to debate). However, it is definitely a case of obtaining money by deception, and perhaps that would have been a better charge to prosecute on.

My aunt, who is frankly getting a bit mentally frail, gives me a gift of money. Is that theft?

It all depends on her state of mind: if she decides to make a valid gift to you, then that should be sufficient. For example, in one case a maid who received gifts of large sums of cash from her employer (whose mind was going) was cleared of theft on that basis. However, in a similar case where two owners of a care home received gifts from one of their charges, the courts decided that the owners were guilty of theft; because of her confused state, the lady could not give unconfused and proper consent and the court felt that the care home owners had dishonestly taken advantage of her frailty.

'Bilking'

This lovely word means making off with goods without paying for them, and is an offence under the Theft Act 1968. Usually it involves 'doing a runner' from an Indian takeaway, or failing to pay after filling a car with petrol. If you have not actually left the premises – or the garage forecourt – it would be difficult to establish that you intended to make off without paying. Leaving an inadequate amount of money on the restaurant table and walking out counts as bilking, as does using foreign currency. However, if you have filled up your tank of petrol and realised you had not brought your wallet and drove off to get it, then you would not be guilty – just as in the case of theft, there must be an intention to permanently avoid paying.

What is burglary?

The definition of burglary is entering a building, or part of a building, or a vehicle, with people in it, or a boat, as a trespasser with intent to steal, commit rape, commit an act of grievous bodily harm, or commit criminal damage. Similarly, if someone enters as a trespasser, and then decides to commit one of the acts mentioned above then they would be guilty of burglary. If you are convicted of burglary, the maximum penalty a magistrate can impose is six months and impose a £5,000 fine (14 years and unlimited fine at a Crown Court).

How much of my body has to 'enter' the building before I am classed as trespassing?

Common law rules apply, as no definition of 'entering' is given in the Theft Act. This means that if any part of your body goes into a building, or any part of a tool is inserted into a door or window frame or other part of the structure to gain admission, then you are deemed to have entered it.

What if I am invited in?

If you are invited in, and then do anything that would violate the conditions on which you were allowed in – and form an intention to commit theft, criminal damage, grievous bodily harm or rape would certainly violate those conditions – then you have become a trespasser. In one strange case, a naked man climbed onto a windowsill with the intention of getting into a woman's bedroom to rape her; the woman woke up, and half asleep, thought the man was her boyfriend and invited him in. The couple made love, and then the woman discovered her mistake. The courts decided that, despite having gone with the intention of committing rape, he was invited in (admittedly under the mistaken belief that he was the boyfriend), and had not committed burglary because he had not entered as a trespasser, but as a guest. The judges reached this decision with reluctance, as it appeared the man had indeed gone there with the intention of committing rape, but he had not entered the premises as a trespasser, and sadly, the woman's mistaken identity did not change that fact. In another case, two men went into the house of one of their parents and stole two televisions; it was decided that they had committed burglary because the implied permission to enter lasted only as long as a person makes 'an ordinary and reasonable use' of the property. Once the men had gone beyond that permission expired and they became trespassers, and then burglars once they removed the TVs.

What is the difference between theft and 'obtaining property by deception'?

If you steal something, you are taking goods dishonestly without the owner's consent; in contrast, here the owner actually hands the goods over to you because of your fraud. The actual obtaining of the goods must be induced by the deception. However, if your action does not deceive the other person then there is no offence. For there to be a deception, the other person would not have provided you with the property, but for your actions.

A deception can be through words or conduct, including concealing something from the person you are trying to deceive. For example, concealing defects would amount to conduct. A perfect example of obtaining property by deception would be to go into a restaurant, order the meal and then refuse to pay in the following circumstances. By going into the restaurant and ordering the meal, you are representing yourself as being prepared to pay for your dinner. If you went into the restaurant intending to pay for your meal, but discovered you had left your wallet at home, in itself this would not constitute 'obtaining property by deception'. But if having learned that you left your wallet at home, you remained in the restaurant, said nothing and continued with your meal, you are continuing to represent yourself as a bona fide customer, and hence would be guilty. In addition, the deception must be 'deliberate or reckless' as well as being dishonest. There is a separate offence of obtaining a pecuniary advantage by deception, which involves dishonestly obtaining things such as:

- An overdraft
- An insurance policy

- A job
- Improved terms for any of the above

So a teacher who was paid a basic salary would be guilty of obtaining a pecuniary advantage by deception if he claimed an additional allowance for graduate teachers, even though he only had a basic teaching certificate. In addition, Section 1 of the Theft Act 1978 creates the offence of obtaining services by deception, where a service is defined as a benefit someone would be willing to pay for. Section 2 of the 1978 Act creates the offence of evading liability by deception, for example by applying for goods on credit with no intention of paying for them.

I'm worried because I have written some cheques that have bounced...

If you write a cheque, there is an implied representation that the cheque will be honoured by your bank when it is presented. If you use a cheque card to guarantee your payment, you are representing not only that the bank will meet the cheque but that you are authorised to use a cheque card. The law seems to be that:

- If you write a cheque unsupported by a cheque card for some books, let us say, knowing there are insufficient funds in your account to cover the transaction, you would be guilty of obtaining property by deception from the bookseller.
- If you write a cheque supported by a cheque card for the books, knowing there are insufficient funds in your account to cover the transaction, you would be guilty of obtaining property by deception from the bookseller, and additionally, guilty of obtaining a pecuniary advantage by deception from your bank (because the bank is contractually bound by the use of the cheque guarantee card to honour your cheque).

Obviously, if you write cheques on someone else's account, forging their signature, then you are obtaining goods or services by deception, in that you have represented yourself as the person entitled to draw the cheque. For a while, there was a loophole in the law that meant that if you obtained a mortgage by giving false information, the transfer of money between banks did not constitute obtaining property by deception. However, parliament passed the Theft (Amendment) Act 1996 which creates the offence of obtaining a money transfer by deception.

What is robbery?

A simple definition of robbery is theft with violence or use of force, or threat of violence or use of force. If people are subjected to force and put in fear of their safety while you are carrying out a theft, then it may be classed as a robbery. The threat of violence need not be against the owner of the property – 'Hand over the gold or the wife gets it!' would be a robbery. But the threat of violence or act of violence must be made solely to allow the theft to take place – it must be used to encourage the victims to hand over their property. For this reason, the violent acts must be carried out or threatened before the theft takes place; using force after the theft will not amount to robbery – though some courts look at the robbery as a continuing act and see violence perpetrated a little time after the actual theft as being part and parcel of it. Exactly how much time can elapse is a matter for the jury to decide – an act of violence within a few seconds would certainly be part of the theft, an act of violence some minutes after may be, but an act of violence an hour after the actual act of theft took place would probably not be.

What is blackmail?

Put simply, blackmail is demanding money with menaces. If a person, either for his own gain or for someone else's, makes an unwarranted demand then it is blackmail. Menaces do not have to mean threats of violence, but can include threats of some action – 'Give me £5,000 or I'll tell your husband we had an affair!' would be blackmail. For a demand to amount to blackmail, the demand must be unwarranted, and if the person makes a demand believing he has reasonable grounds for making it and that the use of the threat is a proper way of enforcing the demand then there is a defence.

What about 'stealing' electricity?

As we said earlier, electricity does not constitute the sort of property that can be stolen, but Section 13 of the Theft Act makes it an offence to use without due authority, or dishonestly cause to be wasted or diverted, any electricity. The maximum penalty is five years' imprisonment. However, there must be some dishonesty – if the electricity board cuts you off and you reconnect your electricity supply and inform the electricity board, then there is no offence because there has been no dishonesty.

I've bought a radio in the pub from a man whose name I don't know. I've just discovered that it was stolen. Am I in trouble?

You are guilty of handling stolen goods if, knowing or believing them to be stolen, you dishonestly receive the goods or dishonestly keep, remove, dispose or sell them for the benefit of another. This means you can be charged with handling if you:

* Took possession of the stolen property.
* Moved it from one place to another.
* Destroyed or concealed the stolen property.

If you bought the radio in good faith, and only discovered later that it was stolen, you would not be guilty of handling stolen goods. However, if the goods were sold to you in some way that a reasonable person might have been suspicious, for example the man took you into the toilets and showed you the radio in a locked cubicle, or outside the back of the pub in darkness, then a jury is entitled to conclude that you believed the radio was stolen. Also, if the radio is stolen and a case goes to court, if you have some previous convictions for handling stolen goods, that can be brought to the attention of the jury (unlike in all other criminal cases where evidence of previous convictions cannot be bought up unless you question the honesty of police evidence) and they will be allowed to infer that you believed the radio was stolen. If you kept the radio after discovering it was stolen, and tried to sell the radio on once you discovered that it had been stolen, you would also be guilty of obtaining a pecuniary advantage by deception. If you are convicted of handling the maximum penalty is six months' imprisonment and £5,000 fine (14 years and an unlimited fine at a Crown Court).

What offences of dishonesty should I be aware of when running my business?

There are a number of potential pitfalls businessmen should worry about in terms of criminal prosecutions:

- False accounting, defined as where someone, with a view to gain for oneself or another (or intending to cause someone else loss) destroys, conceals or falsifies any account or record or document made or required for any accounting purpose, or produces a false document or record which may mislead or deceive over a material fact. This applies to ledgers, cash books, tills or meters – anything used for accounting purposes.
- If an offence of obtaining property or a pecuniary advantage by deception, or an offence of false accounting is shown to have been committed by a company or organisation with the consent or connivance of a director, then the director is also guilty of the offence (Section 18, Theft Act 1968).
- If a company officer publishes a written statement or account which the officer knows to be misleading, with the aim of misleading creditors about the company's affairs, that is a criminal offence.
- Anyone who dishonestly destroys, defaces or conceals any valuable security or a will, in order to gain a benefit or cause someone else a loss, is guilty of an offence.

What is criminal damage?

If you damage or destroy another person's property, you can be prosecuted for causing criminal damage. For a prosecution to succeed, it would have to be shown that you did the damage recklessly or intentionally.

If the damage is less than £5,000, the case can be dealt with only at a magistrates' court, and is punishable by a maximum £2,500 fine and three months in jail. For damage with a value of more than £5,000, the case can be tried at a magistrates' or a Crown Court with a maximum penalty of £5,000 and six months in jail (ten years and an unlimited fine at Crown Court).

There is also an offence of threatening to destroy property, which has a maximum penalty of ten years' imprisonment and an unlimited fine.

Section 5.3 Crimes of violence

Crimes of violence are normally thought of as offences against the person, and many of the statutory provisions are contained in the Offences Against the Person Act 1861. Offences against the person include murder, manslaughter, assault, wounding and battery.

What counts as an assault?

Assault is a common law offence and is defined as any act by which one person intentionally or recklessly causes another to fear unlawful personal violence. Notice that there does not actually have to be actual physical contact, just the fear of it. Strictly speaking, a violent act is actually a battery, which is the intentional or reckless infliction of unlawful personal violence on another person. In practice, however, courts talk about assault even when they mean battery, the actual physical attack.

In terms of the threat of violence, if you do not see or hear the action or words then it cannot be an assault, similarly if an action cannot be carried out then it cannot be an assault. If convicted of an assault, the maximum penalty is six months' imprisonment and a £5,000 fine.

Can I consent to an assault?

Consenting to an assault or a battery can provide a defence. For example, whenever you play a contact sport you consent to a certain amount of physical contact, some of which may even go beyond the rules of the game. But your consent will not cover deliberate attempts to injure you, hence the numbers of prosecutions for foul play arising out of acts on both rugby and football fields. Similarly, as the merest touch can constitute a battery, you consent to being touched during everyday work, play and social occasions. However, you cannot consent if you are too young to understand the nature of the act you are consenting to, or where the consent is obtained by fraud; similarly children can never consent to a sexual assault.

What can constitute an assault?

At various times, courts have found that the following have all constituted an assault:

*   A man staring through a window at a woman.
*   A silent telephoned call, where the silence is felt to convey a threatening message.
*   Touching a person's clothing.
*   Threatening someone by waving a baseball bat.

- Parking your car on someone's foot.
- Taking part in a bare-knuckle boxing bout voluntarily.

I've been charged with causing actual bodily harm; what does that mean?

Causing actual bodily harm (ABH or 'assault occasioning actual bodily harm' to use its precise legal term) is the next most serious form of assault after common assault, and is covered by Section 47 of the Offences Against the Person Act 1861.

Actual bodily harm has been defined as to cover any hurt or injury calculated to interfere with the victim's health or comfort; a bruise would qualify as actual bodily harm, as can silent phone calls. It can cover psychiatric injury, but not emotional upsets such as fear, distress or panic. In order to establish a Section 47 assault, the prosecution would have to show that you intended to cause injury or hurt, or were reckless as to whether your acts would cause hurt or injury in that you consciously took an unjustified risk as to the effect of your actions.

If you are convicted of ABH, the maximum penalty is six months in jail and a £5,000 fine (five years and an unlimited fine at a Crown Court).

I hit someone over the head and he turned out to have a particularly thin skull. Am I responsible?

There is a general rule of English law known, appropriately enough, as the 'eggshell skull rule' which broadly states that you must take your victim as you find them. If you hit someone who turns out to have a thin skull, then it is pretty much your tough luck.

My partner and I have indulged in sado-masochistic sexual practices; we both enjoy them, but are we guilty of assault?

It had been established that consent is not relevant in cases of sado-masochism, following a case in 1992 where a group of men were prosecuted for a number of sado-masochistic acts, against one another, which all consented to. The case was appealed as far as the European court, but there it was decided, as a matter of public policy as much as anything else, that while it is possible to consent to some assaults, it is not possible to consent to sado-masochistic acts.

But more recently in 1996, the Court of Appeal found that where a husband burnt marks onto his wife's body at her insistence, was not guilty of causing actual bodily harm. So the law is a little inconsistent on the subject, but it is probably safer to conclude that getting sexual gratification by means of violent acts is an assault, and to behave accordingly.

What is malicious wounding?

Malicious wounding or causing grievous bodily harm (GBH) is an offence under section 20 of the Offences Against the Person Act 1861. The 'grievous' in grievous bodily harm means really serious, and a wounding would have to draw blood, by penetrating both layers of a victim's skin; the use of the word 'malicious' means that the act must have been committed deliberately, or recklessly as to whether some physical harm would be caused. If you are convicted of GBH, the maximum penalty is six months in jail and a £5,000 fine (five years and an unlimited fine at a Crown Court).

What is the difference between malicious wounding and wounding with intent?

Section 18 of the Offences Against the Person Act 1861 covers an even more serious assault or a greater intent, that of wounding with intent, which involves maliciously wounding or causing grievous bodily harm with intent to do some grievous bodily harm to any person, or with intent to prevent someone being arrested. To prosecute you for causing GBH, the prosecution would have to show that you intended to cause some harm to the other person; to prosecute for wounding with intent, they would actually need to show that you intended to do grievous bodily harm to that person, rather than just 'rough them up a little!'. The maximum penalty for wounding with intent is life imprisonment if tried at a Crown Court.

What is murder?

The age-old definition of murder provided by Lord Justice Coke is:

> 'Murder is when a man of sound memory, and of the age of discretion, unlawfully killeth within any country of the realm any reasonable creature in rerum natura under the king's peace, with malice aforethought, either expressed by the party or implied by law, so the party wounded, or hurt, die of the wound or hurt within a year and a day of the same.'

(The year and a day rule has been scrapped by the Law Reform (Year and a Day Rule) Act 1996).)

'A person of sound memory, and of the age of discretion' means a person of full mental capacity who is capable of committing a criminal offence. 'Under the king's peace' means not in time of war and offers a 'get-out clause' to soldiers. And geographically, British citizens can be charged with murder if they commit the crime on a plane or boat, or outside the UK. What distinguishes murder from manslaughter is 'malice aforethought' – the mental element of the crime. If you are charged with murder, the prosecution must show that you did some act with the intention of killing your victim, or causing them grievous bodily harm. So if you deliberately set out to wound someone and they die as a result, you could be looking at a murder charge. If it is not obvious that you intended to kill or cause grievous bodily harm, the jury would have to consider whether you foresaw death or grievous bodily harm as the result of your actions, and to convict you they would have to be satisfied you foresaw these options as virtually certain to happen.

What if I have attacked someone and they are placed on a life support machine, and doctors decide to switch the machine off – I didn't cause the death did I?

Even if, as a result of your attack, the victim is on a life support machine, and doctors decide to switch off the machine in good faith, then your acts could still be held to have caused the death. However, if you attacked someone who subsequently died because of incorrect or negligent medical treatment, you would not be charged with murder. You can only be held liable if your act was a substantial cause of death.

I attacked someone who turned out to be a Jehovah's Witness and refused a blood transfusion. The victim died – can I be charged with murder?

There is a common law rule that if a victim neglects their injury, this will not exempt you from being convicted of murder. The fact that your victim does not allow a transfusion to take place does not affect the chain of causation – you attacked her, she died.

Can I plead any defences to murder?

You would be acquitted of murder if you can show that your victim's death happened in the execution or administration of justice, for example if you were an armed police officer forced to bring down a suspect with your firearm. Alternatively, you might be able to plead self-defence, in that you had to kill your victim in order to prevent him/her killing you. Another defence would be if the death was accidental – in which case there would be no 'malice aforethought'.

I have been convicted of murder – how long will I serve?

Murder has only one penalty – life imprisonment. Judges can make recommendations as to how long you serve, or say you will never be released. It is not binding on the Home Secretary of the day, but it is usually followed.

What is the difference between murder and voluntary manslaughter?

There are two types of manslaughter – voluntary and involuntary. Legally there is absolutely no difference between murder and voluntary manslaughter, in terms of the act you do and your state of mind at the time you do it; but there are four 'defences' that can reduce the crime in seriousness to manslaughter:

- Provocation, defined as some act or series of acts done by your victim to you which would cause in a reasonable person – and actually did cause in you – a sudden loss of self-control. In order to find you guilty of voluntary manslaughter rather than murder, the jury would have to be satisfied that you lost control as a result of the provocation, and that the provocation was enough to make a reasonable person act as you did. How much delay there is between your victim's final act that caused you to lose control and your violent act is important – there may be some delay, but your lack of self-control must still be sudden and temporary.

- Diminished responsibility, which is defined as some abnormality of the mind, arising from a mental condition that arose naturally or subsequent brain damage, which substantially impairs your mental responsibility for your acts or omissions. For this defence to work, you have to prove that you are suffering from diminished responsibilities, and the burden of proof is 'the balance of probability'. Diminished responsibility will also cover an irresistible impulse – where you felt compelled to do something.

- Infanticide, where a woman kills her child before it reaches the age of 12 months, provided there is evidence that at the time of the child's death the balance of her mind was disturbed. What counts as a disturbance of the mind could be the actual act of giving birth, or lactation.

- Suicide pact, where you and some other person resolve to die together but you survive. Suicide used to be treated as crime (though why – because what possible penalty could be imposed – was always a matter of some confusion), but aiding, abetting, counselling or procuring the suicide of another remains a criminal offence. If you carried out the act that led to your co-suicide pactee's death, then you can be charged with manslaughter; if not, you can be charged with aiding, abetting counselling or procuring suicide.

What about battered wives and domestic violence? Can being battered provide a defence of provocation?

Over 40 per cent of all female murder victims are killed by their partner – that is certainly an indicator of widespread domestic violence. However, only eight per cent of male murder victims die at the hands of their partner; it is likely that many 'wives' have been subjected to physical violence over a period of months or years before they finally 'snap' and do something about it. The question is: whether a sustained series of attacks and indignities spread over a comparatively long period of time can amount to provocation? Obviously, women and men are likely to react differently in the face of the same provocation; the stronger, more aggressive male may react immediately, whereas the female, in most cases physically weaker, sometimes with family ties – like children – that would make reacting to their partner's violence difficult or impossible, tend to react differently. Research suggests that a female's anger bottles up, then erupts as she kills while her normally dominant victim is vulnerable, sleeping, drunk, or helpless in some other way. For this reason, a woman's loss of self-control is unlikely to be the 'sudden and temporary' sort that is usually associated with the defence of provocation. As the result of a 1992 Court of Appeal case, judges now accept that women can suffer a delayed reaction, as their anger slow-burns –

however, at the time of the killing there still had to be a sudden and temporary loss of self-control (though it does not have to be immediate any longer), and the longer the delay between the last act of provocation and the violent act the harder it is to show provocation. So battered women can claim they were provoked to kill, even if some preparation had been done to allow the killing to take place, provided there is a loss of self-control. Battered women can also claim a defence of diminished responsibility, for example if the acts of violence have led to depression. However, women's groups do not like this defence, suggesting as it does that a woman kills a vicious partner because of some mental abnormality of her own.

What is involuntary manslaughter?

Voluntary manslaughter involves acts that would amount to murder, but for the mitigating circumstances outlined above. Involuntary manslaughter is different again:

- **Killing by gross negligence.** If you do some violent act with such a disregard to the life and safety of others that it would amount to a crime, and this act results in someone's death then you can be charged with voluntary manslaughter.
- **Constructive manslaughter.** If you do some unlawful and dangerous act that leads to the death of another person, you can be charged with involuntary manslaughter. To argue constructive manslaughter, the prosecution would have to prove that you intentionally committed a dangerous act that all sober and reasonable people would recognise would subject some other person to at least a risk of harm. The harm must be physical as opposed to emotional harm. Also the act must be illegal, but does not have to be an illegal act aimed at the ultimate victim; for example if you dropped a stone off a bridge onto a car and killed the driver, you could be convicted of manslaughter as your aim was to cause criminal damage to the car.
- **Causing death by dangerous driving.** If a motorist kills someone in the course of an accident, it is unlikely that a charge of manslaughter would be brought. Instead 'causing death by dangerous driving' is the likely charge. For you to be convicted of causing death by dangerous driving, the prosecution would have to show that your driving fell far below the standard of a reasonably competent driver, and that it would have to be obvious to a careful and competent driver that driving in the way you did would lead to a danger of serious injury or serious damage to property.

What are the penalties for manslaughter?

There is a range of penalties available for manslaughter, ranging from life imprisonment, for those acts of manslaughter that fall just below the level of murder, to jail terms of a few years imprisonment or even fines and probation in the case of 'mercy killings'.

A man kicks his wife in the stomach and she loses her unborn child because of the attack; is that murder?

The definition of murder does not cover an unborn foetus; only if a foetus is capable of existence outside its mother's body, and indeed does exist outside its mother's womb, can killing it amount to murder. However, there are a number of statutes that seek to protect the life of an unborn child:

- The Abortion Act 1967 (and subsequently amended) legalises abortion in certain specifically defined cases:
    1. Where two doctors take the opinion that to continue the pregnancy would pose a risk to the mother's physical or mental health, or risk to her life.
    2. Where there is a substantial risk that if the child is born, it will suffer from mental and physical difficulties so severe as to render the child handicapped.

    Abortions must be performed at an NHS hospital or an approved place, otherwise they would be illegal and an offence under the Offences Against the Person Act 1861.
- The Infant Life (Preservation) Act 1929 makes it an offence of child destruction if any person who, with intent to destroy the life of a child capable of being born alive, by any wilful act, causes a child to die before it has an existence independent of its mother, providing the act was not done in good faith for the purpose of protecting the life of the mother. Any unborn child in the twenty-eighth week of pregnancy is considered to be capable of existing outside its mother's body.
- The Offences Against the Person Act 1861 criminalises illegal abortions, makes it an offence to procure a miscarriage or administer any poison or substance, or use any instrument designed to make a woman miscarry, whether or not she is pregnant.

I am a member of a political group. Is it an offence to dress up in a uniform?

This was made an offence in the 1930s, when the spread of fascism and the blackshirts in the UK started to worry the government of the day. As a result, it is still an offence to wear a uniform signifying association with any political organisation or object, in any public place or at any public meeting. This seems to imply that uniforms can be worn at private rallies where no members of the public can be upset.

What are public order offences?

The Public Order Act 1986 codified a number of public order offences such as riot and bound them together.

What is a riot?

A riot takes place if twelve or more persons together use, or threaten to use, unlawful violence for a common purpose in such as way that 'a person of reasonable firmness' who saw them would fear for his personal safety. The maximum penalty is life imprisonment and an unlimited fine.

What is violent disorder?

Violent disorder is a mini-riot, where more than three persons (but fewer then twelve) use, or threaten to use, unlawful violence for a common purpose in such as way that 'a person of reasonable firmness' who saw them would fear for his personal safety. The maximum penalty six months' imprisonment and a £5,000 fine (five years and an unlimited fine at a Crown Court).

What is affray?

A person is guilty of affray if he uses or threatens unlawful violence towards another, and his conduct is such as would cause a person of reasonable firmness present at the scene to fear for his personal safety. The maximum penalty for affray is six months' imprisonment and £5,000 fine (or three years and an unlimited fine at a Crown Court).

What is threatening behaviour?

There are two different forms of threatening behaviour:
- You are guilty of an offence if you use threatening, abusive or insulting words or behaviour to another person, with intent to cause that person to believe that immediate unlawful violence will be used against him or another by any person. The maximum penalty is six months' imprisonment.
- You are guilty of an offence if, with the intention of causing a person harassment, alarm or distress, you use threatening, abusive or insulting words or behaviour or disorderly behaviour, or if you display any writing, sign or other visible representation which is threatening, abusive or insulting, thereby causing that (or another) person harassment, alarm or distress.

The offence may be committed in a public place or private place but there is no offence if the act is done by a person inside a dwelling and seen only by a person also inside that dwelling. The maximum penalty is six months' imprisonment and a fine of £5,000.

Section 5.4 Sex crimes

I have been accused of rape. What does that mean?

The legal definition of rape is that a man commits rape if he has unlawful sexual intercourse with a woman who at the time of the offence does not consent to having sex, and – and this is the important part – that at the time he knows she does not consent to sex, or is reckless as to whether she consents or not. If there is no genuine consent, then there is rape. For example, if the woman is drunk and you have sex with her, then you can be found guilty of rape. Intercourse does not have to be completed for you to be guilty of rape; penetration will be sufficient. The maximum penalty for rape is life imprisonment.

My wife is accusing me of raping her. Can a husband rape his wife?

The old legal position was positively Victorian in tone, emphasising the subservient nature of a wife to her husband. Under the old law, a man could not be guilty of raping his wife because it was felt, by the act of marriage, both had consented to have intercourse with each other. The only exceptions were where a husband and wife had divorced, or where the couple had legally separated and there was an order in place forbidding the husband from molesting the wife, or where the wife had taken out an injunction against her husband, ordering him not to molest her. However, pressure from women's groups and lawyers who felt it was manifestly absurd – and bad law – for a woman to have the right to consent to sex with her husband removed from her, led to changes in the law and now marital rape is an offence.

Can a woman change her mind during sex?

A woman who has consented to sex can change her mind at any time. If the man continues, not knowing or caring whether she means it when she tells him to stop, then he can be charged with rape.

What about the 'when a woman says no, she means maybe' tease?

The definition of rape is clear. If you honestly believe that she is consenting to have sex with you, then you have a defence – as long as the jury believes you. If the jury does not accept that you could have honestly believed the woman was consenting, then you have a problem!

Can a woman be charged with rape?

If a woman has sex with a man against his will, the law will not allow this to be classified as rape. The law is very clear: 'A man commits rape...' according to Section 1, Sexual Offences Act 1956, and Section 1, Sexual Offences (Amendment) Act. Instead, she would be guilty of committing an indecent assault.

Can a teenager commit rape?

There was a presumption that a boy under the age of 14 would not be capable of committing rape, and any sexual offence would be an indecent assault; however, a recognition that sexual activity actually started in teens younger than 14 was incorporated into law in the Sexual Offences Act 1993, which abolished the assumption that boys aged under 14 could not commit rape.

Can a man rape another man?

The offence of male rape has become more common over the past decade, as more and more men are prepared to come forward and report the crime to police. Effectively, male rape is anal intercourse without consent, and carries the same penalties under the law.

What is date rape?

Date rape is a term used in newspapers and magazines to convey a particular type of incident where a rape follows some sort of social event – for example where a blind date ends up with the man forcing the woman to have sex – or where the woman and man have been in some sort of relationship. But the basic principle of the law on rape is that if the man knows or thinks the woman is not consenting to sex (or is reckless as to whether she is consenting), then it is rape.

What is an indecent assault?

Any form of sexual activity that is forced upon someone without their consent is an indecent assault. For an assault to be indecent, there must be some hint of indecency, though it is not necessary to actually touch bare flesh for an assault to be indecent. A woman can indecently assault another female, or a man. Examples of indecent assault are kissing a woman or man, or touching her/him, without permission or against her/his will. If the matter is dealt with at a magistrates' court, the maximum penalty is six months' imprisonment and a £5,000 fine. If the case is dealt with at a Crown Court, the maximum penalty is 10 years' imprisonment and an unlimited fine. Obviously, the length of sentence will depend on the severity of the indecent assault. For an indecent assault to have taken place under normal circumstances, the victim must not have consented to the activity. However, if you indulge in sexual activity with a person under the age of 16, of either sex, then it is an indecent assault, regardless of whether they consented or not. The Indecency with Children Act 1960 makes it an offence to commit an act of gross indecency on or with a child under the age of 14, or to incite a child under that age to commit an indecent act on some person. The penalty is six months in jail and a £5,000 fine (two years and an unlimited fine at a Crown Court).

I've just discovered my '19-year-old' girlfriend is only 15! We have been having sex; have I committed a crime?

If you have sex with a girl who is under the age of 16, even if she consents, you can be charged with unlawful sexual intercourse. If the girl is aged 13 or under, you can be jailed for life. If the girl is aged between 13 and 16, the maximum penalty is two years' imprisonment. However, you have a defence (known as the 'young man's defence') if you are under the age of 24 and reasonably believe that the girl is aged 16 or above, provided you have not been charged with this offence on a previous occasion. So, if you met the girl in a nightclub, you might be able to rely on the defence; meeting her at an under 14s netball trial would tend to ruin it. The circumstances surrounding your relationship are very important, if you need to rely on this defence.

Can cousins marry and have children?

If a person has full sexual intercourse with another person who he/she knows to be his/her: mother/father, daughter/son, granddaughter/grandson, sister/brother or half-sister/half-brother (whether legitimate or illegitimate), then the offence of incest is committed. It doesn't matter if both parties consent, the offence is one involving public policy, as incest is considered morally wrong. The maximum penalty for incest is seven years' imprisonment, unless the female is aged under 13 years, the maximum penalty is life imprisonment. There is no legal prohibition on cousins marrying, and hence no prohibition on them having children.

I've heard that the government is planning to change the laws relating to sex crimes. Is that true?

The Home Office has launched a package of proposals in a report, *Setting the Boundaries*, which will redefine many sexual offences in this country. These include decriminalising gay sex in public places, and redefining consent in rape cases by making those accused of rape show that they had taken 'reasonable steps' to ensure sex was consensual. The report also proposes toughening up sentencing to punish those who sexually abuse children. The Home Office has pledged to put them out to consultation before any are introduced in Parliamentary Bills.

Section 5.5 Motoring offences

With the introduction of motor vehicles to this country in the early years of the last century, a whole new class of legal problems was developed, many of them affecting the criminal law. Most motoring law is designed to prevent or reduce accidents on the road. Approximately 400,000 motoring accidents occur on British roads each year, injuring some 180,000 people; over 5,000 of these injuries result in death. There are also laws that relate to the police power to stop, and laws applicable to cyclists. Most motoring offences are covered by the Road Traffic Acts, and many of the minor ones are offences of strict liability – that means you are guilty unless you can prove otherwise, rather than the usual burden of proof. The problem with motoring offences is that a culture of 'there but for the grace of God...' has grown up; everyone double-parks, many people would say: it's not really a crime, is it? Granted, some offences may seem not too serious, for example parking on double yellow lines; but imagine the chaos and confusion if everyone parked where they were not supposed to – towns would be gridlocked and people would not be able to get into their places of business. It can't be all right for one person to break a law, but everyone else uphold it – so the standard is applied to all. The punishment handed out by the courts for motoring offences can broadly be divided into three categories: fines, endorsements on a driver's licence, and disqualification.

What is an endorsement?

An endorsement means that the conviction has been endorsed (i.e. written) on the driver's licence and will be recorded on DVLA records; in certain cases this can be removed after four years (except in the case of a drink driving offence). Each endorsement has a number of penalty points attached to it, which can accumulate to a number where disqualification could be ordered. Motoring convictions are spent after three years.

I am out driving and get flagged down by a police car. Do I have to stop?

The police can stop any motorist and question him, whether or not they suspect him of an offence, so you would have to stop. However, they are not entitled to delay you for longer than you reasonably want to stay, unless they have a search warrant or are going to arrest you. (If you are flagged down by a civilian, you are not obliged to stop – even if he turns out to be a plain clothed policeman – because you have no way of knowing for sure who he is.)

If you are stopped by a uniformed policeman, you must give your name and address when asked. However, if you are in a genuine hurry, for example to see someone that is seriously ill in hospital, you can explain and ask to give the details later. The policeman may not agree to this and if that is the case, he can insist for the details on the spot. If you are carrying motoring documents with you (you are not obliged to carry them), show them if asked. If you do not show them the police can insist that you produce them at a police station within seven days. You must obey a policeman if he asks you to move your vehicle; you can be prosecuted for obstructing the police, regardless of the circumstances. If the police are looking for a stolen car, they may ask you questions about your car (registration, make of tyres, etc). You should answer their questions as much as you can, as this helps to confirm that the car is yours. Do not answer any questions that you think could incriminate you – after all you are under no legal obligation to do so – but be polite and co-operative.

What is careless driving?

Careless driving, or 'driving without due care and attention' covers drivers that drive negligently. The test that courts will apply is whether you were exercising the care and attention that a reasonable and prudent driver would exercise in the circumstances? If convicted of careless driving, you can be fined a maximum of £2,500 and have your licence endorsed with between three and nine penalty points.

But I'm a learner driver – surely they will take that into account?

The same standard must be applied by learner drivers as experienced motorists, so it is not enough for you to say 'I'm a learner, you should expect less of me!'

What about inconsiderate driving?

There is an offence of driving motor vehicles without reasonable consideration for other persons using the road or pavement, including pedestrians. Under this section, you can commit an offence by driving too slowly, or driving too near the kerb and going through a puddle to splash pedestrians.

I've been charged with inconsiderate driving but the road (or pavement) was empty....

Then you're going to get off! For the charge to stick, other people must be using the road. If you are convicted the maximum fine is £2,500 and between three and nine points.

What is dangerous driving?

If you drive recklessly rather than negligently, you can be charged with dangerous driving. The maximum penalty on conviction is a six-month jail term and a fine of £5,000; in addition, your licence will be endorsed with between three and eleven penalty points. Reckless driving could involve driving at excessive speed down a narrow road, for example.

Causing death by dangerous driving

This offence arose because juries were incredibly reluctant to convict someone of manslaughter following road accidents where someone died. If you are convicted, you can be sentenced to up to ten years in jail, an unlimited fine, a two-year ban and a re-test. You may also have points on your licence. To show dangerous driving, the police will only need to show you drove badly – the fact that someone died as a result will establish the charge.

I have been stopped by police when I was driving home after a night out. They want to breathalyse me.

The laws relating to drink driving are exceptionally tough – though few people would say they are too harsh. Motor cars are dangerous machines if the driver loses control accidentally; to drive having taken something that reduces your ability to manage the vehicle is genuinely criminal, and the law punishes this severely as a result. Although random breath testing does not exist, the police can stop you and ask you to give them your details (e.g. your name, address, insurance policy details, or ask you to produce your driving licence) and if officers smell alcohol on your breath, they can quite lawfully request you to supply a specimen of breath; this will involve a road-side breath test which is merely a preliminary screening test. The Association of Chief Police Officers (ACPO) have been asking for the right of police to conduct random breath tests since 1998.

I've only had two pints... will I be all right?

It is an old wives' tale that if you have only drunk two and a half pints of beer or less (or the equivalent of spirits) you would pass a breath test. This always was, and still remains, nonsense! It depends on your weight, how much food you have eaten, the state of your health and many other factors.

What is the legal limit?

The legal maximum is 34 microgrammes of alcohol per 100 millilitres of breath.

How do roadside tests work?

If the police stop you and believe that you have been drinking, they will ask you to take a roadside test. The roadside test uses a machine, the successor to the 'blow in the bag' breathalyser, which acts as a screening test, to tell whether you are above the limit, on the borderline, or below it. If you are above the limit or borderline, the policeman will arrest you and take you to the station where you will be asked to supply two samples of breath on an intoximeter, which is a computerised breath test machine.

What about the test at the police station?

You will be asked have to blow into a tube until the operator tells you to stop, and you will be required to give two samples of breath within two minutes. These samples are then analysed by the machine which measures the alcohol concentration in your breath. The legal maximum is 34 microgrammes of alcohol per 100 millilitres of breath. If it is below that you are free to go and if between 35 and 39 microgrammes you may be let off with a warning. But if your level is between 34 and 50 microgrammes and you query the police reading, you are entitled to give a specimen of blood. The police have no discretion in these circumstances and must ask you if you wish to give such a sample of blood and then the blood analysis will be relied upon rather than the intoximeter read-out. The legal limit is 80 milligrammes of alcohol in 100 millilitres of blood; if your reading is over 50 milligrammes the police can rely on the intoximeter print-out and that will form the basis of their case against you. It is also possible to give a urine sample, in which case the prescribed limit is 107 milligrammes of alcohol in 100 millilitres of urine. However, most people choose to give a blood test.

I've heard of something called the 'hip flask' defence...

There used to be a defence known as 'the hip flask defence' where people who had been involved in drink-drive accidents did not stop, went home and drank half a bottle of spirits, then claimed they had only been drinking since the accident when they were interviewed later. The police would be unable to prove exactly how much alcohol was in that person's body at the time the accident had occurred, and the case would fall. But the law has been changed, and it is up to you to prove that you were below the legal limit at the time of the accident, whether or not you have been drinking since. This will be difficult for you to prove, so in practice the defence is dead and buried.

What if I lock myself away at home and refuse to let the police in?

It used to be the case that if you had an accident and ran away to your home, then if the police called, you could tell them to go away, and they would be unable to come inside to collect any evidence of drink-driving. This is no longer the case; if an accident has happened and the police have reasonable grounds to believe that someone was injured, they are entitled to force entry into any premises where they have reasonable cause to believe that the driver is, to make an arrest. You can ask what the reasonable grounds for believing someone is injured are.

I have been charged with drink-driving. What happens now?

The law makes it an offence to drive or attempt to drive a motor vehicle when unfit through drink or drugs, or to be in charge of a motor vehicle in that state, or to drive or attempt to drive a motor vehicle with a blood/alcohol concentration above the prescribed limit or to be in charge of a motor vehicle in such a condition. If you are convicted of any of these offences you will be normally disqualified for a minimum period of 12 months – though it could be longer, and the higher the concentration of alcohol found in your sample, the longer the disqualification and the higher the fine that is likely to be imposed. If the reading is more than two-and-a-half times the legal limit, you also face going to jail, even for a first offence. If, after being convicted of one of these offences, you are convicted of a second drink-driving offence within three years, you will be banned for a minimum of three more years; there is also a real possibility you will be jailed, even if your reading were 'just over the limit'. Where blood-alcohol readings are very high, courts must inform the Home Office and then you may well have your licence revoked until you can supply medical evidence that you do not have a drink problem. But the consequences do not end with a fine or jail term and ban. When your licence is returned after you have served your ban, you will find motor insurance much more expensive. Moreover, you will not automatically get your licence back after a ban: you can be ordered to undergo a medical examination to prove you are fit to drive if your alcohol level at the time of the offence was over a certain limit or if you have been convicted of a similar offence.

What does 'in charge' of a vehicle mean?

The concept of being 'drunk in charge' is potentially very wide, and all that is required is for the police to establish some connection with the accused, who is drunk, and the mechanically propelled vehicle (a car, bus, taxi or bike). If someone is sleeping off a drinking bout in the back of a car he might well be charged with being drunk in charge, but if he can prove on the balance of probabilities that at the time of his arrest he was not going to drive the car as long as he was over the limit, then he might get off. So, being asleep in the back of the car in a sleeping bag, or with your shoes off is more likely to get you acquitted than being fully clothed and slumped over the steering wheel. If you are convicted of being 'drunk in charge' you are liable to a fine of up to £2,500 and three months' imprisonment, and ten penalty points on your licence.

I've been stopped by the police. I have been drinking. Can I refuse to give a test, so they can't ban me?

It is also an offence to fail to supply a specimen of breath if properly requested so to do. The same penalties apply for refusing or failing to give a sample of breath as if you fail a test.

I'm a cyclist. The road laws don't apply to me surely?

Although cyclists cannot be imprisoned or disqualified, they are subject to the same laws as other road users. In addition, there are various provisions that apply only to cyclists. For example, it is an offence to wheel your bike past red traffic lights, or to leave your bike on a footpath or in a dangerous position. Contrary to popular belief, a cyclist can be convicted of being drunk in charge of a bike, but the normal breathalyser laws do not apply, and though cyclists cannot be disqualified, there can be a fine of up to a maximum of £400.

Motoring offences

There is a host of motoring offences, with different penalties as set out below. Some can be dealt with as fixed penalties; some will require you to go to court.

- **Abandoning a motor vehicle**: if convicted you face a maximum fine of £2,500 and six months' imprisonment.
- **Failing to give particulars of an accident** (AC20): if convicted you face a maximum fine of £5,000, 5–10 penalty points and six months' imprisonment. Your licence is endorsed.
- **Failing to report an accident** (AC20): if convicted you face a maximum fine of £5,000, 5–10 penalty points and six months' imprisonment. Your licence is endorsed.
- **Failing to stop after an accident** (AC20): if convicted you face a maximum fine of £5,000, 5–10 penalty points and six months' imprisonment. Your licence is endorsed.
- **Defective bicycle brakes**: if convicted you face a maximum fine of £1,000.
- **Careless bicycle riding**: if convicted you face a maximum fine of £1,000.
- **Dangerous bicycle riding**: if convicted you face a maximum fine of £2,500.
- **Inconsiderate bicycle riding**: if convicted you face a maximum fine of £1,000.
- **Carrying a second person on a bike**: if convicted you face a maximum fine of £200.
- **Riding a bicycle when unfit through drink**: if convicted you face a maximum fine of £1,000.
- **Defective brakes, private vehicle** (CU10): if convicted you face a maximum £2,500 fine, three penalty points and your licence may be endorsed (but not if you can show you were not aware of the defect). Can be dealt with via fixed penalty notice.
- **Defective brakes, goods vehicle** (CU10): if convicted you face a maximum £5,000 fine, three penalty points and your licence may be endorsed (but not if you can show you were not aware of the defect). Can be dealt with via fixed penalty notice.
- **Defective bicycle brakes**: if convicted you face a maximum fine of £1,000.

- **Driving on common land**: if convicted you face a maximum £1,000 fine. Can be dealt with via fixed penalty notice.
- **Car dumping**: if convicted you face a maximum £2,500 fine and three months' imprisonment.
- **Using private vehicle in dangerous condition** (CU20): if convicted you face a maximum £2,500 fine and three penalty points. Your licence may be endorsed (but not if you can show you were not aware of the defect). Can be dealt with via fixed penalty notice.
- **Using goods vehicle in dangerous condition** (CU20): if convicted you face a maximum £5,000 fine and three penalty points. Your licence may be endorsed (but not if you can show you were not aware of the defect). Can be dealt with via fixed penalty notice.
- **Dangerous load on private vehicle** (CU50): if convicted you face a maximum £2,500 fine and three penalty points. Your licence may be endorsed (but not if you can show you were not aware of the defect). Can be dealt with via fixed penalty notice.
- **Dangerous load on goods vehicle** (CU50): if convicted you face a maximum £5,000 fine and three penalty points. Your licence may be endorsed (but not if you can show you were not aware of the defect). Can be dealt with via fixed penalty notice.
- **Leaving vehicle in dangerous position** (MS10): if convicted you face a maximum £1,000 fine and three penalty points. Your licence will be endorsed. Can be dealt with via fixed penalty notice.
- **Failing to give date of birth**: if convicted you face a maximum £1,000 fine.
- **Defective tyre, private vehicle** (CU30): if convicted you face a maximum £2,500 fine and three penalty points. Your licence may be endorsed (but not if you can show you were not aware of the defect). Can be dealt with via fixed penalty notice.

- **Defective tyre, goods vehicle** (CU30): if convicted you face a maximum £5,000 fine and three penalty points. Your licence may be endorsed (but not if you can show you were not aware of the defect). Can be dealt with via fixed penalty notice.
- **Careless driving** (CD10): if convicted you face a maximum £2,500 fine and 3–9 penalty points. Your licence will be endorsed.
- **Dangerous driving** (DD30): if convicted you face a maximum £5,000 fine, six months' imprisonment and 3–11 penalty points. Your licence will be endorsed. Case can be head at crown court or before magistrates.
- **Driving while disqualified** (BA10): if convicted you face a maximum £5,000 fine, six months' imprisonment and six penalty points. Your licence will be endorsed.
- **Driving excessive periods**: if convicted you face a maximum £2,500 fine.
- **Driving without insurance** (IN10): if convicted you face a maximum £5,000 fine and 6–8 penalty points. Your licence will be endorsed.
- **Driving without tax disc**: if convicted you face a maximum fine of £1,000 or five times' the duty payable.
- **Driving without reasonable consideration for other road users**: if convicted you face a maximum £2,500 fine and 3–9 penalty points. Your licence will be endorsed.
- **Driving without private test certificate**: if convicted you face a maximum £1,000 fine.
- **Driving without goods test certificate**: if convicted you face a maximum £2,500 fine.
- **Failing to display excise licence**: if convicted you face a maximum £200 fine. Can be dealt with via fixed penalty notice.
- **Making false statements to obtain excise licence**: if convicted you face a maximum £5,000 fine. Case can be head at crown court or before magistrates.
- **Using/keeping vehicle without excise licence**: if convicted you face a maximum fine of £1,000 or three times the duty payable.
- **Driving with defective eyesight** (MS70): if convicted you face a maximum £1,000 fine and three penalty points. Your licence will be endorsed.
- **Failing to comply with traffic sign**: if convicted you face a maximum £1,000 fine and three penalty points. Your licence may be endorsed. Can be dealt with via fixed penalty notice.
- **Failing to obey policeman or traffic warden on traffic duty** (TS40): if convicted you face a maximum £1,000 fine and three penalty points. Your licence will be endorsed.
- **Failing to give name and address to police** (AC20): if convicted you face a maximum £5,000 fine and six months' imprisonment.
- **Failing to give specimen of breath** (DR70): if convicted you face a maximum £2,500 fine and four penalty points. Your licence will be endorsed.

- **Failing to give specimen of urine/blood/breath if driving or attempting to drive** (DR30): if convicted you face a maximum £5,000 fine, six months' imprisonment and 3–11 penalty points. You will be disqualified from driving.
- **Failing to give specimen of urine/blood/breath if driving if in charge** (DR60): if convicted you face a maximum £2,500 fine, three months' imprisonment and 10 penalty points. Your licence will be endorsed.
- **Failing to give statement by owner**: if convicted you face a maximum £1,000 fine.
- **Failing to produce driving licence**: if convicted you face a maximum £1,000 fine.
- **Failing to produce driving licence for endorsement**: if convicted you face a maximum £1,000 fine.
- **Failing to produce insurance certificate**: if convicted you face a maximum £1,000 fine.
- **Failing to produce test certificate**: if convicted you face a maximum £1,000 fine. Can be dealt with via fixed penalty notice.
- **Failing to wear front seat belt**: if convicted you face a maximum £1,000 fine. Can be dealt with via fixed penalty notice.
- **Failing to stop at school crossing** (TS60): if convicted you face a maximum £1,000 fine and 3 penalty points. Your licence is endorsed.
- **Making a false statement to obtain driving licence**: if convicted you face a maximum £2,500 fine.
- **Making a false statement to obtain insurance**: if convicted you face a maximum £2,500 fine.
- **Forging driving licence**: if convicted you face a maximum £5,000 fine. Case can be head at crown court or before magistrates.
- **Forging insurance certificate**: if convicted you face a maximum £5,000 fine. Case can be head at crown court or before magistrates.
- **Forging test certificate**: if convicted you face a maximum £5,000 fine. Case can be head at crown court or before magistrates.
- **Carrying child in front seat**: if convicted you face a maximum £1,000 fine. Can be dealt with via fixed penalty notice.
- **Driving heavy goods vehicle (HGV) without LGV licence**: if convicted you face a maximum £1,000 fine.
- **Overloading HGV**: if convicted you face a maximum £5,000 fine. Can be dealt with via fixed penalty notice.
- **Parking HGV on verge**: if convicted you face a maximum £1,000 fine. Can be dealt with via fixed penalty notice.
- **Using HGV without plating certificate**: if convicted you face a maximum £1,000 fine.
- **Using HGV without test certificate**: if convicted you face a maximum £2,500 fine.
- **Holding onto vehicle to be towed or carried**: if convicted you face a maximum £200 fine.

- **Insecure load, goods** (CU50): if convicted you face a maximum £5,000 fine and three penalty points. Your licence may be endorsed (but not if you can show you were not aware of the defect). Can be dealt with via fixed penalty notice.
- **Insecure load, other** (CU50): if convicted you face a maximum £5,000 fine and three penalty points. Your licence may be endorsed (but not if you can show you were not aware of the defect). Can be dealt with via fixed penalty notice.
- **Jay walking**: if convicted you face a maximum £1,000 fine.
- **Driving or parking without lights (goods)**: if convicted you face a maximum £2,500 fine. Can be dealt with via fixed penalty notice.
- **Driving or parking without lights (other)**: if convicted you face a maximum £1,000 fine. Can be dealt with via fixed penalty notice.
- **Motorcyclist not wearing helmet**: if convicted you face a maximum £1,000 fine.
- **Causing unnecessary obstruction (goods)**: if convicted you face a maximum £2,500 fine. Can be dealt with via fixed penalty notice.
- **Causing unnecessary obstruction (other)**: if convicted you face a maximum £1,000 fine. Can be dealt with via fixed penalty notice.
- **Driving wrong way down one-way street**: if convicted you face a maximum £1,000 fine. Can be dealt with via fixed penalty notice.
- **Owner failing to identify driver**: if convicted you face a maximum £1,000 fine and three penalty points. Your licence will be endorsed.
- **Parking on yellow lines**: if convicted you face a maximum £500 fine. Can be dealt with via fixed penalty notice.
- **Parking in on-street parking places**: if convicted you face a maximum £500 fine. Can be dealt with via fixed penalty notice.
- **On-street parking places, abuse of parking for the disabled**: if convicted you face a maximum £1,000 fine.
- **Parking in off-street parking places**: if convicted you face a maximum £500 fine. Can be dealt with via fixed penalty notice.
- **Off-street parking places, abuse of parking for the disabled**: if convicted you face a maximum £1,000 fine.
- **Failing to pay initial or excess parking charge**: if convicted you face a maximum £500 fine, plus the unpaid amount.
- **Interfering with meter with intent to defraud**: if convicted you face a maximum £1,000 fine.
- **Pedestrian failing to comply with direction of police officer on duty**: if convicted you face a maximum £1,000 fine.
- **Not giving precedence on pedestrian crossing** (PC20): if convicted you face a maximum £1,000 fine and three penalty points. Your licence will be endorsed. Can be dealt with via fixed penalty notice.

- **Overtaking on pedestrian crossing** (PC20): if convicted you face a maximum £1,000 fine and three penalty points. Your licence will be endorsed.
- **Stopping on pedestrian crossing** (PC20): if convicted you face a maximum £1,000 fine and three penalty points. Your licence will be endorsed. Can be dealt with via fixed penalty notice.
- **Defective silencer (goods)**: if convicted you face a maximum £2,500 fine. Can be dealt with via fixed penalty notice.
- **Defective silencer (private)**: if convicted you face a maximum £1,000 fine. Can be dealt with via fixed penalty notice.
- **Speeding (ordinary roads)** (SP30): if convicted you face a maximum £1,000 fine and 3–6 penalty points. Your licence will be endorsed. Can be dealt with via fixed penalty notice.
- **Speeding (motorway)** (SP50): if convicted you face a maximum £2,500 fine and 3–6 penalty points. Your licence will be endorsed. Can be dealt with via fixed penalty notice.
- **Stealing (or attempt) vehicle** (UT20): if convicted you face a maximum £5,000 fine and six months' imprisonment.
- **Taking motor vehicle without consent** (UT60): if convicted you face a maximum £5,000 fine and six months' imprisonment.
- **Tampering with motor vehicle**: if convicted you face a maximum £1,000 fine and six months' imprisonment.
- **Defective steering (private vehicle)**: if convicted you face a maximum £2,500 fine and three penalty points. Your licence may be endorsed (but not if you can show you were not aware of the defect). Can be dealt with via fixed penalty notice.
- **Defective steering (goods vehicle)**: if convicted you face a maximum £5,000 fine and three penalty points. Your licence may be endorsed (but not if you can show you were not aware of the defect). Can be dealt with via fixed penalty notice.
- **Using vehicle without test certificate**: if convicted you face a maximum £1,000 fine.
- **Refusing a breath test at roadside** (DR70): if convicted you face a maximum £1,000 fine and 3–11 penalty points. Your licence will be endorsed. You may be banned from driving at the court's discretion.
- **Driving with excess alcohol** (DR10): if convicted you face a maximum £5,000 fine, six months' imprisonment and 3–11 penalty points. You will be banned from driving for a minimum of 12 months'. Your licence will be endorsed
- **Driving under the influence of drink or drugs** (DR20): if convicted you face a maximum £5,000 fine, six months' imprisonment and 3–11 penalty points. You will be banned from driving for a minimum of 12 months. Your licence will be endorsed
- **Drunk in charge** (DR50): if convicted you face a maximum £2,500 fine, six months' imprisonment and 10 penalty points. Your licence will be endorsed. You may be banned from driving at the court's discretion.

Section 5.6 Weapons

What is the law relating to firearms?

Anyone who owns or possesses a gun of any kind should normally have a certificate of some kind issued by the police:

- A shotgun certificate covers smoothbore weapons with barrels longer than 24 inches. Shortening a shotgun barrel (to make a 'sawn-off' shotgun) is a serious offence. If you are caught in possession of a shotgun without a permit, you can face fines of up to £5,000 and a six-month jail term. Possession of a sawn-off shotgun in punishable by a five-year jail term and an unlimited fine.
- A firearms certificate covers rifles; since the Dunblane massacre a total ban has been placed on the public ownership of handguns with a calibre of .22 inch or more, despite outcry from target-shooting fraternities across the country.

The firearms certificate will specify what ammunition you can buy for your weapon. (An all-party group of MPs has called for all firearms to be regulated by certificates, including comparatively low-powered air rifles, and the prevention of young children having any access to firearms of any kind.)

I have an airgun. Do I need a firearms licence?

That depends on the airgun. Low-powered airguns do not need a licence but it is possible to buy high-powered weapons that will need to be licensed. It is best to check with the gun seller or police. Though, if the all party MPs group gets its way, you may need a permit for that as well in a few years' time. In addition, if you are a member of a gun club or cadet corps and use the gun for drill or target practice only, you do not need a licence.

How can I get a shotgun certificate?

As the law stands, almost everyone who owns a shotgun and ammunition needs a certificate to hold it lawfully. There are exceptions, however:

- People shooting at artificial targets – clay pigeons for example – with police permission.
- Someone who borrows a shotgun from the owner of private property, and who subsequently uses it on that property.
- Someone carrying a gun belonging to a certificate holder, under the holder's instructions, to use for sporting purposes.

Unlike America, you do not have a right to possess a firearm. Police can refuse to grant you a firearms certificate, but you may appeal against their refusal to a crown court.

What do I need to be aware of when using my gun lawfully?

The first issue is storage. Your firearm should be kept in a safe place, such as a gun cabinet secured to a wall or floor, with your ammunition stored in a separate location. The way you transport your guns is also important. It is an offence to have a firearm uncovered in a public place, and you can be fined up to £5,000 and jailed for six months (five years if you are tried at a Crown Court) as well as forfeiting the gun.

What is an offensive weapon?

Anything that can cause injury to someone else can be classed as an offensive weapon – it is all a question of the circumstances at the time – so it is possible that something that an lawfully be owned, such as an umbrella, can become an offensive weapon if you were to stab someone with it, for example. Some items are obviously offensive weapons, as they are meant to cause injury – for example a knife, broken bottle or razorblades embedded into a lump of four-by-two – and possession of such objects without a lawful reason is illegal. Other items such as a steel toe-capped boot or a baseball bat will classed as offensive weapons if the prosecution can show that there was an intention to use the objects as weapons. So if you flail about you wildly with a bat and lash out with your feet, the prosecution could make a pretty good case that you had them as offensive weapons. If you are accused of possessing an offensive weapon, the case will normally be tried before magistrates, and if convicted you will be fined up to £5,000, with a maximum six-month jail term. If the case goes to a Crown Court, you could be jailed for up to two years, with an unlimited fine.

However, you would be allowed to have a knife in a public place in some circumstances – for instance if you were wearing a kilt and had a dirk tucked in your sock, if you are a Sikh or if the knife is a tool of your trade. And obviously, a knife being used to peel an apple is allowed, but not if it is later used to threaten someone.

I'm carrying the weapon to defend myself. The courts will allow that surely...

Not a chance. Courts will only allow you to carry a weapon in self-defence if there is an imminent threat, for instance if you were surrounded by a mob and picked up a cricket bat to protect yourself. Taking the bat out on the off-chance that someone might decide to threaten you would not wash with magistrates – you may not carry a weapon regularly for self-defence.

Section 5.7 Stalking

For many years, there was a loophole in the law that allowed stalking. Stalking is behaviour that stops short of an assault or threatening behaviour, but that can still put you in fear. For example, if a man became attracted to a woman and decided to sit outside her home every night, not saying or doing anything, but just watching, then this would not be an assault or threatening behaviour, but it would certainly be unnerving. There are civil remedies that you could pursue, for example an injunction, but these are time-consuming and costly. But in 1997, the Protection from Harassment Act was enacted by parliament.

What does the Protection from Harassment Act prevent me from doing?

Essentially the Act law states that you should not pursue a course of conduct that amounts to the harassment of someone else, and which you know amounts to the harassment of someone else. Basically, the law says that you are guilty of harassment if a reasonable person in possession of the same information would think that your behaviour amounts to harassment. If you are convicted or harassment, you could be jailed for up to six months in prison, or be fined, or both. Harassment is a pattern of behaviour, so one-off bad behaviour may be unpleasant, but it would not constitute harassment; it is likely that to succeed in a prosecution for harassment, the Crown Prosecution Service would have to show at least two instances of conduct which constitutes a harassment. 'Conduct' includes speech, as well as actions.

Does the Act prohibit any other conduct?

In addition to criminalising unnerving behaviour, it also tackles more specific, systematic threatening behaviour. If it can be proved that you have caused another person to fear, on at least two occasions, that violence would be used against them, you would be guilty of an offence if you knew that your behaviour would create the fear, or a reasonable person would know this. The maximum penalty for this offence is five years' imprisonment, along with a restraining order that would prohibit you from doing anything set out in the order, for example approaching or contacting the person you have been convicted of threatening. The order can have a time limit, or be perpetual and apply for the whole of your lifetime, and the maximum penalty for breaching its conditions is an additional five years in jail.

A court can also make a restraining order if you have been convicted of the lesser charge of harassing someone, with the same penalty for breaching it. One limitation on this law is that the prosecution would have to prove harassment beyond all reasonable doubt, which may be difficult to do in practice.

What about sending an ex girlfriend an e-mail?

Sending a barrage of offensive or threatening e-mails would count as harassment.

I've been harassed by a former lover, but I don't think I can prove harassment beyond all reasonable doubt. Is there anything else I can do?

You could seek a civil injunction if you can show, on the balance of probabilities, that your harasser has done at least two things to you that a reasonable person would consider would cause alarm, distress or harassment, provided that your harasser knew that it would have this effect on you, or that a reasonable person would think that. If granted, the injunction would have the effect of restraining your harasser from doing anything that amounts to harassment. Also, the court can award you damages for any anxiety caused by the harassment and any financial loss resulting from it. If your harasser ignores the injunction, police can arrest him and he be charged with breaching the injunction (a criminal offence) and, if convicted, face a jail term of up to five years. However, as the injunction is a civil remedy, you will have to go through the civil courts to get it, and meet the legal costs yourself, unless you qualify for Legal Aid.

Are there any other laws that can be used to stop stalkers?

- Civil injunctions, which have already been discussed. Taking out a civil injunction is likely to cost at least £600 if you do not get Legal Aid.
- The laws that criminalise assault can be applied in some cases. Stalkers can be convicted of causing grievous bodily harm by causing a psychiatric injury, if it can be shown that you have suffered clinical depression as a result of the stalking. For lesser harm, a charge of actual bodily harm (psychiatric injury) can be brought.
- The Mental Health Act might provide an option, but only if there is evidence that your harasser is suffering serious mental illness.
- If you are receiving malicious telephone calls, it may be possible to prosecute your harasser for a breach of the Telecommunications Act 1984, which deals with obscene or persistent telephone calls.
- Obscene letters and parcels can be similarly dealt with, by prosecuting for a breach of the Malicious Communications Act 1988. But for this prosecution to succeed, you would have to have been sent something of an indecent or grossly offensive nature and which was intended to cause distress or anxiety.
- If you believe that immediate unlawful violence would be used against you, then the Crown Prosecution Service could prosecute under the Public Order Act 1986; but for this to succeed, they would have to prove that your harasser intended or was aware that his or her behaviour was threatening, abusive or insulting.

Section 5.8 Drugs

The possession of drugs in the UK is very closely regulated. Many drugs can only be held through a medical prescription, while others must not be held at all. The Misuse of Drugs Act 1971 sets three categories of drug that cannot be held.

What are the police powers in respect of drugs?

Police can stop and search anyone reasonably suspected of possessing controlled drugs, but need a warrant to search a house or premises (though cars and vans, etc. can be searched without a warrant).

I have been searched and a brown substance found in my pocket...

If police find what they suspect to be drugs on someone, they can send the substance off for analysis. While they are waiting for results, they can grant you police bail, and order you to report to the police station regularly.

What are the drug categories?

- Class A drugs include heroin, morphine, LSD, injectable amphetamines, mescaline, medicinal opium, dipopanone, ecstasy and cocaine.
- Class B drugs include cannabis, cannabis resin, codeine, Benzedrine and marijuana.
- Class C drugs include lucofen, villiscan, amphetamines and Mandrax.

What are the penalties?

The law distinguishes between having drugs for personal use, or with intent to supply them to other persons. The quantity of drugs that are found on you when you are stopped will determine the likely charge – a few Es would probably be for personal use, while a suitcase would be to supply them.

Class A drugs
For personal use: six months, £5,000 fine (seven years and unlimited fine at a Crown Court).

Supply: six months, £5,000 fine (life and unlimited fine at a Crown Court).

Class B drugs
For personal use: three months, £2,500 fine (five years and unlimited fine at a Crown Court).

Supply: six months, £5,000 fine (14 years and unlimited fine at a Crown Court).

Class C drugs
For personal use: £1,000 fine (two years and unlimited fine at a Crown Court).

Supply: six months, £2,500 fine (five years and unlimited fine at a Crown Court).

Section 5.9 Children and crime

I've heard of the age of criminality. Does that mean a child can be too young to commit a crime?

Not exactly. It does mean that a child under the age of ten cannot appear before magistrates charged with any offence; this is based on the view that below this age, children do not know whether their acts are legally and morally wrong. Youth courts deal with accusations of criminal behaviour made against children and young persons aged between 10 and 17 years and 364 days at the time an offence is committed.

So a child aged under ten can never appear in court?

Magistrates in family proceedings can make a child safety order which places a child aged under ten under the care of a local authority, to prevent the repetition of objectionable behaviour that would be a criminal offence if the child were aged over ten years. Magistrates in civil courts can also make anti-social behaviour orders against adults and children including the under-tens.

Can a young person be tried at magistrates court?

If a young person is jointly charged with an adult with the same offence, then they will appear before magistrates together.

What do youth courts do?

Youth courts deal with young offenders committing the less serious crimes, in the same way that magistrates' courts deal with summary offences and cases that are triable either way, meaning the case can be heard by a youth court, magistrates or at Crown Court, but are being dealt with before magistrates. More serious cases will be sent up to the crown court for trial by the youth courts.

What penalties can a youth court impose on a juvenile that appears before it on criminal charges?

Courts have a range of penalties available to deal with juvenile offenders:

- Youths aged over 16 can be placed on probation if the court feels that guidance is needed; the order would be for a set length of time, placing the offender under the guidance of a probation officer.
- Offenders aged over 16 can also be given community service orders, where, for a set number of hours, they will have to carry out unpaid work for the good of the community at large, for example painting, rubbish clearance or gardening.
- Where the offence requires a period in custody, a youth court can sentence an offender to a spell in a young offenders' institution, which is akin to a spell in an adult jail.
- Magistrates can also make child safety orders (already mentioned).

Can I appear in court as a witness if I am not aged 18?

A person of any age can be a witness in court. In some cases a judge may ask members of the public to leave the court to protect a young person giving evidence, or a video link may be used. If the police interview you as a potential witness, you have the right to remain silent. If you so wish you do not have to appear as a witness in court, unless a witness summons has been issued. Should you still fail to appear you could be fined or sent to prison for contempt of court.

I've heard that young people that appear in court do not get identified. Is that true?

As a matter of policy, the government is keen to give young people who get into trouble the chance to rebuild their lives. Adults benefit from the Rehabilitation of Offenders Act, which allows former offenders to treat some convictions as spent after the passage of time (which means they do not have to identify them when applying for jobs). Young offenders get even more protection, as successive governments since the 1930s have imposed restrictions on the way newspapers report court cases involving juveniles:

- If a juvenile appears in a youth court, a newspaper cannot report the name, address or school of the offender, or any material that might lead to the identification of that person. Nor can pictures of the offender be published. (This protection also extends to any young persons involved in the proceedings as a witness.) The amount of detail that will identify a young person depends on the circumstances; saying a 14-year-old boy was from London would not identify, whereas saying the boy was from a small village, which was then named, probably would.
- If a young person (under the age of 18) appears at an adult court as a defendant or witness, either at Crown Court or at a magistrates' court, there is no automatic ban on identification, but the court can impose a ban, either of its own volition or on the application of either prosecution or defence counsel. If an order is made, newspapers cannot publish the name, address or school of the young person, or any other information that might lead to identification. The ban also prevents photographs. (This order can also be made in civil

courts.) The Youth Justice and Criminal Evidence Bill also wanted to ban publication of a details of a young person's workplace.

Can this anonymity ever be lifted?

A youth court or (in exceptional cases) the Home Secretary can allow a young person to be identified in media reports, where it is in the young person's interests to prevent injustice to that person. This might happen if one young person who gave evidence in a case was actually suspected of committing the crime; the youth court could intervene so that they young person could be named and identified as a witness, rather than continue to be suspected of committing the offence. In addition, magistrates and judges can lift the cloak of anonymity when young people are convicted of serious offences, on the principle of 'naming and shaming', as happened in the case of the killers of little Jamie Bulger.

Section 5.10 Private prosecutions

What is a private prosecution?

Most private prosecutions begin when the Crown Prosecution Service (CPS) decides to bring a case. However, for whatever reason, the CPS may choose not to follow through a case, perhaps because the police have recommended that no action be taken, or because they do not believe there is a chance the case will succeed on the evidence, or because they may have identified procedural errors that mean the case will fail. But that does not mean that alleged criminals will not be charged, for it is possible to bring a private prosecution. Private prosecutions can be brought in a number of cases, the most recent and possibly well-known is the case of Stephen Lawrence, who was murdered at a London bus stop in 1993 by a gang. Two men were charged with murder, but the case was dropped when the CPS decided a prosecution would fail. When the CPS failed to prosecute three others allegedly involved in Stephen's death, his parents brought a private prosecution against the men. However, their case collapsed when evidence was ruled inadmissible and the three men were acquitted. Private prosecutions can be brought – and usually are brought – in less weighty matters; for example, if you insist on taking action against your neighbour after he hits you (though the CPS decides that it does not want to proceed with the case), or if you want to prosecute a motorist for careless driving.

How do I go about bringing a private prosecution?

Private prosecutions are usually heard in magistrates' court, though prosecutions for murder would involve a jury and go to the Crown Court. The first step is to get the permission of the magistrates' bench where the accused person lives, to bring the private prosecution. You will have to go into a witness box at the magistrates' court and be asked to give details of the person you want to prosecute, and the nature of the crime you are alleging took place. Remember that you can only prosecute someone for offences that exist in law: if the act you are complaining about is not a crime, you cannot prosecute them for doing it. If you can convince the magistrates that you have the basis of a case – you don't have to prove that the person you want to prosecute actually committed the crime at this stage – then the bench will give you permission to bring a private prosecution, and a summons will be issued by the court and served on the accused person.

The court will arrange the time and date of the hearing, and inform you accordingly so that you can arrange for your lawyers to be in court. Because it is a private prosecution brought by you, you will have you take on the costs of bringing the case yourself. Occasionally the CPS will take over a private prosecution, and then you would no longer be responsible for the cost element of the case, though cases are sometimes taken over and then withdrawn.

I have been summonsed to appear in court by my neighbour after a fight. The police decided not to bring charges. Is there anything I can do?

If you feel that you might have a case against your accuser, and if there was a brawl then at first sight you arguably have as much of a case against him as he has against you, then you can also issue a summons. In such cases of two opposing allegations, neither you nor your neighbour are likely to be satisfied – if the magistrates cannot get to the bottom of the affair (and bear in mind the police decided that they could not, or would not waste their time doing so) then they will probably bind you both over to keep the peace.

What happens if the private prosecution succeeds?

If the prosecution case is proved, the penalty for the offence will be imposed in the same way as if it were a CPS prosecution. If you should lose. however, you could be sued for damages for malicious prosecution, provided that the other party can prove you acted maliciously. Even worse though is the award of costs; if your private prosecution fails you could be ordered to pay defence costs as well as your own side's.

I am unhappy with the way the police and CPS have dealt with a case – they say the evidence isn't strong enough yet and they are still building a case. Should I bring a private prosecution?

This is the big issue as far as private prosecutions are concerned; if you bring a private prosecution, say for murder, and it fails, then no matter how much evidence the police get hold of, what the Americans call 'double jeopardy' – the concept that you can't be tried for the same offence twice – means that the guilty person will not face another trial. However, the Home Secretary has announced that he is reviewing the 'double jeopardy' rule.

This 'double jeopardy' rule has been highlighted recently by the case of a man who was cleared of murdering a woman, only to confess to the crime several years later; all that the CPS can now do is to put him on trial for committing perjury at his previous trial by lying in the witness box. If your prosecutions should fail, you may never get justice, so consider the pros and cons carefully before deciding.

Section 5.11 Compensation for victims of crime

Can victims of crime get compensation for injuries suffered when a crime is committed?

If you are a victim of crime, you can get compensation in a number of ways:

*   You can sue for damages in a civil court.
*   A judge or magistrate hearing a criminal case against the person that hurt you can order them to pay you compensation, either at once or in instalments.

Both these remedies are limited in a number of ways:

*   The criminal must have means to pay you: if a judge orders a poor person to pay you compensation, or makes an order against a person of no means who is also going to jail, your chances of getting cash are very limited.
*   There must be someone to make the order against, or someone for you to sue. If you are the victim of an unsolved crime, a judge has no-one to order to pay compensation; or you were attacked by an unknown assailant say, who could you sue?

A third option would be to apply to the Criminal Injuries Compensation Authority for compensation under its scheme.

How does the Criminal Injuries Compensation Scheme work?

The scheme will compensate victims of 'criminal injuries' which include victims of crimes of violence, arson or injuries you incur while trying to restrain or detain a criminal. Mental injuries and disease can also be compensated, for example if you were traumatised by a crime of violence. Injuries sustained in motor accidents will not be considered, unless you were the victim of someone trying to deliberately run you down, or a road-rage incident.

How do I claim for my injuries?

You can obtain forms from the Criminal Injuries Compensation Authority (see Appendix). Often, a final assessment of what compensation should be paid takes place when an injury has had time to stabilise. Compensation is normally paid as a lump sum, but if a claims officer thinks it is appropriate, interim payments can be made while the final calculation is being made.

How much compensation can I claim for my injuries?

The Criminal Injuries Compensation Authority has a comprehensive tariff that covers virtually all types of injury. Rather than list every category, here are a few examples of compensation figures that the Authority can order:

*   Sprained ankle (keeping you off work) for 6–13 weeks £1,000
*   Front teeth cracked (needing crown) £1,000
*   Multiple first degree burns (at least 25 per cent of body) £30,000
*   Loss of sight in one eye £20,000
*   Loss of sight in both eyes £75,000
*   Rape £10,000–17,500
*   Permanent, serious brain damage £250,000
*   Death (payment to one relative) £10,000

Can I claim for loss of earnings as a result of my injuries?

If your claim succeeds, you can be compensated for loss of earnings, though any social security payments or benefits you have received while you are off work will be deducted from the payment. Compensation will begin being calculated from 28 weeks after you sustained the injury that led to you going sick.

My wife was brutally raped while I was forced to watch. Can I claim for mental injuries?

Yes. Relatives of loved ones that suffer physical injury (including being killed) arising from a crime of violence, arson or attempting to arrest a criminal, can claim damages for mental injury, providing the relationship still exists (unless your wife had died) and you either witnessed the attack or was involved in the aftermath of it.

Can my claim be limited or reduced?

Awards can be withheld or reduced if you do not take all reasonable steps to inform the police or the authority the circumstances surrounding your injury as soon as is practicable. Failing to co-operate with police in bringing the criminal to justice, or with processing the application or compensation could also lead to the award being reduced or withheld. More importantly, your conduct before, during and after the incident that led to your claim can affect the making of an award, as can evidence as to your character – namely if you have any criminal convictions.

If I decide to apply for compensation from the judge or magistrates, what should I do?

You should contact the police or Crown Prosecution Service before the case goes to trial to tell them you want to be compensated. You will have to account for the claim you are making – loss of earnings, injuries, etc. If your attacker is convicted, the prosecution will then ask the court to make a compensation order, though a judge may decide to do so unbidden. The court will apply standard rules to calculate compensation for your injuries, and this will either be made in a lump sum, or in instalments over a two-year period. If a judge orders compensation, this liability takes precedence over fines or costs, and must be paid first. If your attacker defaults, he can be brought back to court. If you are awarded compensation you can still sue for damages in a civil court, but to get anything, the accused person must be convicted. No conviction, no compensation.

Section 5.12 Defences

There is a number of defences that are available if you have been accused of a crime. Some, such as the 'young man's defence' (for allegations of unlawful sexual intercourse) have been dealt with in the sections that cover the crimes. Others are outlined here.

I've been charged with an offence but I can't recall committing the crime. Can I plead insanity?

If you claim to have been suffering from some kind of mental disturbance or impairment at the time of the offence, it is possible to raise a defence of insanity (in murder cases, diminished responsibility) or automatism. Insanity can be an issue at the time of the trial, where your counsel might argue you are unfit to stand trial, but impairment at the time of the offence is a defence, rather than a procedural manoeuvre designed to prevent a trial taking place.

How can I claim a defence of insanity?

In order to succeed with a defence of insanity, you would have to prove on a balance of probabilities that at the time of the offence, a disease of the mind prevented you being aware of the nature and quality of your actions, or if you did know what you were doing, the disease of the mind meant you did not realise the actions were legally wrong. So, if you committed a crime while you suffered from a blackout, you could plead not guilty by reason of insanity. However, if despite your mind being diseased, you knew your actions were legally wrong then you cannot succeed with a plea of insanity. Effectively, what you are saying is that you were insane at the time you committed the offence. This defence has a number of serious consequences for you if it succeeds.

What counts as a disease of the mind?

A variety of conditions count as diseases of the mind, and medical expert testimony will be vital here. Anything that seems to affect the mind's functioning could be classed as a disease of the mind. Examples include epilepsy, blood clots on the brain, tumours, diabetes, arteriosclerosis, diabetes and even sleepwalking.

However, if the mind's malfunction is caused by an external factor, for example drink or drugs or a blow to the head, a defence of insanity cannot be raised (but if it resulted in a total loss of the mind's control of the body, it could allow you to plead automatism).

So if my plea of insanity succeeds, I walk free then?

Not exactly. If you are found not guilty by reason of insanity, you will be sent to a mental hospital for an indefinite period for observation.

What if I am unfit to stand trial?

If your counsel argues that you are suffering from a mental disorder that makes it impossible for you to understand the proceedings and exercise your rights in court, if the judge agrees then you cannot stand trial. Your counsel would have to prove that your state of mind was such that you could not stand trial. But again, this route should not be taken lightly. If the judge finds you are unfit to plead, you will be committed indefinitely to a mental hospital; if you should then 'regain' your sanity proceedings could be reopened.

What about diminished responsibility as a defence to murder?

If you have killed someone (or been party to the killing), you will be able to plead guilty to manslaughter on the grounds of diminished responsibility if you can show that you were suffering from an abnormality of the mind (caused by disease, injury or arrested mental development) that substantially impaired your mental responsibility for your acts and omissions in connection with the killing.

What about automatism?

To succeed in a defence of automatism, you would have to prove that your body acted outside the control of your mind. To succeed with a defence of automatism, you need to show that the loss of control was caused by an external 'trigger', such as a blow to the head. If the loss of control was caused by internal factors, a defence of automatism will fail and you will have to rely on insanity.

Are there any other defences to a charge of murder?

A possible defence to murder arises if the killing was provoked. This was discussed in detail in **Crimes of violence**.

Is the fact that I was drunk or had taken drugs any defence?

Intoxication can provide a defence. If your drinks were spiked and you then committed a crime that you would not have done had you been sober, then you can claim a defence of involuntary intoxication. If you were accused of stealing a policeman's helmet, and you claimed your drinks had been spiked without your knowledge, it would not matter that, once you became drunk, you decided to steal the helmet. If you would not have done such a thing while fully sober, then you can claim the defence. If it just loosened your inhibitions then you will not have a defence.

Intoxication does not provide an absolute defence to murder, but may allow you to argue for manslaughter. If you are an alcoholic and suffer from delirium tremens, then you might be able to claim temporary insanity.

My friends were feeding me double whiskies when I thought I was drinking singles...

In this case, you cannot rely on the defence as you knew you were drinking alcohol – it was just the strength of the drinks that fooled you.

I have been charged with a crime but I was blackmailed into doing it. Can I claim that as a defence?

Courts recognise the defence of necessity, which works on the principle that you committed the crime in order to avoid an even greater evil. But actually using the defence is quite difficult; for example, you would think that if you were starving, a defence of necessity might work if you were accused of stealing food. As a matter of public policy, courts would not seek to punish defendants for doing something that reasonable people in the same circumstances would have done. But a defence of necessity will never succeed if you are charged with murder.

They were threatening to hurt my mother... surely I was under duress?

The defence of duress is closely related to necessity. The legal definition of duress is that you felt compelled to commit a crime because of an immediate threat of death or physical bodily harm by some other person. However, the threat must be made against you directly, rather than a member of your family or a friend. But duress is no defence to a charge of murder.

I was attacked by a gang and I defended myself. Is that a defence?

Courts recognise that there are occasions when people have to protect themselves from threats of violence or violence itself, and as a matter of public policy it would be wrong to prosecute people who defend themselves from unlawful attacks, provided they use reasonable force to do so. In fact, self-defence is the only absolute defence to a charge of murder – kill or be killed. In order to succeed with a defence of self-defence, you would need to show that the force you used was reasonable. What is reasonable depends on the circumstances – for example if you are facing an unruly grandmother, then just holding her down until police arrive would be reasonable, whereas if faced by a mob of football fans, defending yourself with a golf club or baseball bat might count as reasonable force. What is reasonable ultimately depends on the jury at the time of the trial.

What about consent?

In most crimes, there must be a victim, so if the 'victim' consents to the criminal act then it is not a crime. For example, if you 'steal' a friend's pen, if the friend does not count it as stealing then it cannot be theft. Similarly, as the whole point of rape is that the there is no consent, consent means there is no rape. However, a defence of consent cannot be brought in cases of murder or manslaughter, in fights (except as parts of sports which are played according to the rules) or the deliberate infliction of harm for no purpose. Note that children and young persons cannot consent to indecent acts by adults, however, as a matter of public policy.

Chapter 6
You and your leisure

Section 6.1 Shopping

We all shop. Whether it's a bottle of perfume, a sandwich for lunch or a holiday in paradise, we are all consumers of goods and services. Almost every trader is a scrupulous, fair and honest individual or company, but there are one or two sharks out there. How much protection does the law give us from these sharks? The Romans had a phrase '*caveat emptor*' which means 'buyer beware'. Thankfully English law is not that harsh, as it recognises that skilful conmen can deliberately mislead and big companies draft tough contract terms that may put ordinary people at a disadvantage. A range of Acts of Parliament protect the rights of ordinary consumers, and limit the rights of companies against them. In addition, the Office of Fair Trading oversees commercial activity in the UK, as do trading standards departments (sections of your local authority or council).

Do goods on sale have to meet any legal requirements as to their condition?

The Sale of Goods Act says that goods must be:

1. **Of satisfactory quality.** They must be what a reasonable person would consider to be an acceptable standard, taking into account the description, cost and any other relevant factors. 'Satisfactory quality' covers the good's finish and appearance, safety standards and how hard-wearing they are. Unless they have been brought to your attention before you buy (and in which case you should expect a reduction in price), goods must be totally defect-free.
2. **Fit for their purpose** (and this includes any particular purpose mentioned by you to the seller). If you buy a computer game and tell the shop you want to play it on a particular type of machine, the shop cannot sell you a game that cannot be played, and then claim it was fit for its purpose.
3. **As described.** If you are told that a shirt is 100 per cent cotton, then if it turns out to be cotton and polyester, you have a right to complain. This also applies to labelling on the item or packaging, or to displays and signs.

These are statutory rights. All goods bought or hired from a trader or any kind – a shop, market trader, mail-order catalogue or door-to-door salesmen – are covered, including goods bought in sales.

What if the goods I have bought do not meet these standards?

Once you discover that something is wrong with the goods, you need to contact the seller as soon as possible to complain, either in person by bringing the goods back to the shop or by telephoning (but if you use the 'phone make a note of the conversation, and the name of the assistant you speak to, as this avoids any difficulties later if the assistant can't remember talking to you). You are entitled to have faulty goods replaced or get a refund if you notify the shop promptly. But if you keep the goods for too long without complaining after discovering the defect, or if you have not checked the goods for defects and too much time elapses, you may be considered to have 'accepted' the goods in that condition. 'How much time can elapse?' depends on the circumstances; you are certainly able to take the goods home and try them out. In most cases, shops tend to be good about damaged goods because of the PR value, but legally a significant delay in reporting damaged goods can affect your rights to replace them or claim a refund.

Once goods have been legally accepted, you can't claim a refund, only reasonable compensation, and would have to accept an offer to repair the goods (but shops may well replace the item if it would work out cheaper than repairing it, as is often the case with small electrical or computer goods, for example) or its cash value if it cannot be replaced.

Can I always insist on a refund or the right to exchange goods?

You cannot always demand a refund or an exchange. You may not be able to exchange goods if you took too long to return them, or if you knew of the defect when you bought the goods, or if you damaged the goods carelessly or by not following instructions, or if you have just changed your mind about wanting the item – that's just your bad bargain (though big stores do exchange goods that are not defective as a courtesy not as a right).

The goods were delivered and I signed an acceptance note. Does this mean I have signed away any right to complain?

You can check goods delivered to your house to see that they are not defective, and the law allows a reasonable time for this, so as long as you send back defective goods as quickly as possible your statutory rights are unaffected.

Do I have to accept a credit note because the shop wants me to?

No. You can insist on your money back, as credit notes cannot always be exchanged for cash if you don't see anything else you want to buy, and then you would be stuck! In addition, some credit notes expire after a period of time, which would mean you would need to 'spend it' quickly.

The goods were given to me as a present. Can I complain?

Strictly speaking, as the contract of sale was between the buyer, who gave you the present, and the shop, it is the buyer who should complain. But the buyer can authorise you in writing to complain on their behalf, and in most cases, if you have the receipt then shops would rather negotiate with you rather than get bogged down in contract law!

Do I need a receipt to claim a refund?

No. To claim a refund for faulty goods, all you have to prove is that you bought the goods from the shop. Of course, it is easier if you have the receipt...

Am I responsible for paying the cost of taking faulty goods back?

You are not legally obliged to pay to return faulty goods to the seller, so if an item is big and bulky, ask the shop to collect it! But, if you received the item as a present or if you complain about faults after accepting the goods (in the legal sense, by keeping them for a period of time without complaint) then you may have to pay.

The shop says that I have to deal with the manufacturer as 'it is the manufacturer's fault'. Is that correct?

Traders can't opt out of the responsibilities. The law says it is up to the seller to deal with complaints about defective goods; – they can't pass the buck to manufacturers. But if the product comes with a guarantee, you may have additional rights against the manufacturer. These will be discussed in more detail in **Conditions, warranties and guarantees**. (The seller can still take the matter up with the manufacturer and seek and indemnity from them, but that is not your concern.)

I bought some goods in a sale and they were faulty. The shop says they were on sale so I have no rights to refunds of any kind (and there were signs on show saying just that). Is that true?

The fact that the goods were bought in a sale does not affect your statutory rights as to the quality of goods. Signs can't limit your statutory rights either. But you should think twice before shopping in a place that displays notices like that; it is against the law, and local authorities can prosecute the trader.

I ordered goods and paid a deposit, but now I have changed my mind about them. Can I get my deposit back?

There is no automatic right to the return of your deposit if you have changed your mind about the purchase; some deposits may not be returnable. It all depends on the terms in the agreement you signed when handing over your deposit; so read the small print carefully!

What if I buy goods using a credit card?

If you buy goods on your credit card that cost more than £100, but not more than £30,000, your credit card company is also liable for any claim you make against the seller. This gives added protection, especially if the seller goes bankrupt or disappears.

If I have bought something on a credit agreement, what rights do I have to change my mind and cancel?

Credit agreements have a 'cooling-off period'; if you change your mind within this period, you may be able to cancel. The credit agreement must state whether you can cancel in this way, and how long the cooling-off period is. But this does not apply if you did not make the agreement with the seller in person (so purchases made on the telephone are excluded) or if the agreement was signed at the supplier's business premises.

How are my rights affected if I buy something in a private sale?

If you buy goods privately, you have fewer rights than when you buy from a trader. Privately-bought goods do not have to be free of faults, but must be as described, so a leather coat that turns out to be plastic would be a ground for complaint. The rule for private sales is buyer, beware; so make sure you check that you are getting a good buy. But if you are injured by defective goods, or they cause property damage of more than £275, you have rights regardless of how they were bought or if they were a gift.

If the seller says anything misleading about the good's condition, and you buy on that basis, only for the statement to be false, you might be able to sue. But this would be difficult to prove, however, and a witness to what was said in the run-up to the sale would be very useful if you had to go to court. So, it might be an idea to take someone with you when you buy anything privately, or ask for a written description of the goods. You have fewer rights buying from private sellers; unscrupulous traders know this and some pose as private sellers, for example in car boot sales or via newspaper ads. A clue would be if you see a lot of different adverts, all with the same telephone number. This is against the law, and if you buy defective goods and suspect the seller was really a trader, contact your trading standards, who should be able to confirm whether the seller is a trader, in which case your statutory rights apply. Trading standards may also prosecute the seller.

Are my rights different if the goods are bought second-hand?

When you buy second-hand goods from a trader, you have the same rights as when buying new ones, but with the qualification that second-hand will be of a lesser quality as brand new. But you can ask for a refund or the cost of repairs if the goods are faulty, unless the faults are from normal wear and tear, or if the defects were pointed out before you bought.

A salesman called at my house and showed me a demonstration vacuum cleaner, which I liked very much and bought. Now I have opened the box of my new cleaner and it is not the same. What can I do?

The vacuum cleaner must be the same model and quality (though not necessarily identical, for example the colour may be different) as the sample, and you must be able to compare the sample and your cleaner. In addition, there must not be any faults that could not be detected by examining the sample in a reasonable way. If these conditions are not met, you are entitled to a refund or a new cleaner.

I'm going to an auction to buy some furniture. Do I have the same rights as if I bought from a shop?

This is another place where 'buyer, beware' is important, as auctioneers can refuse to accept responsibility for the quality of the goods they auction; if they do, exclusion clauses to exclude this liability will probably be displayed on notices in the saleroom, in the catalogue or any promotional material. Another thing to remember is that once the hammer has fallen that's it; you cannot back out on the sale.

What are exclusion clauses?

Some traders may try to evade their liabilities in contracts by using exclusion clauses, for example saying they will not accept any liability for loss or damage. But if an exclusion clause is unfair it is legally void and cannot be used against you. Generally only a court can decide whether a contract term is unfair, but trading standards will be able to advise whether you have a good case to complain. **But any exclusion of liability that tries to exclude or limit liability for death or personal injury is always void, whether it appears in a contract term or on a notice.** A sign limiting statutory rights is also void, for example a sign saying 'No refunds given'. Attempting to limit statutory rights is a crime, and trading standards departments can prosecute. But in the case of services, statements limiting liability are not automatically illegal, for example a clause that reads 'No responsibility for loss or damage to garments, however caused' on the back of a dry-cleaning ticket.

What about buying a service?

When you pay for a service, for example, from a dry-cleaner, a hairdresser or builder, you are entitled to certain standards:

*   The service should be performed using reasonable care and skill, and with the proper standards of workmanship.
*   The service should be performed within a reasonable time, even if a completion date has not been agreed.
*   If no price has been fixed in advance, the charge for the service should be reasonable. If the price was fixed at the outset, you cannot complain subsequently, not if a method of calculating the price was agreed before work started. For this reason, it is best to get a quotation (which is a fixed price) rather than an estimate (an informed guess); that way you know where you stand, and if the tradesman pitches his quotation too low, he is bound by the price too

If any materials are used in providing the service or if the service involves fitting goods (bricks, wallpaper or radiator pipes, for example) then you are protected by the same statutory rights over these materials as you would if you had bought them yourself from a builders' yard or wherever.

Some tradesmen are members of a trade association; in itself, this does not guarantee that the workmanship will be satisfactory, but does suggest that the tradesman has some standards and that it might be possible to remedy any problems if things go wrong; many associations have codes of practice, which may help you if the trader is a member of the association and something goes wrong.

I've been sold some unsafe electrical goods. What can I do?

It is an offence for a supplier to sell unsafe goods (either new and second-hand). But this does not apply to antiques or to goods that you were sold on the basis that they needed to be repaired or reconditioned. Trading standards may prosecute the sellers of unsafe goods, and you can also take action against the manufacturer of defective goods for any injuries or damage caused.

A door-to-door salesman has called at my house to sell me some goods. Are my rights the same?

When a salesman calls, don't sign anything until you have had a chance to compare prices with other companies. You may be offered gifts or incentives to sign, but ignore the pressure; don't sign until you know how the price compares with other sellers, or until you understand fully what the agreement you sign commits you to. Anyone signing an agreement at home, or buying goods worth more than £35 from a salesman that calls without an appointment, has several days to cancel (you should be given a written confirmation of your cancellation rights) though there are exceptions (in the case of perishable goods – which is understandable – and home extensions –which is not). But if the seller is calling by appointment, there may not be a right to cancel, so be wary of sales visits masquerading as surveys, prize draws, etc.

If you buy anything costing more than £50 on credit, you can cancel, regardless of whether the trader called by appointment, provided the deal was discussed face to face with the seller and the agreement was not signed at the seller's offices.

Members of the Direct Selling Association have a code of practice covering doorstep and party-plan selling, which gives buyers a 14-day cooling-off period on most goods.

If you decide to cancel, act fast. Send recorded delivery letters, so you have proof of delivery if the company tries to play hard-ball.

What about buying goods by mail-order?

You have the same statutory rights buying via mail-order as from a shop; but there are other things you need to consider, such as the risks of handing over credit card details to some company that you might only know of by their advert. Delivery should be within a reasonable time (normally 28 days, or whatever the advert may state), or you can cancel the order and ask for your money back. Once they are delivered, you have a reasonable time to examine the goods. If there are any problems, send them back at once, explaining why; otherwise you may be held to have 'accepted' them, and if you have to pay to send the goods back, you can claim the cost of this. If you decide to order, don't send cash – cheques or credit card is a better way to pay. But if you do send cash, send it by registered letter to prove delivery, though of course this does not prove you sent cash at all, only an envelope You'd be better advised getting a friend to write a cheque on your behalf.

Some mail order purchases do not involve one-off purchases, for example book or record clubs, and most require that you buy a number of books or records over a period to qualify for the introductory offer, which is usually reduced or free records, tapes or books. Before signing up, find out what the conditions are. Most newspapers and magazines operate mail order protection schemes (MOPS), which protect you if you respond to an advertisement, paying in advance for goods, only for the firm to go bust before your product is delivered. If this happens to you, write to the paper or magazine's advertising manager.

Is it wise to pay for mail-order goods in advance?

If you pay in advance for goods and services and the firm goes out of business, you could get little or nothing back, so the best course is not to pay in advance unless you have to, though in some cases, for example, home improvements or made-to-measure goods, you have to. Try to find out about firms you have never heard of before sending them cheques, and check if deposits are refundable if you cancel. Above all, if you pay in advance, get a receipt with the company's name and address on it.

I have been sent some goods in the post that I did not order. What do I do?

If you receive unsolicited goods through the post, you do not have to accept them and should write to the firm saying that you don't want them. If they are not collected within 30 days they become yours. If you decide to do nothing about contacting the firm but put them to one side, after six months they become legally yours too! If the firm contacts you asking for payment, contact trading standards.

Section 6.2 Guarantees, warranties and trade descriptions

What is a guarantee?

Because of the concept of privity of contract (which means that only the parties to the contract – which means the buyer and the seller – can sue on it) if you buy goods from a shop and they turn out to be defective or broken, then your contract is with the shop and not the manufacturer, so you should complain to the shop as your rights are against them. But in certain fields, namely cars and electrical goods in the main, manufacturers accept they have some responsibility to deal with defects (partly because of the damage to their reputation that a customer complaining about a defective washing machine might have, for example). As a result, manufacturers often offer a guarantee for the goods, which is good PR and because the manufacturer has more experience in repairing or servicing the goods than the store.

Guarantees normally run for a fixed length of time, usually six or 12 months, and which normally runs from the date of purchase. This is an additional right; you can still insist on your statutory rights against the store that sold you the defective goods.

What rights do I have under a guarantee?

Your rights under any guarantee depend on the wording. Most are concerned with defective components and poor workmanship, and will often promise to repair faulty parts and goods, or replace them if the manufacturer prefers (and in some cases it is cheaper to replace than repair). Sometimes guarantees are limited only to the cost of parts, so you have to pay for the labour costs, and other guarantees pass on to you the costs of packaging and returning goods. But remember, guarantees do not take away your statutory rights, so if your goods are defective, you still have rights against the seller, so if the guarantee requires you to pay to ship the goods back to the manufacturer, you can claim the costs back from the retailer even if it was not their fault. But guarantees aren't always as good as they sound, for example, if the company ceases trading. Insurance-backed guarantee schemes are available from some trade associations to cover building work; if you go for this option, make sure the insurance covers the same time span as the guarantee or you might lose out at the end of the term.

I didn't send back the guarantee card that came with my vacuum cleaner. The cleaner is broken and the manufacturers say the guarantee is not in force.

Strictly speaking, the manufacturer is within its rights to insist that terms it has built into its agreement for activating guarantees must be honoured. Therefore, if you are asked to send back a registration card then you should do so. But in most cases, manufacturers don't bother to check precise dates if they are satisfied that your goods are within the guarantee period, or you have a sales receipt; after all, it's good PR for them. On the other hand, remember that your statutory rights still exist against the store, so even if the guarantee is not active you can exercise your rights against the store instead.

What about extended guarantees?

Some electrical goods manufacturers that produce TVs, cookers, home computers or washing machines may offer extended guarantee or warranty, which you normally pay extra for, and which is really a service contract for parts and labour. For large, high value items such as TVs, fridges or washing machines, this can be a good idea, because call-out charges can bump up the costs of repairs considerably, but this may not be the case for smaller items; look at the value for money offered by extended warranties, as it might be more expensive to take out the warranty than to get your own repair man, or even buy a new item!

What is a warranty?

A warranty is another name for a guarantee, especially in the motor trade. Vehicle warranties will be discussed in more detail later.

What is a trade description?

A trade description is a description of any goods or service given by a trader acting in the course of their business, and the law says this description must be accurate and not misleading. So if an estate agent tells you a house has a 30-foot driveway, or if a shop assistant tells you that you will be able to play a particular game on your home computer, then it may be a trade description. A description can be given verbally, in writing (for example, in an advert or brochure or as an invoice or order form), through an illustration (for example, in advertisements or on packaging) or by implication. Under UK law, the Trade Descriptions Act makes it is an offence if a trader applies a false or misleading description to goods (which can be by writing it down, making a verbal statement or by turning back a car's odometer) or if a trader supplies, or offers to supply, goods to which a false or misleading trade description is applied. This would cover goods on display in a shop or in a storeroom ready for sale.

What sorts of statements can be classed as trade descriptions?

Trade descriptions can include statements as to an item's size (length, weight etc.), how it was made, what it is made from, statements as to its strength, performance, behaviour or accuracy (in car adverts, it would include statements such as 'immaculate condition', 'mechanically superb' and 'in excellent condition'), saying that it meets certain standards, like the BS Kitemark and many others. If you want to know if a term is a trades description, ask trading standards. Remember too that logos can be trades descriptions.

In the case of services, it is also an offence to make a false or misleading statement, deliberately or recklessly about the nature, location or providers of any service, accommodation or facilities, or about any examination or approval of the services, facilities or accommodation (for example, saying that the Holiday programme gave it a four star rating when it was panned, or had not even appeared on the show).

If I think that I have bought something to which a false trade description has been applied, what can I do?

Really there are two issues here. One is to act like a consumer and complain to the trader. The trader may not want bad publicity and may give you your money back, reduce the price or offer you a satisfactory replacement. The other issue is the criminal one. By selling an item with a false trade description, your trader has broken the law. Report the matter to trading standards; they will investigate and prosecute if they feel you have a case.

I am a trader being sued for making a false trade description. Do I have a defence?

If you made the trade description yourself, then you are stuck – you said it, so it is your misdescription, even if you thought what you had said was the truth. But if the manufacturer provided the misdescription and you repeated it, you could get off provided that you took reasonable steps to ensure that the goods conformed to the description.

What about bogus goods? I bought a branded sweatshirt but it's a fake...

A trade mark is used to indicate a link between goods and the company having the right to use the mark (for example the Nike 'tick' or the Adidas trefoil or three-stripe logo). In addition, many famous household brand names are registered as trade marks – this may cover a logo, name, word or signature. Trade marks are trades descriptions because they tell you that the goods are produced and manufactured by the company whose logo is displayed on the shirt or label;

there is also the quality issue (you expect a branded shirt to be manufactured to a high quality standard). It is illegal to apply a registered trade mark (or something that looks like it) to goods or packaging. Trading standards departments and the courts take the importation, manufacture and distribution of counterfeit goods most seriously, and come down hard on offending retailers; the 'Del Boy' image of 'cheeky chappies selling slightly hooky gear to people that know it's dodgy anyway' cuts no ice in court! However innocently a retailer may have acted in taking delivery of fake goods, once they sell (or attempt to sell) or hire them, a prosecution is likely unless it can be shown that all reasonable steps were taken to confirm that the goods were genuine. So if a retailer collected a supply of branded goods from the supplier company's warehouse, it is reasonable to expect them to be genuine; it is not so reasonable if he collects them at 11.30pm from the back of a van in a pub car park! Be wary if goods are priced too cheap for what they are supposed to be, and be especially dubious if you are told that the goods are 'seconds' or 'rejects' – they may be fake, or they may be stolen. They could be genuine too, but if you can't confirm it the risk may be too great to take.

What are the penalties for selling bogus goods?

If trading standards mount a prosecution for offences under the Trade Descriptions Act 1968, Trade Marks Act 1938 or Copyright, Design and Patents Act 1988, a trader can be fined up to £5,000 in the magistrates' court and/or jailed for up to six months.

Section 6.3 Travel, holidays and transport

We all look forward to holidays, a chance to have a well-earned break, to relax and have fun. So it can be very disappointing, frustrating and expensive if things go wrong. When you book a holiday, you enter into a contract, usually with a tour operator, and the law gives you automatic statutory rights.

I booked a holiday with a travel agent rather than with the tour operator. What does this mean in terms of my rights?

In most cases, you book your holiday with a tour operator, via a travel agent; your contract for the holiday itself is with the tour operator, who must accept liability for all the holiday's elements: the travel, accommodation, pre-booked car hire, etc. The travel agent acts as an agent for the tour operator, but it also has an obligation to process the booking correctly and efficiently. The agent may also be liable for other extras not connected to the holiday advertised in the brochure but which they have sold on top of the booking, like currency exchange, arranging airport car parking, etc.

Under the Supply of Goods And Services Act 1982 (amended by the Sale and Supply of Goods Act 1994), the contract for the holiday should be booked using 'reasonable care and skill', which means both tour operator and travel agent should ensure that they carry out the booking correctly, that the holiday itself should be of a generally satisfactory standard, and that it matches its description.

Booking a holiday is entering a contract, so if you make any special requests, make sure they are entered on the booking form and passed on to the tour operator. Read the small print: once you have signed, the law assumes you have read them and are bound by them; keep a copy in case you need to refer to the conditions later if anything goes wrong. The terms and conditions must be fair and reasonable, so if in doubt, take legal advice before you sign (you could cross out the offending terms, but the operator does not have to accept this revision of the contract).

Soon after you book through the agent, the operator will send a confirmation notice, which you should check carefully as it is your proof of the contract and what you have booked. The confirmation usually has details about flights and accommodations, dates and times of departures and any special requests that have been booked. Check anything that does not match with what you booked with the agent – it may be an oversight, or mean that your request will not be met. Now is the time to query and try to get it sorted out, as spotting problems or omissions at this stage can obviously avoid a lot of hassle and upset later on.

I booked a holiday and now the tour operator has gone bust. What can I do?

The Package Travel, Package Holidays and Package Tour Regulations 1992 require tour operators to ensure that the money you have paid out for your holiday is protected by the company having adequate insurance bonding (or some other method of protection). If the company ceases trading while you are abroad, arrangements must be made to repatriate you. The regulations also impose further controls on tour operators about the overbooking of hotels and false or inaccurate descriptions of resorts and hotels made by representatives while you are on holiday, as opposed to statements in the brochure or made by booking clerks.

Do I need travel insurance when I book a holiday?

Most tour operators require you to have adequate insurance cover (the travel agent will probably try to sell you cover when you book) but the choice is yours, so shop around and compare prices and levels of cover first. Travel agents used to offer great discount deals on holidays provided you took out their insurance, but this is now illegal. If you are planning to hire a car while on holiday, check that your cover extend to this, and that medical cover is adequate (in some cases, you may need to take out extra insurance cover locally, for example, to hire a car in the USA). Make sure your policy covers cancellation, because if you cancel, the operator will almost always charge a penalty which varies in amount depending on how much notice you give.

Are there any other steps I can take to protect the money I 'invest' in my holiday?

If you have a credit card, and your holiday costs more than £100, it is worth paying for the holiday using this facility, or even just for a part of it, such as the deposit. This is because the Consumer Credit Act 1974 makes the credit card company equally liable for any breaches of contract, including the trader going bust, or your having a nightmare holiday. But this only applies if you book direct with the tour operator and not via an agent. If the travel agent and operator are members of holiday trade associations, such as ABTA (Association of British Travel Agents), AITO (Association of Independent Tour Operators) or IATA (Independent Air Travel Association), they will be covered by the body's code of practice and the association may step in if problems occur.

Also, you should ask about bonding; even though it is a legal requirement for a tour operator to have bonding, it is better to check specifically. If the company ceases trading before you fly, you should get your money back; if you are already abroad, you should be able to continue your holiday and fly home without having to pay extra, but you may have to pay some expenses up front and then claim them back, if your tour operator is not a member of ABTA or AITO and does not hold an ATOL (see below).

Package holidays that include flights must be protected by an ATOL (Air Travel Organisers' Licence) which is granted by the Civil Aviation Authority (CAA), and which carries out an examination every 12 months to ensure the companies are fit to hold a licence and are financially sound. (This makes it less likely that a travel company will collapse and catch people unawares.)

I booked a holiday in one hotel in a resort. Now the travel agent says that hotel is overbooked and I've been moved to a new hotel in a different part of the resort (which we don't like because it is too quiet). What can we do?

Sometimes, the tour operator might change important parts of the holiday after you have booked. If the change is a significant one, such as moving you to a different hotel that you are not happy with, they are probably in breach of contract, and should give you the option to cancel and receive a full refund if you want to. Altering the itinerary or making significant changes in flight times would also fall into this category. If you don't want to cancel, you can always try to negotiate a change in the booking to another holiday for a similar price. Another option, if you still want to go on the trip and/or it is too short notice to arrange an alternative, is to write to the operator, telling them you are unhappy with the situation, but will assess the effect of the changes on your holiday when you have travelled or are at the resort. This has the effect of reserving your right to complain – you are effectively travelling under sufferance and the operator would find it difficult to show that you accepted its holiday revisions once you sent this letter to them. Then, you could try to claim compensation on your return, for example if the hotel was a three-star and you had booked a four-star.

The hotel is nothing like the description I read in the brochure. Facilities were not as described, excursions and views did not exist and all in all I felt like I had been sent to a different hotel. Can they do this?

If you book a holiday from a brochure, you are entitled to assume that the descriptions contained in it are neither misleading nor inaccurate, and this includes photographs. We are all familiar with the goldfish-lens, touched-up picture that makes the garden pond look like an Olympic swimming pool, but some claims go far beyond salesmanship. The Supply of Goods And Services Act 1982 (amended by the Sale and Supply of Goods Act 1994) makes it the tour operators' responsibility to ensure that holidays described in their brochures should accurately reflect the holidays they sell; if it does not you can sue for breach of contract. In addition, the

Trade Descriptions Act 1968 makes it an offence to make any factual statements that are not truthful and accurate. So, if your hotel is 'a stone's throw from the beach' but you need a catapult to throw the stone then you have a right to take action! If you want to make a criminal complaint, contact your local authority's trading standards department.

So how do I complain if something goes wrong on the holiday?

Make sure you take a copy of your holiday insurance policy with you, as well as copies of the relevant page of the brochure, so that you can check anything out quickly and easily. If something is wrong with your holiday, you should complain to the tour representative as soon as possible. Make sure your complaint is in writing too, and keep a copy in case you need to refer to it later. If they can, they will solve the problem at once: a complaining guest unsettles the rest of their holidaymakers and is bad PR for the company. But if this does not happen, you may need to consider taking the following action:

1.   Ask for an official company complaint form to fill out at the resort.
2.   Take photographs or videos of any problems, such as poor accommodation, building work, etc as evidence, to back up your complaint to the company, or to show a small claims court.
3.   Keep a brief log of the problems with dates, action taken, etc., so that you have an accurate account of events on your return.
4.   Try and get fellow travellers to act as witnesses, backing your complaint preferably in writing. Make sure you have their names, addresses and telephone numbers before they and you depart. Holiday high spirits and solidarity may evaporate once they are back in the UK.
5.   If you incur extra costs on holiday because of the problem you are complaining about, for example unexpected travel costs, eating out, replacement clothing, medical fees, etc., keep bills and receipts to support your claim.

When you get home, write to the tour operator as soon as possible, giving details of the problems and copies of any receipts, pictures, statements etc to support your claims (keep the originals in case you have to go to court), and what compensation you want. You may have to be persistent, so be prepared to have to write more than once, or supply additional information. But try to be reasonable, realistic and objective about any problems you experienced on your holiday, and bear in mind that tour operators have no control over local customs and cultures. I remember booking a holiday to Spain one half-term for a week's break, and landed in Alicante on the day that their head of state, President Franco, died. Days of official mourning with nothing going on, bars closing early and the worst rain in October for 15 years made it a truly miserable holiday. But no-one was to blame!

I have complained to the tour operators but feel they have fobbed me off. Can I go further?

If all else fails, you may have to consider legal action, probably through the county or small claims courts (if your claim is for £5,000 or less, it will probably be heard as a small claim, which keeps costs down). If the tour operator is an ABTA member, you could go through their documents-only arbitration scheme (but take advice on this first, though).

If you feel any facilities or other aspects of the holiday were misrepresented, either verbally or in writing, you should complain to trading standards as this is a crime, and if they feel there is enough evidence they may prosecute, but this will be as well as, and not instead of, your civil claim against the company.

What about booking flights only?

If you are booking flights only, check whether the agent, or any intermediary, has an ATOL (Air Travel Operator's Licence), which is issued by the Civil Aviation Authority (CAA), and is guarantees financial protection. It is particularly important to check about the ATOL licence if the travel agent does not issue the flight tickets direct.

My luggage has been lost in transit while I was in the airport and I had some very expensive gear in the cases. What can I do?

The Air Carrier Liability Order 1998 makes airlines liable for loss or damage to personal property and luggage while in the carrier's care. There are no limits on the carrier's potential liability for financial losses, for example if you were shipping rare paintings or wine in the cargo hold. Many carriers try to limit their liability for lost luggage to a certain amount, so before travelling, you should check just how much compensation would be paid if cases go astray. In addition, make sure your holiday insurance covers lost luggage. To calculate compensation, most countries follow one of two versions of the Warsaw Convention. The most used option specifies a limit of 17 'special drawing rights' per kilogram for luggage stored in the hold, (a special drawing right is a unit of exchange listed in the Financial Times each day, the British value of which currently stands at approximately 85p) which works out at around £14.50 per kilogram. Some airlines, for example BA, assume that your checked baggage weighs 30 kilograms with a compensation limit of around £435, while others weigh the luggage and note the total on your ticket. For hand luggage, the most commonly followed version of the Convention specifies a flat rate upper limit of 332 special drawing rights, which, at a rate of 85p, would equal £282.20 per passenger. Obviously, this fluctuates according to the exchange rate.

I fancy an adventure holiday. What should I be aware of?

Adventure holidays – whitewater rafting, canoeing, gliding, sailing, etc. – are becoming more and more common as people decide that getting away from it all on a beach may be a waste of two weeks away from home. Holidays like this are particularly attractive to younger adults and teenagers.

But there are risks involved and accidents can happen. So if you are planning such a holiday, make sure you have the right insurance; some holiday policies don't cover skiing let alone gliding or rafting. That way if you have any injuries, your policy will pick up the cost (this is particularly important abroad in countries like the US where everything costs, especially medicare). The Lyme Bay canoe tragedy focused attention on outdoor pursuits holidays, and many companies demand highly qualified instructors to minimise the risks to holidaymakers. Lifesaving skills, yachting proficiency and experience and first-aid are (and should be) even more highly prized than culinary and social skills. You have a right to expect that the staff working with you are reasonably competent instructors, and should any accident be caused by their incompetence you may well have the right to sue them for negligence. If you can prove they were negligent or at fault, and the injury you suffered was reasonably foreseeable, then you should be able to recover damages as compensation for your injury or loss. Remember too that any attempt to limit liability for accidents (either on site, or in the booking form you sign or the brochure you book the holiday from) is invalid as an unfair contract term. Should you become injured on an adventure holiday, the best advice is to contact a lawyer that deals with personal injury claims as soon as you return to the UK, or sooner if you are hospitalised abroad. They can advise you.

I'm buying a second-hand motor car. I'm afraid of buying a stolen vehicle or a cut-and-shut (a car built from two broken ones welded together). Is there any way of reducing the risk?

The safest way of buying a car is from a car dealer, as this gives you the maximum protection under the law in terms of making false trade descriptions, and your statutory rights. Tales of cowboy car dealers abound, though most are reliable and many sell second-hand cars as an adjunct to their main business of selling new cars. If the dealer is a member of a trade association, for example the Society of Motor Manufacturers and Traders, and will follow a code of practice that is supported by the Office of Fair Trading. Some dealers also subscribe to quality checking schemes, like Ford Direct or Vauxhall's Network Q. Any car sold by a dealer must be of satisfactory quality, be as described and be reasonably fit for its normal purpose or any purpose that you specify to the dealer, for example if you say you want to buy a car to tow your boat. A dealer following the codes of practice would normally inspect the car before sale, and would allow you to see the vehicle check-list so you would know what you are getting. In addition, dealers would try to verify the mileage shown on the 'clock', though most will apply a sticker saying that the mileage cannot be verified. Any paper work, service records, repair invoices and inspection reports that have been supplied when the garage took possession of the car would also be available for you to see.

What about buying a car in a private sale?

If you buy a car in a private sale, if the car turns out to be stolen you may not have any rights of ownership, and could lose both the vehicle and the money you paid for it. But there are some steps you can take to minimise the risks:

- When you check over the car you plan to buy, look for the vehicle's identification number (VIN); is the metal plate that it is inscribed on where it should be? (This is usually in the engine compartment.) Check that the 17-digit VIN matches the VIN on the registration document. Does it show signs of having been fitted recently or tampered with? If there is no plate, find out why, fast! The VIN is also stamped on the vehicle body, often under the bonnet; has this been altered? Check window etchings too; if the VIN has been etched on the glass, make sure it matches.

- Beware of advertisers with only a mobile phone number, as they are virtually untraceable. Ads specifying a time to call (e.g. 'between 5pm and 6pm') could mean a call box so, be suspicious. If the seller is not keen to have you view the vehicle at his or her home, alarm bells should definitely start ringing, so don't agree to having the car brought to your home or some public place for you to look it over.

- Is the seller familiar with the car controls? If not, why not? Isn't it their car?

- The person whose name is on the vehicle registration document may not be the legal owner, but only the registered keeper. The log book does not confirm that someone owns the car, so you have to be sure that the 'seller' has a right to sell the car.

- Never buy a vehicle without a registration document, whatever excuses or reasons you may be given. The reasons may be genuine but can you take that risk? If there is a log book, check the watermark to se that it has not just been printed onto the paper.

- Does the engine number match the registration document? Has it been altered or the engine changed? There can be legitimate reasons to change an engine, but also criminal ones, so ask!

- Is there any sign that locks have been changed recently (perhaps if they had been forced)? Are the different locks on the ignition and the door?

- Think about taking an independent qualified examiner with you to see the vehicle, and check with one of the companies that hold information on vehicles, if your dream car has been reported as stolen, seriously damaged or is still under a finance agreement.

- Never pay cash.

Might the second-hand car I'm buying still be covered by a finance agreement?

If the previous owner bought your car on hire purchase, it belongs to the company that provided the finance until all the payments have been made. In layman's terms, what this means is that if the previous owner has not paid off the finance agreement when you buy the car and there is outstanding finance on it, you may lose the car (though if you were not aware that the car was subject to an outstanding credit agreement and bought it in good faith, you may be allowed to keep it – but this would not apply to cars subject to a hire agreement). You can sue the person who sold it to you for your money, but you'll have to find them first. There are companies that have records of credit agreements affecting cars: they will be able to tell you whether your car was previously bought on credit, and if so whether there are any credit agreements outstanding. If you are buying from a dealer, ask whether they have checked about credit agreements.

How do I get a driving licence?

The first step is applying for a provisional driving licence and then having lessons either from a qualified driver or an approved driving instructor before taking a driving test at a driving test centre.

Learner drivers must be supervised by another driver that must be at least 21 years old and have held a full EC licence for the appropriate category of vehicle for at least three years. Anyone giving driving lessons that is not qualified to do so could be liable to a maximum fine of £1,000, discretionary disqualification or up to six penalty points (as could the learner driver). Tests are two-stage, a practical driving test and a theory paper on the Highway Code. Once you pass the test you can apply for a full licence. When a learner is driving a car or bike, the vehicle must display an 'L' plate to show other road users that an inexperienced learner is driving, so they can take special care if needs be.

The fees are £36.75 for the practical test (£46 for evenings and weekends), and £15.50 for the theory.

What about motorcyclists?

Before becoming a 'learner' cyclist on the road, you have to undergo compulsory basic training (CBT) involving on-site and on-road training and riding; when you pass you will be given a Certificate of Completion, valid for three years, and which you will need to produce if stopped by the police and when you take your motorcycle practical test. (You don't need to take the CBT if you are provisionally qualified to ride a motorbike because you hold a full moped or full car driving licence.) Learner moped or motorcycle riders cannot carry pillion passengers. Learners aged 21 or over are allowed on any size motorcycle over 125cc, but must be accompanied by a fully qualified instructor on a separate machine. There are two types of full motorcycle licence: the light motorcycle licence (when the test is taken on a bike with engine capacity 75–125cc) that allows you to ride bike of up to 125cc; and the standard licence (for bikes with engine capacity of 120–125cc and a speed of at least 100km/h). Motorcycle tests cost £45 (£55 for evenings and weekends) and £8 for the CBT certificate.

What does every motorist need to take a vehicle on the road?

To drive alone on public highways and places, you will need to hold a full driving licence rather than a provisional licence. Learner drivers are allowed on roads and in public places provided they are accompanied by a driver with a full licence sitting beside them to advise.

In addition, the car must be fully taxed and have a valid MOT certificate, and you would need a valid policy of insurance that covers you to drive on the road in that vehicle.

These requirements apply to other motor vehicles, though to drive motorbikes, heavy goods vehicles or buses and coaches, you would need to have a licence that shows you are 'qualified' to drive these classes of vehicles.

As regards the vehicle itself, you would need to ensure that the brakes (both foot-brakes and parking brakes) and windscreen wipers with washers are in working order, and that clean, clearly readable (at seventy-five feet on a clear day) and valid number-plates are displayed front and back ('valid' means with evenly spaced letters of the correct sort). All vehicles except works trucks and pedestrian-controlled vehicles must have horns that play a single note – two-tone (or more) horns are illegal.

You must have two rear facing mirrors, one of which must be on the driver's side and which must have a rounded edge to limit the risk of injury.

Your tyres must have a sufficient amount of tread on them to grip the road. A minimum of 1mm is required, with no bald patches; and there must be no deep gashes in the side wall of the tyre. Steering wheels must be properly adjusted so as to have the right amount of play – if the steering wheel can be turned more than thirty degrees without the front wheels moving, then it is unsafe.

Speedometers must be fitted and in working order on non vintage-type vehicles, and it is an offence to have one that has a margin of error of more than ten per cent (e.g., reads 30 mph when you are doing 33 mph).

All vehicles must have white lamps at the front and red ones at the rear, and cars built after 1981 must have rear fog lamps. The lights must be fitted so as to show the width of the vehicle – so a truck can't be fitted with a single, centrally mounted light or a motorist might think a bike was coming up behind. Cars must have direction indicators at least one pair centrally mounted each side (or one set in front and one at the rear), and rear. Cars must also have stop lamps (brake lights as they are often called) that light up as soon as the brake pedal is depressed.

Other lights (for example, front fog lamps) need not be fitted by law, but if they are on your car then they must work properly. (Interestingly, reversing lights need not be fitted by law.)

Lights must be used within half an hour of sunset and half an hour before sunrise – but of course, you can have them on at other times if the road conditions require it. In poor visibility, full or dipped headlamps must be used, day or night.

Where fitted, seatbelts must be properly fixed, and it is an offence not to make passengers use belts that are fitted.

Are there any additional requirements for motorcycles?

Bikers can only carry one passenger, riding pillion, but if a sidecar is fitted a third person may ride on the combination. Crash helmets must be worn by all passengers and riders (except for members of the Sikh religion) and bikes must have at least one rear-view mirror.

What is an MOT certificate?

Three years after the date of first registration (the date the car is bought by someone as new, or registered in the case of demo vehicles), all vehicles must undergo an annual check-up to establish that the vehicle is roadworthy. Ministry of Transport certificates (MOTs) must be carried out by authorised MOT examiners (most garages have them) and the test normally takes no more than an hour to complete.

The test checks brakes, lights, suspension, seatbelts, horn, tyres and wheels, windscreen wipers and washers. The test will also involve a check of the bodywork to ensure there are no fractures or stresses that might adversely affect the brakes or steering. If the vehicle passes the test, a certificate is issued; if not, a fail certificate is issued listing work that needs to be completed before the vehicle is 'passed'. Tests can take place up to one month before the renewal date, and if issued a new certificate will run from the expiry of the old one.

It is illegal to keep a car or vehicle on a public road or place with an invalid MOT certificate, or drive a car without a valid MOT… and it may invalidate your car insurance, too.

MOTs for cars cost £32.11 and £13.04 for bikes. But garages often do them cheaper as a loss-leader, so they get your business for the service and any repairs that might be needed to get your car through the test.

What sort of insurance do I need?

Whenever a motor vehicle is on a road, either driven, parked or stationary, the owner or registered keeper must be covered by a valid policy of insurance at least for the risk of injury to other people. A vehicle owner must provide at least insurance cover for other road users ('third party' insurance) and is responsible for ensuring that other users of the vehicle have at least that level of cover, too.

Almost any vehicle owner with a valid driving licence should be able to get insurance from one of the many companies, either directly or via a broker. They may charge higher premiums for inexperienced drivers, or for drivers who have been involved in road accidents and/or made claims on other motor insurance policies.

The precise terms of your insurance cover will depend on your policy – with different excesses (how much you pay on a claim before the insurance company takes over the rest of the claim), but there are three main types of insurance available for cars:

- Third party, which covers damage and personal injury to other people if your vehicle is in collision with theirs. However, if your car is damaged in the smash, you will have to pay for those repairs yourself. Third party cover also provides cover for legal costs you may incur defending yourself for claims for damage in an accident, as well as for appeals against court decisions. It will also provide for the cost of legal representation at an inquest if your vehicle is involved in an accident in which someone dies.
- Third party, fire and theft, which is the same as third party, but also covers you if your car is stolen or damaged by fire. It also covers damage caused by the thief, so if locks have been chiselled out, or if luggage has been stolen, the insurers will pay (subject to any excesses).
- Comprehensive policies cover most sorts of damage to your car, as well as the cover offered by third party and third party, fire and theft… and it does not matter whether the accident is your own fault or not, or even if in the course of the accident you break the law, provided you have a valid driving licence. Cover would include damage to your car, personal injury benefits, medical expenses and personal possession cover.
- There is a fourth, very basic cover known as 'Road Traffic Act only' cover, which just offers cover for personal injuries sustained by others when they are in collision with your vehicle. Any damage to their vehicle would be paid out of your pocket as would any costs for injury to yourself or your vehicle. This cover is the statutory minimum you can have, and you would be better getting more protection.

Motorcycle insurance is broadly similar to car insurance, but with slightly less cover, for example no provision for personal accident benefits for you or your passenger, nor medical expenses, loss or damage to personal possessions or theft cover for accessories unless stolen with the bike.

I am applying for insurance. Do I need to tell them I made a claim last year with another company?

You certainly do. You must disclose all facts about your vehicle and your personal details, including any modifications you may have made to the car – sunroof fitted, bodykit, etc. – which could affect the insurance premium you pay. In addition, if you have made a claim, whether it is your fault or the other driver's, you should inform the new company. One reason is legal; you are making a legal application for insurance cover, and lying on your proposal could void the cover. The other reason is practical; if you change insurers and try to claim a no-claims bonus discount from them, they will want a letter from your previous insurer certifying your no-claims status; that letter will show that you had in fact made a claim. So you will be caught out eventually.

How do I claim if I am involved in an accident?

If you are involved in an accident, you should inform your broker or the insurer direct, giving full information of the accident, times, dates and locations, names, addresses and insurance details of other parties involved.

Most insurers will advise you to say nothing to the other party that suggests that you were at fault over the accident, and some policies will not pay if you admit liability. The best advice is to say nothing and wait until you can calmly set down what happened in writing, usually after talking to your insurer.

The other person may not want to get their insurer involved, and would prefer to settle the claim privately. That is a matter for you, but it might be as well to notify your insurers, so there is no comeback later. But mark your letter 'for information only' and make it clear in a covering letter that you don't want your insurers to act on your behalf. You do not have to inform the police of an accident, unless you have been unable to get insurance or other details from the other motorist. Then your insurer will send you forms and ask for more details, and arrange for the repair of your car if your policy provides that cover. Negotiations between the two companies will settle the bills, though you may end up having increased premiums the following year if you are considered to have borne some responsibility for the accident. In some cases where liability cannot be decided, the matter is heard at court, with your insurers paying for legal representation and footing the repair bill if you lose (if your policy covers it).

If your policy does not cover repairs to your vehicle, you will have to arrange your own repairs and pay for them up front; so the next step would be to write to the other party telling them that you hold them responsible for the accident and that a claim will be submitted in due course. Send the letter by recorded delivery, and if there is no reply send a second letter by recorded delivery making your claim once again and pointing out the next step will be to take legal action. If the other party and his insurers reply, send details of the accident and any repairs estimates that you have obtained. It is possible that the other party may want his insurance company or an assessor to look at the damage before deciding how to answer the claim.

The insurers will then accept liability or attempt to negotiate a settlement with you. If they contest liability, you make have to sue for your repair money, and at this stage it might be best to speak to a solicitor to get impartial advice on the strength of your claim.

What is motor tax?

All motor vehicles that are not exempted must have a road fund licence, or a tax disc to give it its more usual name. To get a tax disc you should go to your local post office with your registration document, a valid certificate of insurance or cover note and an MOT certificate.

Tax discs for cars with engines over 1100cc cost £155 (£85.25 for six months) and £100 (£55 for six months) for cars with engines under 1100cc. Tax for motorbikes over 250cc costs £60 (£40 for 150–250cc, and £15 for bikes under 150cc). Tax for private HGV vehicles is £165, while the tax for buses and coaches ranges from £165 for a nine-seater to £500 for a sixty-one seater.

Currently cars with an engine size of 1100cc or less pay in the Private Light Goods (PLG) class a 'reduced rate' of £100. From March 2001 the 'reduced rate' will be increased to £105 and extended to cars with an engine size of 1200cc or less.

Cars with an engine size of above 1200cc will pay the 'standard rate' of £160 for a vehicle licence taken out from March 2001

Are there any health requirements I should be aware about when driving?

You must be fit to drive every time you get behind the wheel of your car or sit astride your bike. Obvious concerns like drink-driving or driving while under the influence of drugs have already been discussed. But other impediments can affect your fitness to drive. For example the sight requirement means you must be able to read a standard number plate at 75ft, with or without glasses.

In addition, other conditions such as epilepsy, diabetes, Parkinson's Disease, multiple sclerosis, stroke or heart condition can affect one's consciousness, and it would be wise to consult a doctor before deciding whether you are fit to drive.

Can I tow a trailer behind my car?

You cannot tow a trailer before you have passed your test in category B, C1, D1, C or D. However, you may tow a trailer when learning to drive in category B+E, C1+E, D1+E, C+E, D+E or an agricultural tractor (category F).

I've heard a lot about child safety on buses. Are there any requirements for children to wear safety belts?

Because of concerns about child safety, legislation has been passed so that when groups of three or more children are carried on minibuses or coaches on organised trips, each child must be seated in a forward-facing seat with a seat belt (at least a lap belt without a shoulder restraint). This legislation ends the 'three kids in two seats' policy, which was common on bus trips in days gone by.

Each child (aged from three to 15 years) must have at least a lap belt and a seat space of 40 centimetres (16 inches).

The new requirements apply to minibuses and coaches, whether or not privately owned or used for hire and reward. A minibus is a motor vehicle constructed or adapted to carry more than eight passengers plus a driver, while a coach is defined as having a weight of more than 7.5 tonnes and carrying 16 or more passengers plus a driver and a maximum speed of more than 60 miles per hour. The legislation does not apply to buses.

This legislation applies to a journey wholly or mainly organised to carry a group of three or more children on a trip in a minibus or coach, and this includes school outings, trips by youth organisations and voluntary organisations where transporting the children is the key element, and even journeys to or from school, even when accompanied or driven by parents (though not if using a service bus).

If a trip is wholly or mainly for children, the driver of the coach/minibus and his employers are responsible for ensuring that a suitable bus fitted with seatbelts is provided; for this reason, organisers should notify companies as soon as possible if buses with belts are needed.

In the front seats of coaches or seats in front of the driver's seat, it is his responsibility to ensure that children wear their belts (this does not apply to front-seat passengers on the upper deck of double-deck coaches): a child restraint for children under three years, child belts or adult safety belts for children aged three to 11 years, and adult belts children aged from 11 to 13 or larger children. In seats further back, the driver must ensure the right belts are used if available and fitted (children under three in child restraints, others up to 11 in child restraints or adult belts, and children aged between 11 and 13 or larger children in adult belts).

Children aged 14 years and over must wear a seat belt if one is fitted and available to be used, and they (not the driver) are responsible for doing so.

In the rear seats of coaches and larger minibuses there is no statutory requirement for children to wear a seat belt or child restraint, but they should always be encouraged to wear belts when available.

I'm taking the car abroad. What should I be aware of?

Motorists abroad need three documents – a driving licence, proof of third-party insurance and car registration papers. How far your existing documentation will cover you abroad depends on the country; check with the embassy of the country you plan to drive in before setting out.

You may require an international driving permit in some countries, especially if you plan to hire a car so check, check, check.

Your insurance policy will give you minimum third-party cover in EU countries and some others; for more than third-party cover you may have to pay an additional premium to cover the time abroad. You can get additional policies to bring the car back in case of accident or breakdown.

Registration papers and a valid UK tax disc are also required. If you are planning to drive in another country for more than a few months, check whether you need to pay for a tax disc for that country too. And don't forget the GB plate.

Section 6.4 Timeshare

What is timeshare exactly?

Timeshare is a system that gives buyers the right to spend a holiday in their 'own' villa or apartment (most timeshares are self-catering) for a fixed time for a given number of years. Timeshare buyers can go to the same destination, or 'swap' their week, and go to another destination at another time of the year by trading their slot with timeshare users worldwide. Depending on the laws of the country that the timeshare is located in, ownership may be in perpetuity or for a few years. The key issue here is exactly what the timeshare owner 'owns'. Rather than buying the property, the 'owner' owns the slot, the week or two-week period of time that they can use the property for. Often timeshare owners do not take up their week's holiday, but will either let it to friends or exchange it for a week in another timeshare development.

Unfortunately, timeshare is also associated with less pleasant experiences. Most holidaymakers in Mediterranean countries will have been approached by some English-speaking tout with tales of a competition that had been won, a free drinks party or some other implausible reason to spend three or more hours being coerced into signing up for timeshare. Developers have built 'clubs' or complexes across the region, often some way away from the main resorts, and then hire PRs (as touts in Spain now like to think of themselves) to attract customers who can be pitched to in marathon sales pitches reminiscent of the Battle of the Somme in terms of attrition.

In the UK, more and more developers are cold-calling householders to persuade them to attend holiday presentations with an incentive of a 'free' holiday at home or abroad. Beware these calls – there is no such thing as a free lunch, let alone a free holiday and the chances are that if someone calls you to invite you to a presentation that involves a 'free holiday' it is either a timeshare company (regardless of what they try to call themselves) or a firm offering you the chance to pre-book your holidays for years in advance, and then swap the slot with other similar holidaymakers if you don't want to go to the same place every year. Sounds familiar?

But there are benefits in timeshare. A friend actually has two, one near Marbella and another on the Canaries, and uses them to provide family holidays and to exchange with other users for trips to other resorts. The family have two guaranteed holidays abroad each year, for a total of four weeks, and can count on picking up cheap last-minute flights from the airlines so giving them affordable family holidays abroad. The self-catering aspects suit that particular family (though some wives and husbands like to get away from the cooking on their holiday) and gives them what they want. At the time they chose to buy, they had some spare cash and it seemed like a good idea – and for them it is. Timeshare does not suit everyone, but for every buyer that was 'coerced' into taking up a slot, there are others that leapt at the chance.

What protection is there for consumers from high-pressure selling?

Lots of companies sell timeshare by inviting you to presentations, usually with the tempting offer of free gifts. But once you get to the presentation, you will probably be given a hard-sell aimed at getting you to sign up for a slot. So remember this when the call comes, and think carefully before going just to collect your 'free gift'. These gifts often include hidden extra charges, anyway, such as booking or administrative fees for taking up 'free' holiday/flight vouchers or postage and packaging costs for highly priced designer watches you will never have heard of.

Any business selling 'new' timeshare in a European Union country must:

- Provide a 'cooling off' period to buyers, allowing them to cancel without losing any deposit within ten days (14 in the UK) of signing an agreement, and includes the automatic cancellation of any finance agreement linked to the purchase. So, if you are taken to a timeshare and sign up, you have time to change your mind. (Up to half of all timeshare are cancelled within this period.)
- Not ask for any deposit payment. If anyone asks you for cash up front, walk away – it is against EU law and if you do pay up then cancel, you may never see your cash again because a firm that breaches EC law by asking for a deposit is not likely to hand it back later.
- Give full details of the developer, resort, contract of purchase, cancellation rights, management fees for running the timeshare, etc., in the buyer's language. Beware if the brochure is 'temporarily out of print'.

These are statutory rights (set down in English law by the Timeshare Act 1992 in the UK and the European Directive on Timeshare in other EU countries), and if your timeshare contract attempts to 'sign them out' of the agreement, that contract term is invalid.

(But be careful if you are being pestered by touts while on holiday abroad, because if you sign up for timeshare abroad, you may not automatically have any cancellation rights because the European Directive has not been fully implemented in all EC countries.)

Timeshare sales conducted in the UK can also fall foul of the Trade Descriptions and Consumer Credit Acts, no matter where the resort is located. If the resort, amenities and operation of the club and management fees are not accurately described, Trading Standards might be able to prosecute for a criminal offence of breaching the Trade Descriptions Act.

But, sales between private individuals are not regulated by the Timeshare Act; nor are sales for periods of three years or less, though in both cases the protection offered by the Trade Descriptions and Consumer Credit Acts would apply.

I've looked into timeshare and I still like the idea. Are there any hidden pitfalls I should be wary of?

There is a number of hidden ownership problems and issues that are linked to timeshare holidays, especially if the company is not entirely reputable:

1. The large profits made by management companies. Most timeshare resorts are managed on a day-to-day basis by the developer or a subsidiary companies, and these established the resort constitution long before any owners were signed up. These constitutions will state who carries out the maintenance (the developer or subsidiary company) and who manages the resort (the developer or subsidiary company again). This monopoly position allows unscrupulous companies to impose high charges for performing these duties, and it is not possible to get other firms to tender to perform the services at a lower cost, for where resorts have been able to put their management out to open tender, the owners have made good savings.

2. The difficulties of resale. The constitutions may hinder sales, as they often give the developer effective control of the selling process by making owners put their slots up for sale only through the developer as sole agent. This has led to sales going through, or sales at low prices, and a falling morale among timeshare owners.

3. The management fee. Many owners' clubs or management companies have the right to terminate the membership of owners who do not pay their fees. But deciding not to pay your fees is not a clever way to end the timeshare agreement, especially if the decision is prompted by money worries; it would be better to let out your slot or try to sell it through a reputable resale broker.

4. Independence. Despite claims that resorts are 'run by the owners', this is rarely the case, as developers often retain substantial measures of control in the resort and owners' club. Attempts have been made by the Office of Fair Trading to control the developers, but they took little or no notice, as the high maintenance charges, etc. suggest.

I am still interested in timeshare. Is there any other way of limiting my liabilities and getting more protection?

Any purchase transaction of more than £100 using a credit card automatically makes the credit card company (or issuing bank) jointly responsible, with the seller, for ensuring that the product or service is as promised; if problems arise, you can try to obtain repayment of your cash from the card company, but this would not be the case if you used a debit card, or used your credit card to get a cash advance. Since 1998, UK credit card companies will refund any payment made on a credit card for a timeshare bought anywhere in Europe, provided you cancel in writing within 10 days and keep a copy of the letter for the credit card company.

If you are interested in timeshare, do your research first and get all the relevant details in writing. The Organisation for Timeshare In Europe (OTE) (see Appendix) will be able to advise on which companies are reputable.

If I never own the timeshare, who looks after it? If someone is there the week before me, I don't want to come into a dirty apartment?

To maintain the apartment and facilities in 'nearly new' condition for the whole period of use, owners pay a management fee to the resort company that manages the timeshare, ranging from under £200 to well over £500 a year per week of ownership.

What sort of cost would I have to incur to buy a timeshare? And what might its resale value be?

It costs between £1,000 and £2,000 to construct a week of timeshare, including land, infrastructure and leisure facilities shared between all the weeks on the resort. So, allowing for reasonable marketing costs and profit, a week would be expected to sell for between £2,000 and £3,000. But of course, you have to be able to sell it. Many timeshare businesses are perfectly respectable and responsibly run, but it is because of the few sharks that buyers have to beware.

Section 6.5 Pubs, clubs, hotels and restaurants

What is a public house?

A public house is actually a private house in law, and the landlord has the discretion to ask people to leave, or bar them. The law does not give members of the public an automatic right to enter a public house, unless the pub is really a 'hotel', offering accommodation and food.

I'm a landlord. A transsexual comes into my pub and frankly the regulars don't like it. Can I bar him/her?

Strictly speaking, a landlord does not have to serve anyone whom he does not want to, but to discriminate on grounds of sex (or race) is an offence under sex (or race) discrimination laws. So if you want to exercise the bigot's right to exclude a customer on grounds of sexuality, you can, provided you don't tell them why. If you do, the law will come down on you like a ton of bricks.

What licences does a pub need to operate?

To sell alcohol on the premises, you will need an 'on-licence'. This allows you and your staff to sell alcohol on the premises (or be taken away as a 'carry-out').

Licences are granted by magistrates, acting as the local licensing authority. Each year there is an annual 'Brewster session' where licences are granted or renewed, and magistrates will also grant temporary liquor licences where people have just taken over pubs or clubs.

(There is also an 'off-licence' which allows businesses to sell alcoholic drinks that are not consumed on the premises but can only be taken away.)

I live near a pub and it is very disorderly. Can I object to the licence being renewed?

Anyone can attend Brewster sessions, which are effectively open-court hearings at the local magistrates' courts. Dates of hearings are usually advertised in the local papers, or you can telephone the magistrates' court office to find out when your particular pub's licence is up for renewal.

Strictly speaking, if you want to object to a licence being renewed, you should give the licensee seven days' notice as required by law (though no notice is required if you are objecting to a licence being granted for the first time). However, magistrates can waive the need to give notice if you turn up in court and object, so it is possible to 'ambush' a licensee in this way.

You may be asked to give evidence in the witness box under oath – remember that to lie under oath is perjury. Then it is up to you to convince the magistrates that the pub is not providing a proper service to its customers, or that it is a disorderly house.

You might not be alone, however. The police are keen to keep their patches under control, and if your landlord cannot keep his customers under control, the local licensing sergeant may be in court also objecting to the granting of a licence.

Are there any rules about pubs selling the same quantities of alcohol?

The growth in the sale of bottled beers – the designer lagers, strong ciders, etc. – has made some licensees' jobs so much easier, because it removes the need for concern about short measures. But draught beers and wines and spirits sold direct from the bottle must be sold in specified measures.

Beers, porters and lagers from the keg or draught barrel are usually sold in pints and half-pints, and glasses used to sell beer must have the same capacity as the drink ordered (so you can't sell a half-pint of beer in a pint pot) unless there is an engraved or marked line to show the correct measure, or the pub has an automatic measuring pump.

Spirits such as whisky, rum, gin and vodka must be sold in measures 25ml and 50ml measures, though liqueurs can be sold in any measure that a landlord chooses. Wine is normally sold in 125ml and 250ml glasses, where a normal bottle of wine is 750ml.

What criminal offences can a customer commit in a pub?

There are some offences that can only be committed in public houses:

- Drinking after hours, which means having a glass in your hand with alcohol in it more than ten minutes after the last bell.
- Buying alcoholic drinks when aged under 18, or buying an alcoholic drink for someone aged under 18.
- Being drunk, violent, quarrelsome or disorderly, and refusing to leave a public bar when asked to do so.

And what about offences committed by a publican?

- Selling alcoholic drinks without a licence.
- Selling alcohol to someone knowing they are under 18, or to someone knowing the drink is for another person aged under 18. (The law treats under-age drinking seriously, and repeat offences can lose a landlord his licence.)
- Allowing drinking after hours.
- Supplying alcohol on credit – i.e. drinks 'on the slate' rather than paid for by credit card.
- Selling alcohol to someone that is already drunk.
- Allowing illegal gambling on the premises.
- Permitting violent, quarrelsome or riotous conduct, or drunkenness.
- Employing someone aged under 18 behind the bar.

Are children allowed in a pub?

Children under the age of 14 are not allowed into the bar of a public house though they can pass through the bar (or anywhere alcohol is sold on the way to a toilet, playroom or restaurant). Children aged over 14 but under 18 can go into bars but cannot buy or drink alcohol, but children aged sixteen and over can buy beer or cider to have with a meal in a pub restaurant.

At what times can pubs be open?

Gone are the days when licensing laws were so strict that pubs closed during the day and opened not at all on Sundays (the classic definition of boredom was 'Merthyr Tydfil – a town in South Wales renowned for the number of pubs it had – on a rainy Sunday afternoon'). Pubs tend to be open from 11am to 11pm, though some premises that serve food are licensed later than that. Once closing time has passed, customers have ten minutes to finish their drinks and leave the premises. If you haven't finished your drink after ten minutes, you can be asked to leave, and it would be an offence to take the drink outside with you.

I think my local landlord is messing about with his beer. Can I do anything?

Since the beginning of time, landlords have been accused or watering their beer or spirits (diluting it to sell more). If you are concerned that your pub is selling watered-down beer, or that the landlord is selling short measures, you can complain to the local trading standards office (part of your local authority). After your complaint, an officer may drop by in 'undercover' to buy a pint for himself. In cases of short-measure allegations, the drink will be measured (and several test purchases may be carried out to establish whether there is a pattern of offending). Watered-down beer will be sent off for analysis. If your landlord is selling short measure, the local authority may prosecute.

What about clubs?

In terms of drinks licensing, nightclubs are regarded as being the same as public houses, though they may serve much later, normally 1am or 2am depending on the local licensing magistrates, and would also have a music and entertainment licence to allow dancing and live bands to entertain on the premises. You normally need a public entertainments licence if you plan to stage musical or dance entertainment for gain (but you don't need a public entertainments licence if the entertainment is to take place in a private club, or if it is a private function, like a wedding or a company 'do'. A public entertainment licence cannot be granted unless a fire officer has issued a fire safety certificate for the premises, certifying the building is a 'safe' place to hold a dance or concert. Usually, 21 days' notice is required by a local authority before granting a public entertainments licence (including notice to the police). But for a one-off event in a building not normally used for such entertainment, 14 days is sufficient. If your licence is turned down, or if conditions are imposed on the grant of the licence (no loud music after 11pm for example), you can appeal to the magistrates' court.

I'm booking into a hotel. What should I expect?

Booking accommodation in this country is just the same as booking a holiday abroad. You are entitled to assume that the descriptions contained in any brochure or sales material are neither misleading nor inaccurate, and this includes photographs. If you booked through a brochure, you have a right to complain. The Trade Descriptions Act 1968 makes it an offence to make any statements that are not truthful and accurate. So, if your hotel is 'a stone's throw from the town centre' but you need a catapult to throw the stone, then you have a right to take action. If you want to make a criminal complaint, contact your local authority's trading standards department.

Any hotel with more than four bedrooms or eight beds is obliged to display a price notice, listing the costs of rooms in a prominent place, where new guests can see the prices before they check in, and if the room tariff includes meals (and if so, which meals).

If because of shoddy service or poor facilities, you feel that your stay in the hotel has not been what you expected, you should speak to the managers to complain and ask for a refund. Try to be as polite as possible and factual about what you feel were the deficiencies in the service you expected and were charged for, and what you got in fact. Most managers will do their best to deal with valid complaints, as they know the potential good public relations that a customer who leaves delighted that their complaint has been resolved fairly can give them. But be reasonable: some things may be unfortunate, such as not having the toilet paper folded each morning by the cleaner, but could hardly have spoiled your enjoyment of the stay as a whole; on the other hand, staying in a room overlooking the bins when you expected and booked a lake view is worth a complaint, and you should get compensated. So be firm and prepared to stick to your guns. If you don't get any joy, you can complain to trading standards and they will take up your complaint. You can also pursue a civil claim for damages in the small claims court, seeking compensation for what went wrong. Refusing to pay is an option, but don't be surprised if the hotel calls the police. In their eyes, you will have received a service and then not paid for it, and the police might see it that way and think you were bilking on the bill (trying to make off without payment). It would be wise to take advice before deciding whether to withhold further payment

Hotels in the UK also have star ratings, offered by groups like the AA, RAC or Les Routiers. If you feel that the facilities do not match the rating, and you feel very strongly about the way your legitimate complaint was handled, you can complain to the organisation, which may want to reclassify the hotel.

I've bought some food and I think it is 'off'. What can I do?

It is a criminal offence to sell food for human consumption that is does not satisfy the buyer's requirements as regards its nature, quality and substance. Even if the seller took precautions to avoid selling unfit food, or was not negligent, or that the unfit food was not harmful, an offence would still be committed. If convicted at magistrates' court, a seller could be fined up to £5,000. Environmental health departments of local authorities investigates complaints about selling unfit food. So if you are concerned about an item you have bought, they are your first port of call. However, you are unlikely to be compensated for your loss, though magistrates occasionally award compensation.

I bought some meat from a butcher's stall at a market. The conditions there were disgusting. What should I do?

Environmental health is concerned about hygiene regulations too, so you should complain to them. They might prosecute, if they feel your complaint is well founded, as it is a criminal offence for shops, restaurants, pubs or anywhere where food is prepared or sold for human consumption not to comply with food hygiene regulations, and if convicted at magistrates' court, traders face a £5,000 fine.

Food regulations concern issues such as the cleanliness of premises (and making sure they are free from vermin and insects), the provision of clean lavatory facilities for staff, ensuring staff don't smoke while handling food, and that open wounds are covered while food is handled.

How should food be labelled?

The Food Labelling Regulations 1996 require most packaged foods to carry a name, a date mark, a list of ingredients, and the name and address of the manufacturer or packer. There are specific further requirements for some foodstuffs (for example, alcoholic drinks must indicate their strength, and nutrition labelling must be provided when claims like 'low fat' are made). Weights and volumes, where given, must be metric.

There's been a lot on the news about genetically modified foods. What are they and are they safe?

Genetically modifying food is a comparatively new way of producing foods, by taking DNA from one species and inserting it into another. However, opponents of GM foods, such as the Friends of the Earth, argue that because there have been no long term safety tests carried out the effects of GM food are unknown.

As far as the safety aspects are concerned, the Ministry of Agriculture, Fisheries and Food say that all GM foods approved for use in the UK have been assessed by independent experts as being as safe as non-GM food of the same type.

If you are concerned about eating GM food by accident, don't worry. All foods that have GM ingredients must be labelled as such. But some GM rapeseed imported from Canada in 1999 has been found to have been contaminated with a GM variety; however, there are no food safety concerns in this, according to the Ministry of Agriculture, Fisheries and Food, as this particular modified seed type was tested in 1995 and found to be as safe to eat as its GM-free equivalent, and has been cleared for food use.

I've ordered a meal in a restaurant but the meal isn't up to scratch. What can I do?

Any sort of complaint in restaurants conjures up images of irate managers like Basil Fawlty, or the restaurateur Peter Langan, rounding on anyone who sees fit to question their cuisine. However, diners are consumers too; you have the right to be served the meal you order, and to question the food if it does not come up to scratch. The same rules regarding hygiene and quality apply to restaurants as they do to shops that sell food. Food and drink must be of the nature, quality and substance that you would expect. So if your meal is brought to the table and it does not match up with your expectations, you should complain to the manager at once. If you asked for your steak rare and ended up with a burnt offering, you have a right to complain. Most managers will get you what you ordered; but if not, you are entitled to send back the meal, and refuse to pay for it.

If you eat the meal and then complain about its quality, you can still complain, but you are contractually obliged to pay for the food you have eaten, and the strength of your complaint is somewhat diminished. After all, to some extent you have rubbished your own argument before you start: how can it be 'good enough to eat' but 'not good enough to pay for'? Obviously some things might only be discovered as the meal draws to a close, but it would seem strange to complain about the soup and main course only after finishing the dessert, cheese and biscuits and coffee. If your complaint is not dealt with, you can refuse to pay, but then the restaurant can sue you to recover the meal's costs, and for this, the manager is entitled to ask for your name and address (in order to have papers served on you so the restaurant's solicitors know who to contact); if you don't supply the information, the manager is perfectly obliged to keep you at the restaurant and call the police, because now it is starting to look like you are trying to make off without paying for the meal, rather than standing up for your contractual rights over a meal that was not up to standard. If you have eaten the meal and subsequently go down with food poisoning, you can claim compensation from the restaurant (but if you had taken guests with you, they could not claim unless they could establish that the restaurant had been negligent in cooking or preparing the meal). But if the restaurant is prosecuted by the local authority's environmental health department as a result of your making a complaint, then magistrates can make a compensation order for you and your guests.

I've heard of 'nouvelle cuisine', but these portions are miniscule!

Unlike wines and beers, there is no minimum size of portion specified in law, so you could get a pile of chips or just a few arranged artistically on your plate. But if the menu specifies a particular weight, for example a '16oz sirloin', then you are entitled to have just that.

Chapter 7
You and your rights

Section 7.1 Immigration

People from other countries who want to come into the UK have to meet our immigration rules, and will have to satisfy immigration officers at the port or airport they arrive at that they do before being allowed in. Immigration policy is set and managed by the Immigration & Nationality Directorate, and officers from this government agency run our entry and after-entry controls. Another unit, the Joint Entry Clearance Unit, runs pre-entry control via an entry clearance operation overseas.

I want to come to Britain on holiday. How do I qualify to come to the UK as a visitor?

To be granted the right of entry to the UK as a visitor, you must be able to show you want to come here for no more than six months, that you intend to leave at the end of your visit, and you have enough money to pay for food, drink, accommodation, etc. without having to apply for benefits or state aid while you are here. Depending on where you come from, you may also need a visa. You will need to have filled in an application form before arriving in the UK, so immigration officers can process your application swiftly. Visitors cannot extend their stay beyond six months – if you came over for two months but wanted to remain in the UK for longer than that, you can extend it to a maximum of six months, but no longer. Any requirements to visit the police, etc. will be stamped into your passport on arrival, and you must register within seven days of landing. The local police force can tell you where the nearest police registration office is, and what its hours of opening are.

Can I work while in the UK as a visitor?

While in the UK as a visitor, you can conduct business in connection with your work in your own country, but you cannot work here, either paid or unpaid, for yourself or someone else. This covers manufacturing and service occupations. You can meet UK companies to negotiate contracts for your firm in your own country, visit trade fairs, conferences, etc.; you can even come here for training. But you cannot work. If you are visiting the UK on business, your salary should be paid by your employer (overseas) but you are entitled to reasonable expenses from UK firms while you are here for travel or living expenses. In addition, the concept of 'business visitor' includes people delivering goods from abroad (lorry drivers for example), computer or manufacturers' representatives, guest speakers at a conference (or a conference organiser, for no more than five days) or to provide training or consultancy services for a company, or 'experts' coming to the UK to brief British businesses on overseas opportunities.

How often can I visit the UK on business?

Rules are flexible, but normally you are allowed to spend no more than a maximum of six months in the UK as a business visitor during any 12-month period. If you apply to stay longer then six months, it might suggest you are basing yourself in the UK. In such cases, your application might be refused.

I have a lot of money to invest in the UK. Am I allowed entry?

People have been able to come to the United Kingdom as businessmen or people of independent means for more than 20 years, but major investors may also apply to come to the UK. These major investors cannot work as employees of companies, but may run their own businesses or hold non-executive directorships in other firms (though husbands and wives of investors, and their children, are allowed to take jobs).

All investors, like businessmen and people of independent means, need to obtain entry clearance at a British Diplomatic Post abroad before they will be allowed in. To do this, they will have to satisfy entry clearance officers that there is no reason for their entry to be blocked because of criminal convictions, or in the light of their character or conduct (as do other people coming for business or employment). But in addition to these general requirements, investors must also show that they intend to bring at least £1m of their own money to the UK, and to invest not less than £750,000 of that in government bonds, shares or loans to UK companies (except those involved in property investment). The investor must also make the UK his main home – though this does not mean that the investor can't live in other countries too. Investors who meet these conditions would be eligible to settle in this country. You can't just claim to have £1m to be allowed in as an investor though – you would need to prove that you have the financial wherewithal to come to the UK and support yourself, and not just claim you have £1m in the bank.

How long can investors stay in the UK?

Normally investors are granted a 12-month stay; near to the end of this time, you can apply for an extension, when you will have to show once again that you have met the entry qualifications. It is normally possible to extend your stay for a further three years, and after four years you have the right to apply for indefinite leave to remain provided you have kept (at least) £1m in the UK during that time, whether invested, in cash balances, etc.

I would like to work as an au pair. Can I come to the UK?

An au pair arrangement is where a single person aged over 17 and under 27 comes to the UK to learn English and lives for up to two years as a member of an English-speaking family. The au pair does a maximum of five hours' work around the house each day (with two full days off per week) in return for an allowance, room and board. The allowance has to be 'reasonable', so slave labour wages are not acceptable. Au pairs can come from a variety of countries including Andorra, Croatia, Cyprus, the Czech Republic, the Faroe Islands, Greenland, Switzerland and Turkey. EC nationals can come to work and study in the UK without any need for such formalities. Au pairs from some countries may need a visa before coming to the UK (for example Turkey or the Slovak Republic). To qualify as an au pair, you must fall within the age range, be unmarried with no dependants, be not applying for state aid and not intending to stay in the UK longer than your two-year au pair hitch. During the two-year period, au pairs can move from family to family provided they continue to meet immigration rules.

I am a student from overseas who has been offered a place to study at Oxford University. Can I come into the UK for that purpose?

To qualify to come to the UK as a student, you must show that you have been accepted for a course of study at a publicly funded university or college of further or higher education, a bona fide private college or an independent fee-paying school, and that while here you will be following a full-time degree course, or receiving a minimum of 15 hours' organised daytime study per week, or courses at an independent school. In addition, you will have to show that you can meet the cost of course fees, food and lodging without having to work or apply for benefits or state aid, and that at the end of your course/degree, you will be going home. You can work part-time or during the holidays, provided you do not work more than 20 hours a week and are not running a business (unless it is a study placement as part of your course). Overseas students can bring their husband or wife, and any children aged under 18 provided they can pay for their family's board and lodging (though husbands/wives can take jobs if the student has been granted leave to remain in the country for more than 12 months).

In addition, prospective overseas students are allowed into the UK to arrange a course, provided they intend to enrol on a course within six months of arriving, intend to leave at the end of the course and can meet all the costs of study, board and lodgings themselves. Once students have been granted leave to enter, they can apply for an extension to follow further courses of study, for example to do a Ph.D (or D.Phil, as they call it at Oxford). There are special rules for doctors and dentists that want to pursue postgraduate work in the UK; it would be advisable to get in touch with the General Medical Council or General Dental Council to register and get details of entry qualifications.

How do I apply for the right to remain in the UK?

You should contact the Immigration & Nationality Directorate if you want to extend your stay in the UK; if you have stayed in this country legally (not as an illegal immigrant) for four years, you are eligible to apply for permanent residence.

Can I bring my wife or fiancé to the UK?

Your wife (or husband or fiancé of either sex) may apply to join you or accompany you in the UK provided you are settled here (living here legally and not having been given a date to leave the country) or you are coming back to the UK at the same time as your wife (or husband or fiancée). To qualify, your wife must be able to show that you are lawfully married and both intend to live together permanently, that you have actually met, that you have adequate accommodation and can support yourselves and any dependants without applying for benefits, and that your wife is not aged under 16 years. (In the case of wives that are polygamously married, she must be the first wife seeking to join her husband here.) Once your wife is here, she will be given 12 months' leave to stay and work, and after that time, if you are still married and intending to live together, your wife may apply to remain here permanently.

If you are not yet married, your fiancée would have to show that you plan to marry reasonably soon (usually in six months), that both of you intend to live together permanently after the ceremony, that your fiancée has somewhere to live until you are married without seeking state benefits, and that your fiancée will not have to get a job to support herself or her dependants. Then, once you are married, your (by now) wife can apply to stay her and will be granted 12 months' leave.

I'm an EU national. What rights do I have?

Nationals from the EU and the European Economic Area (Austria, Belgium, Denmark, Finland, France, Germany, Greece, Ireland, Italy, Luxembourg, Netherlands, Portugal, Spain and Sweden, and Iceland, Liechtenstein and Norway respectively) have a right to live and work in the UK, with EEA citizens having the same rights as European Union citizens. This right exists if you are working here or, though not working, you are supporting yourself financially without applying for benefits. Once here, you have the right to accept job offers, to work (as an employee, self-employed or in business) and to set up business or manage companies, without needing a work permit; you should not be the victim of discrimination because of your nationality, in terms of conditions of employment, pay or working conditions. Family members that are EEA nationals have the same rights to live and work in the UK as you; if your wife/husband and her/his dependants are non-EU or EEA nationals then they are treated as other non-British or non-EU spouses and dependants seeking entry to the UK.

Section 7.2 Asylum

Why do we have to let asylum seekers into this country?

The UK signed a 1951 convention on refugees, so we have an obligation to consider all applications for asylum made within the UK. Applications are considered on their individual merits, and asylum seekers would have to show that they have a fear persecution within their particular country for one or more of a number of reasons, such as race, religion, nationality, membership of a particular social group or political opinion. You can't seek asylum on the grounds that the state is persecuting you for being a criminal or a terrorist. But it is not enough to fear persecution: the fear must be well-founded. A vague unease would not be enough.

How do I go about applying for asylum?

The first stage of applying for asylum, which takes place at the Asylum Screening Unit (ASU) in Croydon, is to establish who you are, what country you are from and how you came to the UK. Your wife (or husband) and any dependent family members will come to the interview with you, and you will have to bring your passports, other ID material (birth certificates, ID cards, etc.), two colour photographs for you and each member of your family and evidence of your address (bank statements, utility bill or a letter from the householder at the place you are staying if you are not paying rent, etc.) You will be fingerprinted, to prevent fraudulent applications by known criminals (these are only used for asylum purposes); if you refuse to be fingerprinted, an acknowledgment letter of your application for asylum cannot be issued and you will be turned down. Once your identity, nationality and current address have been confirmed, immigration officers will give you a standard acknowledgement letter (SAL), which confirms you have applied for asylum. It is not an identity document but you may be asked to produce it from time to time. Once you have gone through the initial interview, you should keep the Home Office informed every time you change addresses, so they can keep track on you and send any papers to the right address.

How will my application be assessed?

The Integrated Casework Directorate (ICD) will assess your application against the criteria laid down in the 1951 United Nations Convention – that there must be a well-founded fear of persecution because of race, religion, nationality, membership of a particular social group or political opinion. Under UK law, certain countries are designated as countries where there is, in general, no serious risk of persecution. If your country is designated as one of the 'safe' ones, to succeed in an application for asylum you must show that there are special circumstances in your case that give you a well-founded fear of persecution. If your application is refused, you can still appeal to a special adjudicator; the appeal will be fast-tracked and if that is turned down, you have no further avenue of appeal.

What happens at the asylum interview?

Your asylum interview is your chance to paint the picture that will support your claim of a fear of persecution. You need to explain as clearly as possible why you live in fear of returning home, to establish full details of your claim. You may already have submitted evidence in written statements; you don't need to repeat this, but you must paint the fullest picture possible. It is in your interests to do so. You will almost certainly be asked why you fled your country to travel to the UK, and you should tell the officers everything, however painful or embarrassing it may be. If you only volunteer information later, at an appeal hearing for example, it would not be unreasonable of the tribunal to wonder whether you had made up the second story to support your application when the first was not considered strong enough. So try to remember any incidents of persecution, harassment or detention you suffered in your homeland that you think are relevant to your application. The interviews are confidential, and nothing said within the four walls will get back to your own country or the authorities there, so you can be frank about what has happened to you, without fear of reprisal. But don't invent anything – if you are found out it may harm your application. Interpreters are available for applicants that do not speak English well, and you can bring a friend or representative into the interview with you as an observer, but they will not be allowed to take part. A written record will be kept of your interview, which will be read back at the end so you can confirm it is an accurate record of what you have said. If you disagree with any part of the written record, you can have the record amended accordingly at that point, then sign off the report as an accurate record of the interview.

Can I submit additional information in support of my application after the interview?

You should bring any additional written evidence of your experiences in your home country to the asylum interview with you; if you don't bring the papers, you must send them in within five working days, having told the interviewing officer what additional evidence you plan to submit. Not submitting evidence at the first time of asking can affect your credibility as a witness, and harm your case.

What happens then?

Your application is 'considered' and a decision may be some time in coming. Once a decision has been reached, you may be notified of the outcome in writing; on the other hand, you may be called to a meeting to discuss your immigration status and be told what has happened to your application then. There are four possible findings:

1. You are recognised as a refugee, and will be issued with papers granting you asylum and confirming your right to stay in the United Kingdom.
2. You are granted exceptional leave to remain for a limited period. This means that, even though the Home Office does not accept you have a well-founded fear of persecution within the meaning of the 1951 Convention, for compassionate or humanitarian reasons it has decided you should not be made to go back to your homeland for the time being.
3. You are refused refugee status, and, unless you appeal, are expected to arrange to leave the country as soon as possible. Sometimes, a deportation notice will be served along with the notice turning down your asylum application, but will not be acted upon unless and until all appeals have been exhausted.
4. In some cases, your application is 'certified' by the Home Secretary, if your application has been refused. If your claim has been certified you can still appeal, but your case is fast-tracked; if your appeal is also certified then you have no more options and will have to leave the UK.

How can I appeal against a decision to refuse my application?

If your application is refused, you can appeal to a special adjudicator, who will review your case and the Home Office decision. Any appeal must be lodged within seven days of your application being turned down, or you could lose the right to appeal. If your appeal succeeds you will be contacted as soon as possible to confirm your right to remain in the UK; if it fails you may be allowed to appeal the adjudicator's decision – you will be told whether you have any further right of appeal – and this must be lodged with five days of being notified that your appeal failed. You do not have to appeal, and can terminate your application at any time; but having sought asylum, it would be silly not to pursue all available avenues before admitting defeat.

What happens if I travel outside the UK while my application is being decided?

If you leave the UK while your application is on the table (or if you leave while any appeal remains outstanding), then that will be treated as your withdrawing your application for asylum.

Can my dependants apply to remain in the United Kingdom with me?

Your husband or wife and children aged under 18 who have accompanied you to the UK can be included in your application. If you are granted refugee status, they will normally be allowed to remain with you. Any family members who fear persecution in their own right (and not just because they are related to you) should make their own claim for asylum too – but such claims should be made at the same time you do, and not only after you have been turned down for asylum as this would be seen as a delaying tactic.

Can I take legal advice about my application?

You may seek legal advice throughout the process. But, not seeking legal advice until late in the day will not delay the speed at which your application is processed. So you can't hurry it up, or slow it down by calling in lawyers.

What about the new asylum laws?

The Immigration and Asylum Act 1999 aims to make fundamental changes to the asylum system to protect genuine cases while catching bogus asylum seekers. The Act will create a single right of appeal to speed up the system and help to decide, by April 2001, most initial asylum decisions within two months and most appeals within a further four months.

A system of providing economic and benefit aid in kind or via vouchers or though limited cash payments is planned, to reduce the economic incentive for migrants to claim asylum falsely. More controversially, the Act aims to disperse destitute asylum seekers around the UK, allocating accommodation on a no-choice basis, creating fears of 'floods' of bogus asylum seekers descending on areas. In addition, tough new measures are being brought in to combat smuggling immigrants into the UK, with a new (civil) penalty for drivers of vehicles found to be carrying illegal immigrants, of £2,000 for each person found. This is particularly topical, since the incident at Dover where 58 illegal immigrants were found dead in a container lorry that had brought them in from the Continent. The driver has since been charged with manslaughter.

Section 7.3 Defamation

Our reputation is important to all of us, as private family members and in our jobs, and anyone that spreads false rumours or accusations about us does us the gravest injustice. Defamation law protects us from the publication of falsehoods that damage our reputation, and people that have been defamed can sue for damages as compensation.

What is defamation?

Defamation can either be made through words, when it is slander (for example if someone falsely tells your friends in a pub that you have been having an affair with his wife) or if it is in permanent form, when it is libel. 'Permanent form' obviously means newspaper articles or magazine reports, but also includes television broadcasts, films, radio broadcasts, plays and books. Generally speaking, statements can be defamatory if they tend to expose you to hatred, ridicule or contempt, cause you to be shunned or avoided, lower you in the estimation of right-thinking members of society or disparage you in your business, trade profession or calling. The key to all of this though is that the statements are untrue. Telling people things that, though damaging to your reputation, are true are not libellous or slanderous. So, if you were convicted of fraud a few years ago and now are running a charity, if a newspaper decides to run the story you may not be happy... but it's not libellous.

What can be classed as a defamatory statement?

Examples of defamatory statements are:

- Claiming that a retail manager has their hand in the till.
- Claiming that someone who presents himself as being 'liberal' actually holds extreme political views.
- Claiming that someone is a drug addict.
- Claiming that someone has been convicted of a crime.
- Claiming that someone is bad at their job.
- Claiming that an athlete takes performance-enhancing drugs.
- Claiming that an amateur sportsman is being paid to play (for example an amateur golfer).
- Claiming that someone has been raped (this is slightly different in that while right-thinking members of society would not hate, ridicule or hold someone in contempt because they had been raped, or cause them to be shunned or avoided, being told that someone has been raped would affect the way we treat them).

Can statements be defamatory even if they don't appear to be?

The concept of innuendo means that a statement that appears to be fine at face value can be defamatory to those people with special knowledge. For example, your calling someone a socialist is not obviously defamatory, but would be to that person's friends who know that he is a member of the Conservative Party.

A newspaper article has alleged things about me that are untrue. Can I sue for libel?

In order to succeed with an action for defamation, you would have to show that the article was defamatory (that it damaged your reputation), that the article referred to you and that it has been published to someone else. You don't have to show that you suffered any damage as a result of the defamatory statements (though if you were suing for slander, you would have to show that you had suffered in some way, for example if because of the allegations you lost your job or were forced to resign from your local club except in a few specialised cases). You do not have to prove that the defamatory statements are false – it is for the newspaper to show that the statements you are complaining about are true, and if they can't, they lose. In America, the press has a defence to libel called 'absence of malice', which means that provided a newspaper does not deliberately publish something defamatory about you, knowing that it is untrue, they cannot be sued for libel. This does not exist in the UK.

An article about drug dealing does not name me, but my friends all think I am the person referred to. Can I sue?

If people that you know would believe that you are the person referred to in an article, then you can sue for libel. Even if the article contains some references that friends would recognise as not being connected with you at all, if these friends skimmed the article and felt that it referred to you, you could succeed with an action.

A newspaper report of a court case said that someone with my name and who lives in the same town has been convicted of drug smuggling. It's not me; can I sue?

Just because the story is true of one person does not matter, if it is untrue of someone else, that second person has been defamed. For this reason, newspaper reports of court cases tend to put in as much detail as possible, to avoid this very glitch happening. Local papers tend to use identification details like name, address, age and occupation to help 'identify' the person concerned.

This is particularly bad in Wales where a street may have four of five Joneses or Davieses, and I can remember an occasion as a young journalist when a story inadvertently defamed another person of the same name, and the correction ended up inadvertently defaming a third person. National papers tend to be less detailed, and often refer only to the accused's town and age. From your point of view, provided that the paper was negligent in compiling the report, by leaving out age, detailed address information ('Railway Cuttings, Tooting' rather than 'Tooting') and occupation, then you can sue. If the paper took all reasonable care, it could claim unintentional defamation and offer a correction and apology.

How can I show that the defamatory statement was published?

If the article appears in a newspaper, magazine or is broadcast, publication is automatically assumed. You do not have to show that anyone saw the programme or read the article. If the libel is in a letter, properly sealed and sent to you, then you could not claim that it had been published. (If it were on a postcard, which the mailman could read, then that is another matter.)

How soon after the defamatory statement was made do I have to start legal action or complain?

There is a limitation period of one year, after which an action would only be allowed if the High Court intervened.

I am being accused of slandering someone. What defences do I have?

There is a number of potential defences to actions for libel and slander:

Justification – that the allegation is true. You cannot defame someone if what you say is true. But you have to be able to prove that what you say is true on the balance of probability.

Fair comment – this refers to statements of opinion, which are made honestly on a matter of public interest. An example would be saying that a politician's conduct was disgraceful after a report that the politician had accepted money to raise questions in parliament. In such cases, you could claim 'fair comment'. However, if the politician has not been paid money to ask questions (and the report was in fact wrong), the defence of fair comment fails.

Privilege – which covers speeches made in parliament, or in a council chamber, where it is recognised that people must be able to speak freely because of the public interest. In the same way, fair and accurate reports of council proceedings and parliamentary debates are also privileged. This is why MPs sometimes use the cloak of parliamentary privilege to name people accused of some wrongdoing, knowing they cannot be sued for libel, and allowing the press to report it with the same protection.

Privilege also covers proceedings in courts, and reports of them that appear in the newspapers or on television provided that they are fair, accurate and contemporaneous (that means that they appear as soon as possible, which means the next day in a daily paper of the next available issue in a weekly or magazine). The important thing here is that it does not matter whether the statements are true or false; the person making them is protected from being sued for slander (and the newspaper that reports it is protected from being sued for libel). So if your neighbour appeared in court accused of hitting you and said he did it because your son had indecently assaulted his daughter, this could be reported in the paper even though it were untrue and your son had never met the girl.

'Accord and satisfaction' – where the matter has been raised and dealt with. For example, if a newspaper carried a defamatory story about you, and you agreed to them publishing a correction and apology in settlement, and you both agreed the wording, where the correction would go and any compensation, costs for lawyers, etc., you would not later be able to sue them for defamation.

A defamatory article has appeared about me in the local newspaper. How should I handle it?

Defamation is a difficult area of the law to handle, so if the allegation about you is particularly damaging and/or you have a high profile, you should speak to your lawyers as soon as possible (though the chances are you already will have done so). If you are determined to seek damages they will issue proceedings for libel, instruct counsel and take the matter all the way to court. Libel actions have seen big payouts and massive costs (which had the effect of making the act of protecting one's reputation a game for the very rich), but in a bid to allow the less well-off to protect their reputations, a summary procedure for damages of less that £10,000 has been introduced; your solicitor will be able to advise you. But the days of large libel pay-outs are long gone, and judges are restricting the bigger claims juries were wont to hand down. More pertinently, if the defamatory article is a grey area you could end up losing your action and having to pay costs – so it really can be a gamble.

On the other hand, you may not want it to go that far, but just want the matter corrected. In this case, contact the newspaper's newsdesk. Try not to get too angry or shout at this stage, even if your blood is boiling; human nature being what it is, if you are aggressive they will become defensive and are less likely to be receptive to your point of view. Explain why the story was inaccurate and how it damaged your reputation. Listen to their response – which may be a request for you to allow them to investigate the matter and get back to you. (If the story arose from a court report you could have difficulties in getting a correction if the court report is accurate – and this means an accurate report of what was said in court and not an accurate representation of the facts as they exist outside the courtroom – because if the newspaper doubts the story given by someone in court, it is calling them a liar and the other party can sue. It might be you will have to ask your local court to allow you to make a statement in court which the paper can then report without fear of being sued.) News editors are far too busy to want to be tied up dealing with corrections and clarifications forever, and while from a professional point of view they will defend their reporters, it is not in their or the paper's interests to try to bury the matter, so you will get a fair hearing from them, and it is in their interests to get back to you. Otherwise you can complain to the newspaper editor direct.

If the investigations confirm that you have been unfairly slated, the paper will undoubtedly offer to correct the story. You will want to be sure that the 'correction' does indeed correct the wrong impression, and that the paper apologises for its error. Another issue is where the correction appears; if the defamatory story was the front page lead, you are not likely to be satisfied if the correction appears on the last news page before the advertisements at the bottom of the page. There is room for some horse-trading: no one likes being seen to have made a mistake, but the correction must be in proportion to the error. If you are 30 and the paper said you were 45, that is a small error (unless you are an actress!); if you are married but the paper said you lived with your mistress, the damage is far more serious and the correction must, of necessity be far more prominent. Often, solicitors are better at negotiating the position of the correction than members of the public, partly because they have a greater understanding of the law and the consequences of breaching it and can turn the screw more effectively. Once the correction and its position in the paper have been agreed, you may be asked to confirm in writing that the correction and apology (and any costs you have incurred and the paper has agreed to pay) are satisfaction for the error. Once you sign this, you will not be able to sue for libel later. But don't assume that because the paper asks you to sign, that they are afraid of losing and you have a good case; it's a formality that libel insurance would require.

If the newspaper ignores your request for a clarification or correction and you don't want to sue, you can complain to the Press Complaints Commission on the grounds that the story is inaccurate. The PCC will investigate and if it finds in your favour, can order the paper to print a correction and publish the PCC decision in your case. For this reason, if your case has merit most editors prefer to get it out of the way with a correction rather than have the matter chewed over by a bunch of other newspaper editors with the same end result. The PCC will also investigate complaints over breaches or privacy, stories involving children misrepresentation or other press concerns. If your complaint is about a radio or television story, you should complain to the station and if they do not deal with your complaint, to the Broadcasting Standards Commission.

Section 7.4 Copyright

The law of copyright is designed to protect the rights of people over their work. It protects the products of people's skill, creativity, time or labour. The Copyright, Designs and Patents Act 1988 protects any literary, artistic, dramatic or musical work, sound recording, film or broadcast.

Do I have to register copyright to protect any work I do?

No. But in order for a work to be protected, it must be 'original', in that some effort and work has gone into its production. There is no copyright in history, facts, news or ideas. But the way these things can be used and applied can be copyrighted. What happened at the England-Portugal football match is a fact and cannot be copyrighted, though a report of the game as it appears in a newspaper can be. The copyright is in the words used, not the report itself.

When does a piece of work become copyrighted?

Copyright protects all literary work – and this includes books, poems or newspaper reports – as soon as it is written.

Who owns the copyright of work I do?

That depends on what sort of work you are talking about. The first owner of a copyright work is the author, except in the case of work done in the course of your job. In these cases, the copyright belongs to your employer, unless you have an agreement to the contrary.

I hired a freelance photographer to take a picture of me. Surely I own the copyright?

No. Where you commission a portrait photographer to take your picture (or a picture of anything else come to that) the freelancer owns the copyright of the picture. This is true for private individuals and companies and newspapers. So, if you wanted to use the picture in a newspaper, the newspaper would have to get a licence from the photographer to use that picture. (If the picture was one taken before the 1988 Act came into force, the copyright belongs to the person or company that commissioned the picture.)

There was a big row over the copyright of pictures taken of Prince William for the celebration of his 18th birthday. Pictures taken by Ian Jones, a *Daily Telegraph* photographer, were to be supplied to the world's press (this thing happens with royal and state visits as a matter of course) but because the issue of copyright had not been addressed, any future use of pictures would have had to be agreed with the *Daily Telegraph*, which would have been within its rights to charge a fee for using the pictures (or with Ian Jones if he were a freelance rather than staff photographer), and which naturally upset the other newspapers. Buckingham Palace was concerned at the apparent lapse, and the matter was quietly sorted out after a few days' protracted rowing when the *Telegraph* assigned the copyright of its pictures to the palace.

We commissioned a photographer to take a picture of me, and now I am involved in a scandalous news story. Does that mean that the freelance can sell the picture to a newspaper and make money out of it?

No. If you have commissioned a picture for private or domestic purposes, you can assert your 'moral rights' over the picture – this means you can prevent pictures being issued to other people or companies, even though you don't actually own the copyright. Using the Prince William case again, Buckingham Palace could not have asserted moral rights over the pictures to prevent them being used or sold on, because, as the pictures had been taken for press purposes, this was outside the 'private or domestic purposes' over which moral rights can be asserted.

How long does copyright last?

Copyright exists for 70 years after the year in which the 'author' of a work dies (this includes images). The copyright in a broadcast lasts for 50 years.

My copyright has been breached. Can I do anything about it?

Under the civil law, you can get an injunction from the High Court to restrain someone from infringing your copyright. You can also seek a share of profits, damages and an order for possession of the work and material used to infringe your copyright. So if you drew a picture and it found its way onto a cover of a book, you can claim damages. Breach of copyright can also be a criminal offence, though most people prefer the civil route. However, if the person breaching your copyright did so innocently, you can only claim profits and not damages for the breach. If you give permission for your work to be used, this may reduce your chances of claiming breach of copyright. You can be considered to have given permission by doing nothing after discovering that your copyright has been breached – for example if you discovered that your picture was being used but only complained of the breach several years later, you could have been said to have acquiesced to the use of your picture.

Section 7.5 Medical negligence

Medical negligence is a significant issue in the UK, with the NHS estimating that £84 million was paid out in settlement of claims in 1998 (the last year where figures are available), and with experts suggesting that outstanding claims could run as high as £2 billion.

What is negligence?

Negligence is a tort that relates to damage caused by one person to another with whom they have a 'relationship'. In order to bring an allegation for negligence you will have to show three things:

1. That the person whose actions you are complaining about owed you a duty of care.
2. That there had been a breach of that duty in that the other person had not performed his or her actions to the acceptable standard of care.
3. That you suffered damage as a result of the breach of the duty of care.

You can only accuse someone of negligence if they had a duty not to be negligent towards you, so there is some element of relationship. It can be informal, for example the relationship between drivers on the road who owe each other a duty of care to drive with reasonable skill, or it can be more formal, as in the relationship between employer and employee or doctor or patient or solicitor and client. The duty of care is best illustrated by 'the neighbour principle', as outlined by Lord Atkin in the case of *Donoghue v Stevenson*, which explained how the duty of care operates. In basic terms you should take care of those acts and omissions that might affect your 'neighbour'; your 'neighbour' is any person who is so closely and directly affected by your acts that you ought to reasonably have them in mind as being so affected when you are considering the acts or omissions that are being called into question. Obviously the relationship between professional people and clients – which must include that of doctor (or dentist) and patient – is one where a duty of care is owed. But in day to day situations it can apply to anyone who ought to be thinking of you – including your neighbour who might be building an unsafe extension that falls into your garden, for example.

How must a professional person behave?

Once you have established that your doctor owes you a duty of care, the next step is to determine whether the doctor's actions breach that duty of care. To do this, you need to look at the doctor's performance and skills. A court would apply the test of reasonableness to decide whether the doctor has breached the standard of care you are entitled to expect. If a doctor does not take reasonable care in treating a patient and the patient suffers harm as a result, the patient can sue for negligence.

In all your dealings with medical (and indeed other) professionals, you are entitled to expect as a standard of care that they will have a skill and competence level equivalent to a reasonable member of the profession at their level. So if you are dealing with a junior house officer, a lower level of skill and experience would be expected than if your complaint was against a consultant or registrar. It is whether they are above or below the particular norm of their peers that is important – whether they are an average or below-average house officer – and not whether a consultant would have been able to do what the houseman failed at. To establish whether a doctor has acted negligently, it is necessary to obtain the opinion of a doctor of the same specialty, to find out if they would have acted differently and whether they agree that the standard of care afforded to you fell below that of a reasonably competent doctor.

My doctor failed to diagnose a very rare condition I have. Was he negligent?

If a doctor misdiagnoses, leading to the wrong treatment being given or no treatment being given, the doctor may be negligent, for example if obvious symptoms were missed or standard tests not ordered. But in the case of very rare or difficult-to-detect conditions, the doctor's failure may amount to negligence, depending on the presenting symptoms, and whether for example a GP should have arranged an earlier referral.

I'm allergic to penicillin and told a nurse who clerked me in that I was. The doctor prescribed penicillin anyway, even though it was on my chart. Was he guilty of negligence?

Failure to ensure that you had the right drugs, or the right dosage of the right drugs is prima facie negligence. Similarly, if he prescribed a new drug and failed to warn you of any side-effects that were known, that would also be negligence. But to obtain compensation you have to prove that you suffered some damage.

I think an operation I went though was botched, because I am in a lot of pain. What can I do?

The first step is to go back to the consultant and explain the pain to see what can be done. Not everyone wants to take legal action, only to stop the pain. If you want to take legal action, the next step is to get medical and legal advice as to whether you have a case for negligence. Examples of possible negligence could involve the removal of the wrong organ, performing the wrong operation or operating on the

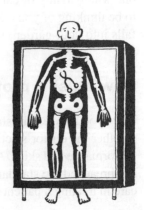

wrong patient. It would also be negligent if the operation made your condition worse, or if the surgeon injured you during the course of the operation.

Who would I take action against?

That depends on the circumstances of your complaint. If you were visiting a dental surgery or GP, you would be looking to sue the doctor or dentist themselves, and for the negligence of anyone working for them. If your injury came about as a result of a hospital stay, you would sue the hospital or NHS trust that employed the doctor, as well as the doctor or the doctor personally in the case of a private operation. Your solicitor would be able to advise whom to complain to.

Can I get medical information about my treatment?

Under the provisions of the Data Protection Act, you can apply for a copy of your medical records and notes by writing to the hospital. You can be charged £10 for the administration costs of this, plus any reasonable costs of copying documents, etc.

How do I go about lodging my claim?

The very first step is to find a solicitor to represent you. It is important that you go to a specialist clinical negligence solicitor. With the advent of the Community Legal Services Commission and their rules for funding cases, you would need to find a firm of solicitors that have a franchise in the field, and who can prove that they specialise in this field. (The idea is to stop firms of solicitors that do not have the depth of expertise trying to do the work, to the detriment of the client.) The Legal Services Commission has a list of franchised firms, so you can find one in your area. Community Legal Services funding may not be available as a matter of course, so you may need to find a law firm prepared to act for you on a conditional fee arrangement. Once you have found a lawyer, they will be able to review your medical condition from your notes and give you some idea of the level of compensation you might get if you can prove your case. But remember that if you agree a conditional fee for your solicitors, a proportion of what you win goes to them. If you decide to proceed, your solicitor will interview witnesses and call on expert witnesses to support your contention that the treatment you received was negligent. The court will give your solicitor a timetable, with dates by which time certain things will have to have been done to get the case to trial. In order to do this, you will need to give your solicitors all the help and information they need as soon as they ask for it.

Will the opposing side see the documents and statements that my witnesses and experts provide me with?

Some of the documents on which your case is based will have to be sent to the lawyers representing the doctors, but your side will get the opportunity to see some of their evidence too.

Does the case have to go to trial?

Unfortunately, medical negligence cases can often be compared to motor insurance claims, because of the role of the insurers. The insurers may decide that it would be cheaper to settle a case at an agreed sum, rather than go to trial, lose and be ordered to pay a higher sum plus legal costs. This may sound callous when you are suing because you were injured by someone's negligence, but to the insurers it is all a question of money, which can mean that very fair offers of settlement will be made (to avoid the additional costs if the doctors lose). However, settlements are usually made without admissions of liability, so if part of your motivation in bringing an action is to punish a wrongdoer, this will not happen. You or your opponent can offer to settle the case 'without prejudice' before it reaches court, but neither of you will be bound by the negotiations if you change your mind and decide to go on to court.

My opponent has offered to settle but I don't want to. What happens then?

If your opponent makes an offer to settle the case with a particular amount of compensation and damages, and the court is notified of the offer, you will have a time limit of 21 days on whether to accept or reject it. If you accept, the other side must also pay all reasonable legal costs up to the date that the money was paid into court.

Should time run out or you reject the offer, and your case goes to trial and you win, if you are awarded a greater sum in compensation that the other side offered, they will have to pay the compensation plus your costs. However, if your compensation figure is set equal to or less than the amount offered by the other side, your opponent will only have to pay their costs up to the moment they paid money into court; you will have to pay all your costs and the remainder of your opponent's costs. If you lose, you get nothing.

Medical negligence cases no longer take a long time to bring to court because of the new civil procedures. In the most serious cases, where patients lives have been blighted forever because of negligence or because procedures unfortunately went wrong, calculating compensation can be very difficult, in terms of calculating how much would be needed to give the injured person a reasonable standard of living, or support them in the same standard of living that they enjoyed before the operation, and with as good a quality of life as possible. The effects on families must also be taken into account. Personal injury and medical negligence law is a real minefield, and any but the most simple actions are best left in the hands of specialist medical neglicence lawyers.

Section 7.6 Challenging local authorities

What is a local authority?

In the same way that central government – parliament and the departments of state such as the Home Office, Foreign Office and the Ministry of Defence – run the day-to-day lives of the country at large, local authorities administer the minutiae, concerning your everyday life as an individual. Local authority services include provision of schools and libraries, housing and social services, leisure environmental health, highways, planning, rating, refuse collection and cemeteries. In addition, police and fire services are run by committees composed of representatives from the local authorities included in its force area. However, while its powers are comparatively wide-ranging, they are illusory – local government powers extend only as far as parliament allows them to. Its powers arise as delegated legislation via Acts of Parliament or regulations. These may be 'mandatory' (the council must do as the Act says), 'adoptive' (where the council can assume powers in a certain case but must vote to adopt the Act before exercising the powers granted by it) or 'permissive' (where it is up to the authority whether to use the powers).

How do local authorities operate?

Local authorities are managed by two sets of people, councillors and paid officers. In its simplest form, councillors decide the broad strategy that the council will follow and the officers (who head the main departments) put that strategy into effect and are responsible for the day-to-day running of the council. In most councils, the full council considers the most important issues, such as the setting of rates; other matters are dealt with by committees and sub-committees of councillors that oversee the departments. The number of committees and their terms of reference is a matter for the council, though by law there must be an education committee.

Powers can be delegated by the local authority to the senior officers, except the setting of a rate which must be set by the full council. For the rest, the extent to which officers can make decisions depends on each local authority's standing orders.

How do local authorities raise finance?

Local authority funding comes from rates, both domestic and business, and via a block grant from central government which varies from authority to authority, depending on the size, population and commitments of the local authority. In addition, central government pays grants for specific things such as the police, and supplementary grants for particular services such as a National Park.

Can local authorities extend their powers?

Any time a local authority wants to do anything that effectively extends its powers, for example if it wants to pass a by-law preventing people drinking alcohol on the streets outside pubs, then it would need approval from the relevant secretary of state and central government department. Once it had been confirmed, the by-law would be printed so members of the public could read it, before it came into effect.

Can local authorities be challenged?

If a local authority acts beyond its powers, it is said to have acted 'ultra vires', for example if a by-law is unreasonable and the council has acted beyond the powers it has available to it. To challenge a council, you need to make an application to the High Court for a judicial review of the council's actions, which is expensive and not an action to be taken lightly. The High Court can prevent the council from continuing to overstep its powers, or order it to do something it is not doing. If you feel so strongly that the council is doing something wrong, you should discuss the matter with your solicitor.

What if I want to challenge the council about something smaller that I think is wrong?

You can complain to the local government ombudsman if you feel that the council has acted incorrectly. The ombudsman has the same power as the High Court to order authorities to produce documents, and investigations take place in private. Unlike a High Court Action, you will not have to pay to get the ombudsman to investigate your case. The ombudsman is a watchdog – his function is really to highlight bad administration and criticise the guilty parties; the ombudsman cannot fine local authorities or officers that transgress, or reverse decisions made by councils. But councils that the ombudsman criticises usually change their decisions quickly.

What authorities can the ombudsman investigate complaints against?

Ombudsmen can investigate complaints of maladministration against district, borough, city or council councils, school governing bodies, education appeals panels, housing action trusts, fire authorities, police authorities (but not the actions of individual officers), National Park authorities, the Greater London Authority, the London Transport Users' Committee, the London Development Agency, the Commission for New Towns (housing matters only), English Partnerships (planning matters only), the Norfolk and Suffolk Broads Authority and the Environment Agency (flood defence and land drainage matters only).

What sort of complaints can the ombudsman investigate?

The ombudsman can only investigate allegations of maladministration – you can't go to the ombudsman simply because the council did something you don't agree with; what the council did must have been 'wrong'. Examples of maladministration are:

- Failing to follow a statutory procedure.
- Failing to follow internal department rules (if there is no discretion).
- Discrimination against a Council Tax-payer on grounds of race, sex, religion, social status, etc.
- Delay caused other than by overwork.
- Misfeasance in office, for example abusing the local authority for your own ends by getting council gardeners to dig your garden.
- Inefficiency.

It is not enough to show maladministration; the ombudsman can only investigate if you show that you suffered 'injustice' as a result of the maladministration, for example by failing to get a benefit you were entitled to, suffered some financial loss or were distressed by the council's actions. But there are some cases when the ombudsman cannot get involved:

- If the action you are complaining about happened more than 12 months ago.
- If you have already taken legal action against the council, or raised the matter with a tribunal or government department.
- If you could have appealed to a tribunal or government department (unless the ombudsman thinks you have a good reason not to have appealed).
- If the claim is too large and affects too many people, such as a claim that a council wasted public money (which would be dealt with by the district auditor).
- Personnel matters (so complaints of nepotism cannot be investigated by the ombudsman).
- Internal management of schools and colleges.
- Contracts for the supply of goods and services.

And before the ombudsman can get involved, the council must have an opportunity to answer the charge. If an inadvertent error has been made, the council may want to rectify it. So if you have a grievance against the council and have not complained to them, you must do so. If you are not happy with their response, or it is not forthcoming with a reasonable length of time, the next step is to complain to the ombudsman. Your local councillor can complain or you can write to the ombudsman direct (see Appendix).

What happens next?

If the complaint is one the ombudsman can investigate, he will gather the relevant facts from any councillors, officers or departments involved, and call for any papers or files that are needed; given that the ombudsman has the same powers as a High Court judge in compelling evidence, there is rarely any attempt to hinder the investigation. You will usually be interviewed as well, and you can have a friend, councillor, MP or lawyer on hand to help you and advise you. But you won't have to face the councillor or officers you have complained about. The council may offer to right the wrong during the course of the investigation, and if the ombudsman think their offer is fair, he may accept and stop the investigation. Once the investigations have been completed, a report will be sent out to you and the council, and subsequently notice of the report's existence will be published in the local press and the council will have to make copies of the report available for scrutiny. You will not be named in the report.

If the council has been found at fault, the ombudsman will recommend what course of action should be taken to remedy matters, but he cannot compel the council to accept its ruling.

Can I make a complaint on behalf of a dead neighbour?

Complaints can be made to the ombudsman on behalf of people you think were treated unfairly, who are dead or unable physically or mentally to make the complaint for themselves.

Section 7.7 Discrimination

Equality in society is very important to us all. No one should be discriminated on grounds of sex, race, creed, colour or physical state. Obviously, we are concerned about discrimination in the workplace – it is unfair that someone should be paid more because they are a different gender, or race, or because they are able-bodied. However, discrimination in other parts of our everyday life is also contrary to law.

We have already looked at discrimination at work; this chapter seeks to examine discrimination elsewhere.

Is sex discrimination a problem beyond the workplace?

The Sex Discrimination Act 1975 says that it is unlawful to discriminate against someone in the workplace on the grounds of his or her sex. However, it also makes it unlawful to discriminate in the areas of education, consumer services (including housing) and advertising.

If you want to complain about sex discrimination in these fields, generally you have to bring the matter before a county court no more than six months after the issue was first raised.

What about discrimination in education?

No-one attending, school, college, a college of further education, university or polytechnic can receive less favourable treatment on the grounds of their sex. Schools that are single sex may refuse to accept a member of the opposite sex because they fall outside the provisions of the 1975 Act, but if a school is mixed, it can't turn down a girl pupil on the basis that it already has 'enough' girls there. Similarly, schools can't prevent girls doing what are traditionally considered 'boy's subjects' such as woodwork or metalwork, or boys doing 'girl's subjects' such as cookery or domestic science. Nor would it be lawful for a school to penalise boys that want to do 'girl's subjects' by making them give up a free period to do so, for example; this would count as indirect discrimination.

What about school uniform?

For some years after the 1975 Act was passed, it was considered that school uniform provisions would not be affected by it, and schools could insist that only boys wore trousers and girls would have to wear skirts. However, a recent case may have weakened this position. A girl took her school in Gateshead to court claiming that it was discriminating against girls by preventing them wearing trousers, especially in cold weather. The case, which had been backed by the Equal Opportunities Commission, was settled out of court, and the ban lifted, so there is no direct legal precedent. Schools do have responsibilities under the Sex Discrimination Act, but ultimately the question of uniform is for the governors at each school. Of course, if uniform bans are lifted, there is nothing to stop boys wearing skirts!

I think I have been discriminated against by my school on grounds of sex. What can I do?

The first step would be to complain to the head teacher about the fact you feel to have discriminated against you. If no action is taken, the next step is to write to the chairman of governors at the school, and if no action is taken then, write to the Department for Education and Employment. The Department then has two months to deal with your complaint, or write informing you why nothing is to be done. If nothing is done, or if you disagree with the course of action taken, you can take out a summons against the school in your local county court, provided not more than six months have elapsed since the incident.

Can people discriminate against consumers?

Discrimination in any form against consumers is prima facie unlawful – anyone providing goods and services is not allowed to treat a woman less favourably than a man (or vice versa) on grounds of sex, regardless of whether any charge is made for the goods and services. For example, pub landlords cannot bar women from using the pool tables, nor can breweries run men-only darts leagues and competitions. But a private 'men only' competition, for example a squash ladder, would be allowed if the members are in favour of it, because non-professional voluntary groups do not fall within the terms of reference of the 1975 Act.

Banks, building societies and other companies are not allowed to ask discriminatory questions on their applications forms, for example requiring women seeking loans or opening bank accounts to give details of their husband's job but not asking the same of men making the same application. Any special conditions that apply to one sex and not another would be counted as discriminatory, for example asking a woman's husband to act as a guarantor on a loan application, but not extending the same request to men. If you think you have been discriminated against over the provision of goods or services, or over the sale or rent of property, you can issue proceedings in the county court against the person or company involved within six months of the incident taking place.

I want to rent out my flat. Can I only rent it to a woman?

You are not allowed to make special conditions that would exclude one sex or the other when selling or renting a house, flat or commercial property. However, private sellers of houses can sell to whomsoever they wish, and can impose whatever criteria they wish – though if you were discriminated against by such a person, would you really want to buy the house anyway?

I am planning a house-share. Can I stipulate 'women only'?

House-shares are totally different – you can specify the sex of the person you want to share with and rightly so. After all, a woman might not want to share a two-bedroom flat with a bloke; or vice versa.

What about single-sex clubs?

There are some exceptions to the general rule that people offering goods and services cannot discriminate on grounds of sex. Private clubs – for example golf clubs, London 'gentlemen's' clubs, many working-men's clubs, sports clubs and the like – are able to discriminate against men and women, in the case of golf clubs by giving lady members less advantageous access to the course, for example. As private clubs, they are allowed to impose their own code of conduct for members. Recently, however, after 212 years, one of the last bastions of male supremacy, the Marylebone Cricket Club (the MCC) voted to allow women members. (Partly due to a desire to move into the 20th century, cynics suggested the decision was also prompted by the fact that failing to do so would prevent the club from applying for and receiving National Lottery cash.)

And there were the women-only shortlists for MPs' seats...

The Labour Party flirted with the idea of women-only shortlists for some seats to increase the representation of women in parliament. However, a man complained and the courts decided that this was unlawful because of the discrimination that it brought. It is possible to run women's sections within political parties, but to discriminate against potential candidates purely on grounds of sex would be wrong.

What about race discrimination?

The same principles that apply to sex discrimination apply in race discrimination. Treating someone less favourably because they are a different colour, race or nationality is contrary to the provisions of the Race Relations Act.

Can you discriminate in the case of housing?

Any terms that would not be applied to all races, creeds or colours would be prima facie discriminatory, for example charging a higher rent to a black family than a white family, or refusing to sell or rent a property to someone who is ready to buy or rent purely on the grounds of their ethnic origin or background. Councils that allocate council housing on a points system would not be able to discriminate against black or Asian families in the way that points are awarded. However, the same principles tend to apply in the case of house-shares as for sex discrimination. People renting rooms within their own houses can decide for themselves who they wish to rent to, outside the Race Relations Act (but if someone did not want you as a lodger because of your colour, would you want to live with someone like that anyway?). In addition, private sellers of houses who are not using an estate agent can sell to whom they wish, but of course an advert for sale saying 'Three bedroom house for sale £90,000. No Irish need apply.' would be unlawful.

Can providers of goods and service discriminate on grounds of race, creed or colour?

Everyone has the freedom to enter and use the facilities of any place that is open to the general public, book rooms in guesthouses or hotels, use facilities offered by banks, building societies or other financial institutions, travel companies, pubs, clubs and sports facilities, and employ the services of any trade or profession, without expecting to be discriminated against on grounds of race, creed or colour. Providers of goods and services cannot impose different qualifications for people of different ethnic origins, charging a higher price for non-white people for example, or preventing non-white people playing on snooker tables in a club. Discriminatory questions on application forms are not allowed, nor the imposition of special conditions for one race.

Can a publican refuse to serve a customer because they are black?

Publicans are not obliged to serve anyone, and they can bar members of the public from their premises, but if a publican barred a customer because of his or her colour, the landlord would be guilty of discrimination.

Can clubs discriminate against ethnic groups?

Any club or association with vacancies for new members cannot discriminate against members trying to join, provided that it has more than 25 members, and that it was not set up to benefit a particular group of people. For example, if a local authority set up a club for Asian youngsters in an area, it could restrict membership to Asian youngsters. In the case of most clubs, however, if a club continued to discriminate against potential members on grounds of colour or race, you can apply to a court for an injunction to prevent the club from continuing to discriminate in this way. The club would then effectively have to offer you membership. You could also claim compensation for injured feelings.

Are there any exceptions to the law relating to race discrimination?

There is a number of circumstances where you cannot complain about discrimination:

- The Race Relations Act does not expressly cover discrimination on grounds of religion, but you may be able to complain if the discrimination is also on grounds of national or ethnic origin.
- At present, law enforcement (police, Crown Prosecution Service, courts, etc.) is exempt from the provisions of the Act, though this is likely to change under the terms of the Race Relations (Amendment) Bill which is currently going through parliament.
- Certain jobs where the Crown is the employer are exempt, for example, at the Bank of England, embassies and consulates and some jobs within the civil service. Discrimination on grounds of nationality, ethnic or national origin is not unlawful, but discrimination based on colour is.
- Work where race is a 'genuine occupational qualification' for the job, such as certain roles in plays or films, or working with people of a particular racial group in a welfare or social services support-type role.

What changes is the Race Relations (Amendment) Bill likely to bring?

The Bill's main effects will be in terms of spreading race relations provision to public authorities that were previously exempt, and in terms of halting indirect discrimination. If the Bill goes through in its present form, public authorities will have a positive duty to promote racial equality. The Race Relations Act will then be extended to cover a number of bodies and authorities for the first time, including:

- Policing, including all aspects of criminal investigation, arrest, bail, detention.
- Prisons, including discipline and punishment.
- Immigration, including the regulation of entry, detention, asylum decisions, prosecutions and deportation.
- The Customs Service.
- The criminal justice system and probation service.
- Local authority enforcement powers over private landlords, street trading and environmental health.
- The Health and Safety Executive.
- Local authority powers regarding child protection.

The benefit of removing all exceptions for indirect discrimination in the Bill is that the full Race Relations Act would then apply to all functions of all public authorities.

What about disabled people?

The Disability Discrimination Act 1995 protects the rights of people suffering from a disability that makes it difficult for them to carry out normal day-to-day activities; the disability can be physical, sensory, or mental, but must be substantial and have a long-term effect (that last for 12 months), though conditions which have a slight effect on day-to-day activities, but are expected to become substantial, are also covered. Anyone who provide goods and services will have to take reasonable steps to ensure that they are not discriminating against disabled people, as will people who sell or let property.

Under the Act, it would be against the law to refuse to serve someone who is disabled, or to refuse them entry, for example a supermarket cannot bar wheelchair shoppers because they shop too slowly. Nor can businesses offer a worse service to disabled people, for example seating people that have a visible disfigurement out of sight of other customers. However, it would not be against the law to refuse to provide a service to a disabled person if their health and safety might be affected by it, or the health and safety of other patrons or consumers.

I'm blind and have a guide dog. Can a restaurant refuse to let me in on the grounds that it does not allow animals on the premises?

It is against the law for anyone to run a service, or provide goods or facilities, in a way that makes it impossible or unreasonably difficult for a disabled person to use the service or goods. In the light of this, the restaurant's ban on guide dogs is unlawful. However, in other circumstances a company can provide its services in a way that do make it impossible or difficult for disabled people, if it is fundamental to the service itself, for example a complaint about dim lighting in a night club from someone with poor eyesight would not be upheld.

Do service providers have to make special provision for disabled people?

Businesses will be required to provide equipment or other helpful items that will make it easier for disabled people to use their services, provided that it is reasonable to do so, for example induction loops for people with hearing problems, or handrails.

Physical obstructions will have to be removed, or disabled access provided, and service providers will not be able to charge disabled people more for using their services. But if it is not reasonable to expect businesses to change their facilities, then they will not have to.

What about property?

It is against the law for anyone selling or renting land to unreasonably discriminate against disabled people, in terms of price or rent for example, though this would not apply to landlords renting out rooms in their own home (unless they are renting more than six rooms). But sellers or renters of property do not have to make adjustments to property to improve disabled access.

I'm disabled and feel I have been discriminated against. What can I do?

If you think that you have been wrongly excluded from receiving or enjoying goods or services, or buying or renting land, you can take legal action to claim damages for any financial loss they have suffered and for injury to your feelings.

What about transport?

The Disability Discrimination Act allows the government to set minimum standards for new public transport vehicles (trains, taxis, buses, coaches, etc.) so that disabled people, including wheelchair users, can use them. For example, disabled people who use wheelchairs will eventually be able to hire taxis in the street or at a taxi rank like everyone else.

And what about disabled students?

Under the Disability Discrimination Act, schools will be required to explain their arrangements for admitting disabled pupils, how they will help these pupils gain access and what they will do to ensure they are treated fairly; in addition, local education authorities will have to provide information on their further education facilities for disabled people. Further and higher education institutions that receive their funding from the Further and Higher Education Funding Councils have to publish disability statements containing information about facilities they offer for disabled people.

Chapter 8
You and your money

Section 8.1 Data protection

What is data protection?

Concerns about the vast body of personal data held on computers by marketing and other companies, as well as banks, councils and government departments grew in the late 20th century. Concerns were expressed over the privacy issue, that data could be misused or passed onto third parties that were not entitled to have it. Just as bad was the concern that information stored about individuals might be wrong and adversely affect them in some way – for example incorrect information about debt might affect credit references. But by the same token, it was recognised that companies and organisations needed to hold data on people in computerised record banks. The Data Protection Acts 1984 and 1998 have tried to strike a balance between individuals' entitlement to privacy in the handling of information about them, and information users' needs in processing information to provide the services which individuals require.

What is personal data?

The Data Protection Act only concerns the holding of personal data. Personal data is defined as data that relates to an identifiable living individual (the data subject), and which is:

* Being processed by computer or other automatic equipment; or;
* Recorded with the intention that it should be so processed or;
* Forms part of a relevant filing system or accessible record.

Employee records, assessment results and research data resulting from surveys would all be classed as personal data, as are bibliographies, e-mail directories and lists of suppliers.

What is a relevant filing system?

A 'relevant filing system' is any set of information structured in such a way so that specific information relating to individuals can be accessed simply, despite not being held on a computer. So files would be included, but a morass of paper on a manager's desk would not be.

What are 'accessible records'?

Accessible records are a special class of personal data consisting of health records, educational records in state schools, and local authority housing and social services records, which must be treated as if it were valuable or potentially confidential data.

What are the rules concerning the handling of data?

Anyone processing personal data must comply with the eight enforceable principles of good practice, that say data must be:

- Fairly and lawfully processed.
- Processed for limited purposes.
- Adequate, relevant and not excessive.
- Accurate.
- Not kept longer than necessary.
- Processed in accordance with the data subject's rights.
- Secure.
- Not transferred to countries without adequate protection.

Anyone who stores personal information about living individuals should have an entry in the register.

What is the register?

The Data Protection Commissioner maintains a public register of data controllers – organisations that store data on individuals. Each register entry includes the name and address of the data controller and a general description of the processing of personal data, so you can tell what each data controller does with its data stores, for example constructing mailing lists. Once data users have registered, they can disclose information to organisations or persons described in their register entry without committing a criminal offence, provided that the data is handled in accordance with the eight principles.

What rights do I have as an individual with regard to personal data about me held by companies or organisations?

Almost all of us are data subjects; data users will hold information about us, our creditworthiness, etc. Your rights as a data subject are:

- To be told if a data user holds information about you, and why.
- To have a copy of that information, and an indication where it came from.
- To prevent the information being processed in a way that is likely to hurt or upset you.

- To be compensated if you are hurt or distressed because the Data Protection Act is not complied with.
- To correct inaccurate personal data.

What does my business need to do to keep on the right side of the law?

Every business that holds data is required by law to nominate a data controller (a person who oversees the processing of personal data), and to notify the Data Protection Commissioner. When you register, you do not have to outline the content of every file; all that is required is for the data user to declare the general purpose for which the data is held, the type of information that is held, the categories of people or organisations it has been sourced from and will be revealed to, and whether data will be transferred overseas. For example, a university's registration may cover 'Education and Training Administration', with a declaration that the university holds information about current, past and potential students, including their academic record; that information has been obtained from, amongst others, LEAs and the students themselves; and that it may be disclosed to various professional and government organisations.

What about sensitive information held about me?

Some data is considered so sensitive that the 1998 Act created a new category of sensitive personal data that must be handled more carefully. Sensitive personal data is any personal data that includes information on:

- Racial or ethnic origin.
- Political opinions, religious or similar beliefs.
- Trade union membership.
- Physical or mental health.
- Sexual life.
- The (alleged) commission of any offence, subsequent proceedings or sentence.

Sensitive personal data should normally only be processed if the data subjects have given explicit consent to this processing; it can be processed without consent, however, if it is necessary for other reasons, for example because of obligations imposed by employment law, or for medical purposes (including research) or for equal opportunities monitoring. This would allow personnel departments to collate information not strictly related to how you do your job, but which is still important to an organisation. But if it were collected for any other purpose, you would have to give consent.

Do I have a right to know why companies collect data on me?

The 1998 Act imposes an obligation to ensure fair processing by telling you what is happening to your data. In simple terms, if a company asks you for data about yourself, it should tell you who will process the data, and for what purpose, any consequences of processing the data (whether you will end up on a mailing list) and whether the information is likely to be disclosed. If your data were provided by someone other than yourself (a market research company, for example), the company would have to provide the same information to you, unless 'the provision of that information would involve a disproportionate effort'; in practice this means that companies that sell mailing lists can do so without having to contact you each time.

Can a company that holds personal data about me pass it on to someone else?

Companies that hold your personal data can only disclose it to those people that the company has notified the Data Protection Commissioner about. For example, a credit reference agency can disclose information to bona fide clients, but not to your next-door neighbour who calls in to be nosy.

How can I find out what information a company holds on me?

If you make a formal application, the company must tell you within 40 days about all the data they have on you. Companies cannot delete the information to avoid telling you what they are holding about you. You are also entitled to know where the data came from, why it is being processed, whether it will be passed on to companies or persons, and if so to whom.

Who can data controllers disclose information to?

A data controller is allowed by law to disclose information to 'employees and agents', though such disclosure should be kept to the minimum necessary to do whatever the information is required for. Data controllers must take reasonable care to ensure any employees with access to personal data are reliable, for anyone that knowingly or recklessly obtains or discloses personal data without authority is committing a crime.

Can companies hold onto my data for ever? And can they use it for different purposes?

Data protection principles require that data is held only for specified purposes, and will not be kept longer than is necessary. So, databases can't be built up and then the information used for purposes other than it was compiled for. But companies can keep any data indefinitely for historical, statistical or research purposes, regardless of why it was collected. Personal data held only for statistical analysis or research still has to be registered, but if it is not used or disclosed for any other purpose and if the information is used so subjects cannot be identified, you don't have a right to see your file.

Are there any exemptions?

Business reasons can give companies a justification not to release information about you. For example, companies do not have to give data subjects access to management planning or forecasting data if doing so might harm the company's business activities. Also, if a company is negotiating with you, it does not have to say why it is holding data if that might prejudice the negotiations. On the other hand, companies are able to disclose any personal data urgently required to prevent injury or damage to the health of anyone, or personal data that must be disclosed because of an Act of Parliament or court order, to safeguard national security, prevent or detect crime or the assessment or collection of any tax. But the company is responsible for checking that anyone requesting the information is entitled to have it, otherwise they will be in breach of the Data Protection Acts.

Can I do anything about junk mail?

If you suffer from 'junk mail', Section 11 of the Data Protection Act 1998 gives you the right to serve notice in writing on a data controller to cease processing personal data about you for the purposes of direct marketing. You can also write to The Mailing Preference Service (see Appendix) to have your name and the household removed from mailing lists of companies who send out unsolicited mail.

I have a home computer. Should that be registered?

You may have a computer at home and be wondering if, as an individual, you should register under the Act. If you hold personal data, other than that needed for your work (which would be covered by your company's registration) you should certainly consider an individual registration. This might, for instance, be necessary for data used in connection with private consultancy work or, for instance, as a church officer or member of a neighbourhood watch scheme. You will not normally need to register if you only hold manual data. You also do not need to register if you hold only data concerned with personal, family or household affairs, or recreational purposes. The same advice applies to individual holdings of data as it does to those held by a large organisation: if in doubt, register. The Act requires no more than ordinary good practice in the handling of personal data.

Section 8.2 Obtaining credit

If you buy something now, and agree to pay in instalments or pay later, then that's buying on credit. A deferred payment is a form of credit; so is getting a loan for a car from your bank or finance company. Credit agreements are contracts, which impose rights and obligations on you as the borrower and the bank or finance company as the lender; if you break the agreement you can be sued, and can sue to enforce your rights too

How are credit agreements regulated?

Credit cards, charge card, cheques, overdraft facilities, loans – these are all types of credit agreements, and agreements for loans up to £250,0000 are covered by the Consumer Credit Act 1974. Lease-hire and hire purchase (HP or the 'never-never' as our parents used to call it) are also forms of credit agreement. HP is where you pay by instalments to use the goods, but have an option to buy the goods if you want to after all the instalments have been paid. But loans from a friend or relatives are not credit agreements protected under the Act.

I've seen a car I want to buy. How do I go about getting credit?

Let's assume you have saved some money for the deposit for your car (say ten per cent) and you want to borrow the rest. You could go to your bank and ask for a loan repayable over up to four years, or if you are very well-paid you could even ask for an overdraft to cover the purchase price of the car. If you go to your own bank, you have the advantage that they know you as a customer, and have seen how you manage your money on a monthly basis; they will know if you are a 'good risk' for them to lend to. On the other hand, there is nothing stopping you shopping around and finding the best possible deal from other banks or building societies, or finance companies.

Alternatively, the car dealer may offer finance themselves – they won't actually lend you the money, but will have a tie-in with a bigger finance company. Before buying anything on credit you need to know much will the loan cost in total. Check the AER (or Annual Equivalent Rate, which illustrates what the gross interest rate is if the balance is compounded on an annual basis); normally the lower the rate the better the deal for the less you pay in interest. Beware 'free credit' – there's no such thing and the purchase price is often higher to cover the interest that you are not being charged. Be sure you can pay back the loan, given all your other commitments. Make sure that the loan interest rate won't change, because if the interest rate should go up you will have to pay more each month – will you be able to afford it if that happens? If you are sure, send the forms in. Many places can approve loans within hours, or over the telephone so the car of your dreams may be only a short step away.

I've had some county court judgments in the past few years. I haven't paid them off yet, and if I admit it I will be turned down for the loan. Can I get away with lying?

Fill the form in honestly. If you have had bad debts in the past, you should admit them. Remember, obtaining a loan by deception is a crime, and if the finance company decides to press charges you could go to court and, if convicted, to jail. You will get found out, because, before giving you credit, lenders will want to check whether you are an acceptable risk, often by using a credit reference agency to get some details about you and your credit record. So you would have to lie about your address... and when there was no trace of you at the address you gave, alarm bells might start to ring.

How do credit checks work?

A lender can run a check on you through a credit reference agency before deciding whether or not to lend you money (most lenders do this). Another approach is 'credit scoring', where you fill in a form about yourself and your circumstances, and the lender allocates points to you depending on the information you give. Lenders have different systems of scoring, and being rejected by one does not mean a rejection from all so you can apply again – though you will almost certainly be asked if you have been refused credit.

How does credit scoring work?

Many credit scoring systems allocate points to various pieces of information that you provide on your application form, such as your age, occupation and whether you live with your parents, rent or own your own home These points are added together to produce a credit score; this acts as an indicator of whether you are an acceptable risk. Lenders do not have to tell you why you have been turned down, but they should give an indication of the reason.

What about credit reference agencies?

Credit reference agencies have access to various sources of information:

- The electoral register (this confirms that you live where you claim to).
- The register of county court judgments and bankruptcies (this will act as a guide to your credit history, and will show whether you have ever had a court order made against you for non-payment of debts; this is why lenders like to know your addresses for the past three years).
- Details of current (and previous) credit agreements with other lenders (this shows your payment history).

Taken together, this information gives lenders a fairly accurate snapshot of your financial circumstances at any given time, as well as your financial history; if you have previously made a habit of not paying loans, it will show up in the credit reference.

I've been turned down for a loan and they won't tell me why... that's not fair, surely?

Lenders do not have to tell you why they have turned you down, only that you did not pass their credit scoring, or that information from a credit reference agency suggests you are a bad credit risk. But knowing how you came to fail means you might be able to solve the problem for a future application, or find out if the wrong information has been given by a credit reference agency.

I've been told that my credit reference was the reason I did not get a loan. But I've never owed anyone anything. If they've made a mistake, is there anything I can do?

If you are turned down because of an adverse credit reference, you are entitled to know which agency supplied the reference. You have 28 days to decide to ask which agency was used; the lender must supply the agency's name and address within seven days of your application. The next step is to write to the agency, enclosing a £2 fee and your full details (name, address, date of birth, etc.); within seven working days of receiving your letter, the agency must send you a copy of your file. If any of the details are incorrect, write back to the agency and ask them to remove or change the information; they have 28 days to comply. If the agency refuses you can send a statement of up to 200 words (a 'notice of correction') giving your side of the story and ask the agency to add this to your file. A copy of the notice must then be sent to each lender that contacts the agency for your file. If the agency refuses to add the notice of correction, you should write to the Director General of Fair Trading, asking them to decide whether the notice should be added to your file. If your file contains information about family members that you have no financial connection with, you should write to explain this to the agency, and ask to be disassociated from them. If the agency does not comply, you can ask the Data Protection Registrar to review your case. Remember, credit reference agencies do not keep 'blacklists' or offer any opinion about whether or not you should be given credit; they only provide information about your credit record. The final decision is the lender's.

I've applied for a loan governed by the Consumer Credit Act. What protection do I get?

1. **The right to cancel.** If you have signed a credit agreement, you can cancel it within a certain period of time, provided you did not make the agreement over telephone, or sign the

agreement at the seller's shop, office or workplace. So, if a double-glazing salesman or vacuum cleaner rep calls at the house, and after a four-hour demonstration forces you to sign, you can cancel. When you sign the agreement, you should be given a written notice telling you how to cancel; write to the address within the cancellation period (it's best to send a recorded delivery letter). Any deposit or goods offered in part-exchange must be returned or refunded if the agreement is cancelled in time.

2. **Protection against early payment demands.** The lender cannot ask you to make early payments, or try to terminate the agreement early or try to get the goods back without serving a written default notice on you first; this then gives you seven days' notice of their intention to take such action. This notice must tell you how much is owed in arrears, when they should be made, and what will happen if the arrears are not paid and the agreement can be terminated.

3. **Protection against the seizure of HP goods.** If you have paid one-third of the total price of the goods under an HP agreement, the creditor cannot take the goods back without getting a court order (which you can oppose). If the creditor repossesses the goods without a court order or your permission, you can sue, claiming back all the money you paid under the agreement. The creditor cannot come into your property to repossess goods without permission or a court order.

4. **Protection against unfair agreements.** If a credit agreement appears to be unfair, for example if the interest rate is excessively high, then you can ask a court to look at the agreement and replace or alter it. The court will only do this if it can be shown that the agreement is 'extortionate', and will look at the circumstances surrounding the agreement, including your age and business experience, etc. The court will consider whether you were a 'bad risk' (which would mean a lender might be justified in asking for higher interest repayments as 'insurance') or if the price was inflated to make the credit terms look more attractive.

5. **Protection against sellers and third-party credit brokers.** A seller may offer credit, or arrange for you to get credit from a third-party. If the agreement is defaulted upon, you can choose whom to sue. For example, if the trader ceases trading, you can sue to recover your money from the credit provider instead.

6. **Information about the credit agreement must be given to you.** This information includes the goods' cash price, the total credit charges and costs and the Annual Equivalent Rate (loans used to have interest calculated using the Annual Percentage Rate or APR).

Are all agreements covered by the Consumer Credit Act?

Not all credit agreements are covered by the Consumer Credit act, so you will not have the same protection. Loans for more than £25,000 are exempt as a matter of course, but so are credit agreements involving building societies, local authorities, limited companies and PLCs, insurance companies, friendly societies, charities, housing and land companies.

Are there any advantages in buying on credit?

Buying on credit does give you some extra rights, for example if goods are faulty. If you pay by credit, you have extra protection if the goods cost more than £100, as, in cases of a breach of contract or misrepresentation by the trader, the credit company is equally liable. For example, if the goods are not delivered or are not what you ordered, or a holiday was wrongly described or you did not get what you paid for, you may be able to claim from the credit card or finance company. This does not apply if you pay by charge card or debit card.

I want to pay the loan back early. Can I do this?

When loans are taken out, the total amount is calculated on the basis of a monthly repayment of a proportion of the capital and interest. For example, if you borrow £1,000 over 24 months, you will usually pay 24 equal instalments of capital plus interest, one instalment per month. However, you may find that half way through repaying your loan, you have enough money to pay off the whole amount outstanding in one go. You may be entitled to a rebate of some of the charges you would have paid over the rest of the life of the loan, but it depends on the agreement you signed.

What are credit unions?

A credit union is a savings and loan co-operative set up for the mutual benefit of all its members. It is a non-profit-making, voluntary organisation. By law, credit unions must be registered with the Registrar of Friendly Societies. Two-thirds of UK credit unions are 'community' credit unions, where the main eligibility criterion for membership is residence in a particular area. A credit union must have a minimum membership of 21 people. Anyone who is aged 16 or over, and meets the requirements, is eligible to become a member. People aged under 16 may also save with a credit union, but cannot be members. Savings with a credit union are called shares, and each pound saved is one share. Credit unions make loans to members at a maximum rate of interest of one per cent per month on the outstanding amount. By law, the maximum amount a member can save with a credit union is 5,000 shares or £5,000; the maximum amount which a member can borrow is £5,000 plus their shareholding (a total of £10,000). Credit unions do not pay interest on savings, but once a credit union has met all its annual operating expenses, any surplus can be returned to the members in the form of a dividend on each share (the decisions on what to do with a surplus are taken by the members at the AGM). Members apply for loans to the credit committee, which will take into account the purpose of the loan and the applicant's savings, borrowing and repayment record in reaching a decision on whether or not to offer a loan, and if so, how much.

Section 8.3 Debt, small claims and bankruptcy

Debt is all around us. Loans, overdrafts and credit cards are all forms of consumer debt, and by and large, few societies operate without some level of debt. Don't forget, banks generate much of their revenue by charging interest on loans and credit cards. But when debt becomes unmanageable, problems start. Changes in circumstances, for example rises in interest rates, losing your job or your wife becoming pregnant and having to give up work for a while, can all change your income and expenditure patterns, and it is then that problems ensue as it becomes harder to meet that monthly repayment.

I'm finding it harder to meet my monthly payments. Is there anything I can do?

It is important to come to terms with financial troubles quickly. They won't go away if ignored, and you could end up in a small claims court, with your credit record in tatters. The first step is to work out exactly how much you owe, to whom and how much you can pay back. This will help sort things out in your mind, and help your creditors see where you stand. Get in touch with your creditors to explain your situation as soon as possible and try to reach an agreement about repayments. Your debt won't be written off, but you might be able to pay it back in smaller payments over a longer period of time, or you might be given a few months' leeway to sort yourself out before commencing repayments again. This will probably mean an increased total payment, because of the increase in interest payments in the long term, but it may be more manageable now. But don't mislead your creditors either. If you don't think three months' grace will help, say so. Nothing would be more annoying for a creditor to give you time only to discover you still can't make the payments. It would be better to negotiate a lower payment up front – that way you can always increase it when times get better. Your creditors are not soft touches. They won't be fobbed off with a phoney sob story if you are just trying to avoid paying what you owe, but they may surprise you by being very understanding and reasonable if you explain the problems to them, and how you propose to get out of trouble. Part of this is self-interest: once they take you to court, the 'clock' stops in terms of interest payments on any outstanding debt, so if you keep paying they will still be able to charge you interest that will ultimately make their understanding worthwhile financially. To convince your creditors to accept a lower payment you will need to show them:

- **How much you owe.** List your debts. Work out when payments fall, and identify important debts.
- **How much you earn.** Work out how much money you have coming in.

- **What you spend.** List your essential and less essential spending. Compare it with your income, and calculate how much you can pay your creditors.
- **Any other sources of money.** Is there any way you can reduce your spending, or generate extra income to pay them?

Show your creditors your calculations. Be fair to them – creditors won't be happy if you pay more pro rata to one creditor than another.

How do companies normally pursue their debts?

If your creditor won't accept your repayment proposals, there is normally a fairly standard pattern companies follow in collecting debts. After you fail to pay the outstanding arrears, the company will send you a formal demand for payment, which must state who you are and be delivered to your home or place of work; the notice will also identify the creditor's name, address and contact details, the amount of arrears and what it is owed for, a deadline for you to pay the arrears and the course of action the company will follow if you do not pay up – usually legal action. If you ignore the demand, the creditor will sends you a claim form demanding that you send payment within 14 days, or submit your defence in writing.

If you ignore the claim form, your creditor can ask the court to enter a default judgment (a county court judgment or CCJ), because you defaulted on an opportunity to deal with the creditor's claim. The CCJ will be sent to you, and you have 28 days to pay in full; if you pay the total plus any court costs, that is an end to the matter and no judgement will be recorded against your name on the county court register. If you ignore the CCJ, it will be entered and will stand against your name for six years and make it impossible for you to get credit easily. You will then have to agree payment terms via the court and your creditors. If you satisfy the debt after the 28-day period, an entry can be made on the register indicating that the debt has been settled. However, the CCJ will still 'stand' against your name for six years.

A business acquaintance owes me money. How can I recover the debt?

Actions to recover smaller debts (£5,000 or less) are normally heard in the small claims court, where cases are usually heard by a district judge. In addition to claims for money owed, the court will hear cases regarding contracts, housing repair and personal injury claims. However, complex cases can be referred to a more senior circuit judge, or in some cases an outside arbitrator will be appointed, if both sides agree. Small claims courts are a simple system of settling claims; in theory you should be able to deal with your own case from start to finish without using a solicitor.

How do I bring an action in the small claims court?

You would need to fill in a claim form from your local county court, giving your details and those of your creditor. The claim form will detail the nature of your claim, the amount you are claiming and whether you are claiming any interest. You will have to supply a copy of all the paperwork for the court, and one for your opponent. The court will affix a seal to the papers and send them to your opponent, along with a form to defend the claim, another form to admit the claim and a third form to acknowledge service of the papers. Once your opponent replies, the court will send you a copy along with instructions on what to do next; or the court may fix a hearing date when you will have to appear before the judge, who will tell you what the next stages are. Small claims hearings usually last no more than a day, but the court can deal with your case without holding a hearing, and will just consider your case on paper (if your case is to be dealt with on paper, the court will contact both sides to notify you). The court can also deal with your case via a telephone hearing if you and your opponent agree, and as long as you are both legally represented. The telephone hearing will be conducted via a BT conference call system. If the court has video conferencing facilities it may also be possible to hold a hearing by video link. If your opponent does not send in the acknowledgement of service or forms to defend the claim within the time limit (normally 21 days), you may be able to get a 'judgment in default' without the need for a hearing; this can also happen if your opponent admits some or all of the claim. (If he contests part of the claim, judgement can be entered for the amount agreed but a court case will be needed to resolve the disputed matters.) Remember, you can't get a judgment in default for delivery of goods that are subject to an agreement covered by the Consumer Credit Act 1974.

Do I have to attend the hearing in person?

You do not have to attend as long as you give seven days' notice to the court and your opponent that you will not be attending. You can submit written evidence to the court, which will be taken into account in reaching a decision.

The case has been proven. How do I get my money?

Once you have a judgment recorded against your opponent, the court may order an oral examination where your opponent provides the court with details of income, capital and savings. You can then decide from this information whether they can repay the debt. You do not have to attend, but you can ask the court to put any questions you would like asked to your opponent. If your opponent refuses to answer questions or produce documents, you can apply for a penal notice ordering him to do so. If they ignore that, they would be in contempt of court and you could apply to the judge to commit your opponent to prison for breach of the order.

Once a judgment has been made, your opponent has to pay, and if he or she does not, the court has various means of ensuring that the debt is not avoided. The court can order attachment of earnings, the return of goods or grant bailiffs a warrant of execution to recover property to repay the debt. It can even order third parties that owe money to your opponent to pay the money direct to you instead. Or it can order a charge to be registered on any property your opponent has (this makes it a secured debt).

Someone owes me money and won't pay. Can I have them declared bankrupt?

If the debt owed to you is for more than £750 you can apply to make that person declared bankrupt. Before going to court, however, you must first ask for the money by serving a statutory demand form on your debtor; if the money is not repaid within three weeks and your opponent has not applied to a court to set aside your statutory demand, you can proceed. You must send a creditors' petition form to the court, which you can obtain from the court, and show that your opponent has not paid the debt and there is no possibility that they will be able to do so. The court will fix a hearing date to decide whether to make your opponent bankrupt. If your opponent is declared bankrupt then the court will appoint a Trustee in Bankruptcy or receiver to look after your opponent's affairs. The receiver will share out any money or property your opponent has between the creditors. But even if you applied to have someone made bankrupt, it does not mean you will be paid first, as the receiver pays out in a special order. And once you have made your opponent bankrupt, you cannot start any other legal proceedings against him, so you cannot go on to try a different method of enforcement. Once a Trustee in Bankruptcy is appointed, no legal action can be started against a bankrupt without the court's permission.

Can my debtor avoid bankruptcy?

If you have started bankruptcy proceedings against a debtor (or if the debtor fears you are about to do so) he could ask the court to make a voluntary arrangement; this will prevent you starting or continuing with bankruptcy proceedings. Instead, your opponent will submit a report outlining proposals to pay off the debts to the court. A meeting of creditors will take place, and everyone at the meeting can vote to accept or reject the proposals. If the majority of those at the meeting reject the proposals, then you can continue the bankruptcy proceedings. But if most creditors vote to accept the offer, you will have to accept too, even though you may not get all your money back.

Chapter 9
You and the courts

Section 9.1 County courts and county court judgments

What is a county court?

County courts were first set up in the reign of Queen Victoria, by the County Courts Act 1846, as a means of providing justice locally and cheaply, taking away the need to bring actions to London. Subsequent Acts have enlarged the court's jurisdiction. Most civil actions are heard at the county court; for example, landlord and tenant disputes, claims for damages as a result of accidents, claims against manufacturers for faulty goods and actions to recover debt.

Who sits at the county court?

Circuit judges are the most senior county court judges, appointed by the Lord Chancellor. They must have been a barrister or solicitor for 10 years (or be a recorder – a very part-time judge) before they can be appointed to the bench.

District judges keep records and perform the administrative work. They must be solicitors of at least seven years' call. They also hear court applications taken out during the course of a case and 'try' (hear) cases on their own, including small claims.

What sort of cases can the county court hear?

A number of different cases can be brought at the county court:

- Actions in respect of contracts up to £50,000.
- Actions in tort (except defamation – slander and libel and including personal injury) up to £50,000.
- Equity actions (trusts, mortgages, etc.) up to £30,000.
- Bankruptcies (except in London).
- Actions for recovery of land, and title issues, where the land has a net rateable value of less than £1,000.
- Probate proceedings where the estate is worth less than £330,000.
- Winding-up proceedings where the company has a pre-paid capital of less than £120,000 (except in London).
- Supervision of the adoption of infants.
- Actions relating to hire-purchase agreements, rent-restriction, landlord and tenant, etc.
- Divorce matters – some county courts are designated divorce county courts, which can hear undefended matrimonial petitions.

- Small claims – the district judge acts as an arbitrator in disputes for debts up to £5,000, for goods sold, money lent, etc.

What are county court judgments?

Most people have heard of county court in connection with actions for debt – a successful claim for which leads to a county court judgment (or CCJ in its often shortened form). If you want to recover money that someone owes you, for work you have done for them for instance, you would first have to start county court proceedings. To do this, you – or your solicitor – will have to issue a claim form (formerly a 'default summons'). This requires the debtor to admit or deny your claim within 14 days.

The claim form may encourage the debtor to pay up – if so, that is the end of the matter. If the debtor disputes or ignores the claim, it goes to trial at the county court. If the case goes to trial and you are given judgment, that is an official confirmation that the debtor owes you money. For more information about debt and county court judgments, see **Debt and bankruptcy**.

Section 9.2 Magistrates' courts – civil and criminal

Magistrates' courts are the lowest tier of the English court system, certainly as far as criminal law is concerned; they have been in existence for more than 600 years. But despite their lowly position, they deal with more cases than any other court, hearing almost all criminal prosecutions brought by police and Crown Prosecution Service. In addition, they perform other administrative functions.

What is a magistrate?

A magistrate, or justice of the peace (JP), is a layperson (that means they have no specific specialised legal training) who hears cases locally. They are appointed on the recommendation, in counties, of the relevant Lord Lieutenant, or in large urban areas by the advisory committee. Magistrates receive some legal training before they can hear cases, but essentially their job is to decide on the facts of the case, almost like a mini-jury. In this, they are advised in their deliberations by a legally qualified clerk. A minimum of two magistrates is required to hear a case, though normally a bench will have three JPs sitting (when magistrates try cases, as many as seven justices can sit). Magistrates are not paid for their work, which is essentially voluntary in nature (though out-of-pocket expenses are paid). There are 30,000 magistrates in England and Wales.

What does the clerk do?

The clerk (now called the legal adviser) advises his bench of magistrates on points of law or procedure, records evidence as heard in the case and prepares depositions (statements sworn on oath in the presence of an accused person) made by witnesses in cases sent to be tried at Crown Court. When the magistrates retire to decide their verdicts after hearing the evidence and arguments of both sides, the advisers do not retire with them. However, they will be on hand to offer advice on any points of law as required. Each magistrates' court has a senior legal adviser responsible for the administration of the courts, called 'clerks to justices', who must be a barrister or solicitor of five years' calling.

Stipendiary magistrates

Stipendiary magistrates are paid magistrates, and unlike the JPs, they are legally trained. To become a stipendiary magistrate you must be a barrister or solicitor of at least seven years' standing. Stipendiary magistrates (or 'stipes') sit at the larger cities and towns. They hear cases alone, and do not need to get legal advice from their clerks in the same way as their lay brethren.

Most stipendiary magistrates are based in London, where 40 hear cases around the capital; another 10 hear cases across England and Wales.

What do magistrates' courts do?

Magistrates' courts have three functions:

1. A court of trial – hearing cases and handing out punishments.
2. A court of preliminary investigation – conducting what are called committal proceedings, deciding whether accused persons should be sent to stand trial before the Crown Court.
3. Administration of other jurisdictions, which are not criminal.

Trying cases

Criminal offences can be divided into three broad types:

- Indictable offences – these are cases that can only be tried by judge and jury at Crown Court (an indictment is the document used in jury trials that states the offences and gives particulars of them). Murder, rape and arson are examples of indictable offences.
- Summary offences – these are offences that can only be tried by magistrates, for example drunk and disorderly, riding a bike without lights or having a bald tyre on your car.
- Offences that are triable either way – there are some cases that can be heard either summarily by magistrates or on indictment by a judge and jury. You can choose where you want to be tried – accused persons are offered the choice of being tried by magistrates or by a jury. But in some cases, a magistrates' court can also refuse jurisdiction if they feel the matter is one that should be tried at Crown Court. Examples of offences that are triable either way include theft, burglary and assault.

If the case is one that can only be heard summarily by magistrates, or if the accused chooses to have his case heard in the lower court (and the justices accept jurisdiction), then the case will be set down for trial and a date set. Cases are not heard as soon as an accused person appears in court unless they plead guilty, in which case the prosecution outlines the case, and magistrates adjourn proceedings for pre-sentence reports (compiled by probation officers) that look at the accused's home life, employment and other circumstances and give advice to the magistrates on the most appropriate punishment. When the magistrates reconvene at a later date for sentence (which can be anything from two to four weeks after the accused pleads guilty), the prosecution solicitor (a Crown Prosecution Service solicitor) will once more outline their case, and the defence solicitor will speak on behalf of the accused, offering mitigating circumstances why the court should be lenient. The magistrates will read the social enquiry reports before passing sentence.

If the accused has pleaded not guilty, the case will be adjourned for a trial date, which would be normally in four to six weeks' time. When the trial begins, the prosecuting solicitor will outline his case and then call all witnesses – police officers, victims of the crime, etc. The accused's solicitor can cross-examine these witnesses after they have given their evidence. The defence will follow, calling witnesses where they can to refute the prosecution case – but the prosecution solicitor can also cross-examine the defence witnesses.

Once both sides have presented their cases, the magistrates will retire to consider their verdict, with the clerk advising on points of law or any difficult procedural matters. If they return a not guilty verdict, the accused is free to go. If they convict, they may adjourn for pre-sentence reports, remanding the convicted person on bail or in serious cases, custody, before sentencing at a later date.

In some cases, the magistrates may pass the case up to the Crown Court for sentence (see below).

What punishments can magistrates give?

Magistrates can impose a maximum penalty for one offence of a fine up to £5,000, and up to six months' imprisonment. However, if they feel their sentencing powers are insufficient, and they want a harsher punishment given than they can hand down, then the justices can commit the guilty person to the Crown Court for sentence.

Magistrates have a number of punishments at their disposal:

- Imprisonment.
- Fines.
- Suspended sentence – where a jail term is suspended for a period of time and you don't have to go to jail. But if you commit further offences the sentence can be activated and you will have to serve the jail term.
- Community service order – where you perform acts of public service as a punishment, such as gardening, graffiti removal or litter picking.
- Conditional discharge – similar to a suspended sentence, but where no penalty is imposed. If you commit a further offence and appear in court, you will receive a punishment for the first offence as well. If no offences are committed during the period that the sentence is suspended for, then you will not be punished for it should you offend after that time.
- Probation – where the probation service helps to address the problem that made you commit the offence, to stop you offending again.
- Absolute discharge – where the court thinks it would be inappropriate to impose any punishment (for example, if you were convicted on a technicality and the court felt your conduct was blameless), magistrates can impose an absolute discharge. However, a conviction is recorded against you, so you will have a criminal record.
- Binding over – in cases of breach of the peace, an accused person may be bound over in a sum of money. This means that if they commit a breach of the peace or some other offence in the future, they will have to pay the bind-over sum as well as any penalty imposed for

the future offence. Normally bind-overs are for a 12-month period, and no-one can be bound over without their assent (but as the alternative is imprisonment for up to six months, very few people refuse the offer). Often, courts suggest binding over at an early stage in proceedings, and this may mean that you have not been convicted of any criminal offence.

Triable either way offences

If a person is brought to court accused of a triable either way offence (one that can be heard by magistrates or at crown court before a jury), they must be asked whether they intend to plead guilty or not guilty. If a guilty plea, magistrates must hold a summary trial and cannot commit him for trial at crown court. Usually there is some dispute over the facts as to how serious the offences were; in this case, the magistrates must accept the accused's version of the facts unless the prosecution can prove their more serious version is the truth. Then, after hearing the facts and any mitigation, magistrates may adjourn for reports or, if they feel their sentencing powers are insufficient, they must commit the case for sentence to the Crown Court. If the accused intends to plead not guilty, magistrates must decide whether the case is one they can try summarily. If they decide they can try it, the accused must agree to keep the case in magistrates' court, but he has the right to a jury trial, and if he decides to exercise it, magistrates must commit the case for trial at Crown Court. The Criminal Justice Act 1967 established a procedure known as a 'paper committal' where the case is automatically passed to the Crown Court without the defence testing it or opposing it at magistrates' court. However, the defence could argue that the prosecution does not have a case, in which case the magistrates will hear the committal. The prosecution and defence will put legal arguments to the court and the magistrates will decide whether there is a case to answer. If the magistrates feel there is no case to answer, they can order the accused's release. If they feel there is a case to answer, they will commit the case to the Crown Court for trial. Although one magistrate alone can hear a committal, normally two or three lay magistrates hear the case. Stipendiary magistrates hear a committal alone.

Indictable offences

A new fast-track scheme for sending indictable-only charges to Crown Court for people aged 18 and over is to be brought in after a series of pilot schemes across the UK. As a result, as soon as an accused person is brought into court, the court must send the accused to trial. The prosecution must serve copies of evidence on which the charges are based to the court and the accused's lawyers. But there is no hearing of evidence, no test of whether there is a case to answer and no right of appeal against sending a case to trial. But once the accused's legal team has received the evidence, they can apply to a Crown Court, orally or in writing, for any or all charges to be dismissed on the grounds of insufficient evidence.

Do magistrates do anything else?

Magistrates' courts also act as licensing justices, granting and refusing liquor licences for pubs, clubs and hotels (approving both prospective licensees and their premises), betting and gaming licences, cinema and theatre licences.

Magistrates also can make matrimonial orders for separation and affiliation orders, consent to marriage orders, guardianship orders, adoption and mental health orders, and orders for children and young persons.

Can magistrates grant bail? If so, on what conditions?

Magistrates' courts do not deal with cases as soon as an accused person appears before them; there may be a number of court appearances between the first appearance, which is little more than a formality, and the final appearance at magistrates' court, when they are either sentenced or committed to stand trial at the Crown Court. So what happens to the accused person between hearings? Magistrates can grant bail, allowing the accused person to remain at liberty and continue his life as normally as possible, or they can remand the accused person in custody, which means he will be held in a jail or remand centre, and then brought by officers to court for his appearances. If magistrates grant bail, they can either grant unconditional bail, which as its name suggests, imposes no restrictions on an accused person, or in more serious cases grant conditional bail, which imposes restrictions. Ignoring or breaking bail conditions is very serious, as you can be brought back before magistrates for breach of bail conditions and held in custody until your next hearing. Bail conditions might be to order an accused person to stay away from licensed premises (which might be imposed in the case of someone accused of committing an offence while drunk) or a curfew order (which might be imposed if someone is accused of committing house burglaries at night) or ordering someone to stay away from a particular area (which might be imposed in assault cases, to reduce the possibility of repeat offences). One condition that is often imposed is to order the accused to stay away from prosecution witnesses, the reason for which is quite obvious!

Sureties

A special bail condition is when bail is granted if the accused can provide sureties – people that undertake to pay a certain sum if the accused fails to turn up for trial or his next appearance at court. If someone offers to act as a surety, the magistrates have to decide whether the person has the financial assets and character to be acceptable – and if the surety is found to be unacceptable, the accused will remain in custody until a suitable surety is found. If you are asked to act as a surety, then you have to be very sure of the person whose behaviour you are effectively guaranteeing. Will they abscond? If they do, you will lose your money.

If you have offered to stand as surety for someone only to have second thoughts, you can inform the court and they will cancel the surety.

Is bail always granted?

For most offences, while the accused person is awaiting trial, bail will be granted unless the prosecution fear that further offences will be committed, or that prosecution witnesses will be interfered with, or that the accused person will not turn up for his next court appearance. So, it is for the prosecution to oppose bail. If bail is refused, magistrates must give their reasons why it is being refused. If the offence is not one punishable by a jail sentence, then bail must be granted unless the accused has previously absconded, and the court fears he will do so again.

If a bail application is rejected, the accused person has three options:

- To wait for his next appearance before magistrates (which will be within eight days) and re-apply for bail.
- To apply for bail to the Crown Court.
- To appeal against the magistrates' decision to refuse bail to a High Court judge.

Youth courts

Certain magistrates form a special panel that can hear cases concerning offences committed by children and young persons (under the age of 18). The three lay justices, one of whom must be a woman, sit separately from adult courts. Youth courts have a number of sentences, unique to children, that they can hand down to help control and rehabilitate younger offenders (see **Children and crime**).

Section 9.3 Crown Courts and trial by jury

Before the reorganisation of the courts system in the 1970s, serious criminal offences were tried by High Court judges at courts known as 'assizes', or by recorders at 'quarter sessions'. But this system was swept away by the 1971 Courts Act, and in its place the Crown Court was installed as the court of first instance for serious offences.

What cases are tried at Crown Court?

The Crown Court has jurisdiction to try all cases involving indictable offences, and offences triable-either-way, either when the accused person has elected to be tried at Crown Court, or when a magistrates' court has declined jurisdiction. In addition, the Crown Court has sentencing powers over magistrates' court cases, where the bench feel their sentencing powers (up to six months' imprisonment or a fine of up to £5,000) are insufficient. The Crown Court is also the first court to hear appeals from magistrates' court, either against conviction or sentence. It can revoke community service orders imposed by a magistrates' court and can substitute it with a sentence of its own, though this substituted sentence cannot be a greater punishment than the magistrates could have imposed.

Who sits in judgement at a Crown Court?

Three types of judges sit at Crown Court:

- High Court judges from the Queen's Bench division.
- Circuit judges, who can sit in Crown and county courts.
- Recorders, who are part-time Crown Court judges (and are barristers or solicitors of 10 years' standing).

High Court judges will always try murder cases, and will usually try manslaughter and rape cases, too. Most triable-either-way cases are dealt with by circuit judges or recorders.

Magistrates will also sit at Crown Court to hear appeals and committals for sentence from magistrates' courts – there will be at least two magistrates and no more than four. In addition, no more than four magistrates can sit with the judge to hear cases on indictment. In the City of London, the Lord Mayor and aldermen can sit at the Old Bailey in the same way.

Isn't the right to jury trial being amended?

The government is introducing a bill to remove a defendant's automatic right to trial by jury in up to 80 per cent of cases. The move comes amid fears that 'professional' criminals opt for jury trials to slow down the justice system and thus evade trial and sentence for as long as possible. Under the Criminal Justice (Mode of Trial) (No 2) bill, magistrates, instead of defendants, will choose whether cases involving triable-either-way offences such as theft and burglary are heard by a Crown or magistrates' court. The Home Office say it would mean 14,000 fewer cases tried by the Crown Court, saving about £128 million a year. However, another key part of the bill which allowed magistrates to decide whether defendants would face jury trial on the basis of the possible effect to their reputation of a conviction has been withdrawn, after critics suggested it could lead to 'trial by postcode' with people from wealthier areas being tried by juries while those from less affluent areas appearing in magistrates' courts to be tried for the same offences. Now only the circumstances of the offence will be considered. The right of appeal will also be toughened up, as the bill requires magistrates to give reasons for their decisions, and any appeal against a decision by magistrates not to allow jury trial will be heard by a judge.

Who can sit on a jury?

Crown Courts provide trial by jury, though the government is looking to abolish the right of trial by jury in certain cases (as described above), on the grounds that it will speed up justice and prevent miscarriages of justice. Under normal circumstances, anyone aged 18–65 in England and Wales can serve on a jury, but there are exceptions:

- Legally qualified people – magistrates, coroners, barristers, solicitors, legal executives, members of the police and prison services (including special constables) – and clergy, nuns and ministers of religion, are ineligible to serve on a jury. This disqualification lasts for 10 years after a person leaves a job that would bar him from serving on a jury.
- Anyone who has been convicted of a criminal offence and sentenced to a jail term or a community service order in the past 10 years, or placed on probation in the last five years, is disqualified from serving on a jury.
- Anyone who has not been resident in the UK or Channel Islands for at least five years since the age of 13 is disqualified from serving on a jury.

Jury panels are selected at random from the electoral register, and a jury summons is normally sent out six weeks before the date on which you will be called to serve. You will be summoned to a specific court building, for example Kingston Crown Court, but not allocated a specific courtroom or case until you have arrived at court.

A summons will give a start date for the beginning of jury service, but not an end date, because it is often impossible to know when a trial will end, though the summons will often indicate a minimum period of service, say two weeks. A panel of more than 12 jurors will be called for a case – because some will have excuses for non-attendance – and the members are chosen by ballot on the first day of the trial.

Can I be excused jury service?

Because of the length of time a trial can take, jury service is not popular with people called to sit on juries or with their employers, but ignoring a jury summons is a criminal offence. However, it is possible to be excused jury service: peers of the realm, Members of Parliament, doctors, dentists, midwives and members of the armed services can be excused jury service if they wish. If you have served on a jury panel in the last two years you can be excused – unless it was a coroner's jury. Otherwise, you will need a valid excuse – 'because I don't want to' or 'it's not convenient' is not enough. To be excused you will have to attend court at the time given on your jury summons, ask the court officials to inform the court of your wish to be excused and state your reasons for doing so. The court has discretion whether or not to accept your reason as a 'good one', but examples of excuses that have been considered valid are:

- Illness, deafness or blindness.
- Pregnancy.
- Holiday arrangements.
- Running a one-man business.
- Difficulty in getting a child minder.

Do I get paid to serve on a jury?

Jurors do not get paid for serving on a jury, but they can claim cash allowances to cover meals and other expenses, travel (mileage claims, second-class rail or bus fare, though taxi fares will only be paid if there is no other alternative transport available) and financial loss caused through not being able to attend work.

Your employer is not obliged to pay your salary while you serve on a jury, but if you were sacked because of that jury service, you would have a strong claim for unfair dismissal.

If I am selected by ballot, will I definitely serve?

Even if you have been selected by ballot, it is still possible for the prosecution or defence to object to your serving as a juror. The defence has three peremptory challenges, where they can object to a juror without giving any reason. The prosecution cannot peremptorily challenge any jurymen, but can put you on 'stand by' which means that you will not take part in the trial unless there are insufficient qualified jurors. If you are rejected as a juror for a particular case, that does not mean you can go home. You would return to the jury pool and wait to be selected for another case.

Challenges for cause

Both prosecution and defence can challenge a potential juror 'for cause' if they feel his presence on the jury panel would jeopardise the fairness of the trial. An example of a challenge 'for cause' would be if the potential juror knows the accused, or someone else involved in the case, or has read something about the case that might colour their judgement and make them act less impartially than they should do. The decision on whether a challenge is valid is up to the judge, who may decide to question the juror himself to decide if the challenge is valid. Once the jury has been selected, the members take an oath or make an affirmation (in the case of non-religious or agnostic members).

How trials take place

Once a jury has been sworn in, the clerk of the court reads the charges to them, and the trial then begins. The sole role of the jury is to decide questions of fact – namely, did the accused commit the crime? Questions of law – such as whether evidence should be admitted or the jury allowed to hear certain things about the accused or witnesses –will be discussed when jurors are not in court by the barristers and the judge. These discussions are referred to as 'legal arguments', because they are arguments about law – whether evidence is admissible, the interpretation of laws, etc. So from time to time, jurors can be asked to leave the court while these discussions take place.

The jurors listen to the opening statements of prosecution and defence barristers (where each side summarises the evidence they will be presenting to the jury) and then the evidence of witnesses for the prosecution and defence (who will also be cross-examined by the opposing side) and then to closing arguments by the barristers, and finally the judge's summing up, where he attempts to lead them through the decision-making process, summarising the evidence they have heard and advising them how much weight they can give to certain parts of the case they have heard. The judge's summing up is vitally important, because not only does he tell the jury what evidence they should take account of, but he will also direct them to ignore certain things which may be inadmissible (pieces of information or evidence that are not relevant to the case in hand, but which may colour the jury's impressions). Then the jury will go to the jury room to discuss the evidence they have heard and try and reach a verdict.

Can jurors take notes?

Jurors are not allowed to have copies of the evidence, but they are allowed to take notes during the case if they think that this may help them follow and understand the evidence, for when they have to reach a verdict. If you are serving on a jury, you are not allowed to ask witnesses questions directly yourselves, but a note can be passed to the judge via the court usher, asking the judge to raise the matter with the witness. The judge can then put the question, or he may say that the question may not be asked.

What is 'the presumption of innocence'?

There are two important principles of law that dominate jury trials in England and Wales.

The first is the presumption of innocence. This means that the defence do not have to prove that the accused did not commit the crime – although it would certainly help a jury if they could prove this. It is for the prosecution to prove its case, for the accused is 'innocent until proven guilty'. If the prosecution cannot prove its case, then the accused is not guilty.

What is 'the burden of proof'?

Closely linked to the presumption of innocence is the burden of proof – this is the standard by which all the evidence has to be judged.

In criminal cases, the burden of proof is 'beyond all reasonable doubt', which means that a jury cannot convict anyone if they have any doubts that he is guilty. The prosecution is bound to prove that the accused did commit the crime, but if the defence can raise any doubts or uncertainties in the jury's minds, then a 'not guilty' verdict must be returned.

How do juries decide?

Once all the evidence and summing up has been heard, the jury are taken away to a jury room where they can discuss the case without outside interruption. The jury must choose a foreman (a man or a woman) who will act as the chairperson of the jury discussions, and who will announce the jury's verdict at the end of the case. Foremen can be chosen by drawing lots, but there is no set procedure for selecting a foreman. Similarly, there is no set procedure to follow in deciding guilt or innocence – how the jury reaches its verdict is very much up to the jurors. But discussions within the jury room are confidential, and it is a criminal offence to reveal jury discussions (in a newspaper article after a sensational trial, for example).

What happens if jurors are confused about evidence?

If the jury is confused about a point of law or point of evidence, they must ask the usher to take a message to the judge, who can recall the jury and repeat the question, and give the answer in court. Juries must try to reach unanimous verdicts where possible, but if it has not done so within a couple of hours the judge must be informed, and he can recall the jury to tell them he will accept a majority verdict. But a majority verdict must have the support of at least 10 of the 12 jurors. If the jury has been reduced by illness or other absences (a jury trial can continue as long as there are nine jurors able to serve), majority verdicts are allowed as long as no more than one jury member dissents. If a jury cannot reach a verdict by the end of the first day's deliberation, they will be sent home for the night. But they must not discuss the case with anyone outside the jury panel. It used to be the case that juries were put up in hotels once they had been sent out to deliver their verdicts, so keeping the panel together and preventing outside 'contamination' of the jury process, but cost issues mean that judges tend to send jurors home now.

What if a jury cannot agree?

There is no set time limit for a jury to deliberate, but if it is not possible to even reach a majority verdict, then the judge can discharge the jury and order a new trial.

What happens once a verdict is reached?

Once the jury has reached a unanimous or majority verdict, they send a message to the judge who will reconvene the court. Then the foreman of the jury will be asked whether the accused has been found guilty or not guilty on each of the charges he has been accused of. Once all the verdicts have been delivered, the judge will either free the accused (if a not guilty verdict has been delivered) or remand the accused while pre-sentence reports are prepared. If the accused has been convicted of murder, there will be no adjournment because there is only one sentence – life imprisonment.

Section 9.4 Higher courts

Civil law

The House of Lords

The House of Lords is the final court of appeal in civil and criminal matters, unless the legal issue is a matter of EU law in which case it can be appealed to the European Court of Justice. Usually five in number, the Law Lords comprise the Lord Chancellor, the Lords of Appeal (judges appointed to sit as the final court of appeal) and other lawyers that have held high judicial office.

The House of Lords hears appeals from lower courts: the Scottish Court of Session, the Northern Ireland Court of Appeal and the Court of Appeal (Civil Division) in England and Wales. You can't automatically appeal your case, rather you must be granted leave to appeal.

It is possible to leapfrog the Court of Appeal and go directly to the House of Lords, but your appeal must involve a point of law of 'general public importance'. This means it is likely to be of interest to law students and lawyers in terms of precedent, but it is unlikely to be the sort of case you would be involved in, so comparatively rare are they.

The Judicial Committee of the Privy Council

The Judicial Committee is made up of Privy Councillors who hold, or have held, high judicial office in the United Kingdom and judges from the Commonwealth who are Privy Councillors. Former Lord Chancellors are also members.

The Privy Council mainly hears appeals from some Commonwealth countries (which makes it the only British court capable of confirming a death sentence in time of peace), but it also has some input in the justice system of this country, hearing appeals from:

- Prize courts – those determining claims over ships captured in time of war.
- Ecclesiastical courts.
- Courts of the Isle of Man and Channel Islands.
- Tribunals of the medical, opticians' and dentists' professions.

Decisions of the Privy Council are not binding on English courts in terms of setting precedents, but they are persuasive – they are treated with the utmost respect, as the Privy Council is essentially the House of Lords by any other name.

The Court of Appeal (Civil Division)

The Court of Appeal comprises the Lord Chief Justice, the Master of the Rolls, the President of the Family Division and around 30 other Lords (and Ladies) Justice of Appeal. Normally, the Master of the Rolls will sit with two Lords Justice, or three Lords justice will sit in judgment, but other judges can be drafted in to sit on the Court of Appeal as the Lord Chancellor commands.

The Court of Appeal hears appeals from the High Court, county courts and other tribunals such as the restrictive practices court, and employment appeal tribunals.

The High Court of Justice

The High Court has three divisions:

- The Queen's Bench Division, headed by the Lord Chief Justice.
- The Chancery Division, headed by the Vice Chancellor (the Lord Chancellor is the official head).
- The Family Division, headed by the President of the Family Division.

In addition, there are around 80 other justices who try cases in these High Court divisions. But don't confuse these justices with the lay magistrates that hear cases at the local magistrates' court – they are knights of the realm and have considerable legal experience in their fields, all having been QCs.

The Queen's Bench Division

The Queen's Bench Division (QBD) is the largest of the three divisions, and exercises three kinds of jurisdiction:

1. Original – hearing cases for the first time. The QBD is a 'catch-all division', hearing all the cases that are not Chancery or Family cases. Contracts cases (though not requests for specific performance), torts and some land cases fall within its scope, as do Admiralty and Commercial Court matters such as insurance claims. Usually judges sit alone, but sometimes juries may be empanelled to assist in cases of libel and slander.
2. Appellate – where two or three justices sit as a divisional court to hear appeals, for example, under the Rent Acts or from a Solicitors' Disciplinary Tribunal.
3. Supervisory jurisdiction – overseeing the operation of administrative authorities acting in a 'quasi-judicial manner' and inferior courts and tribunals, for example, overturning the actions of a local council when it has exceeded its powers.

The Chancery Division

Chancery courts deal with the same sorts of cases that they dealt with in the days of the old Court of Chancery, though some additional workload has been added, for example, bankruptcy cases.

The Chancery Division has original jurisdiction over a number of matters including:

- Private and public trusts.
- The administration of estates of people that have died.
- Bankruptcy matters.
- Specific performance of contracts.
- Probate (for contentious matters, for example, questioning the validity of a will).

It also hears appeals from lower courts on bankruptcy and trust matters.

The Family Division

The Family Division deals with predominantly family matters such as:

- Divorce.
- Granting orders of judicial separation.
- Adoption and guardianship of minors.
- Probate matters (non-contentious).

Criminal law

The House of Lords

The House of Lords hears appeals from the Court of Appeal, Divisional Court of Queen's Bench Division and the Court Martial Appeal Court. Either prosecution or defence can appeal to the Lords, provided there is a point of law of public importance that needs determining and that leave to appeal has been granted. The House of Lords is concerned primarily with the law, rather than individual cases. A minimum of three Lords will hear a case, and majority verdicts are allowed.

The Court of Appeal

The Court of Appeal hears appeals against sentence or conviction from Crown Court, or appeals against sentence if the case has been committed to the Crown Court for sentence by magistrates. Three judges hear appeals, and a court is usually composed of Lord Justices of Appeal and justices of the Queen's Bench Division.

The Court of Appeal can reject or allow an appeal, ordering that any verdict and sentence be set aside, or ordering a retrial depending on their view of the case. Appeals will be allowed if sentences are unsafe or unsatisfactory according to the evidence, or if a wrong decision had been reached on a question of law. This can result in a retrial being ordered, or the accused being set free.

With regard to appeals against sentence, either the Attorney General or a convicted criminal can appeal. If the Attorney General appeals, the Court of Appeal can increase or decrease the sentence, but if the convicted person appeals the sentence can only be reduced.

The Divisional Court of the Queen's Bench Division

The Divisional Court hears appeals from magistrates' and Crown Courts on points of law. If either side is unhappy with a verdict, they can ask the magistrates' court or Crown Court to 'state the case' for the divisional court to review. The appeal cannot be on questions of fact, only law.

Section 9.5 Coroners' courts

Coroners' courts provide an important part of the legal process, as they investigate deaths and the circumstances surrounding them. Originally appointed as administrators in the 12th century, their powers and duties are now regulated by the Coroners Act 1988 and Administration of Justice Act 1982.

What do coroners do?

A coroner's main duty is to investigate deaths that are sudden, violent or unnatural. A coroner will also investigate, as a matter of course, deaths of prisoners in police custody or those involving the police, deaths of prisoners in jail, and the deaths of inmates in mental institutions where there is no satisfactory supporting medical evidence. The coroner must be informed of any deaths where a doctor has not been consulted in the previous 14 days, accidental deaths, apparent suicides, deaths from drug overdoses, violent deaths and deaths caused by industrial poisoning.

How does a coroner become involved?

The police will inform the coroner of any deaths that have occurred in suspicious circumstances, though members of the public can also notify the coroner of any deaths they feel should be investigated. Registrars of births, marriages and deaths who have not been given a doctor's certificate giving a cause of death will also notify the coroner.

Does a coroner always hold an inquest into every reported death?

Not every death brought before the coroner will actually end up in a coroner's court. Once a death has been reported, the coroner's officer, who is almost always a police officer, will question doctors, policemen, relatives of the deceased and anyone else who can offer any insight into the circumstances that surround the death. In around 75 to 80 per cent of cases, the coroner's officer will find an acceptable reason for the death with no need of further action.

But if the coroner is not satisfied with his officer's investigations, he can order a post mortem examination of the body, which will almost always be followed by an inquest, possibly delaying the funeral, which cannot take place until the coroner is satisfied as to the cause of death.

What is an inquest?

An inquest is the hearing that investigates the circumstances surrounding the death of a person, and the cause of death. The coroner must ascertain three things:

- The identity of the deceased.
- The place and cause of death.
- Any other circumstances surrounding the death.

Usually the coroner will sit alone, deciding the facts for himself based on the evidence called before him. But sometimes a jury will be called to hear the evidence:

- If the suspected cause of death is murder, manslaughter or infanticide.
- If the death arose out of a road accident.
- If the suspected cause of death was a notifiable disease.

A coroner's jury must have at least seven members, but no more than 11.

Inquests must be held as soon as possible after the death. Unlike murder trials, it is not possible to hold an inquest unless a body has been recovered, so if someone is believed to have been murdered and the body disposed of, or if a body is lost at sea after a boating accident, no inquest can be held.

Where are inquests held?

Inquests are court proceedings, with coroners being the most powerful judges in the land in terms of the rights they have to investigate deaths. For this reason, proceedings are essentially formal in nature, and are usually held in magistrates' courts – though they can also be held in other buildings, private houses and, as happened on one occasion, in a car. Inquests are open to the public, and representatives of the press can attend and report proceedings fully.

Will an inquest mean delaying the funeral?

Inquests can take place weeks and sometimes months after a death, but coroners will normally release the body for burial once the inquest has been opened and its formal identification has taken place. Obviously, if the inquest can be conducted quickly, the disposal certificate will be issued at the end of the hearing; otherwise it will be issued once identification has taken place. An inquest can even be opened and adjourned over the telephone, then re-convened at a later date in a more convenient location for the formal hearing.

But, if a death may have been caused by a crime and someone has been arrested in connection with it, then no disposal certificate can be issued unless and until the arrested person or his lawyer agrees to it. This is because the accused person has a right to have a post mortem performed on the body by their experts, the results of which may differ from the Home Office pathologist's report.

What happens at the inquest?

An inquest is formally opened when the coroner has the body identified formally, then is adjourned while burial or cremation takes place. Some time later, usually a few weeks but occasionally months later, the inquest will be re-opened. Then the coroner can call any witnesses whom he feels can cast light on the circumstances surrounding the death, including friends and family, and/or witnesses (in the case of accidents). Evidence can be admitted by witnesses giving evidence from a witness box (as in any other court) or the coroner can admit evidence in writing (as will often happen in the case of a post mortem finding that is not contentious).

I am giving evidence at an inquest: do I need a lawyer?

Anyone called to give evidence before an inquest can be legally represented by a solicitor, though very few people are involved in such a way that they feel they need to be protected by their lawyer. But a lawyer can only ask questions on the evidence presented at the inquest, and only then if the coroner allows a specific line of questioning. Anyone giving evidence in an inquest can be questioned by the deceased's close relatives (or their legal representatives) and any other persons (or their legal representatives) that might have an interest in the hearing's decision such as:

- Any person that might have been responsible for the death.
- A trade union, if the death was caused by industrial accident or disease.
- Representatives from any insurance company liable to make payments because of death.
- Anyone that might benefit from a life insurance policy.

What verdict can a coroner give?

When all the evidence has been heard, the coroner can deliver a number of verdicts. The most usual are:

- Misadventure – when someone dies in an accident that may have been partly their fault, for instance, a boating accident where the dead person was driving too fast or had been drinking.
- Accidental death – where death is caused by some mishap that is not the dead person's fault, for example, a road accident.
- Suicide.
- Unlawful killing – murder or manslaughter. Since 1978, juries at inquests and coroners have no longer been allowed to say who they think carried out an 'unlawful killing', only that an unlawful killing took place.

- Lawful killing – for example, if armed police shot dead a man who was brandishing a firearm.
- Death from industrial disease – as might be the case in verdicts handed down into the deaths of workers who had been exposed to asbestos or of miners suffering from pneumoconiosis. Such a verdict would obviously raise a compensation issue with the deceased's previous employers.
- Natural causes.
- Open verdict – where there is not enough evidence to give a more specific verdict, a coroner will return an open verdict. This verdict can be set aside and a new one substituted if new evidence emerges and the inquest re-opened.

In addition, coroners can substitute other specific verdicts; for example, there have been occasions where an inquest has returned a cause of death of 'solvent abuse', which some years before would have been termed 'misadventure'.

Anyone who is called to give evidence before a coroner but who does not attend can be summoned to appear and fined an unlimited sum for non-attendance, or sentenced to three months' imprisonment. Coroners can also find anyone who does not obey their directions or who behaves improperly to be in contempt of court, and impose fines for that.

What happens if an inquest is investigating a death that has arisen out of a crime?

The Criminal Law Act 1978 laid down that inquest verdicts are not allowed to prejudge criminal or civil proceedings. If someone has been arrested or charged with murder or manslaughter, then the inquest would be adjourned after formal identification of the body and until criminal proceedings have been concluded. Then the inquest would be reconvened.

Challenging a coroner's verdict

Coroners' verdicts can be challenged, though it is very difficult to do so. If you think a coroner has brought in a wrong verdict in the case of a loved one, you might be able to challenge it (except in the case of suicide); but any appeal can only be brought on a point of law – i.e. if the coroner did not follow the correct procedure or if his verdict could not be supported by the evidence.

The Criminal Law Act 1978 laid down the rule that coroners are not allowed to apportion blame by suggesting that any person is responsible for a death. No-one can take action over remarks made by a coroner which criticise anyone (short of blaming them for causing a death) provided the remarks refer to conduct strictly related to the case being investigated. If his remarks go beyond this, a coroner can be sued.

Do coroners do anything else?

Coroners are also responsible for determining the ownership of treasure trove. Treasure trove is the technical term for money, bullion, gold, silver, plate and coins found in the earth or in a private place. Treasure trove belongs to the Crown, but when people find what appears to be treasure trove, a coroner will hold an inquest to find out the circumstances in which the items were discarded. If he finds that something is treasure trove, the Treasury will usually compensate the landowners for their find.

Section 9.6 Tribunals and other courts

There is a number of other tribunals and courts you may come across in your dealings with the law, though some are more common then others. Tribunals have sprung up over the past few decades to regulate relations between individuals and employers, and individuals and the state – the administrative tribunals. The advantages of tribunals compared with the court structure is that they are quick, cheap (with low or no fees), informal and staffed by experts. However, tribunals often sit in private, leading to allegations (often unfounded) of secrecy. Other criticisms have focused on the impartiality of technical experts, rights of appeal and the non-publication of reasons for decisions.

Rent tribunals

Tenants renting unfurnished accommodation (below a certain rateable value) can apply to a rent officer for a fair rent to be set at their property. In the same way, people renting furnished accommodation can apply to a rent tribunal to have their rent reduced under the provisions of the Rent Acts. If you do not accept the decision of these forums, you can appeal to a rent assessment committee, which is fairly informal (though evidence is given under oath) and consists of a three-person panel, with one legally qualified and one a valuer or surveyor. Hearings are open to press and public (and may be reported in the local paper, though few ever are). Appeals against decisions of rent assessment committees go to the High Court, but on points of law only.

Domestic tribunals

Domestic tribunals are responsible for hearing disputes in trades or professions, and enforce the rules of the union or professional body. Examples of domestic tribunals would be the Solicitors' Disciplinary Committee, which has the power to strike offending members from the roll (with appeals going to the High Court), the General Medical Council for doctors, which can strike off offending practitioners (with appeals going to the Judicial Committee of the Privy Council) and trade unions, which can punish or expel members in line with the union's own disciplinary rules (with appeal to an industrial tribunal).

Social security tribunals

Claims for social security benefits are dealt with at a local level by social security officers. If you don't agree with your benefit assessment, you have a right of appeal to a local social security tribunal, composed of a chairman (who is a lawyer) and two lay members (who will represent employers' and employees' organisations). If you disagree with the social security tribunal's decision, you can appeal to the Social Security Commissioner, a lawyer appointed by the Crown. His decision is final on law or fact, though technical matters such as the means of regulation can be passed to the Minister for Social Security, and the Minister's decision can be appealed to the High Court.

Industrial injury tribunals

A similar system exists for industrial injuries claims under the Social Security Contributions and Benefits Act 1992, where an injured person tries to prove that he was injured during the course of his employment. If his claim is disallowed, the injured person can appeal the decision to a local social security tribunal, composed of a chairman (who is a lawyer) and two lay members (who will represent employers' and employees' organisations). If the injured person can prove the injury did happen during the course of his employment, the next stage is for a medical board of two doctors to decide the extent of the disability. If the injured person is not satisfied with the adjudication, an appeal can be made to a Medical Appeal Tribunal composed of two doctors and a lawyer, with a further appeal to the Social Security Commissioner.

Employment tribunals

Set up initially in 1964, employment tribunals (formerly industrial tribunals) are now governed by the Industrial Tribunals Act 1996, which outline the scope and operation of tribunals. Applicants can be legally represented (or represented by a union official) before the tribunal, which is composed of a chairman (who will be legally qualified) and two lay members; the applicant can also make written representations setting out the case. The tribunal can compel people to attend to give evidence, and demand documents be produced. Decisions can be made by a majority vote, and must be delivered in writing. You can appeal to the Employment Appeal Tribunal on a point of law.

Employment appeal tribunals

Composed of a judge and up to four other members, employment appeal tribunals hear appeals from employment tribunals on points of law. Decisions can be appealed to the Court of Appeal.

Restrictive Practices Court

Restrictive Practices Courts examine and rule on agreements between firms, buyers or suppliers where restrictions might be imposed on the price, quality, quantity and method of distribution of goods and services.

The court was originally created by the Restrictive Trade Practices Act 1956 (now replaced by an Act of the same name that became law in 1976) and is an equivalent tier of the justice system to the High Court. It comprises three High Court judges, a judge of the Court of Session (in Scotland) and a judge of the Supreme Court (Northern Ireland). In addition, there is a number of lay members with experience in industry or commerce, and two of these may sit with a judge to hear cases. Appeals go to the Court of Appeal.

The Fair Trading Act 1973 requires all restrictive practices to be registered with the Office of Fair Trading.

The European Court of Justice

Since Britain joined the European Union, the European Court of Justice has become Britain's highest court, though it rarely intervenes directly on UK law alone. The Court's main function is to help interpret the treaties that established the EU and give preliminary rulings on the validity and interpretation of actions of EU institutions and bodies. National courts can request a ruling from the European Court.

Appendix
Useful addresses

Chapter 1 – You and the law

Community Legal Service (formerly Legal Aid)
Lord Chancellor's Department
54–60 Victoria Street
London SW1E 6QW
Tel: 020 7210 2607
Fax: 020 7210 2608

The Court Service
Southside
105 Victoria Street
London SW1E 6QT
Tel: 020 7210 1818

Justice
11/12 Bouverie Street
London EC4Y 8BS
Tel: 020 7353 5055

The Law Centres Federation
Duchess House
18–19 Warren Street
London W1P 5DB
Tel: 020 7387 8570 Fax: 020 7387 8368
E-mail info@lawcentres.org.uk

Law Centres Federation Manchester
3rd Floor, Elizabeth House
St Peters Square
Manchester M2 3DF
Tel: 0161 236 5333
www.lawcentres.org.uk/

The Law Society
113 Chancery Lane
London WC2A 1PL
Tel: 020 7242 1222
www.lawsociety.org.uk

Law Society of Scotland
Client Relations Office
26 Drumsheugh Gardens
Edinburgh
EH3 7YR
Tel: 0131 476 8137

Legal Services Commission (formerly Legal Aid Board)
85 Gray's Inn Road
London.
WC1X 8TX
Tel: 020 7759 0000
www.legalservices.gov.uk/

Legal Services Ombudsman
22 Oxford Court
Manchester
M2 3WQ
Tel: 0161 236 9532
Fax: 0161 236 2651

National Association of Citizens Advice Bureaux
115 Pentonville Road
London N1 9LZ
Tel: 020 7833 2181
www.nacab.org.uk

The Office for the Supervision of Solicitors
Victoria Court
8 Dormer Place
Leamington Spa
Warwickshire
CV32 5AE
Tel: 0845 608 6565

Parliamentary Ombudsman
Millbank Tower
Millbank
London SW1P 4QP
Tel: 020 7217 4163
Fax: 020 7276 400/4067
www.ombudsman.org.uk

Principal Registry of the Family Division
First Avenue House
42–49 High Holborn
London WC1V 6NP
Tel: 020 7947 6936

Chapter 2 – You and your family

Age Concern England (National Council on Ageing)
Astral House
1268 London Road
London SW16 4ER
Tel: 020 8765 7200
Fax: 020 8765 7211
www.ace.org.uk/

The Association of Workers for Children with Emotional and Behavioural Difficulties (AWCEBD)
Charlton Court
East Sutton,
Maidstone
Kent ME17 3DQ
Tel: 01622 843104
Fax: 01622 844220
www.mistral.co.uk/awcebd/

The Brandon Centre (formerly London Youth Advisory Centre)
26 Prince of Wales Road
Kentish Town
London NW5 3LG
Tel: 020 7267 4792/3
Fax: 020 7267 5212
www.brandon-centre.org.uk

British Agencies for Adoption and Fostering
Skyline House
200 Union Street
London SE1 0LX
Tel: 020 7593 2000
Fax: 020 7593 2001
www.baaf.org.uk

(BAC) British Association for Counselling
1 Regent Place
Rugby
Warwickshire CV21 2PJ
Tel: 01788 550899.
Fax: 01788 562189
www.counselling.co.uk/

BALM, (the British Association of Lawyer Mediators)
The Shooting Lodge
Guildford Road
Sutton Green
Guildford
Surrey GU4 7PZ.
Tel: 01483 235000
Fax: 01483 237004

The British Humanist Association
47 Theobald's Road
London WC1R 4RH
Tel: 020 7430 0908
www.humanism.org.uk

Child Accident Prevention Trust
4th Floor, Clerks Court
18–20 Farringdon Lane
London EC1R 3AU
Tel: 020 7608 3828
Fax: 020 7608 3674
www.capt.org.uk

Child Support Agency
The Waterfront
Pedmore House
Brierley Hill
Dudley DY5 1YL
Enquiry Line Tel: 0845 713 3133
www.dss.gov.uk/csa

ChildcareLink
Opportunity Links
Trust Court, Vision Park
Histon, Cambridge CB4 9PW
www.childcarelink.gov.uk/

Childline
2nd Floor, Royal Mail Building
Studd Street
London N1 0QW
Tel: 020 7239 1000 (admin)
Fax: 020 7239 1001
or

Childline
Freepost 1111 London N1 0BR
Freephone: 0800 1111
www.childline.org.uk

Children's Society
Edward Rudolf House
69–85 Margery Street
London WC1X 0JL
Tel: 020 7837 4400
Fax: 020 7837 4500
www.the-childrens-society.org.uk

The Cremation Society of Great Britain
Brecon House
16/16a Albion Place
Maidstone
Kent ME14 5DZ
Tel: 01622 688292 Fax: 01622 686698
members.aol.com/cremsoc/

Cruse – Bereavement Care
126 Sheen Road
Richmond
Surrey TW9 1UR
Tel: 020 8940 4818
www.cruselochaber.freeuk.com/
about.html

Daycare Trust
Shoreditch Town Hall Annexe
380 Old Street
London EC1V 9LT
Tel: 020 7739 2866
Fax: 020 7739 5579
www.daycaretrust.org.uk

FMA (Family Mediators Association)
46 Grosvenor Gardens
London SW1W OEB
Tel: 020 7881 9400
Fax: 020 7881 9401
www.familymediators.co.uk/

Families Need Fathers
134 Curtain Road
London EC2A 3AR
General Advice: 020 8886 0970
Office: 020 7613 5060
www.fnf.org.uk

The Foundation for the Study of Infant Deaths
Artillery House, 11–19 Artillery Row
London SW1P 1RT
Tel: 020 7222 8001
Fax: 020 7233 8002
Cot Death Helpline: 020 7233 2090
www.sids.org.uk/fsid/

The Funeral Ombudsman
26–28 Bedford Row
London WC1R 4HE
Tel: 020 7430 1112
Fax: 020 7430 1012

General Register Office (Births, Deaths & Marriages)
St Catherine's House, 10 Kingsway
London WC2B 6JB
Tel: 020 7242 0262
Tel: 01704 569824
www.statistics.gov.uk/

Gingerbread (Guidance for single parents and children)
16–17 Clerkenwell Close
London EC1N 0AN
Tel:. 020 7336 8184
Fax: 020 7336 8185
Helpline: 0800 0184318
www.gingerbread.org.uk

Grandparents' Federation
Moot House
The Stow
Harlow
Essex CM20 3AG
Helpline: 01279 444964
Tel/Fax: 01279 428040

Kidscape
2 Grosvenor Gardens
London SW1W 0DH
Tel: 020 7730 3300
Fax: 020 7730 7081
www.kidscape.org.uk

Life Cares
LIFE House, Newbold Terrace
Leamington Spa
Warwickshire CV32 4EA
Tel: 01926 421587
Hotline: 01926 311511
www.lifeuk.org/

London Bereavement Network
356 Holloway Road
London N7 6PN
Tel: 020 7700 8134
Fax: 020 7700 8146
www.bereavement.org.uk/lbn/text/
LBN.html#top

National Association for the Education of Sick Children (PRESENT)
18 Victoria Park Square
Bethnal Green
London E2 9PF
Tel: 020 8980 8523
www.sickchildren.org.uk/

National Children's Bureau
8 Wakley Street
London EC1V 7QE
Tel: 020 7843 6000
Fax: 020 7278 9512
www.ncb.org.uk

National Family Mediation
9 Tavistock Place
London WC1H 9SN
Tel. 020 7383 5993
Fax: 020 7383 5994
www.nfm.u-net.com

National Society for the Prevention of Cruelty to Children (NSPCC)
42 Curtain Road
London EC2A 3NH
Tel: 020 7825 2500
Fax: 020 7825 2525
Helpline: 0808 800 5000
www.nspcc.org.uk

National Stepfamily Association
3rd Floor, Chapel House
18 Hatton Place
London EC1N 8RU
Tel. 020 7209 2460
Fax: 020 7209 2461
Counselling Service: 0990 168 388

National Youth Agency
17–23 Albion Street
Leicester LE1 6GD
Tel. 0116 2856789
Fax: 0116 2471043
www.nya.org.uk

One Plus One Marriage and Partnership Research
14 Theobalds Road
London WC1X 8PF
Tel: 020 7831 5261
Fax: 020 7831 5263
www.oneplusone.org.uk/

Parentline Plus
Endway House
Endway, Hadley
Essex SS7 2AN
Tel: 01702 559900
Fax: 01702 554911
Helpline: 0808 800 2222
www.parentline.co.uk

Relate
Herbert Gray College
Little Church Street
Rugby CV21 3AP
Tel: 01788 573241
Fax: 01788 535007
Helpline: 0870 601 2121

Reunite – National Council for Abducted Children
PO Box 4
London WC1X 8XY
Tel. 020 7375 3441 Fax: 020 7375 3441
Emergency: 020 7724 1435
www.reunite.org.uk

Royal Society for Mentally Handicapped Children & Adults (MENCAP)
123 Golden Square
London EC1Y 0RT
Tel. 020 7454 0454 Fax: 020 7696 5540
www.mencap.org.uk

Terence Higgins Trust
52–54 Grays Inn Road
London WC1X 8JU
Helpline: 020 7242 1010
Tel: 020 7831 0330 Fax: 020 7242 0121
www.tht.org.uk

Voluntary Euthanasia Society
13 Prince of Wales Terrace
London W8 5PG
Tel: 020 7937 7770
Fax: 020 7376 2648
www.ves.org.uk/

Women's Aid Federation
PO Box 391
Bristol BS99 7WS
Admin tel: 0117 944 4411
Fax: 0117 924 1703
Helpline: 0345 023465
www.womensaid.org.uk

Youth Services Unit (YSU)
Department of Education
Sanctuary Buildings
St. Smith Street,
London SW1 3BT
Tel: 020 7925 5000
Fax: 020 7925 6000
www.dfee.gov.uk

Chapter 3 – You and your job

Advisory, Conciliation & Arbitration Service (ACAS)
Brandon House
180 Borough High Street
London SE1 1LW
Tel: 020 7396 5100

Certification Officer for Trade Unions and Employers' Associations
Brandon House
180 Borough High Street
London SE1 1LW
Tel: 020 7210 3734

Commission for Racial Equality
Elliot House
10–12 Allington Street
London SW1E 5EH
Tel: 020 7828 7022
Fax: 020 7630 7605
www.cre.gov.uk

Commissioner for the Rights of Trade Union Members
1st Floor, Bank Chambers
2A Rylands Street, Warrington
Cheshire WA1 1EN
Tel: 01925 415771
Fax: 01925 415772

Companies House
Crown Way
Cardiff CF14 3UZ
Tel: 02920 388588
Fax: 02920 380900
www.companies-house.gov.uk

Department for Education and Employment, Employment Service
Level 6, Caxton House
Tothill Street
London SW1H 9NE
Tel: 020 7273 6111
Fax: 020 7273 6143
www.dfee.gov.uk

Employment Appeal Tribunal
Audit House
58 Victoria Embankment
London EC4Y 0DS
Tel: 020 7273 1040
Fax: 020 7273 1045
www.employmentappeals.gov.uk

Employment Relations Regulatory Guidance
DTI Enquiry Unit
1 Victoria Street
London SW1H 0ET
Tel: 020 7215 5000
www.dti.gov.uk/er/regs.htm

The Employment Service Disability Service Branch
Level 1, 236 Grays Inn Rd
London WC1X 8HL
Tel: 020 7211 4792
www.employmentservice.gov.uk

Employment Tribunal Central Enquiries
100 Southgate Street
Bury St Edmunds
Suffolk IP33 2AQ
Tel: 0345 959775
www.dti.gov.uk/index.html

Equal Opportunities Commission
Arndale House
Arndale Centre
Manchester M4 3EQ
Tel: 0161 833 9244
Fax: 0161 838 8312
www.eoc.org.uk

Federation of Small Businesses Head Office
Whittle Way
Blackpool Business Park
Blackpool
Lancs FY4 2FE
Tel: 01253 336000
Fax: 01253 348406
www.fsb.org.uk

Health & Safety Executive Commission Head Office
Rose Court
2 Southwark Bridge
London SE1 9HS
Tel: 020 7717 6000
Infoline: 0541545500
www.open.gov.uk/hse/hse.home.htm

National Minimum Wage Helpline
Tel: 0845 6000 678

Public Concern at Work
(Whistleblowing)
Lincoln's Inn House
42 Kingsway
London WC2B 6EX
Tel: 020 7404 6609
www.pcaw.demon.co.uk

Race Relations Employment Advisory Service
14th Floor, Cumberland House
200 Broad Street
Birmingham B14 1TA
Tel: 0121 244 8141/2/3

Trades Union Congress
Congress House
Great Russell Street
London WC1B 3LS
Tel: 020 7636 4030
Fax: 020 7636 0632
www.tuc.org.uk

Chapter 4 – You and your home

Architects and Surveyors Institute
St Mary House
15 St Mary Street
Chippenham
Wilts SN15 3WD
Tel: 01249 444505
Fax: 01249 443002
www.asi.org.uk

Association of British Insurers
51 Gresham Street
London EC2V 7HQ
Tel: 020 7600 3333
Fax: 020 7696 8999
www.abi.org.uk

The Association of Building Engineers
Jubilee House, Billing Brook Road
Weston Favell
Northampton NN3 4NW
Tel: 01604 404121
www.biw.co.uk/BIW/register/930.htm

Association of Noise Consultants
6 Trap Road
Guilden Mordern,
Nr Royston
Herts SG8 0JE
Tel: 01763 852958
Fax: 01763 853352
www.isvr.co.uk/anc

British Insurance Brokers' Association
14 Bevis Marks,
London EC3A 7NT.
Tel: 020 7623 9043
Fax: 020 7626 9676
www.biba.org.uk/

British Property Federation
1 Warwick Row,
7th floor
London SW1E 5RE
Tel: 020 7828 0111
Fax: 020 7834 3442
www.propertymall.com/bpf

Building Societies Association
3 Saville Row
London W1X 1AF
Tel: 020 7437 0655
Fax: 020 7734 6416
www.bsa/org.uk

Campaign Against Residential Leasehold Abuse (CARLA)
c/o 6 Pye Corner
Castle Hedingham
Essex CO9 3DE
Tel: 01787 462 787

College of Estate Management
Whiteknights
Shinfield Road
Reading RG6 6AW
Tel: 0118 986 1101
Fax: 0118 975 5344
www.cem.ac.uk

CORGI (Council for Registered Gas Installers)
1 Elmwood
Chineham Business Park
Crockford Lane
Basingstoke RG24 8WG
Tel: 01256 372200
Fax: 01256 708144
www.corgi-gas.co.uk

Corporation of Estate Agents
PO Box 151
Gloucester GL19 3RY
Tel: 01452 840726

Council for Licensed Conveyancers
16 Glebe Road
Chelmsford
Essex CM1 1QG
Tel: 01245 349599

Council of Mortgage Lenders
3 Saville Row
London W1X 1AF
Tel: 020 7437 0075
Fax: 020 7434 3791
www.cml.org.uk

Cleanair
33 Stillness Road
London
SE23 1NG
Tel: 020 8690 4649
www.ezme.com/cleanair

Department of the Environment
Eland House
Bressendon Place
London SW1E 5DU
Tel: 020 7944 3000
www.detr.gov.uk

Estate Agents Ombudsman
Beckett House
4 Bridge Street
Salisbury
Wilts SP1 2LX
Tel: 01722 333306
Fax: 01722 332296
E-mail: mailto:post@oea.co.uk
www.oea.co.uk

Federation of Private Residents' Associations Limited
3rd Floor, Overseas House
19/23 Ironmonger Row
London EC1V 3QN
Tel: 020 7409 7073
Fax: 020 7409 7074
www.deacon.co.uk/fpra.html

The House Building Council (NHBC)
Buildmark House, Chilton Avenue
Amersham
Bucks HP6 5AP
Tel: 01494 434477
Fax: 01494 728521
www.nhbc.co.uk

Housingnet
www.housingnet.co.uk/

Incorporated Society of Valuers and Auctioneers
3 Cadogan Gate
London SW1X 0AS
Tel: 020 7235 2282
Fax: 020 7235 4390
www.homes-on-line.com/isva

Independent Housing Ombudsman
Norman House, 105–109 The Strand
London WC1X 8NB
Tel: 020 7836 3630
Lo-call Tel: 0345 125973
Fax: 020 7836 3900

Institute of Rent Officers
Musgrave House
Musgrave Row
Exeter EX4 3TW
Tel: 01392 72321

Insurance Ombudsman
City Gate One
135 Park Street
London
SE1 9EA
Tel:0845 600 6666
Fax: 020 7902 8197
www.theiob.org.uk

The Land Registry
Lincoln Inn Fields
London WC2A 3PH
Tel: 020 7917 8888
www.landreg.gov.uk

Lands Tribunal
48–49 Chancery Lane
London WC2A 1JR
Tel: 020 7936 7200

Leasehold Advisory Service
6/8 Maddox Street
London W1R 9PN
Tel: 020 7493 3116
Fax: 020 7493 4318
www.lease-advice.org

Leasehold Enfranchisement Association
10 Upper Phillimore Gardens
London W8 7HA
Tel: 020 7937 0866

Mediation UK
Akexander House
Telephone Avenue
Bristol BS1 4BS
Tel: 0117 904 6661
Fax: 0117 904 3331
www.mediationuk.org.uk

National Association of Councils for Voluntary Service (NACVS)
3rd Floor, Arundel Court
177 Arundel Street
Sheffield S1 2NU
Tel: 01142 786636
www.nacvs.org.uk

National Association of Estate Agents
Arbon House
21 Jury Street
Warwick CV34 4EH
Tel: 01926 496800
www.naea.co.uk

National Federation of Housing Associations
175 Gray's Inn Road
London WC1X 8UP
Tel: 020 7278 6571

National Federation of House Co-operatives
88 Old Street
London EC1V 9AX
Tel: 020 7608 2494

National Federation of Residential Landlords
Sackville Place
44–48 Magdalen Chambers
Norwich NR3 1JU
Tel: 01603 762980
Fax: 01603 762981
www.nfrl.org.uk

National Association of Estate Agents
Arbon House
21 Jury Street
Warwick CV34 4EH
Tel: 01926 496800

National Neighbourhood Watch Association
Tel: 020 7772 3348
www.nwatch.org.uk

National Tenants' Organisation
Voluntary Action Centre
51 Grove Road
Hounslow
Middlesex TW3 3PR
Tel: 020 8690 8920

The Planning Inspectorate
Room 14/04, Tollgate House
Houlton Street
Bristol BS2 9DJ
Tel: 0117 987 8927
Fax: 0117 987 8139
www.planning-inspectorate.gov.uk/

Ofgem (Office of Gas and Electricity Markets)
11 Belgrave Road
London SW1V 1RB
Tel: 020 7233 6366
Fax: 020 7233 6449
www.ofgem.gov.uk

Ofwat (Office of Water Services)
City Centre Tower
7 Hill Street
Birmingham B5 4UA
Tel: 0121 625 1300
Fax: 0121 932 1600
www.open.gov.uk/ofwat

Royal Institution of Chartered Surveyors
12 Great George Street
Parliament Square
London
SW1P 3AD
Tel: 020 7222 7000

Scottish Housing Ombudsman
Drumsheugh Toll
2 Bedford Road
Edinburgh EH4 3BL
Tel: 0131 220 0599
Fax: 0131 220 0577

Chapter 5 – You and the police

The Adjudicator
Haymarket House
28 Haymarket
London SW1Y 4SP
Tel: 020 7930 2292
Fax: 020 7930 2298
www.open.gov.uk/adoff/aodemo1.htm

Alcohol Concern
Waterbridge House
32–36 Loman Street
London SE1 0EE
Tel: 020 7928 7377

Association of Chief Officers of Probation
Whitechapel Road
London E1 1BJ
Tel: 020 7377 9141
Fax: 020 7375 2100

Association of Family Court Welfare Officers
Court Welfare Office
The Link Centre
Whitehill Way, Westlea
Swindon SN5 7DL
Tel: 01793 871 333

Criminal Injuries Compensation Appeals Panel
11th Floor Cardinal Tower
Farringdon Road
London EC1M 3HS
Tel: 020 7549 4600
Fax: 020 7549 4643
www.cicap.gov.uk/contact/index.htm

Crown Prosecution Service
Customer Service Unit
50 Ludgate Hill
London EC4M 7EX
Tel: 020 7796 8500
Fax: 020 7796 8092
Public Enquiry Point: 020 7796 8500
www.cps.gov.uk/

Driving Standards Agency
Stanley House
56 Talbot Street
Nottingham NG1 5GU
Tel: 0115 901 2516
Fax: 0115 901 2510
www.driving-tests.co.uk/

The Guild of Experienced Motorists
Station Road, Forest Row
East Sussex RH18 5EN
Tel: 01342 825 676
Fax: 01342 824 847
www.gemrecovery.co.uk/

HM Inspectorate of Probation
Portcullis House
Seymour Grove
Manchester M16 0PS
Tel: 0161 848 0566

The Institute of Advanced Motorists
IAM House
359–365 Chiswick High Road
London W4 4HS
Tel: 020 8994 4403
Fax: 020 8994 9249
www.iam.org.uk/

National Association for Youth Justice
2 Farley Hill
Luton
Beds LU1 5HQ
Tel: 01582 736522
www.nayj.org.uk

National Association of Probation Officers (NAPO)
3–4 Chivalry Road
London SW11 1HT
Tel: 020 7223 4887
Fax: 020 7223 3503

Police Complaints Ombudsman
10 Great George Street
London SW1P 3AE
Tel: 020 7273 6450
Fax: 020 7273 6401

RoSPA (Royal Society for the Prevention of Accidents)
Edgbaston Park
353 Bristol Road
Edgbaston
Birmingham B5 7ST
General Information: 0121 248 2000
Sales: 0121 248 2222
Fax: 0121 248 2001

Victim Support
Cranmer House
39 Brixton Road
London SW9 6DZ
Tel: 020 7735 9166
Fax: 020 7582 5712
Supportline: 0845 3030900
www.victimsupport.com/

Chapter 6 – You and your leisure

Advertising Standards Authority
Brook House
2 Torrington Place
London WC1E 7HW
Tel: 020 7580 5555
Fax: 020 7631 3051
www.asa.org.uk

Air Transport Users' Council (AUC)
CAA House
45–59 Kingsway
London WC2B 6TE
Tel: 020 7240 6061
Fax: 020 7240 7071
www.auc.org.uk

Association of British Insurers (ABI)
51 Gresham St
London EC2V 7HQ
Tel: 020 7660 3333
www.abi.org.uk/

Association of British Travel Agents (ABTA)
68–71 Newman Street
London W1P 4AH
Tel: 020 7637 2444
www.abtanet.com

BBC Television Consumer Programmes:
BBC Watchdog
Room 4225, White City
201 Wood Lane
London W12 7TS
www.bbc.co.uk/watchdog/

BBC Radio Consumer Programmes:
Broadcasting House
Portland Place
London W1A 1AA
Tel. 020 7580 4468

British Holiday and Home Parks Association Ltd.
Chichester House,
6 Pullman Court
Great Western Road
Gloucester GL1 3ND
Tel: 01452 526911

British Insurance Brokers' Association
14 Bevis Marks
London EC3A 7NT
Tel: 020 7623 9043
Fax: 020 7626 9676
www.biba.org.uk/

British Standards Institution
Information Services
389 Chiswick High Road
London W4 4AL
Tel: 020 8996 9000
Fax: 020 8996 7400
www.bsi.org.uk/

The Chartered Institute of Arbitrators
24 Angel Gate,
City Road
London EC1V 2RS
Tel: 020 7837 4483
Fax: 020 7837 4185
www.arbitrators.org

Consumers' Association
2 Marylebone Road
London NW1 4DF
Tel: 020 7770 7000
Fax: 020 7770 7600

The Consumer Gateway
www.consumer.gov.uk/

The Consumer Policy Committee (BSI)
389 Chiswick High Road
London W4 4AL
Tel: 020 7629 9000
www.bsi.org.uk

Consumers in the European Community Group
24 Tufton Street
London SW1P 3RB
Tel: 020 7222 2662

Department of Trade & Industry
Consumer Affairs
Victoria Street
London SW1H 0ET
Tel: 020 7215 5000
www.tdi/gov.uk

Department of Transport
Mobility Unit
First Floor, Great Minster House
76 Marsham Street
London SW1P 4DR
Tel: 020 7271 5252
Fax: 020 7271 5253

Direct Marketing Association
Haymarket House, 1 Oxendon Street
London SW1Y 4EE
Tel: 020 7321 2525
www.dma.org.uk

Direct Selling Association
29 Floral Street
London WC2E 9DP
Tel: 020 7497 1234
www.dsa.org.uk

Food and Drink Federation
6 Catherine Street
London WC2B 5JJ
Tel: 020 7836 2460
www.foodanddrinknto.org.uk/fdf.htm

Institute of Trading Standards Administration
3/5 Hadleigh Business Centre
351 London Road
Hadleigh, Essex SS7 2BT
Tel: 01702 559922
www.tradingstandards.gov.uk

Local Authorities Coordinating Body on Food Trading Standards (LACTOS)
10 Albert Embankment
London SE1 7SP
Tel: 020 77359977
www.lactos.org.uk

Motor Insurers' Bureau
152 Silbury Boulevard
Central Milton Keynes MK9 1NG
Tel: 01908 830001

National Consumer Council
20 Grosvenor Gardens
London SW1W 0DH
Tel: 020 7730 3469
Fax: 020 7730 0191
www.ncc.org.uk

Office of Fair Trading
Fleetbank House
2–6 Salisbury Square
London EC4Y 8JX
Tel: 08457 22 44 99
Fax: 020 7211 8800
0870 60 60 321 (publication orders)
www.oft.gov.uk

Organisation for Timeshare in Europe
15–19 Great Titchfield Street
London W1P 7FB
Tel: 020 7291 0901

Pipedown
PO Box 1722
Salisbury SP4 7US
Tel: 01980 623945
www.btinternet.com/~pipedown

Society of Motor Manufacturers and Traders Ltd
Forbes House, Halkin Street
London SW1X 7DS
Tel: 020 7235 7000
Fax: 020 7235 7112
www.smmt.co.uk/

Trading Standards web site:
www.tradingstandards.net/

Chapter 7 – You and your rights

Action for Victims of Medical Accidents (AVMA)
Bank Chambers
1 London Road
Forest Hill
London SE23 3TP
Tel: 020 8291 2793
Fax: 020 8699 0632

Amnesty International
99–119 Rosebery Ave
London EC1R 4RE
Tel: 020 7814 6200
Fax: 020 7833 1510
www.amnesty.org/

Article 19 (human rights)
90 Borough High Street
London SE1 1NL
Tel: 020 7403 4822

Association of Personal Injury Lawyers (APIL)
33 Pilcher Gate
Nottingham NG1 1QF
Tel: 0115 958 0585
www.apil.com

The Authors' Licensing & Collecting Society
Marlborough Court
14–18 Holborn
London EC1N 2LE
Tel: 020 7395 0600
Fax: 020 7395 0660
www.alcs.co.uk/

The British Deaf Association
38 Victoria Place
Carlisle CA1 1HU
Tel: 01228 48844
Fax: 01228 41420
www.bda.org.uk

British Medical Association
BMA House
Tavistock Square
London WC1H 9JP
Tel: 020 7387 4499
Fax: 020 7383 6400
web.bma.org.uk/homepage.nsf

The Broadcasting Standards Commission
7 The Sanctuary
London SW1P 3JS
Tel: 020 7808 1000
Fax: 020 7233 0397
www.bsc.org.uk/

Campaign Against Racism and Fascism (CARF)
BM Box 8784
London WC1N 3XX
Tel: 020 7837 1450
www.carf.demon.co.uk/

Confederation of Indian Organisations (CIO)
5 Westminster Bridge Road
London SE1 7XW
Tel: 020 7928 9889
Fax: 020 7620 4025

Copyright Licensing Agency Ltd
90 Tottenham Court Road
London W1P 0LP
Tel: 020 7631 5555
Fax: 020 7631 5500
www.cla.co.uk

Criminal Injuries Compensation Appeals Panel
11th Floor Cardinal Tower
Farringdon Road
London EC1M 3HS
Tel: 020 7549 4600
Fax: 020 7549 4643
www.cicap.gov.uk

The Disabled Drivers' Association
Ashwellthorpe
Norwich NR16 1EX
Tel: 01508 489449
Fax: 01508 488173
www.disabilitynet.co.uk

Disability Access Rights Advice Service (DARAS)
Unit 99,
Bow House Business Centre
153–159 Bow Road
London E3 2SE
Tel: 0345 585 445
Fax: 0345 585 446
Minicom: 0345 585 447
www.daras.co.uk

Disability Rights Commission
Freepost MIDO 2164
Stratford-upon-Avon CV37 9BR
Tel: 08457 622633
www.drb-gb.org

Disabled Living Foundation
380–384 Harrow Road
London W9 2HU
Tel: 020 7289 6111
Fax: 020 7266 2922
www.dlf.org.uk

Federation of Independent Advice Centres
4 Deans Court
St Paul's Churchyard
London EC4V 5AA
Tel: 020 7489 1800
Fax: 020 7489 1804
www.fiac.org.uk

General Dental Council
37 Wimpole Street
London W1M 8DQ
Tel: 020 7887 3800
Fax: 020 7224 3294
www.gdc-uk.org/

General Medical Council
178 Great Portland Street
London W1N 6AE
Tel: 020 7580 7642
Fax: 020 7915 3641
www.gmc-uk.org/

Health Services Commissioner
(Ombudsman)
11/13th Floor,
Millbank Tower
Millbank
London SW1P 4QP
Tel: 0845 015403
Fax: 020 7217 4160
www.ombudsman.org.uk

Wales:
5th Floor, Capital Tower
Greyfriars Road
Cardiff CF1 3AG
Tel: 01222 394621
Fax: 01222 226909

Scotland:
28 Thistle Street
Edinburgh EH2 1EN
Tel: 0131 225 7465
Fax: 0131 226 4447

Immigration Advisory Service
County House
190 Great Dover Street
London SE1 4XB
Tel: 020 7357 6917

**Immigration & Nationality
Directorate**
Block C, Whitgift Centre
Wellesley Road
Croydon CR9 1AT
Tel: 0870 606 7766
www.homeoffice.gov.uk/ind/
sitemap.html

**Immigration Law Practitioners'
Association**
Lindsey House
40/42 Charterhouse Street
London EC1M 6JN
Tel: 020 7251 8383
Fax: 020 7251 8384
Email: info@ilpa.org.uk
www.ilpa.org.uk/

Institute of Race Relations
2–6 Leeke Street
London WC1X 8HS
Tel: 020 7837 0041
Fax 020 7278 0623

**Joint Council for the Welfare of
Immigrants**
115 Old Street
London EC1V 9RT
Advice line: 020 7251 8706
Fax 020 7251 8707
www.jcwi.org.uk

**Liberty – National Council for Civil
Liberties**
21 Tabard Street
London SE1 4LA
Tel: 020 7403 3888 Fax 020 7407 5354

Local Government Ombudsman
21 Queen Anne's Gate
London SW1H 9BU
Tel: 020 7915 3210
Fax: 020 7233 0396
www.open.gov.uk/lgo

Wales:
Derwen House
Court Road
Bridgend CF31 1BN
Tel: 01656 661325
Fax: 01656 658317

Medical Protection Society
The Medical Director,
33 Cavendish Square
London W1M 0PS
Tel: 020 7399 1300
Fax: 020 7399 1301
www.mps.org.uk/

**Mobility Advice and Vehicle
Information Service**
'O' Wing
MacAdam Avenue
Old Wokingham Road
Crowthorne
Berkshire RG45 6XD
Tel: 01344 661000 (also on Minicom)
Fax: 01344 661066
www.mobility-unit.detr.gov.uk

The Patients Association
PO Box 935
Harrow
Middlesex HA1 3YJ
Tel: 020 84239111
Fax: 020 84239119
Lo-call: 0845 6084455
www.patients-association.com

Press Complaints Commission
1 Salisbury Square
London EC4Y 8JB
www.pcc.org.uk/

Publishers Licensing Society Ltd
5 Dryden Street
Covent Garden
London WC2E 9NB
Tel: 020 7829 8486
Fax: 020 7829 8488
www.pls.org.uk/

Refugee Council Information Team
3 Bondway
London SW8 1SJ
Tel: 020 7820 3085
www.refugeecouncil.org.uk

**Royal National Institute for Deaf
People (RNID)**
19–23 Featherstone Street
London EC1Y 8SL
Tel: 020 7296 8000
Minicom 020 7296 8001
Fax: 020 7296 8199
www.rnid.org.uk

Solicitors Complaints Bureau
Victoria Court, 8 Dormer Place
Leamington Spa CV32 5AF
Tel: 01926 822007
www.lawsociety.org.uk

**Chapter 8 – You and your
money**
Banking Ombudsman
70 Gray's Inn Road
London WC1X 8NB
Tel: 020 7404 9944
Lo-call: 0345 660902
Fax: 020 7405 5052
www.obo.org.uk

British Bankers' Association
10 Lombard Street
London EC3V 9EL
Tel. 020 7623 4001

British Retail Consortium
5 Grafton Street
London W1X 3LB
Tel: 020 7647 1500

**Building Societies Association and
Council of Mortgage Lenders**
3 Saville Row
London W1X 1AF
Tel: 020 7437 0655

Building Societies Ombudsman
Millbank Tower
Millbank
London SW1P 4XS
Tel: 020 7931 0044
Fax: 020 7931 8485

CCN Credit Systems Limited
Consumer Help Department
PO Box 40
Nottingham NG7 2SS
Tel: 01159 868172

**Consumer Credit Association (UK)
(CCA)**
Queens House
Queens Road
Chester CH1 3BQ
Tel: 01244 312044

**Consumer Credit Counselling
Service**
Tel: 0345 697301

Consumer Credit Trade Association
Tennyson House
159–163 Great Portland Street
London W1N 5FD
Tel: 020 7636 7564
www.cifas.org.uk

Council of Mortgage Lenders
3 Saville Row
London W1X 1AF
Tel: 020 7437 0075
Fax: 020 7434 3791
www.cml.org.uk/

**County Courts Customer Service
Unit**
6th Floor, South Side
105 Victoria Street
London SW1E 6QT
Tel: 020 7210 2266

Data Protection Registrar
Wycliffe House
Waber Lane
Wilmslow
Cheshire SK9 5AX
Tel: 01625 545745
www.open.gov.uk/dpr/dprhome/htm

Experian Consumer Help Service
PO Box 8000
Nottingham NG1 5GX
Tel: 0115 976 8747

**Federation of Independent Advice
Centres**
4 Deans Court
St Paul's Churchyard
London EC4V 5AA.
Tel: 020 7489 1800
Fax: 020 7489 1804
www.fiac.org.uk

**Finance and Leasing Association
(FLA)**
Imperial House
22 Kingsway
London WC2B 6UN
Tel: 020 7836 6511

Investments Ombudsman
4th Floor
6 Fredericks Place
London EC2R 8BT
Tel: 020 7796 3065

Mailing Preference Service
Freepost 22
London W1E 7EZ
Tel: 020 7766 4410
www.asa.org.uk/bcasp/r_mps.htm

**National Consumer Credit
Federation**
98 Holme Lane
Sheffield S6 4JW
Tel: 01142 348101

National debt line: 0121 359 8501

**Occupational Pensions Advisory
Service**
11 Belgrave Road
London SW1V 1RB
Tel: 020 7233 8080
Fax: 020 7233 8016

Pensions Ombudsman
11 Belgrave Road
London SW1V 1RB
Tel: 020 7834 9144
Fax: 020 7821 0065

Personal Investment Authority
Hertsmere House
Hertsmere Road
London E14 4AB
Tel: 020 7216 0016
Fax: 020 7712 8742

Registry Trust
173–175 Cleveland Street
London W1P 5PE
Tel: 020 7380 0133

**Chapter 9 – You and the
courts**

The Court Service
Southside
105 Victoria Street
London SW1E 6QT
Tel: 020 7210 1818

European Court of Justice
Palais de la Cour de Justice
Boulevard Konrad Adenauer
Kirchberg
L – 2925 Luxembourg
Tel: 00 352 4303 1
www.curia.eu.int

Royal Courts of Justice
Strand
London WC2A 2LL
Tel: 020 7947 6000

Glossary

affidavit A written statement of evidence that is used in a civil action (now called a 'statement of truth').

age of criminality Children under 10 cannot be charged with committing a criminal offence.

annulment The setting aside of a marriage on the grounds that it was not validly contracted, for example because one party was already married.

bail The status of a person between being arrested and charged with an offence and appearing in court to have the case heard. If they have not been remanded into custody and held at a remand centre or jail, then they are 'on bail'. Bail is normally granted in most cases, or magistrates must have reasons to refuse it (but in serious cases like rape or murder, the magistrates must have reasons why bail should be granted).

balance of probability Civil burden of proof, whereby a plaintiff has to establish his case is more than 50 per cent likely.

bankruptcy A process where a debtor's assets are taken over by a court, which then appoints someone to manage the assets, on behalf of the debtor's creditors.

barrister A member of one of the four Inns of Court, a barrister's main function is to act as an advocate, representing his/her client and with a right of audience in all UK courts. They may also be asked for a counsel's opinion on points of law and to offer advice on evidence and procedure. Barristers cannot be instructed by a client directly, but via a solicitor.

beneficiary Person named in a will, trust or insurance policy to whom money will be paid or benefits passed onto.

beyond all reasonable doubt Burden of proof in a criminal trial.

bona fide Literally 'in good faith'

burden of proof The standard that is necessary for a case to be proven. In criminal law, the prosecution must prove its case beyond 'all reasonable doubt' (except in cases of insanity which takes the civil burden of proof), whereas in civil cases the burden of proof is 'on the balance of probabilities'.

caveat emptor Buyer beware. A warning that advises buyers, especially in private sales or auctions to proceed with caution as their rights are less than in consumer situations when buying from a shop or trader.

charge One mechanism by which a person accused of a serious criminal offence can be brought to court (the other method for less serious offences is by summons).

codicil A supplement added to an already existing will.

conditional fee A method of funding cases that is likely to increase following reforms of the 'Legal Aid system'. Under conditional fee arrangements, solicitors will act for clients in return for a proportion of the damages they recover if successful. Sometimes called 'no win, no fee' arrangements.

contract An agreement between two or more people that is binding in law. Examples of contracts are the sale of goods, booking a holiday or the buying and selling of houses

contributory negligence A situation where actions (or omissions) by a plaintiff amount to negligence on his/her part and which can reduce a defendant's liability.

copyright A branch of intellectual property law, which protects the products of a person's labours, skill and creativity.

coroner A barrister, doctor or solicitor of at least five years' standing who conducts legal proceedings in the cases of suspicious, violent, unnatural or sudden deaths, deaths while in custody or deaths that might have been caused by industrial disease.

costs The amount a party has to pay to bring an action to court. When a party wines, costs may be 'awarded' against the other side (the losing side pays the winning side's costs).

crime Offences against the public at large which society thinks are sufficiently serious that they should be punished.

cross-petition A situation where both the husband and wife in divorce seek to divorce the other party. Rare.

damages An award made by a court for compensation of a plaintiff's injury, loss or damages, arising from a tort or breach of contract.

decree absolute The last stage of the divorce. Can be applied for six weeks and one day after a decree nisi is issued. Once the decree absolute is issued, either party is free to remarry.

decree nisi A stage in divorce where a county court judge gives provisional approval for the dissolution of a marriage. But the marriage is not over at this point, and if one party dies, the surviving spouse can inherit as if they were still married. Six weeks and one day after the decree nisi is issued, either party can apply for a decree absolute to end the marriage.

deed A formal legal document, often used in transactions of property.

defamation The making of an injurious and false statement about another person that damages their reputation. Spoken defamation is slander, while defamation in permanent form is libel.

defendant The person against whom legal proceedings are brought, either in civil or criminal law.

divorce The legal dissolution of a marriage on the grounds of the irretrievable breakdown of the relationship.

double jeopardy At present the rule against double jeopardy prevents a person being tried for the same crime twice in this country. However, this rule is under review.

duty of care Foundation of an action for negligence. A duty owed by one party towards another to take reasonable care not to cause economic, psychiatric or physical harm or loss.

easement A right enjoyed by the owner of one piece of land over another. Examples of easements are rights of support and rights to air and water.

employer liability The liability of an employer to pay damages to employees that suffer personal injury in the course of their employment, if liability is established.

equity A mechanism developed to fill in gaps in the complex and cumbersome writ procedure and where remedies were not available. It supplemented the common law remedies such as damages with injunctions that would compel performance or prevent something being done. The whole doctrine of equity arose out of principles of fairness and a case's merits.

executor A person nominated in a will to ensure that that a testator's wishes are carried out and the will followed.

ex parte An application made to court by one party in the absence of the other side. Can also mean an application to court by a person who is not a party to the proceedings.

fiduciary duty An obligation to act in the best interests of another party, arising out of the relationship. For example, a trustee has a fiduciary relationship with the beneficiary of a trust.

freehold Land ownership with unlimited rights over the land, in that it is yours forever.

guardian ad litem A court-appointed professional that will act on behalf of the children in family matters, and represent their views.

heir A person entitled to inherit a person's property if they die without making a will.

injunction A court order that either prevents someone doing something, or compels them to do something (which is called a 'mandatory injunction').

intestacy The situation that arises when a person dies without leaving a will that disposes of his/her property.

inquest A legal public inquiry into the cause of death, conducted by a coroner. An inquest's function is to determine the identity of the deceased, an how, when and where death occurred.

joint tenancy A mechanism for more than one person to own property, where on the death of one 'tenant' his/her interest passes to the surviving joint tenant(s). Joint tenants cannot bequeath their share in the property under a will.

judge The legally trained professional (usually a former barrister, though sometimes experienced solicitors become judges) that will hear cases at court. Different types of judges sit in different courts.

jury A panel of members of the public that decide questions of fact in serious criminal cases. The right to jury trial for serious cases is a cornerstone of the English legal system, but is being reviewed. For criminal cases a jury of 12 is selected, and for civil cases like libel and slander or false imprisonment. Coroners' juries must comprise at least seven members but no more than 11.

leasehold Land ownership that confers less rights than owning the freehold, usually for a term of years; for example a 99-year lease.

Legal Aid State funding allowing less well-off people to bring cases to court or to provide a defence in criminal cases. Now administered by the Legal Services Commission.

legal charge A form of legal security that a lender has over property, and which appears on the Land Register. A mortgage is a charge.

libel Defamation in permanent form, for example in a newspaper or television programme.

magistrate Also known as a justice of the peace or JP. Laypeople who are given some legal training and empowered to hear minor criminal cases and transfer the more serious ones to the crown court, as well as deciding some civil and licensing matters. Advised by a legal advisor (formerly the court clerk) who is legally trained.

maintenance Money paid in a divorce or separation by one spouse to another in settling the financial obligations that arose out of the marriage.

minor A person under the age of 18.

negligence A tort. Breaching a legal duty of care, and which causes damage.

nuisance A tort, involving the performance of acts that interfere with another person's enjoyment of their property (like dumping rubbish) or allowing damaging things to escape onto a neighbouring property (like smoke from a bonfire, smells or water). Public nuisances (those which can interfere with and upset the community at large are also crimes.)

occupier liability A property occupant's duty to ensure that his/her premises are not in a dangerous condition and likely to cause harm to visitors or, in the case of premises adjacent to a road or highway, passers-by.

overriding interests Interests in property that cannot be registered but which may still be asserted over an owner of land.

plaintiff The person (or persons) that brings a civil action, against a defendant.

prima facie On the face of it.

privilege A defence to defamation, base don the principle that the proceedings in which the defamatory statement was made, or a report of it was published, are so important that people should be able to express themselves freely, as a matter of public policy.

probate A legal process in which property bequeathed in a will is distributed.

prosecution The bringing of a criminal action

Queen's Counsel (QC) A senior barrister.

remand Where a person accused of a crime is held in custody rather than be granted bail.

settlement, out of court Where the parties in a law suit come to terms before a judge can rule on the merits of the case. Costs and damages may be agreed under a settlement, but often there is no admission of liability, so it would then be inaccurate to say that the case had been won or lost.

slander Defamation in the spoken word.

stipendiary magistrate A legally-trained and salaried magistrate (formerly a barrister or solicitor) that sits alone in magistrates court, hearing cases and committing them for trial at crown court.

strict liability Liability in some cases is 'strict', for example drink-driving (in almost all cases): if you have excess alcohol in your system when you are driving, the offence is proven. The question of intent is not relevant.

solicitor Solicitors deal with criminal and civil matters, both in court and in the office (in big city firms, solicitors tend to specialise while in smaller practices, they tend to do a variety of work). Solicitors have a rights of most courts now, and are instructed by their clients directly.

summons A mechanism for bringing a person accused of a less serious criminal offence before a court.

tenancy in common A mechanism for more than one person to own property, with each 'tenant' holding a share in the property. Unlike joint tenants, tenants in common can leave their share in the property in a will.

tort A civil wrong, for which the plaintiff will bring an action for damages, for example for negligence or defamation. From the French 'tort', which means wrong.

trespass A tort, committed when a person enters someone else's property or goes onto their land without permission. Trespassers are sued, not prosecuted!

trust A mechanism of property ownership where 'property' which can be money, shares, land etc. is managed by trustees on behalf of a beneficiary, who will receive benefits arising out of the trust. Sometimes property may be held in trust for a child until he/she comes of age.

TWOC-ing Police jargon for taking a motor-car without the owner's consent. Used to be called joy-riding.

ultra vires An act that goes beyond one's powers, for example if a local authority does something which it is not empowered to do by statute or delegated legislation.

verdict The decision of a jury, or a coroner.

vicarious liability A situation where one person is liable for the actions of another; for example, through the principle of vicarious liability an employer is responsible for the acts and omissions of employees during the normal course of their employment.

writ The mechanism for bringing proceedings in the High Court.

Index

The index covers all chapters, but not preliminary pages or appendices. Entries are arranged in word-by-word order (spaces and hyphens given filing values, so 'Child Support Agency (CSA)' precedes 'childminders'). *Italic* type indicates titles of Acts; **bold** type indicates a more detailed section within a sequence of locators.